Pulse and Repulse

Pulse and Repulse

Troop Carrier and Airborne Teams
In Europe
During World War II

By H. Rex Shama

EAKIN PRESS ⊣ Austin, Texas

FIRST EDITION

Copyright © 1995

By H. Rex Shama

Published in the United States of America
By Eakin Press
An Imprint of Sunbelt Media, Inc.
P.O. Drawer 90159   H   Austin, TX 78709-0159

ISBN 0-89015-991-2

9 8 7 6 5 4 3 2

Library of Congress Cataloging-in-Publication Data

Shama, H., Rex
  Pulse and repulse: Troop carrier and airborne teams during WWII / by H. Rex Shama
    p   cm.
  ISBN 0-89015-991-2 : $29.95
  Includes bibliographical references, sources, index
  PZ7. W1875M1 1995
  [Bio]--dc20

95-1989
CIP
AC

Contents

Operation Maps

iv

Preface

Of the earlier books about warfare, the best known were by Karl von Clausewitz, a Prussian who became a military theorist after service in the Napoleonic Wars and the Battle of Waterloo. In his seven volumes (1832–1837) the first three, *Vom Krieg* (On War) related war to politics. "War is a continuation of politics by other means," he wrote. That may be a less subtle translation of his conclusions. He reduced military actions to a strategic science.

John Keegan, in his book *A History of Warfare* (1993), disagreed: "War is wholly unlike diplomacy or politics because it must be fought by men whose values and skills are not those of politicians or diplomats." Keegan considered Clausewitz's "thought" to be "incomplete." In his philosophical last chapter, "Conclusion," he closed with, "There is an even greater wisdom in the denial that politics and war belong within the same continuum."

✻　✻　✻　✻

"Airborne" warfare during World War II was not "aerial" warfare as in the sense of aircraft engaging in combat. It was conducted by unarmed Troop Carrier aircraft, often with gliders on tow, carrying armed paratroops and glider troops into the enemy's ground positions. Resupplies of munitions, fuel, food rations, and medics followed, also by aircraft — powered airplanes and gliders.

When I began my research in 1986, my first objective was to learn more about Operation REPULSE, the IX Troop Carrier Command airborne missions in the Ardennes during the Battle of the Bulge. I discovered that a number of very interesting stories about the top command decisions, as well as about those who carried out the missions, had not been brought to light. After researching the other airborne operations in the Mediterranean and Europe, I found more interesting, unpublished facts.

In this book, the result of my research, I do not intend to philosophize to any degree about diplomacy or politics as may be applied to World War II airborne operations. I will present historical facts as I discovered them, facts I invite the reader to consider and evaluate.

*   *   *   *

As glider pilots in one of the Troop Carrier groups in England during October-November 1944, we accumulated little flight time in gliders, or in our L-4 Cubs. We logged more flight time as C-47 copilots on supply missions to the Continent, to airfields at the rear of the U.S. First and Third armies. In December, glider exercises for airborne operations were greatly restricted by poor weather until midmonth when the German counteroffensive began. At times on nonflying days, my secondary assignment was in the squadron's S-2 Intelligence Section, drafting flight charts and maps to show the latest routes between England and airfields on the Continent. It seemed to be an innocuous duty effort, except for the distractions in the S-2 Quonset — those incoming messages updating the ground and air actions in the Ardennes as the 101st Airborne Division at Bastogne was encircled, and the front-line status maps on which S-2 staff made frequent changes. The German salient, outlined by map pins and red strings, grew larger day after day, sometimes hour after hour.

Our group's four squadrons first felt the seriousness of the situation on 18 December, when some of the aircraft were assigned to carry advance personnel and equipment of the 17th Airborne Division to the Reims area in France, close to the Ardennes. Hindered by weather and delayed flights, every available plane and crew of the IX Troop Carrier Command in England was used until 29 December to move the 17th Airborne from England to Camp Mourmelon, France, the previous base of the 101st Airborne Division. That was only one phase of Operation REPULSE in which Troop Carrier Command also flew numerous airborne resupply missions to isolated American army units in the Ardennes. The most notable, in terms of number of aircraft involved, were the missions in support of the 101st Airborne Division at Bastogne, Belgium (named Operation KANGAROO by IX Troop Carrier Command).

In addition, the command was called on for many air resupply missions before and after REPULSE. One of the more unusual ones involved the delivery of dog sled teams to the Ardennes in January-February 1945.

* * * *

None of the many books published about the German counteroffensive in the Ardennes and the Battle of the Bulge have appropriately recognized the extent and importance of the many resupply missions flown by IX Troop Carrier Command aircraft and gliders. Some published accounts are disturbing in their glaring inaccuracy. In one account was a brief, erroneous mention of the XIX Tactical Air Command, Ninth Air Force, sending in L-5 liaison planes with surgical teams and supplies. They were described in references such as, "The cubs . . ." and "The little squadron flew to Bastogne and the medics were landed without mishap." That does not equate to the sixty-one tow planes and gliders that flew toward Bastogne on 26 and 27 December 1944, some with medics and medical supplies as well as gasoline and ammunition.

During my eight years of researching all Troop Carrier and airborne operations in the European Theater of Operations, it became obvious that the popular publications about the Battle of the Bulge were primarily concerned with the ground forces. The same may be said about other published accounts of Allied invasions in the Mediterranean as well as on D-Day in Normandy.

My research in the National Archives in Washington, D.C. and Suitland, Maryland; the Air Force Historical Research Center at Maxwell AFB, Alabama; Bolling AFB, Maryland; and from other military record sources revealed remarkable stories heretofore missed or ignored. Many were further enhanced from correspondence and discussions with all those I could locate who were involved in the Battle of the Bulge or in the other airborne operations of World War II. After more than forty years, the memories of some of the veterans are surprisingly good. Many of them furnished copies of military records, all with sufficient detail to piece together interesting, accurate stories. In addition, another correspondent, a Belgian, was extremely helpful. His dedicated research included numerous personal interviews and provided more invaluable and arresting facts.

To put Operation REPULSE in its proper perspective, I have presented the other airborne operations in the ETO, each with a story not told before. They are about the men and the commanders, their decisions, both good and bad, fortunate and unfortunate. It is my hope that every chapter will be of interest to the general reader as well as to those veterans who "were there" fifty years ago.

H. Rex Shama

Colonel Crouch *left,* CO IX Troop Carrier Pathfinder Group and Lt. Col. James T. Blair, Jr. *right,* group executive officer, in England, 1945.

— Courtesy: Bancroft

Introduction

THE WORD "NUTS" WAS used more than once by Brig. Gen. Anthony C. McAuliffe during World War II to both friend and foe. The first time was on 22 December 1944 at Bastogne, Belgium, while he was the acting commander of the 101st Airborne Division. "Nuts" was his reply to the German commander who had demanded the surrender of the surrounded Americans during the Battle of the Bulge. That one-word message was highly publicized then and is immortal now.

When his forces were relieved by elements of General Patton's Third Army after 26 December, General McAuliffe told his story of Bastogne to war correspondents at the Hotel Scribe in Paris on 2 January 1945. He was quite satisfied with his terse message. However, he added that Col. Joseph H. Harper, commander of the 327th Glider Infantry Regiment, who delivered the note to the Germans, had to explain its meaning: "Go to Hell."

But one week later, General McAuliffe was agitated enough to again send another "Nuts" message, this time to friends. It was published in the 12 January 1945 issue of *Stars and Stripes* under the "B-Bag" column:

AND ORCHIDS TO YOU!

Your Jan 9 issue carried a photo of Ninth Troop Carrier Command dropping supplies to us at Bastogne. The caption refers to the "desperate plight of the defenders." To such nonsense I again say "Nuts." Ask those tough cookies of 101st Airborne, 10th Armored, 705 TD attached artillery and Force Snafu. They really know the score.

It was pretty rough at times but we were hurting badly only

for medical attention and a little bit for ammunition. Our situation was never desperate and I know of no man inside of Bastogne who ever doubted our ability to hold it.

— A. C. McAuliffe, Brig. Gen., USA

That letter was enough to rile members of IX Troop Carrier Command in England and France. Many Troop Carrier men and aircraft were lost on the resupply missions from 23 through 27 December in support of General McAuliffe's forces during the Battle of the Bulge. Was McAuliffe oblivious of the support he was given, or was he interested in adding accolades to the men who had been under his command?

Col. Charles H. Young, commanding officer of the 439th Troop Carrier Group at Chateaudun, France, was so disturbed by the letter that he felt compelled to respond. His letter of 15 January 1945, forwarded through channels, was addressed to Commanding General, IX Troop Carrier Command. The subject of his letter was "Morale." Paragraph 1 stated, "Attention is invited to the following article published in 'The B-Bag' in the Stars and Stripes issue 12 January 1945." After reproducing McAuliffe's letter, Colonel Young's letter continued:

2. A very considerable amount of extremely unfavorable comment on the above statement has been heard in this unit, and it is feared that there may be an effect upon morale.

3. The plain inference from the General's statement is that the Troop Carrier missions were unnecessary. Considering the fact he may be wrong in this conclusion, that someone in authority felt that such combat missions were very necessary, and that a not inconsiderable number of lives and aircraft were lost on this mission — fourteen (14) tow planes and as many gliders were shot down out of fifty (50) — which involved a higher percentage of loss than any other, or the total of all other missions flown by this Group to date, including "D-Day" in Normandy, it is felt that the article is not only probably wrong, but unfair to all personnel of this Command, particularly those who gave and risked their lives.

4. The article was so unfortunate, the suggestion is respectfully made that an apology, in the same column of the Stars and Stripes

would probably help alleviate a regrettable state of mind of Troop Carrier personnel.

5. We were told that we must get ammunition and medical supplies to the Bastogne pocket or the 101st could not survive. A great many of my men died in that task. Many more are missing in action or prisoners of war. They made the sacrifice gladly, anxious to do anything to help the gallant fighters whom we had taken into Normandy on "D" Day.

6. What am I to give as an answer now to those of my men who survived the terrible flak and machine gun fire and to the families of those who did not, when they ask why they were sent in on a task which the General now, in effect, says was not necessary? The word "Nuts" does not seem appropriate.

/s/ Charles H. Young
/t/ CHARLES H. YOUNG, Colonel, Air Corps, Commanding.

By the letter of 17 January 1945 (as first endorsement) General Chappell, commanding general of the 50th Troop Carrier Wing, forwarded Colonel Young's letter to IX Troop Carrier Command with the following statement:

The undersigned concurs with the basic communication as the article referred to does present a definite morale factor in the units that participated in the resupply at Bastogne.

/s/ Julian M. Chappell
/t/ JULIAN M. CHAPPELL, Brigadier General, USA.

General Williams, commanding general of the IX Troop Carrier Command, decided to send Young's letter to General Brereton, commanding general of the First Allied Airborne Army, adding his own lengthy letter as second endorsement. Dated 23 January 1945, it was explicitly critical of McAuliffe's rash and "undignified" letter writing:

1. Attention is invited to basic communication and attached article from the Stars and Stripes, Friday, 12 January 1945. It is believed that the statements contained therein are frivolous, undignified and unwarranted since they tend to minimize the ef-

forts put forth by this Command as well as question the soundness of the Supreme Commander's judgement in ordering air resupply to the 101st Airborne Division isolated at Bastogne.

2. It is a known fact that IX Troop Carrier Command flew some of the most strenuous sorties of its time during this period, from the point of view of weather and enemy action. The glider mission of the 50th Wing on 27 December 1944 resulted in the highest casualty rate during any operation experienced by units of this Command. Published information indicating that the lives of these officers and men have been given in vain for an unnecessary cause is a severe shock to the members of this Command, especially to those who participated at Bastogne with a high sense of duty to a just cause.

3. A feeling of great admiration for the 101st Airborne Division has always existed throughout this Command. Troop Carrier crews have carried them to battle in Normandy and Holland, and cheerfully risked the worst in weather and enemy flak yet experienced to help them out of what they were told was a "desperate position" at Bastogne. This feeling of cooperation between Airborne and Troop Carrier units is highly desired and definitely needed for combined success.

4. The attached article has caused a serious and most regre[t]table morale situation within Troop Carrier units. It is the assumption of this headquarters that missions flown in connection with the relief of the 101st Airborne Division were properly coordinated and ordered by responsible military authorities, and accordingly, remarks of the nature of those attributed to General McAuliffe should find no place in news articles. It is urgently requested that a clarification of this issue be obtained and that a suitable retraction be made using the same medium that disseminated said information.

/s/ Paul L. Williams
/t/ PAUL L. WILLIAMS, Major General, USA, Commanding.

Ten days later, General Brereton forwarded the correspondence to General Eisenhower, supreme commander, Allied Expeditionary Force. He added his 3 February 1945 letter (third endorsement) of one paragraph:

Request that this be referred to Major General A. C. McAuliffe who has been transferred from the First Allied Airborne Army. The letter published over his signature in the Stars and Stripes has been detrimental to the cordial feeling of teamplay which I have been endeavoring to foster between the Airborne Divisions and the Troop Carrier units. In his efforts to defend the record of the 101st Division at Bastogne, General McAuliffe has belittled the action of the IX Troop Carrier Command in carrying out a mission directed by competent authority to assist. I do not feel that General McAuliffe meant to do this and I feel that he will be glad of the opportunity to correct the impression which his letter has been so unfortunate as to cause.

/s/ L. R. Brereton
/t/ L. R. BRERETON, Lieutenant General, USA Commanding.

In the meantime, General Eisenhower had reassigned General McAuliffe to command the 103d Infantry Division, Seventh Army, and approved his promotion to major general. Therefore, the Supreme Headquarters Allied Expeditionary Force (SHAEF) transmitted the accumulated letters on 7 February 1945 (fourth endorsement) to the commanding general, Sixth Army Group. The endorsement was brief.

1. This correspondence will be referred to Major General A. C. McAuliffe for comment with particular reference to 3rd Indorsement.

2. File will be returned to this headquarters. By direction of the Supreme Commander:

/s/ T. J. Davis
/t/ T. J. DAVIS, Brigadier General, USA Adjutant General.

Adding to the growing stack of letters, Headquarters, 6th Army Group sent its transmittal of 11 February 1945 (fifth endorsement) to the commanding general, Seventh Army. It was also brief:

Attention is invited to the preceding indorsement. By command of Lieutenant General DEVERS:

/s/ J. L. Tarr
/t/ J. L. TARR, Colonel, AGD Adjutant General.

On 14 February 1945, the correspondence was forwarded to General McAuliffe by Headquarters, Seventh Army (sixth endorsement). Addressed to the commanding general, 103d Infantry Division, the letter stated:

For compliance with 4th indorsement. By Command of Lieutenant General PATCH:

/s/ W. G. Caldwell
/t/ W. G. CALDWELL, Colonel, AGD Adjutant General.

General McAuliffe's response was prompt and was dated 17 February 1945 (seventh endorsement). It was returned through the channels by which it came. He wrote:

1. Of course I regret exceedingly having given an impression, however misinterpreted, of lack of appreciation of the really magnificent job of air resupply at Bastogne. I submit, however, that my letter, far from belittling the action of IX Troop Carrier Command, is actually a tribute to them. It states that the garrison was never in a desperate state for supplies, which is true. Everyone knows that our only source was by air, that our supply situation was as good or as bad as air resupply made it. Had it not been for air resupply, the situation would have become worse than desperate; it would have become untenable.

2. The letter to Stars and Stripes was occasioned by bad reporting; particularly repeated statements that the garrison at Bastogne was in its last throes and the use of such expressions as "Kiss of death," "Rescued," "in a desperate plight," etc. Actually, a week after ground contact was established, the 101st Airborne Division was still holding about three-fourths of the perimeter, with four regiments on the line. It spearheaded the attack to the North which captured Noville.

3. Air resupply at Bastogne was superior. We recovered more than 95% of ammunition, medical supplies, rations, gasoline and other items.

4. I attach a copy of my letter of January 25th to General Williams, in which I attempted to express our feeling at Bastogne about the air resupply. I expressed this same feeling publicly at a

press conference in Paris on January 2, and privately on many occasions. I have never stated or implied anything different.

/s/ A. C. McAuliffe
/t/ A. C. McAULIFFE, Major General,
United States Army Commanding

* * * *

Colonel Young received General McAuliffe's reply from Headquarters, 50th Troop Carrier Wing (thirteenth endorsement) on 24 March 1945. Perhaps the response would have been faster had Young written to *Stars and Stripes*. But would it have been proper and would the results have been the same?

Of particular interest is the letter of 25 January that General McAuliffe addressed directly to General Williams. Without a doubt, McAuliffe learned about Colonel Young's letter as it moved up through channels and reached General Brereton, CG, First Allied Airborne Army. General McAuliffe wrote:

Dear General Williams:

I would like to express to you and your command the admiration all of us in the 101st Airborne Division feel for the grand job of air resupply you furnished us during the siege of Bastogne. The IX Troop Carrier Command repeated in this operation the gallant performance which it had taught us to expect. Despite intense flak, the much-needed ammunition and medical supplies were dropped just where we wanted them.

Needless to say, Bastogne could not have been held without that excellent support.

Sincerely,

/s/ A. C. McAuliffe
/t/ A. C. McAULIFFE, Brigadier General, USA Commanding.

The wording of this letter was far different in its meaning from the letter published in *Stars and Stripes* almost three weeks earlier. And for the official record, it satisfied IX Troop Carrier Command. Readers of *Stars and Stripes* in other commands, however, saw only the first McAuliffe letter, the one that appeared in the "B-Bag" column, which, by the way, was subtitled "Blow It Out Here."

Every aspect of the Battle of the Bulge has its problems, and

Troop Carrier had its share. Some, in retrospect, defy thorough and simple explanations. One chronic problem, communications, is easier to isolate. The recorded communications between commands during combat can also provide verification of battle accounts. Such communications, especially during the Battle of the Bulge, are both informative and intriguing. But they are only a part of the story that follows.

Charles H. Young, CO 439th Troop Carrier Group, standing beside his C-47, *The Argonia II*, Etain, France. 12 May 1945.

— Courtesy: Young

Pulse and Repulse

PART I

Organization and Assignments

Where is the Prince who can afford so to cover his country with troops for its defense, as that ten thousand men descended from the clouds, might not, in many places, do an infinite amount of mischief before a force could be brought together to repel them?

> Benjamin Franklin, 16 January 1784,
> in France, reporting on history's first
> balloon ascents.

Kilroy was here. Arrived by Troop Carrier.

> Anon.

1

Troop Carrier Command

Git ther fust with the mostest men.
Gen. Nathan Bedford Forrest, 1821–77

IN THE UNITED STATES, Brig. Gen. Anthony C. McAuliffe had been catapulted to fame by his eloquent reply to the German demand for surrender on 22 December 1944. Embittered by the general's letter in the 12 January 1945 *Stars and Stripes*, which belittled the importance of airborne resupply missions, the men of IX Troop Carrier Command often referred to him as General "McNuts."

Bickering between airborne and Troop Carrier commanders did not begin in the Ardennes with Operation REPULSE. Friction often surfaced during their formative period in 1941, and their growing pains became more acute after the United States entered World War II in December 1941.

Lt. Col. William C. Lee, often called the father of U.S. airborne forces, had by July 1941 organized the Provisional Parachute Group at Fort Benning, Georgia. After training three parachute infantry regiments, Colonel Lee moved his Airborne Command Headquarters to Fort Bragg, North Carolina, in April 1942, while the Parachute School remained at Fort Benning. Meanwhile, mounting complaints centered around the lack of aircraft assigned to Fort Benning for training. Only a few "miscellaneous" transports staffed with flight crews had been sent there on loan. "Even in March, the AAF A-3 [operations officer], although agreeing that Benning needed a

2

transport group for its airborne activities, held that the planes simply could not be spared." The Army Air Force had decided that the Douglas C-47s coming off the assembly lines in late 1941 and early 1942 were needed for training its air transport groups.

Transport squadrons, as they were designated before 1942, had few aircraft or qualified crews. To meet the increasing demand for personnel and priority materiel transport, new transport squadrons were activated at various AAF air bases. In April 1942, they were placed under a central command headed by Col. Fred C. Borum. He was given the task of organizing the transport squadrons into air transport groups under his command; thus he was considered the father of U.S. Troop Carrier. One of Colonel Borum's first actions was to call up reservists and others he knew — even "retreads" from World War I — to form his headquarters staff at Stout Field, Indianapolis, Indiana. The air transport squadrons were to be trained for another type of operation — combat. The primary mission of the newly organized Air Transport Command would be to drop paratroopers into battle zones as well as to land airborne troops in gliders also carrying jeeps, artillery, and ammunition. On 20 June 1942, the Air Transport Command was redesignated Troop Carrier Command (TCC).

Subsequently, a new organization was formed out of the Army Air Forces Ferrying Command and the Air Cargo Division of the Air Services Command. Designated the Air Transport Command (ATC), it developed into a successful airline-type transportation system between the U.S. and the ETO via the North Atlantic flight routes.

The Airborne and Troop Carrier commands did not share a clear understanding of programs and problems between them, and friction increased. To alleviate the situation, they began a mutual exchange of liaison officers in May 1942. By July Colonel Borum recognized the need for a higher level conference and invited General Lee for a meeting "in order that we may sit down over a table with our sleeves rolled up and our cards spread out above the board, to determine the most practical and expeditious manner in which we can weld our raw material into a smooth-running tool with which our country may carve out victory."

Without a unified command, some of the training problems persisted. The Airborne Command and the I Troop Carrier Command were both subject to directives and plans from separate, higher headquarters. Serving to unify them, however, each had individual training objectives designed for a common purpose.

The motto of Troop Carrier Command was considered to be a polite steal from General Forrest's prescription for victory. *Vincit qui primim gerit* (He conquers who gets there first) was written on the lower part of the blue and gold insignia of Troop Carrier Command. Above the motto was a falcon carrying in its talons a soldier holding a rifle with fixed bayonet.

*   *   *   *

Among the early birds assigned to Troop Carrier Command during its formation and training period were three commanders who would occupy critical command decision positions during the hastily organized Operation REPULSE.

Brig. Gen. Julian M. Chappell, from Americus, Georgia, was a graduate of the U.S. Military Academy in the class of 1931. After his first assignment at Fort Benning, Georgia, he entered pilot training and earned his wings at Kelly Field, Texas, in March 1933. After service in bombing units, he became commanding officer of the 89th Air Transport Group, which flew B-25 medium bombers. In very early 1942, Major Chappell was transferred to Troop Carrier Command to organize and build from what was a small squadron of nondescript aircraft a unit that would become the 50th Troop Carrier Wing. After intense training, the wing, with its four groups (439th, 440th, 441st, and 442d), moved to England in February–March 1944. On D-Day plus 1, 7 June, Colonel Chappell piloted a pathfinder C-47 into Normandy. He led 100 C-47s towing Horsa and Waco gliders loaded with glider troops of the 82d Airborne Division.

Col. Charles H. Young was commanding officer of the 439th Troop Carrier Group. He was recalled to active duty as a first lieutenant in February 1942. His military service began while attending Phillips University in Enid, Oklahoma. His Army Air Corps flight training occurred at Randolph and Kelly fields, and he graduated on 6 October 1937 at Kelly Field. For most of the next two years, he was assigned to Maj. Paul L. Williams' 90th Attack Squadron, flying the Northrop A-17A, at Barksdale Field, Louisiana, after which he left active duty to become a pilot for American Airlines until his 1942 recall to active duty and subsequent assignment to Troop Carrier. In January 1944, he was placed in command of the 439th Troop Carrier Group in Colonel Chappell's 50th Troop Carrier Wing just before the wing left for England, where it was assigned to Brig. Gen. Paul L. Williams' IX Troop Carrier Command. On D-Day (6 June), Lieutenant Colonel Young flew the lead aircraft of ninety C-47s to drop paratroops of the 101st Airborne Division over Normandy. Included on that mission were Maj. Gen. Maxwell D. Taylor, division commander, and Brig. Gen. Anthony C. McAuliffe, the division's artillery commander.

Lt. Col. Joel L. Crouch was commanding officer of the IX Troop Carrier Pathfinder Group (Provisional). A native Californian, he entered the Army Air Corps flight training program in 1932 and received his pilot rating at Kelly Field in 1933, graduating at the head of his class. Following two years' active duty in the Air Corps he was employed by United Air Lines as a DC-3 copilot. After five years as a captain with United, he was recalled to active duty in February 1942. He was subsequently assigned to Col. Harold L. "Hal" Clark's 52d Troop Carrier Wing Headquarters during the formation of the 61st, 313th, 314th, and 315th groups. As operations officer of the 52d Wing, Captain Crouch was involved with airborne training exercises in the United States for over a year. It was then that he first recognized the need for special "pathfinder" aircraft and paratroop teams to precede large Troop Carrier aircraft formations and locate drop zones (DZs) for paratroop missions, and landing zones (LZs) for glider missions. With lightweight radar-radio transmitters, the advance paratroops could establish the DZs and LZs for the navigators of the main formation to "home-in" on.

Such navigational guidance instructions had not been given to the earliest Troop Carrier groups of the 51st Wing, which had been sent to the European Theater of Operations (ETO) in September 1942 with very little training time. The wing would get its first, costly lessons from actual combat in the Mediterranean Theater of Operations (MTO) before the end of the year. Later missions, principally in the Mediterranean region, provided the American troop carriers with an apprenticeship in airborne warfare.

2

Lesson One: North Africa

OPERATION REPULSE WAS NOT the only hastily planned airborne operation in the ETO. Troop Carrier was even less prepared for its participation in Operation TORCH, the Anglo-American invasion of North Africa during November 1942. Maj. Gen. James H. Doolittle was in command of air operations for the invasion, and not since his bombing mission over Tokyo, seven months earlier, had he experienced enemy fire.

In late October, the 51st Troop Carrier Wing and its three groups (60th, 62d, and 64th) under command of Col. Paul L. Williams, were assigned to General Doolittle's newly formed Twelfth Air Force. Also, two heavy bombardment groups (97th and 301st) from the Eighth Air Force and four fighter groups were transferred to Doolittle for Operation TORCH.

Gen. Dwight D. Eisenhower, in overall command of the North African invasion, decided to direct the operation from Gibraltar rather than from England. He and his staff were flown there by six B-17s of the 97th Bombardment Group's 340th Squadron on 5–6 November. The lead aircraft was flown by Squadron Commander Maj. Paul W. Tibbets, Jr. (Tibbets would later command the B-29 *Enola Gay*, dropping the atom bomb over Hiroshima.) The B-17 with General Doolittle, Brig. Gen. Lyman L. Lemnitzer, and Col.

Thomas J. Davis on board was delayed by hydraulic system problems, but was on its way at dawn, 6 November. Without a fighter escort, the lone B-17 was attacked by four German JU-88s off the west coast of France. They had been on a reconnaissance flight searching for Allied shipping. Low on fuel, they soon retreated, but not until the B-17 had been badly crippled and copilot Lt. Thomas F. Lohr had been wounded in the arm. Earlier in the flight, Doolittle had visited the cockpit, and talked with Lohr and the pilot, Capt. John C. Summers. One of the general's first comments had been, "I've never flown a B-17, but maybe later." His turn came sooner than expected; when Lohr was wounded, Doolittle agreed to replace him in the copilot's seat while the B-17 limped to a landing at Gibraltar.

✳ ✳ ✳ ✳

D-Day for all three task forces was 8 November. The Western Task Force, arriving by sea from the United States, was to take the port of Casablanca, French Morocco. The Eastern Task Force (British) was to take Algiers and drive into Tunisia. One element of the Center Task Force was Doolittle's Twelfth Air Force, assigned to take airfields around Oran, Algeria, before dawn on 8 November. The spearhead role was given to the 60th Troop Carrier Group and the 2d Battalion, 503d Parachute Infantry Regiment of the 82d Airborne Division, both under the command of Col. William C. Bentley. (Bentley had previously been a military attaché in Morocco.) Lt. Col. Thomas J. Schofield commanded the 60th Group and Lt. Col. Edson D. Raff was in command of the 2d Battalion. Operation TORCH was successful, although the Troop Carrier mission was a disappointment for a number of reasons.

The 60th Troop Carrier Group was deemed the most qualified of the 51st Wing but was still undertrained and understaffed. All but one of its thirty-six navigators were fresh out of school, having had about fifty hours of in-flight training. Colonel Raff and his paratroops were trained and briefed with maps for six weeks before the mission. But they were to be flown by air crews who had not shared that training, nor even practiced long range instrument flying at night. For security reasons, the Troop Carrier pilots and navigators were not briefed about the mission until 5 November, two days before the scheduled departure from England. At Lands End, on the southwest coast of England, 531 paratroopers and the crews of thirty-nine C-47s were prepared for a night paradrop operation near Oran. In accordance with an alternate plan, General Doolittle's headquarters at Gibraltar sent a radio signal to delay the mission by four hours, obviating the need for the paradrops and permitting the landing of the Troop Carrier aircraft at La Senia (near Oran) after sunrise on 8 November.

The takeoffs began at 2105 and all aircraft were in the air by 2145. At 2200, they assembled over Portreath and headed southward in three flights. It was about 1,100 miles to Oran by the prescribed route over Spain, too long for maintaining a close formation. Some pilots failed to hold the prescribed airspeed of 135 MPH. The stormy weather at 10,000 feet over the Spanish mountains caused further separations of the flights. Communications by radio between aircraft were poor, even with the newly installed VHF equipment, with which the radio operators had had no time to familiarize themselves.

Most of the planes flew courses over Spain by dead reckoning, but the strong east winds had not been predicted in the weather report during the preflight briefing. Cloud cover precluded celestial navigation. As a result, most of the aircraft ended up fifty miles or more west of their objective over Moroccan terrain, which was covered by thick ground fog at daybreak. Three planes were so far off course that they landed in Spanish Morocco as far as 250 miles west of Oran. One of the planes unloaded its paratroops to save fuel and then flew on to Oran. Two others overran the African coast to land over 100 miles southwest of Oran in French Morocco. A C-47 that was short of fuel landed on the runway at Gibraltar. Thus seven planeloads of paratroops played no part in TORCH. Nine of the pilots did make their way to the Oran area approximately on schedule, between 0515 and 0615. They had gotten little assistance from the beacons. One that was supposed to be broadcasting at 440 kilocycles was actually signaling at 460. Another secret beacon at Tafaraoui Airfield was shut down by the operator, who expected the task force to arrive at 0100, in accordance with the plan that had been changed.

The bulk of the planes in the airborne mission found their way along the unfamiliar coast of Morocco, between 0600 and 0800, making landfall about 100 miles west of Oran. Three were forced down by French fighter aircraft. Two others were attacked and dam-

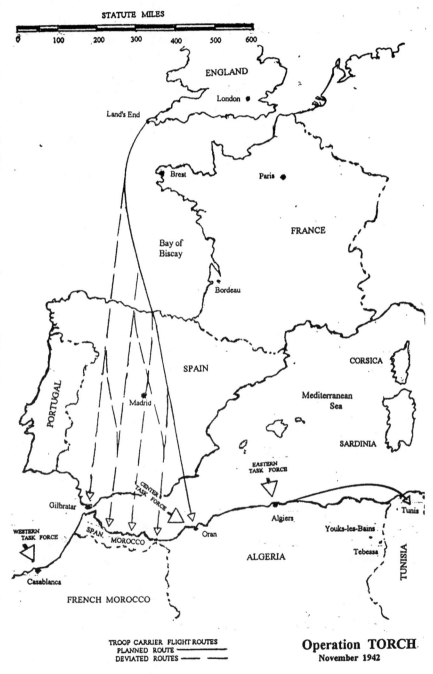

STATUTE MILES

ENGLAND

London

Land's End

Brest

Paris

FRANCE

Bay of
Biscay

Bordeau

SPAIN

CORSICA

Madrid

Mediterranean
Sea

PORTUGAL

SARDINIA

EASTERN
TASK FORCE

Gilbratar

CENTER
TASK
FORCE

Algiers

Tunis

WESTERN
TASK FORCE

SPAN.
MOROCCO

Oran

Youks-les-Bains

Tebessa

TUNISIA

ALGERIA

Casablanca

FRENCH MOROCCO

TROOP CARRIER FLIGHT ROUTES
PLANNED ROUTE ——————
DEVIATED ROUTES ——— ———

Operation TORCH
November 1942

— Map source courtesy Breuer (Phillips Publications)

aged, but managed crash-landings. After searching in vain for a land-
mark, Colonel Bentley landed his plane and found his position by
querying some Arabs. He took off again to guide the other three
aircraft of his contingent toward Oran. At 0810, eight planes of his
Troop Carrier group were seen circling near Lourmel. One was
Colonel Schofield's, with Colonel Raff aboard. After joining up and
heading for Oran, they saw a column of armored vehicles, believed
to be French, headed for the Sebkra d'Oran hills south of Oran. Raff
had a brief radio talk with Bentley and opted for a paradrop to meet
the threat. Thus ten C-47s dropped Raff and his paratroops on a hill
that dominated the northern edges of the Sebkra dry lake bed. After
the jump, all planes (except Bentley's) landed in the Lourmel area.
Bentley flew on to reconnoiter the area around Tafaraoui, where he
was fired on by French artillery near La Senia and landed on the
northeast shore of the Sebkra with engine trouble. While Bentley
was reporting the situation to II Corps by radio, the pilot who had
left his paratroops in Spanish Morocco flew in and landed with fuel
gauges on empty. A few minutes later, both French forces arrived
and apologetically took both planes and crews into custody.

Colonel Raff and his paratroops made a successful jump, but
had been spared combat when they discovered that the armored column was American, moving inland from the coast to take Oran.

And so by 0900, 8 November 1942, the airborne mission of Operation TORCH ended. Of the thirty-three planes that had reached
Oran, twenty-seven were grounded near Lourmel, five were scattered
around the Sebkra, and one was down near Arzeu. Tafaraoui Airfield
was taken around midday by American ground forces. Twenty-five
of the C-47s (two loaded with paratroops) were flown in that afternoon. They were saved from further damage by Spitfires of the 31st
Fighter Group, flying to Tafaraoui from Gibraltar. Spitfires shot
down four French Dewoitines preparing to strafe the airfield.

Some of the paratroops from three of the planes were able to
march and they pressed on by foot to Tafaraoui, arriving there at
dawn on 9 November. The main body of the battalion was picked up
by trucks and arrived at Tafaraoui at about 1600 the same day. The
French at Oran capitulated about noon, 10 November.

*   *   *   *

The Allies' next task in North Africa was to outrace the Germans into Tunisia, and airborne operations again offered a chance for success. On 10 November, General Doolittle ordered every possible plane from the 60th Troop Carrier Group to Maison Blanche Airfield near Algiers. Five days later, Colonel Williams arrived from England with the other two groups (62d and 64th) of his 51st Troop Carrier Wing — all loaded with paratroopers of the 82d Airborne Division. With little preparation, Williams was to fly a mission on 29 November to drop paratroops at Depienne, where they would attack the airfield at Oudna, which was located about ten miles south of Tunis.

The formation of twenty-six planes of the 62d Group and eighteen planes of the 64th Group were loaded with 530 paratroopers and at noon on the 29th, they headed east from Maison Blanche. The prescribed route of some 400 miles along the Algerian coast seemed simple enough, but it was more difficult to follow after it turned south over the Tunisian hills. In the lead plane of the formation, Colonel Williams picked his landmarks precisely and dropped his troops over the Depienne airfield at 1450 from an altitude of 600 feet. By then the formation had become loose and ragged due to the inexperience of the pilots, particularly those of the 62d Group. Troops and supplies were scattered over an area one and one-half miles long and over a half mile wide. Some paratroopers were dropped much farther away and were still missing seven hours later. Fortunately, only a few of them were injured, and all planes returned safely.

This last airborne mission flown in North Africa was a lesson in combat experience that Colonel Williams would never forget. He realized the need for dropping pathfinders with radar-radio navigation aids at the DZ ahead of large Troop Carrier formations. Such techniques would not be properly employed until after the disastrous Sicily missions, in July 1943.

3

Lesson Two: Sicily

MAJ. GEN. MATTHEW B. RIDGWAY, commanding general of the 82d Airborne Division, was in the United States to oversee the formation and training of the division during Operation TORCH. He was disturbed at the heavy casualties that Colonel Raff's 2d Battalion suffered during the four days after the drop at Depienne. By March 1943, it was clear that all of Tunisia would soon be taken from the Germans and that Troop Carriers with airborne troops would be used for the invasion of Sicily. General Ridgway was flown to North Africa to plan the operations and then returned to Fort Bragg on 24 March to get the division ready for deployment to North Africa. With Raff's experience still fresh, he complained that his division had been given a third of the training that most divisions received before being committed to combat.

At the same time, Ridgway was highly critical of Brig. Gen. Harold L. "Hal" Clark's 52d Troop Carrier Wing. As a training partner, he viewed Clark's airmen inept in "precise formation flying and pinpoint navigation required for effective parachute and glider tow operations." Also, because of the shortage of training time, the aircraft crews were particularly poor at finding DZs during night operations, a terribly difficult proposition. Ridgway cabled General Taylor in North Africa, urging him to persuade General Eisenhow-

12

er's planners to change the scheduled airborne operation into Sicily from nighttime to early dawn on D-Day, 10 July. Neither Gen. Bernard L. Montgomery nor his airborne commander and adviser to Eisenhower, Maj. Gen. F. A. M. Browning, were receptive to the advice. When Ridgway and his paratroops sailed for North Africa, he still hoped to change their minds.

On 20 April the 82d Airborne Division left Fort Bragg, arriving at Casablanca on 10 May. General Taylor greeted General Ridgway on the dock, but a more remarkable greeting soon met the not-so-secret arrivals: On the first night ashore, Axis Sally broadcast from Berlin, "Welcome to Africa, Matt Ridgway and your bad boys."

From Casablanca the division moved by truck and train some 400 miles eastward to Oujda, French Morocco. By mid-May they were ready for jump training exercises with Troop Carrier.

The planes and crews of the 52d Troop Carrier Wing — the wing's air echelon — took off from Laurinburg-Maxton AAB on Easter Sunday, 25 April. They flew the South Atlantic route and arrived at Oujda 9–10 May. The sea convoy with the ground echelon arrived in Casablanca on 20 May, reaching Oujda on 24 May while training was already under way.

D-Day had been determined by and based on the phases of the July moon, the assumption being that the evening hours of 9 July would provide enough moonlight for airborne operations. After midnight there would be complete darkness for the amphibious assaults. Reasonable on paper, the nocturnal mission carried huge risks for the poorly trained force, but neither General Ridgway nor General Clark was able to dissuade General Browning from scheduling the night airborne missions.

It was left to Maj. Joel L. Crouch, operations officer of the 52d Troop Carrier Wing, to develop the pathfinder tactics required for night operations. New tactics were not the only challenge the invaders faced. Fierce winds, dust storms, and thunderstorms plagued the training exercises. Aggravating the problem, dysentery struck almost every airman and paratrooper. Time to properly train the pathfinder teams and Troop Carrier crews in night formation flying, navigation, and location of paratroop drop zones simply ran out.

In May the newly organized Northwest African Air Force Troop Carrier Command (NAAFTCC) was placed under the command of Brig. Gen. Paul L. Williams. Recognizing that intricate flight routes were necessary for the airborne missions to Sicily, Williams delegated the planning to General Clark of the 52d Wing, and Col. Ray A. Dunn, commander of the 51st Wing.

Since groups of the 51st Wing had had experience with the British 1 Airborne Division and the men of the 52d Wing had trained with the American 82d Airborne Division, it seemed logical for General Williams to assign together the same teams to the Sicily invasions. The logic was lost at the end of May when General Montgomery decided to add a glider mission to the British airborne operation. The 51st Wing had almost no glider tow experience and no experience at all in night flying. Montgomery's planning, together with advice from Browning, who was in Eisenhower's air force headquarters in Algiers, resulted in a very costly lesson, one that would not be forgotten during planning and preparations for later glider airborne missions in Europe.

*   *   *   *

To accomplish General Montgomery's invasion plans, the Glider Pilot Regiment of the British 1 Airborne Division had enough pilots, but it was short British Horsa gliders — the aircraft the regiment had trained in. However, a plentiful supply of American Waco (CG-4A) gliders had arrived in May and were placed at Montgomery's disposal. Additionally, American glider pilots assigned to the 51st Wing were on detached service to give transition flight training in the CG-4A to British glider pilots. It was a hasty training program ruefully weak in night-flying practice.

The thrust of the British invasion, Operation LADBROKE, to be conducted by Montgomery's Eighth Army, was aimed at the southeast shores of Sicily. It was timed to follow the paratroops and glider troops of 1 Airborne Division after they were inserted into the Syracuse area.

In Operation HUSKY, the American ground forces were to go ashore along sixty-nine miles of the sandy coast of southwest Sicily. From the coast, the newly formed Seventh Army under Lt. Gen. George S. Patton, Jr., and the 1st Infantry Division, of Maj. Gen. Omar Bradley's II Corps, would drive toward Gela. Three hours before the shore landings, aircraft of the 52d Troop Carrier Wing were to drop paratroops of the 82d Airborne Division at a DZ east of Gela, on a high-ground location chosen by General Bradley.

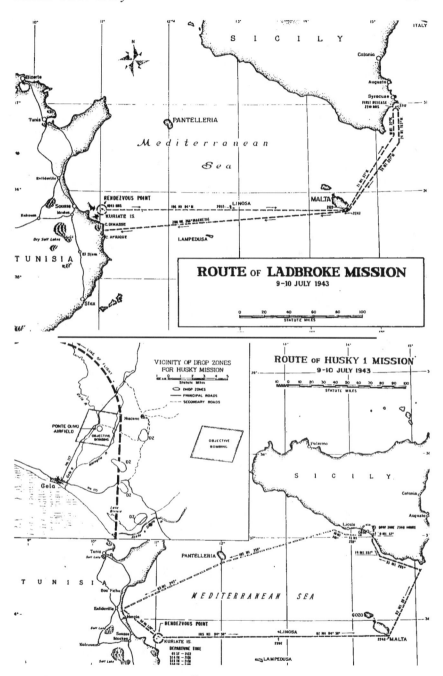

— Maps source courtesy Maxwell AFB, AL. USAF Historical Studies, No. 74

Of the two airborne operations, LADBROKE (the first) was far more disastrous. After a rendezvous off the coast of Tunisia at 1943, 9 July, 130 Waco and seven Horsa gliders loaded with troops of 1 Airlanding Brigade were in tow behind American and British aircraft. The glider pilots were all British with the exception of twenty-eight Americans who had instructed them during the Waco glider transition; the Americans volunteered to fly the mission as copilots. Of the 137 tow planes, 109 were C-47s from the 60th Troop Carrier Group, 51st Wing.

The flight route to Sicily posed a serious challenge to the pilots and navigators who would fly it at night. The first leg was east to Malta — it presented no serious problems. After passing around Malta, the next course heading was north-northeast for some seventy miles to the southeastern tip of Sicily and then north along the east coast to Syracuse. After the formation rounded Malta, the strong, turbulent northwest winds and the dark of night contributed to the breakup of the formation before it reached Syracuse. Many gliders cut off prematurely, or were released and ended up in the sea because the tow plane crews could not pinpoint their own locations and the LZs in the dark.

The flight route of Operation HUSKY No. 1 was to follow that of LADBROKE until it reached the coast of Sicily. From there the flight route went west along the coast to a checkpoint provided by a river mouth and a small lake, then inland to the DZ.

Five Troop Carrier groups (61st, 314th, 313th, 316th, and 64th) of Clark's 52d Wing were in the air over Tunisia by 2045. The 226 C-47 aircraft were loaded with 2,781 paratroops of the 505th Parachute Infantry Regiment, plus 624 of the 3d Battalion, 504th PIR, a company of engineers and other small detachments. Their commander was Col. James M. Gavin. (Later, during the Battle of the Bulge, Maj. Gen. James "Slim Jim" Gavin, at age thirty-seven, commanded the 82d Airborne Division, then the youngest general in the U.S. Army.)

The mission did not go as planned. Visibility became the major problem, particularly after the turn around Malta where each formation of nine aircraft headed northeast toward Cape Passero, Sicily. Navigation was complicated by the prescribed maximum flight altitude of 500 feet. The formation flew under strict radio silence. In the confusion of silence and darkness, and with the winds from the northwest at 25 to 30 MPH, some of the planes veered off course. Fortunately they did not stray far enough from the dogleg route along the coast of Sicily to encounter American naval forces there which were instructed to fire on any and all aircraft.

Unable to accurately identify their checkpoints for the approach to the DZ, the pilots dropped the paratroops by estimation. They were widely scattered; many were unable to join up with their units and some were captured. Despite the inaccuracy of the drop, however, Colonel Gavin's paratroops succeeded in capturing the major objectives supporting the seaborne landings by Patton's and Bradley's forces. To Troop Carrier, it was by no means a "milk run." Eight aircraft were lost to enemy flak and machine guns after the drop. About half of the aircraft crews survived to rejoin their squadrons a few days later.

Allied prisoners were shipped across the Strait of Messina to the toe of Italy's boot. From there, they traveled in boxcars to Rome. One prisoner was S/Sgt. Cecil Owen King, from Geneva, Pennsylvania, a demolition expert who jumped on 9 July with the 505th PIR. While still hanging from his parachute, he was hit by German small-arms fire and shrapnel. He passed out after landing, awaking in a German ambulance thirsty and in a lot of pain. To his surprise, he was given a canteen of wine. In the German hospital in Rome, the surgeon who operated on him had been educated in the U.S. and was fluent in English. He told King that he returned to Germany for a visit in 1934, and was not allowed to leave the country. King credits his survival to him. From Rome the prisoners were moved to *stalags* in Germany.

* * * *

The next mission was even less fortunate. When Colonel Gavin requested reinforcements in the Gela area on 11 July, HUSKY No. 2 was hastily planned. About 2,000 paratroopers of the 504th Regiment were to be dropped around midnight on the 11th. Based on the debriefing information from the Troop Carrier crews that returned from HUSKY No. 1, a repeat mission was decided upon. The flight course around Malta to Sicily was the same as that flown by HUSKY No. 1, except that it turned inland about thirty-five miles from Gela. The route was planned to avoid the Allied naval convoy of the invasion forces, but would go directly over the battle front.

Thirty-five C-47s of the 316th Group led the 144-plane formation. Last off from Tunisia, at 2020 hours, were thirty-eight planes of the 313th Group. At the same time, the German Luftwaffe was over the Allied invasion forces. The last German bombing assaults began at 2010, and for almost an hour American antiaircraft guns on ships and on shore blazed away at the bombers until they broke off their attacks. The gunners expected and were prepared for another wave of bombers in the midnight blackness. But, because of a breakdown in communication channels, they did not expect Allied aircraft.

As the Troop Carrier formations approached at midnight, the entire flight corridor erupted with deadly, heavy flak and machine gun fire from nervous U.S. Navy gunners. Six C-47s were lost on the way in to "friendly forces fire" with paratroopers still on board. On the way out from the Gela DZ, while passing over the east coast, the aircraft again received devastating barrages from one friendly ship after another, for twenty miles. Twenty-three aircraft failed to return from the HUSKY No. 2 mission.

Two days later, General Montgomery wanted another British-American airborne mission into Sicily, also at night and again with gliders. Operation FUSTIAN was yet another airborne disaster. Of the 135 aircraft, the 51st Wing furnished 105 C-47s from the 60th, 62d, and 64th groups, and the British provided eleven Albemarles and Halifaxes from the 38th Group to carry paratroops of the British 1 Parachute Brigade. Nineteen gliders, eight Wacos and eleven Horsas loaded with antitank weapons were to be towed by British Albemarles and Halifaxes.

Takeoffs from two Tunisian airfields began at 1920 on the night of the 13th. Last off at 2200 were the tow planes and gliders. This time British naval vessels did not get the word. The Troop Carriers were mistaken for German torpedo bombers. Eleven C-47s with paratroops aboard were shot down, fifty were damaged, and others turned back rather than endure friendly fire.

* * * *

All major regions of Sicily were in Allied hands by 24 July, and the last German resistance ended at Messina on 17 August. One month earlier, General Eisenhower had requested a full accounting of the airborne missions, especially General Montgomery's Opera-

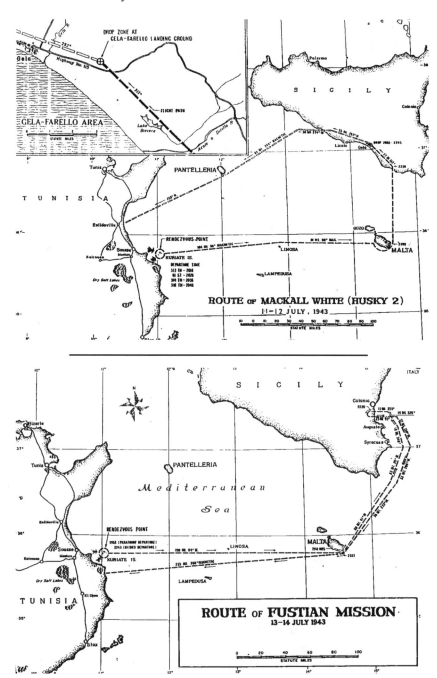

— Maps source courtesy Maxwell AFB, AL. USAF Historical Studies, No. 74

tion LADBROKE, and particularly the glider mission. On 15 July Brig. Gen. Raymond A. Dunn, CG of the 51st Troop Carrier Wing at Goubrine, Tunisia, received the request from Eisenhower's AFHQ in Algiers. Ike wanted an inspection of the gliders that had landed in the Syracuse area of Sicily. The findings of the on-site investigations were to be submitted first to Brig. Gen. Paul L. Williams.

Prior to the investigations on the ground, Col. Elliott Roosevelt's North Africa Photo Reconnaissance Unit furnished photographs which were taken from 30,000 feet on 10 July. They showed only some sixty gliders in the area near Syracuse, seven of which were offshore in the surf. For four days, 17–20 July, a search team traveled the territory within a twenty-mile radius of the designated LZs and located only thirty-five gliders or their remains. Another hundred were unaccounted for. Those that were found were photographed and pinpointed, and were included in the report to Generals Williams and Eisenhower. The information verified what Williams' command already knew and what Montgomery may have disregarded. Unlike bombing missions, airborne missions required pinpoint accuracy — men, unlike bombs, had to be parachuted or landed in gliders; further, once landed, they had to quickly regroup into their units.

This weakness in the command and communication channels was not anticipated. Timing and coordinating combat operations has always been challenging, particularly when land, sea, and air forces are combined. Complicating matters, the airborne operations into Sicily were the first time that combined British and American Troop Carrier aircraft carried paratroops and glider troops into battle.

In the reports to General Eisenhower, various viewpoints regarding the communications problem were emphasized. Eisenhower was highly critical of Patton's command, and he wrote Patton that he should fix responsibility and take disciplinary action. Patton felt that Ike was looking for a reason to relieve him of his command. General "Boy" Browning was Montgomery's man and was on Eisenhower's headquarters staff. He laid the blame entirely on the American Troop Carrier crews. His American counterpart, Maj. Gen. Joseph M. Swing, who had graduated from West Point with Eisenhower, disagreed. Swing had been called to North Africa from his command of the 11th Airborne Division in the U.S. He was more objective than Browning in his report, citing five major weaknesses:

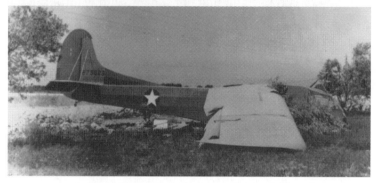

Operation LADBROOKE, Sicily, 9–10 July 1943. Photos of four of the 130 Waco CG-4As on the mission (taken 17 July 1943).

— Courtesy: Fetters

1. Insufficient time spent in coordinating the air routes with all forces.
2. Complexity of the flight route for the low degree of training of the navigators.
3. The rigid naval policy of firing at any and all aircraft.
4. The unfortunate timing of airdrops directly after extensive enemy air attacks.
5. The failure of some army ground commanders to warn all antiaircraft gun units of the impending airborne missions.

General Ridgway reported then and later on his fruitless efforts to coordinate with the naval forces. Contrary to Ridgway's assertions, U.S. Navy commanders claimed that they had not been notified of the airborne missions nor of their flight routes. Even if they had, however, it is unlikely that the entire invasion fleet, which included many merchant ships with U.S. Navy "Armed Guard" gun crews, could have been properly informed or completely controlled after "extensive enemy air attacks."

Eisenhower's headquarters managed to keep the disastrous results of the Sicilian airborne operations secret for about eight months. The first sketchy accounts appeared in the 27 March 1944 issues of *Time* and *Newsweek,* furnished by a *Stars and Stripes* reporter who was in the States on home leave.

4

Lesson Three: Italy

IN FEBRUARY 1943, General Sir Harold R. L. G. Alexander became deputy commander in chief (under General Eisenhower) of all Allied ground forces in the Mediterranean Theater of Operations. Alexander, who had directed the evacuation of the British Army from Dunkirk (May-June 1940), in August 1942, had been appointed commander in chief of British Forces in the Middle East. In North Africa, he had organized the British drive on Tunis (October-November 1942). For Operation AVALANCHE, the planned invasion of Italy, he was placed in command of the seaborne forces of the Allied 15th Army Group, consisting of Lt. Gen. Mark Clark's U.S. Fifth Army and Montgomery's British Eighth Army. Both forces would go ashore south of Salerno. However, Alexander also became unduly involved in planning American airborne operations.

After the fall of Mussolini in July 1943, the newly formed Italian government under Marshal Pietro Badoglio, designated prime minister by King Victor Emmanuel III, decided to join the Allies against Germany. (Since 15 August, Badoglio's chief armistice negotiator, Gen. Giuseppe Castellano, had been secretly negotiating with the Allies.) On 1 September, in an olive grove at Cassibile, Sicily, General Alexander met with the Italian delegation. For the conference, he had changed into his dress uniform — with his decorations extending from his shoulders nearly to his shiny boots. Instead of making peace, however, he and his beribboned staff gave the Italians a harsh talking-to. Disappointed that they had not been given authority to sign the armistice, Alexander gave them another twenty-four hours, after which they could expect the bombing of Rome.

Later the same day, Castellano reported to Marshal Badoglio in Rome that the Allies were threatening to bomb Rome unless their terms were accepted. He had at least obtained a pledge that an American airborne division would be dropped to help protect the Italian government in Rome from German reprisals if the Italians agreed to the Allied demands.

The next day Eisenhower sent Major General Ridgway and Brig. Gen. Maxwell Taylor (liaison officer for the 82d Airborne Division at Allied Force Headquarters) to Alexander's headquarters at Cassibile. There they learned of Alexander's new plan — to drop the largest American airborne forces available on Rome the night before Operation AVALANCHE. Both Ridgway and Taylor questioned the effectiveness and cost in men and machines of such a mission. Alexander brushed their opinions aside.

Back at Bizerte, Tunisia, in Eisenhower's advance headquarters, Ridgway and Taylor persisted in objecting to Alexander's plan. On 5 September, they appealed to Eisenhower's chief of staff, Gen. Walter Bedell "Beetle" Smith. He tried to arrange another meeting with Alexander, who curtly turned it down with the reply, "Don't give this another thought, Ridgway. Contact will be made with your division in three days — five at the most."

All the while at the German headquarters near Rome, Field Marshal Albert Kesselring, fully aware of the Italian switch, was preparing for an Allied airborne assault with the reinforcement of Rome.

Still unconvinced, General Ridgway requested General Smith to arrange for two airborne officers to get to Rome and meet with Badoglio himself. Alexander replied that it was too dangerous. But Ridgway persisted. This time Alexander agreed. However, he did not permit General Taylor and Col. William T. Gardiner, A-2 of the 51st Troop Carrier Wing, to board a British motor torpedo boat at Palermo, Sicily, until 0200 on 7 September.

After landing at Gaeta, seventy-five miles south of Rome, at about 1700 hours, the ride to the city in an Italian staff car and later in a Red Cross ambulance through German check points had all the

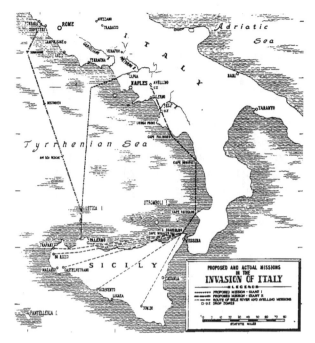

— Maps source courtesy Maxwell AFB, AL. USAF Historical Studies, No. 74

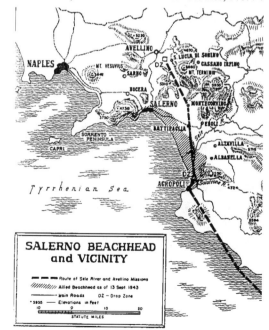

intrigue of a spy novel. To escape detection, the Americans posed as captured fliers.

That night, meeting with General Carboni, they learned that his forces could not protect the DZ and LZ airfields. The airborne operation would be a disaster. He urged a delay of the drop at Rome until Allied ground forces were nearing the city.

Insisting on a meeting with Premier Badoglio, the two Americans were driven in Carboni's limousine to Badoglio's palatial villa around midnight. Badoglio and his staff were present, although they were still half asleep, having just been awakened. He told the Americans that he could not or would not cooperate with an airborne operation around Rome. He definitely wanted an armistice, but not until the Allies occupied the city. The premier wrote a message to General Eisenhower postponing the armistice which Taylor would carry, along with his own coded message, that he sent over the clandestine radio link to Eisenhower's headquarters in Algiers.

After being driven back, again through many military checkpoints, to quarters provided by General Carboni, Taylor and Gardiner knew what their coded message would be: "Situation Innocuous" — an urgent request to cancel the mission. It was sent early on the morning of 8 September. They worried about whether Eisenhower received the message. He did.

It was forwarded to Eisenhower's advance headquarters at Bizerte, Tunisia, where he and his staff were reviewing the final details of Operation GIANT I, the Salerno invasion scheduled to begin at 0330 on the 9th. General Smith gave Ike the message from Allied Forces HQ in Algiers. Ike promptly canceled Ridgway's 82d Airborne Division airdrop (Operation GIANT II) on Rome. General Alexander was disturbed and asked Eisenhower to also send a courier to Sicily to inform General Dunn, the 51st Troop Carrier Wing commander, and General Ridgway of the mission's cancellation. He was concerned that the communication might not get through in time. Brig. Gen. Lyman Lemnitzer, deputy chief of staff of the 15th Army Group, was told to "get an airplane and get over there and ensure that this operation is stopped." When he arrived at Licata airfield in late afternoon, the first element of loaded C-47s was in the air, circling and forming up. After the emergency signals were flashed from Lemnitzer's plane, the runway was cleared. On the ground, General Lemnitzer saw General Ridgway in his parachute and shouted "Didn't you get our message?" "What message?"

Ridgway retorted. One hundred thirty-five C-47s, loaded with two battalions and part of the headquarters of the 504th Parachute Regiment, a battery of antiaircraft artillery, and other support troops were unloaded — and saved from looming disaster.

American commanders under General Eisenhower later expressed gratitude for Taylor's and Gardiner's Rome exploit. As Ridgway wrote, "We were spared that senseless and useless sacrifice." Prime Minister Churchill also mentioned it after his querying telegram of 7 September to Alexander: "Alexander replied that the Italian Government, being unable to announce the Armistice, had forced him to make certain changes. AVALANCHE would go as planned, except no airborne forces would take part."

＊　＊　＊　＊

Prime Minister Churchill was in the United States conferring with President Roosevelt at the White House and at Hyde Park from 1 September until the night of the 12th. During his train ride to Halifax, where he would board HMS *Renown* for his return to Britain, he wrote a message of advice for Alexander. It began, "I hope you are watching above all the battle of 'Avalanche,' which dominates everything. None of the commanders engaged has fought a large-scale war before." It was telegraphed from the *Renown* on the 14th. While messages traveled to and from the ship, the battle near Salerno went on. Alexander's report, received on the 16th, included, "There is little depth anywhere; we have temporarily lost the initiative. Last night our Air dropped a parachute battalion behind enemy lines in Avellino area. Air flew in 1,600 men of the 82d Division last night." By the time the *Renown* reached the Clyde, Scotland, on the 19th, the worried tone of the messages had changed to confidence in a successful invasion.

＊　＊　＊　＊

The seaborne forces of the 15th Army Group attacked on schedule. From Sicily, Clark's and Montgomery's armies went ashore south of Salerno at 0330 on 9 September 1943. On the 11th, General Clark was informed that the Rome airborne mission had been canceled and that American paratroops and Troop Carrier planes were available if needed. The 52d Troop Carrier Wing and the 82d Airborne Division were kept ready.

At the time, all communications were routed through General

Alexander's headquarters at Syracuse, Sicily. From the Salerno beach-head on the 11th, Clark asked Alexander by radio for airborne rein-forcement that night or the next night at the latest. He wanted a bat-talion to drop on Avellino and a regiment to drop northeast of Naples to block German troops coming from the north toward Salerno. The message was not relayed until the 12th. Meanwhile the British-Ameri-can hold on the beachhead was deteriorating. Clark soon recognized the seriousness of the communication delays (not the first experi-enced through Alexander's headquarters). Fortunately he found a quicker way to communicate, one bypassing Alexander.

Early on the 13th, a tired air force reconnaissance pilot, 1st Lt. Jacob R. Hamilton, landed his A-36 — the reconnaissance version of the P-51Mustang — at a crude airstrip about twenty miles south-east of Salerno, near Paestum. He was quickly "recruited" by Clark to deliver a vital letter directly to General Ridgway. After flying the 300-mile course, Hamilton arrived at Licato, Sicily, at about 1330 hours. That afternoon, with Ridgway's response in hand, Hamilton flew back to the Salerno airstrip. While riding in a jeep headed for Clark's command post, he was strafed by German planes, dislocat-ing his shoulder when he dived into a ditch. He was in pain and was thoroughly exhausted when he delivered the message to General Clark. It was classically brief: "Can do."

To avoid a repeat of the faulty Sicily airborne operations, tim-ing and coordination had become paramount planning consider-ations. For that reason, the Troop Carrier wing and group com-manders were at Licata for a briefing on the Naples airborne mission when Ridgway received the revised plan from Clark. After consulta-tion, another briefing was held to finalize the flight routes to the new DZ. By 1600 the commanders left for their airfields to marshal their units for Operation GIANT No. 1. After returning to their 52d Wing headquarters at Agrigenta, General Clark and his opera-tions officer, Lt. Col. Joel Crouch, briefed the three pathfinder air-craft crews and the parachute teams.

The pathfinders were prepared. Since mid-August, Crouch had concentrated their training for the airborne invasion of Italy. A pla-toon of forty-eight paratroopers from Headquarters Company, 1st Battalion, 504th Parachute Infantry Regiment, under a First Lieu-tenant Jones, was organized into three squads or teams. Each of them were assigned specific duties to accomplish after their para-chute landing at the DZ. Jones' first team would carry the lightweight 5G radio homing transmitters, Eureka radar transmitters, and Krypton lights. The second team was the Intelligence and Reconnaissance Squad under 1st Sgt. Milton V. Knight, of LaFayette, Louisiana. The third team was the Defense Squad.

Lt. Col. James J. Roberts, Jr., returned to his 313th Group at Milo-Trapani where the four squadrons (29th, 49th, 48th, and 47th) and the 2d Battalion, with over 600 paratroops of the 504th Parachute Infantry Regiment, were briefed in the late afternoon. As the squadrons' navigators replotted their courses up the southwest coast of Italy to the DZ, they were assured that there would be no friendly fire from Allied naval forces along the way. Friendly fire or no, what was most disturbing to them was that only some of the leading aircraft had the Rebecca radar receivers that displayed the terrain diagrams sent by the Eureka transmitters located at the DZ. Fancy electronics notwithstanding, the Very light could be seen from up to thirty miles away — in good visibility. But to effectively hit the DZ, a close flight formation was essential.

Col. Willis W. Mitchell's 61st Group was based at Licata, yet its planes had to fly in to Comiso to pick up their paratroops from Col. Reuben Tucker's 504th Regiment. It was not until Col. Clayton Stiles returned to his 314th Group at Castelvetrano that his crews were quickly briefed. They too would fly to Comiso to load paratroops. Because they were late in arriving, the plane crews got their final briefing "by the light of a few flashlights and maps held against the side of a plane" while the men of the 504th climbed aboard.

Meanwhile, in accordance with the understanding between Mark Clark and Matthew Ridgway, communications were direct, bypassing Alexander. Ridgway radioed Clark his confirmation of the flight plan and schedules. He explicitly stated that all Allied ground and naval forces must withhold firing on any aircraft after 2100 hours until otherwise notified. Clark was well aware of the Sicily disaster and promptly sent orders to every VI Corps battery on the beachhead and to Vice Adm. H. K. Hewitt, the naval commander of the American Western Task Force. This time, Hewitt could not claim that his forces were not properly informed.

* * * *

Operation GIANT I began at 2045 hours on 13 September, when Colonel Crouch took off from the Agrigenta airfield in the first of three pathfinder C-47s. Passing north of Mt. Etna and Messina, Sicily, they flew off the southwest coast of Italy without encountering any fire from either friend or foe. Favored by fair weather, light winds, and a full moon, the coastal checkpoints were easily discernible. At Cape Palinuro, Crouch headed over Clark's beachhead forces toward the DZ, which was located at the Sele River, sixteen miles southwest of Salerno. As promised by General Clark, a green Very light and flashlight signals were aimed from the DZ toward the approaching planes.

At 2314, directly over the target, Crouch rang the jump bells. While the three teams floated down from a height of about 800 feet, the Fifth Army engineers lit flares around the DZ. The improvised flares were five-gallon cans of sand soaked with gasoline. Less than fifteen minutes later, one of the Eureka radar beacons and a G-5 homing transmitter were in operation, but not in time for the first Troop Carrier formation to home in on.

Eighty-five aircraft of the 52d Troop Carrier Wing and 1,300 paratroopers of the 82d Airborne Division had been marshaled at the two Sicilian airfields. First off from Trapani at 2040 hours were thirty-six planes of the 313th Group (nine each from the 29th, 49th, 48th, and 47th squadrons) loaded with 611 paratroops of the 2d Battalion, 504th Parachute Infantry Regiment. From the Messina checkpoint, they were to fly the same route as the pathfinders — over water up the toe of the Italian boot. The squadrons' navigators calculated that the estimated time of arrival at the DZ would be 2330 hours. They arrived four minutes ahead of schedule. As the four squadrons approached the DZ, each in the nine-plane V of Vs formation, the navigators with Rebecca radar scopes in their aircraft were alarmed — they could not pick up any Eureka radar transmissions.* However the DZ was readily located by the flashes from the Very light and the flares that surrounded it. So well had the pilots kept formation, and so well had the DZ been marked, that nearly all the paratroops landed within 200 yards of its perimeter.

The return route was the same as the one flown by the pathfinders. The planes cut back across the Tyrrhenian Sea to Sicily by way of Cape Palinuro, Stromboli, and Cape Milazzo, thus skirting

---

* The nine-plane V formation consisted of three three-plane Vs, one three-plane V central and leading, with a three-plane V trailing off to its left and one off to its right, forming a compact nine-plane V.

the edge of the navy's restricted area. For added safety, they flew above 6,000 feet. By 0315, all squadrons of the 313th were back in Trapani without mishap.

The other two Troop Carrier groups did not perform as well. At Comiso, some of the forty-two aircraft of the 61st Group had to be removed because of mechanical problems, and takeoffs were delayed until replacements were made. When forty-one aircraft were finally marshaled and loaded, they were nearly three hours behind schedule, with the first departures at 2320. Therefore they could not join up with the 313th Group as planned. Divided into four flights, they flew what amounted to a separate mission. One flight had no operator/navigator competent to operate the Rebecca and it lost contact with the others. The flight dropped B Company of the 504th eight to ten miles southwest of the DZ. The other three flights made good drops with all the paratroops coming down within one mile of the drop zone. The planes of the 61st returned to Sicily by the same route on which they had come.

The 314th Group had more difficulty in dispatching its flight from Comiso than did the 61st Group. Of the eight aircraft assigned, two were grounded by electrical problems. Quickly, the paratroopers were redistributed among the other planes. Then the Rebecca-equipped lead plane had a tire blowout. Finally, fifteen minutes after midnight, six planes took off and flew the prescribed route along the coast of Italy. For the final approach they had only the flares to guide them to the DZ, and all drops were made within a mile of it. They were safely back at their airfield by 0430.

In terms of hitting the drop zone, Operation GIANT I was flawed. Though all pilots found their way to the beachhead, many had not kept close formation and approached from various directions. Certainly, without the Eureka and the flares, the drop could have been chaotic. Fortunately the operation was not affected by enemy action. German planes were reported to be in the air during the mission, but none attacked. And General Clark was highly satisfied. Within fifteen hours of his initial request, he had added a force of 1,300 troops to the center of his lines to counter the German drive down the Sele River valley.

* * * *

The success of Operation GIANT I ensured a request from

Mark Clark directly to Matthew Ridgway for a sequel on the following night. The 505th Parachute Infantry Regiment drop east of Naples at Avellino was canceled and redirected to the DZ along the Sele River. The 52d Troop Carrier Wing got the word at 1340 on the 14th that it was to carry the 505th on a duplicate flight of the previous night's mission. The situation at the front was still so critical that they were told the mission was "most urgent." For the Operation GIANT II mission, the 52d Wing committed 131 planes to carry the 505th PIR and a company of engineers, about 2,100 men in all.

Again Colonel Crouch piloted the first of three pathfinder planes which took off at 2147. From 6,000 feet, they descended to 1,000 feet on the approach to the DZ, again guided by the burning flares placed in T formations. The pathfinder teams jumped at 2338 from 700 feet into the center of the zone. Within three minutes they had a Eureka in operation. Again the pathfinders had proved their worth. However, not all of the following three flight formations performed as expected.

The lead formation of six flights consisted of fifty-four planes from the 313th and 314th groups. Only the first two flights of the 313th (eight planes of the 47th and ten of the 49th squadrons) flew the route to the DZ on schedule. Some of the crew members had been on the previous night's mission. Each lead plane had a Rebecca radar receiver and the squadrons held to a close formation during the approach, made at about 700 feet. The lead navigator of the 49th Squadron, 2d Lt. Donald Q. Paulsel (from Pendleton, Indiana), was elated. Not only did they drop on target, but exactly at the ETA that had been calculated some eight hours earlier: midnight. On his first mission, the pilot of the lead plane, Capt. Ward W. Martindale, was impressed with Paulsel's accuracy. For the latter, it was a repeat of his first mission. (Later in England, Martindale was transferred and subsequently assigned as commanding officer of the 94th Squadron, 439th Group, which was heavily involved in Operation REPULSE.)

The last four flights of the first formation, consisting of thirty-five planes of the 314th Group at Castelvetrano, started having problems before the scheduled takeoffs. Loaded with the 3d Battalion, and the Headquarters and Engineer companies of the 505th PIR, they were an hour behind their formation. En route, the flights did not keep close formation positions and they were separated. The first planes reached the DZ at 0110. Two planes, one a flight leader and the other his wing man, got lost and returned to Sicily with their paratroopers.

The second formation, of thirty-eight aircraft in three flights from the 61st Group, had five Rebeccas to guide them. After flying from Licata to Comise, the second crews were briefed as the paratroopers of the 2d Battalion, 505th PIR, were loaded. Operating over an hour behind schedule, they approached the DZ in close formation, and made an accurate drop by 0135.

The third and last formation was made up of thirty-six planes from the 313th and 316th groups, flown in four flights. Each group had only one Rebecca receiver. They were scheduled to fly to Borizzo, load the 1st Battalion, 505th PIR, and take off at 2200 hours. Their departure was delayed three hours, mainly because of loading problems. On the route to the DZ, three pilots were separated from the formation and found, to their surprise, that they were over Naples. After the rest of the formation dropped their paratroops on the DZ at 0300, one of the lost pilots groped his way back to the DZ and made his drop. The other two pilots gave up and went home to Sicily with their loads of paratroopers still intact.

Both airborne operations, GIANT I and GIANT II, were considered highly successful. A total of 3,300 paratroopers of the 82d Airborne Division had been dropped by Troop Carrier groups of the 52d Wing during the nights of 13 and 14 September as requested by General Clark. But good fortune was shortlived: on the night of the 14th, during another airborne mission flown by groups of the 51st Wing, fiasco struck.

✵   ✵   ✵   ✵

For the Avellino mission, Operation GIANT III, the 64th Troop Carrier Group of the 51st Wing was designated to carry 598 paratroops of the 2d Battalion, 509th Parachute Combat Regiment and forty demolition engineers. It resulted in disappointment for Generals Alexander, Clark, and Dunn. At Licata, on the 12th, they planned the flight route, which would be identical to that of the other missions up to Agropoli. From there it would extend northeasterly up the east coast to Salerno and then north some eighteen miles to the Avellino DZ. On the 13th, they revised the final approach segments from Agropoli to avoid the German antiaircraft fire believed to be concentrated along the road between Salerno and Avellino. Unlike the troop reinforcement missions, this would be an airborne invasion, and the planners were accordingly apprehensive.

The hastily planned new route from the beachhead between Agropoli and Salerno was surrounded by mountains reaching to over 5,000 feet. It was the most difficult terrain encountered by any airborne operation in Europe during World War II.

Compared to the 52d Wing, General Dunn's 51st Wing had less navigational equipment, and it was too late to obtain photographic coverage of the new approach route. Only a photo map of the Avellino area and the DZ was available at the preflight briefing.

A single pathfinder C-47, piloted by the commanding officer of the 35th Troop Carrier Squadron, with a team of eleven paratroopers, took off from the Comiso, Sicily, airfield at 2125 on the 14th. The pathfinder team had only one 5G transmitter and two Aldis lamps. They had no Eureka radar transmitter, since none of the 51st Wing's aircraft was equipped with the Rebecca receiver. After passing through considerable antiaircraft fire, the pathfinder teams were dropped over a mile south of the DZ. Within ten minutes the G5 transmitter and Aldis lamps were in operation. But only a few of the following thirty-nine Troop Carrier planes recognized them. On the final approach route they flew as high as 4,300 feet through the mountains before they could descend to the drop altitude of about 700 feet; most drops on the 14th occurred from 1,500 to 2,500 feet and were far from the DZ. After midnight, between 0003 and 0045, only fifteen planes managed to place their paratroopers within five miles of the DZ. One squadron with eleven planes flew to the right of the mountain range (Mt. Termino) and dropped its paratroops ten miles from the drop area. Twelve other C-47s dropped their troops between eight and twenty-five miles away. One month later, two planes were still unaccounted for. Clearly the formation had not held together.

The paratroops had been briefed to expect a rapid reinforcement by units of Clark's Fifth Army, which did not complete the capture of Avellino until 30 September. Many paratroops lurked in the hills for days before filtering back to the U.S. Army's forward lines. As of 8 October, 118 paratroops (nearly twenty percent of those who had jumped) were listed as dead, wounded, or missing.

Although the 509th Parachute Infantry Regiment (Team) provided a valuable counteraction against Field Marshal Albert Kesselring's peripheral forces around Avellino, the airborne mission was considered a failure, primarily because of insufficient training, a difficult flight route, and inadequate pathfinder equipment.

※　※　※　※

Before the end of the year more invasions were considered and planned, but two which included airborne operations, both with paratroop drops and one with glider landings, were never executed — and both commanded Churchill's personal interest.

The first operation's objective was the Aegean Islands, which Churchill wanted taken as a sequel to Italy's surrender. The chief prize and key to all the islands was Rhodes. The Germans had taken it from the Italians on 9 September. On 1 October, staff officers of XII Troop Carrier Command went to Cairo to plan the airborne support. General Eisenhower, recognizing the still-strong German resistance in Italy, refused to allocate scarce resources for the Aegean operation. Churchill appealed to Roosevelt in lengthy messages on 7 and 8 October. The president's reply of the 8th included the following: "I am opposed to diversion which will in Eisenhower's opinion jeopardize the security of his situation in Italy . . ." A copy was sent to General Eisenhower.

The prime minister persisted in his message writing. On the 9th, he wrote that he was "afraid" that Eisenhower would take the telegram "as an order from you and as closing the subject finally. This I should find it very hard to accept." He added "At the present time General Wilson [Sir Henry Maitland Wilson, commander of Middle East Army — not under General Eisenhower's command] is preparing to attack Rhodes on the 23d with forces from his own command or which have been assigned by General Eisenhower."

Obligingly, the president asked Eisenhower to hold a conference with Wilson and examine the "whole question." On 10 October Wilson flew to Eisenhower's headquarters outside La Marsa in a final effort to win airborne support in the assault on Rhodes. Eisenhower insisted that Italy come first. Wilson's next message to Churchill stated, "I agree that our Rhodes plan as it stood was on such a scale as to incur risk of failure."

The second operation also particularly appealed to Churchill, who attached great importance to the capture of Rome. During the planning, Churchill was in North Africa. On Christmas Day, while suffering from symptoms "adjudged to portend pneumonia," he attended a conference which included Eisenhower, Alexander, and

Wilson. The proposed invasion at Anzio was to cut the main road and rail lines between the German movement and Clark's Fifth Army front. Anzio was about seventy miles beyond the front and thirty-five miles south of Rome. General Alexander proposed to send two divisions plus airborne troops of the 504th Regimental Combat Team from the 82d Airborne Division. His recommendation was vigorously seconded by Churchill.

The 504th began training with groups of the 52d Troop Carrier Wing on 4 January. On the 8th, Churchill, Wilson, and Alexander set 22 January as D-Day for Operation SHINGLE, the seaborne invasion, and for Operation SUN ASSAULT, the airborne paradrop. The latter would consist of 178 C-47s from airfields near Naples with the 504th Regiment, the 376th Field Artillery Battalion and an engineer company. On 19 January General Williams of XII Troop Carrier Command flew to Naples to supervise the operation. The next day Colonel Crouch, operations officer of the 52d Wing, led a flight of nine pathfinder aircraft, newly equipped with the latest SCR 717-C radar, from Sicily to Naples for the mission. But they were not used because early that morning the airborne support mission was canceled by Gen. Mark Clark. Although Clark's motives in canceling the operation have been questioned, it seems clear that no advantage could have been gained from the mission commensurate with its costs.

After being away from England for nearly two months, Churchill left North Africa on 14 January. Flown to Gibraltar, he boarded the *King George V* which took him to Plymouth. General Alexander kept him informed on the Anzio battle but Churchill had questions. In his 6 February message to General Wilson in Algiers, he asked, "First, why was the 504th Regiment of paratroops not used at Anzio, and why is the existing British Parachute Brigade used as ordinary infantry in the line?" Wilson replied that the 504th "was seaborne and not airborne because of a last-minute decision by General Clark. The British paratroops were employed in the line because of an infantry shortage." Churchill learned that both American and British paratroops were used as ordinary infantry at Anzio. One can only imagine his reaction.

Before the end of the year, the paratroops and glider troops of three American divisions (the 101st, 82d, and 17th) would be used as "ordinary infantry" during the Ardennes counteroffensive, better known as the Battle of the Bulge.

5

From Allied Expeditionary Air
Force to SHAEF-AIR

AN ENIGMA TO MANY men in the U.S. air forces in the European Theater of Operations was the top command organization — and the reorganizations in particular. Those in Troop Carrier experienced their full share of changes beginning in late 1943, and they began at the very top.

Since the spring of 1943, the Anglo-American Allies had considered mounting two simultaneous invasions of France. They were even given code names: Operation OVERLORD, the invasion of Normandy, and Operation ANVIL, the invasion of southern France. The supporting airborne operations were named NEPTUNE and DRAGOON respectively.

The supreme commander was to be designated by President Roosevelt. In late September, after the invasions of Italy, Churchill was impatient; the appointment influenced his choice for deputy supreme commander and the reassignment of other British commanders from the Mediterranean Theater of Operations. Roosevelt would not make the decision until he could assess the subject during his visit to the MTO. During the president's meeting with the prime minister in Cairo, 23–27 November, and as the two of them met with Joseph Stalin in Tehran, 28 November–2 December, Roosevelt remained silent on his choice. It was not until the 5th, when they returned to Cairo for further conferences together with their chiefs of staff, that General Eisenhower was named the supreme commander. The next day Roosevelt left to return to the United States. He was flown to Oran in his C-54, the *Sacred Cow*, then sailed home on the battleship USS *Iowa* in a naval convoy.

*   *   *   *

It was in Quebec, earlier in August, that the British and American Combined Chiefs of Staff prepared the outline plan for Operation OVERLORD. There a decision was made to organize the Allied Expeditionary Air Force (AEAF). Air Chief Marshal Sir Trafford Leigh-Mallory, former head of RAF Fighter Command, was designated air commander in chief of AEAF, and he was to operate directly under the Supreme Headquarters Allied Expeditionary Forces (SHAEF).

As a result, on 16 October 1943, all American tactical air units in England were reassigned from the Eighth Air Force to the newly formed Ninth Air Force, commanded by Maj. Gen. Lewis H. Brereton. (During his two previous years, Brereton had commanded U.S. air force units in combat in four theaters of operation.) Simultaneously the IX Troop Carrier Command was activated under the Ninth Air Force. Also transferred from the Eighth Air Force was Brig. Gen. Benjamin F. Giles. He was placed in provisional command of the IX TCC awaiting Brig. Gen. Paul L. Williams' transfer from his XII Troop Carrier Command in the MTO. Under Giles, the first Troop Carrier units consisted of recent arrivals: Brig. Gen. Julian M. Chappell's 50th Wing headquarters, composed of staff and men who had almost three years of Troop Carrier training experience in the United States, and the 434th Group, complete with four squadrons. Transferred from the Eighth Air Force, the 315th Group consisted of the 34th and 43d squadrons. Although the 315th had been in England since December 1942, its aircraft totaled five or less. By April 1944, the IX Troop Carrier Command was scheduled to have fourteen groups in England and be ready for the Normandy invasions.

*   *   *   *

Leigh-Mallory established his Allied Expeditionary Air Force headquarters on 25 November, locating it in the pleasant London suburb of Stanmore, Middlesex. He immediately took over his new subordinate commands, General Brereton's Ninth Air Force and its IX Troop Carrier Command.

In addition to concentrating on building up his command organizations, Brereton encountered a new kind of problem. On 6 December, Leigh-Mallory announced that his headquarters would retain responsibility for all airborne operations. His control was to be unusually direct and comprehensive. During a conference three days later, Leigh-Mallory asserted to Brereton that AEAF should have direct operational control, not only of the British 38 Group, but also of IX Troop Carrier Command. General Brereton wrote about the issue for the record on 9 December:

> At a conference at AEAF headquarters on airborne operations, it was suggested by 21st Army Group (British) and Lt. Gen. Browning, British airborne commander, that all Troop Carrier forces be under a single command. I agreed in principle provided the command is American. This was unacceptable to the British, and ACM Leigh-Mallory finally agreed that the policy would be for American control of American airborne operations and British control of British airborne operations.

Without General Brereton's resistance to British domination by Marshal Leigh-Mallory, the IX Troop Command would have been, in effect, a British unit.

The extent of Leigh-Mallory's opinions was troublesome to American commanders from the start. He had contended that both strategic and tactical air forces should come under one air commander, implying an ambition to also control heavy bomber forces. His American deputy in the new AEAF headquarters, Maj. Gen. William O. Butler, tried in vain to secure capable American AAF officers of sufficiently high rank to make the AEAF a genuine British-American organization. As a consequence, American air force officers in both Washington and England undertook to broaden control of the AEAF. One action was the establishment of the United States Strategic Air Forces (USSTAF) in Europe as of 1 January 1944. It was given administrative control over both the U.S. Eighth and Ninth air forces. ACM Leigh-Mallory's AEAF never really lost its reputation of being a British-dominated command, which was a factor in its diminishing effectiveness. Later, as many important decisions were weighed, it was bypassed.

*   *   *   *

General Eisenhower arrived in London from the MTO in mid-January to take command of SHAEF, his primary concern the planning and preparing for Operation OVERLORD. The target date for the invasion of Normandy was 1 May. Eisenhower soon encountered growing friction among his top commanders planning Operation NEPTUNE.

The major issue concerned the airborne operations by IX Troop Carrier Command in support of the beach landings by Lt. Gen. Omar N. Bradley's First (U.S.) Army. After the first airborne mission with paratroops and glider troops scheduled for D-Day, a second airborne division insertion was scheduled for twenty-four hours later. But the objectives and locations for the assaults were still undetermined in early February, and Bradley and Leigh-Mallory were in strong disagreement. Bradley planned to use the airborne forces to support the very risky assault on Utah Beach. Leigh-Mallory was primarily concerned about the German anti-airborne defenses and predicted high casualties, even disaster, if Bradley's plan was followed. After considerable deliberation by Eisenhower, Bradley's plan prevailed.

Although later the glider operations of Operation NEPTUNE were criticized, Bradley's choice of objectives must escape blame. The culprit was the nighttime landings. The most heated controversy arose in late February over the use of gliders at night. General Bradley insisted on having 260 gliders landed before daylight on D-Day. General Ridgway also wanted the glider troops of his 82d Division brought in as early as possible, preferably with his paratroops to provide artillery against possible panzer attacks. But General Williams and his IX Troop Carrier Command staff knew by experience from Operation HUSKY's night glider missions to Sicily in July 1943, that night landings were impractical. In vain they protested to Leigh-Mallory.

*   *   *   *

After the June invasion of Normandy and the July invasion of southern France, the command issues in the AEAF became more embroiled. The discord reached its peak before the invasion of Holland in September 1944. Real efforts to resolve them remained secondary to supporting the Allies' thrust toward Germany, and they continued to fester. Commanders in the U.S. air forces wanted to answer directly to General Eisenhower (SHAEF), as General Bradley, General Devers, and Field Marshal Montgomery were already doing; thus there would be a parallel in air and ground commands.

The chance came after the September Holland invasion (Operation MARKET-GARDEN), to resolve the issues and in one regard, a solution was resolved. The AEAF was disbanded on 15 October and replaced by Air Staff, SHAEF (or SHAEF-AIR). Air Chief Marshal Leigh-Mallory was reassigned to the China-Burma-India (CBI) Theater only to lose his life in an air accident on the flight there. The new air staff was headed by Air Marshal James M. Robb and, like AEAF had been, it was large and mostly composed of RAF officers. However, Robb's deputy chief, Brig. Gen. David M. Schlatter, proved to be an able and helpful proponent of the American commanders' opinions. But real progress was not made without the cooperation of the top American and British air commanders in SHAEF.* In effect, they left the men of lesser ranks to do the squabbling. In spite of the burden this placed on Allied efforts, it was unavoidable at the time. It was also costly for the airborne operations during the invasions of France and Holland.

---

*Among those to be accredited were: Air Chief Marshal Sir Arthur Tedder, deputy; Lt. Gen. Carl Spaatz, USTA; Air Marshal Arthur Coningham, 2d Technical Air Force; Maj. Gen. Hoyt Vandenberg, CG, Ninth AF, and General Eisenhower.

6

IX Troop Carrier Command

As THE DREARY ENGLISH winter of 1943–1944 passed, Troop Carrier groups of Brig. Gen. Julian M. Chappell's 50th Wing and Brig. Gen. Maurice M. Beach's 53d Wing began arriving from the United States. Each group alighted, usually on a preassigned vacant airfield located close to its wing headquarters.

The arrival of new units was not always a smooth affair. The advance air echelon of the 438th Group (53d Wing) arrived in England with orders sending it to an Eighth Air Force airfield. Its arrival was a surprise to the entire station, which refused it space. The rejected crews began a virtual aerial tour of England looking for where they were supposed to go. Finally they reported to Ninth Air Force Headquarters at Sunninghill Park. From there they were ordered to IX Troop Carrier Command headquarters at Grantham. One week after arriving in England, on 9 February, they reached their airfield at Langar. The rest of the group's planes arrived on the 18th, but stability proved elusive; on 11 March, the 438th was ordered to move to Greenham Common.

The movement of the four groups of the 50th Wing from the United States to airfields in England was less traumatic. While still in extensive airborne training exercises in North Carolina, they received their overseas movement orders. Col. Charles H. Young's

439th Group was the first to arrive in England on 25 February. The other groups, Lt. Col. Frank X. Kreb's 440th, Col. Theodore G. Kershaw's 441st, and Col. Charles M. Smith's 442d, reached their assigned airfields late in March.

By April all of the five groups assigned to the 53d Wing had arrived and were stationed at English airfields. Joining John M. Donaldson's near-orphaned 438th Group were Lt. Col. Fred D. Stevers' 434th, Col. Frank J. MacNees' 435th, Col. Adriel N. Williams' 436th, and Col. Cedric E. Hudgens' 437th groups.

※   ※   ※   ※

As the 50th and 53d wings settled in England, the 52d Wing spent the winter in Sicily, training with the 82d Airborne Division and fighting a plague of yellow jaundice. In late November, Clark and his wing medical officer, Lieutenant Colonel Hudson, inspected the offices and quarters of each group. What they found, or concluded was not recorded.

In January, along with jaundice, rumors about the wing's destination ran unchecked — one was that it would be Karachi, India! At the time, only General Clark, Colonel Crouch, and other select staff officers at wing headquarters knew of General Williams' decision to take the 52d Wing with him to England. The value Williams placed on the wing's experience in the MTO — particularly that of Crouch's pathfinders — was no secret. That experience would be needed for Operation NEPTUNE, the airborne invasion of Normandy. The 51st Wing was to remain in the MTO, Sicily and Italy, except for its glider pilots, who were assigned to the 316th Group of the 52d Wing. The rumors ceased on 10 February, when the four groups of the 52d (61st, 313th, 314th, and 316th) received orders for England. Between 11 February and 5 March, the air echelon of 220 planes, with all flying personnel, arrived in England from Sicily via Marrakech and Gibraltar. The rear echelon of ground support personnel arrived by ship on 18 March. In England since December 1942, the few planes and crews of the 315th Group (34th and 43d squadrons) were assigned to the 52d. Two of its squadrons (the 904th and 910th), which had been sent to North Africa for the Sicily invasion, returned later in March.

※   ※   ※   ※

Maj. Gen. Paul L. Williams landed at the IX Troop Carrier Command headquarters airfield near Grantham on 25 February 1944. The primary task facing him was to organize a new command and coordinate airborne training exercises with the 82d and 101st airborne divisions for Operation NEPTUNE.

The first thing Williams did was establish the IX Troop Carrier Pathfinder Group (Provisional) with Lieutenant Colonel Crouch the commandant and Maj. James T. Blair, Jr. the group's executive officer. (Later Blair would become governor of Missouri.) The group was to provide pathfinder crews and aircraft to precede airborne missions. It was also to be the command's pathfinder school for crews from various Troop Carrier groups and paratroop teams from the 82d and 101st airborne divisions. First located at Cottesmore, it was moved to North Witham, ten miles south of Grantham, on 22 March.

Two officers were assigned from the 82d Airborne Division to head the training of paratroop pathfinder teams at North Witham. Capt. G. Wilfred Janbert, of St. Landry Parish, Louisiana, of the 504th PIR, and Capt. Michael C. Chester of the 505th PIR were both veterans of the Sicily and Salerno airborne operations. The pathfinder school was off to a solid start.

Pathfinder paratroop teams routinely practiced positioning visual aids — ground markers, smoke signals, and lighted T-shaped flares — at DZs and LZs. But to guide aircraft to within visual range of the objective, both paratroops and Troop Carrier navigators and radio-radar operators learned to use the Eureka-Rebecca radar which had been proven in Italy. The ground transmitter beacon, aptly named Eureka, was a lightweight battery-powered unit that pathfinder paratroopers could carry and put into operation within five minutes of the airdrop. Its counterpart in the aircraft was the radar receiver (interrogator) named Rebecca. The Rebecca scope display gave an accurate bearing and a fair indication of distance from the Eureka.

For better accuracy, the aircraft's navigator needed only to apply conventional calculations to verify the distance and time from the objective. From experience in training exercises, the Rebecca was restricted to use by flight leaders in each normal nine-plane formation. Too many aircraft using their Rebecca receivers, possible in a large formation, could overload the Eureka transmitters. The result was distorted and inaccurate information. The radar technicians assigned to the pathfinder groups imposed other restrictions, such as the specific channels chosen for the Eureka transmission and when during the flight the Rebeccas should be operated.

Some pathfinder C-47s were modified for installation of SCR-717C (PPI) radar. The plane was readily recognizable by the added bulge under the belly of the fuselage. An American product, it was an airborne radar sender-receiver which scanned the landscape with its beams. At night, the reflected beams from the scope would show a crude outline map in which water appeared black while land and ships appeared lighter — most useful for the Normandy airborne missions.

* * * *

The IX Troop Carrier Command reached its full complement of fourteen Troop Carrier groups in April while training with the 82d and 101st airborne divisions was under way. Although organized, most of the groups were short of aircraft and crews. However, by the end of May the strength had been increased to 1,116 qualified crews and 1,207 operational C-47s, all available for Operation NEPTUNE. (Each group was authorized sixty-four C-47s and a reserve of twenty-five percent, totaling eighty aircraft, with two combat crews per plane.) The number of CG-4A Waco gliders was adequate. In February about 2,100 of them had arrived in their crates and had been assembled for training and for NEPTUNE. Each group from the United States had brought 104 glider pilots with it to England. In addition, from late March to June, the training of more than 500 glider pilots was expedited to speed their arrival in England. Before D-Day, the command had almost 2,000 glider pilots.

* * * *

Since landing in England, the five groups of the 53d Wing were relocated, some more than once. Finally by March, they were stationed at airfields southwest of London at Ramsbury, Welford Park, Greenham Common, Membury, and Aldermaston. All were located about fifty miles from the Channel. The locations were well-suited for launching glider missions, with less exposure to bad weather and closer proximity to airborne objectives on the Continent. The wing's headquarters at Greenham Common was but a mile from the 101st Airborne Division headquarters.

On 3 March, at a meeting of Ninth Air Force commanders,

General Williams announced that if his IX Troop Carrier Command was to fly 400 gliders in the assault phase of OVERLORD, five additional airfields would be needed in southern England for the 50th Wing. The RAF agreed to furnish them and at a midmonth meeting at Air Marshal Leigh-Mallory's AEAF headquarters, only four suitable airfields were selected, but the move could not be made until the last week of April. Wing headquarters and the 440th Group moved to Exeter, the 439th to Upottery and the 441st to Merryfield. The 442d Group remained at Fulbeck, near Grantham, tentatively attached to the 52d Wing for training purposes.

The five groups of the 52d Wing remained in the Midlands at airfields within twenty-two miles of Grantham. Wing headquarters and the 316th Group were stationed at Cottesmore, the 61st at Barkston Heath, the 313th at Folkingham, the 314th at Saltby, and the 315th at Spanhoe.

✻ ✻ ✻ ✻

The first priority of IX Troop Carrier Command during April and May was the training exercises with the 82d and 101st airborne divisions. It became a command issue between Air Marshal Leigh-Mallory (AEAF) and General Brereton (Ninth Air Force). During the training period, the American commanders objected to Leigh-Mallory's acting as though his operation and planning authority included the right to direct supervision of American troop carrier training. Brereton sharply insisted that such supervision could only be exercised indirectly through his Ninth Air Force. Even this indirect authority was challenged by USSTAF which, as the highest AAF headquarters in the United Kingdom in 1944, claimed to have sole authority over the training of the Ninth Air Force. But in practice, IX Troop Carrier Command was in close consultation with both the AEAF and the Ninth Air Force in training matters.

Another link in the chain of command, favored by Leigh-Mallory to control the airborne operations into Normandy, was added in early April. It was established as the Combined Troop Carrier Command Post at Eastcote Place near AEAF in the Uxbridge area. Under the AEAF, it was to direct and coordinate both the U.S. IX Troop Carrier Command and the British 38 and 46 groups during Operation NEPTUNE.

PART II

Invasion Assignments

This is the day call'd the feast of Crispian:
He that outlives this day, and comes safe home,
Will stand a tip-toe when this day is named,
And rouse him at the name of Crispian.
He that shall live this day and see old age,
Will yearly on the vigil feast of his neighbors,
And say, 'To-morrow is Saint Crispian:'
Then will he strip his sleeve and show his scars,
And say, 'These wounds I had on Crispin's day.'
Old men forget; yet all shall be forgot,
But he'll remember with advantages
What feats he did that day: then shall our names,
Familiar in their mouths as household words . . .
Be in their flowing cups freshly remembered.
This story shall the good man teach his son;
And Crispin Crispian shall ne'er go by,
From this day to the ending of the world,
But we in it shall be remembered . . .

The King's address to his men before the Battle of Agincourt in
France, 25 October 1415. *King Henry the Fifth,* William Shakespeare

There is one great thing you men will be able to say after this war is over
and you are at home once again. And you may thank God for it. You may
be thankful that twenty years from now when you are sitting by the fire-
place with your grandson on your knee and he asks you what you did in the
great World War II, you won't have to cough, shift him to the other knee
and say, "Well, your Grandaddy shoveled shit in Louisiana." No, sir! You
can look him straight in the eye and say, "Son, your Grandaddy rode with
the great Third Army and a son-of-a-bitch named Georgie Patton."

Lt. Gen. George S. Patton, Jr. Address to the men of his U.S.
Third Army before their landing in Brittany, August 1944

47

7

Test One: Normandy

The eyes of the world are on you tonight.

> Gen. Dwight D. Eisenhower addressing men
> of IX Troop Carrier Carrier Command and the
> 101st Airborne Division, 5 June 1944.

D-DAY, H-HOUR, THE MOMENT when Allied assault craft would hit the Normandy beaches, was intricately planned. The approach was to be by moonlight and H-Hour was just after daylight. Among the predictable factors considered were the tides and the moonlight. The first three-day period after 31 May that satisfied all of the desired conditions would be 5–7 June. But the weather then was less predictable and a postponement would mean a delay until the next lunar phase. In early May, therefore, General Eisenhower picked 5 June for Operation OVERLORD.

The American and British airborne assaults, Operation NEPTUNE, was meticulously timed to precede H-Hour — and daylight. It was rehearsed within Britain on the night of 11 May. The command exercise, EAGLE, was the most exhaustive rehearsal of an American airborne operation in World War II. It also served as a test to determine whether IX Troop Carrier Command could carry out its controversial, perilous nighttime role. In addition to the seven pathfinder aircraft, the exercise consisted of 432 planes of the 50th and 53d Wings with paratroops of the 101st Division, and 369 planes of the 52d Wing with paratroops of the 82d Division. One hundred four C-47s of the 434th and 437th groups towed a mixture of Waco CG-4A and Horsa gliders. Although imperfect in some respects,

48

General Williams and Air Marshal Leigh-Mallory were impressed. In effect, EAGLE induced a mood of optimism regarding Troop Carrier capabilities. But the American commanders had their doubts.

On 31 May Leigh-Mallory announced that a high-level briefing could begin and Williams called the meeting for the next day. It was held at Northolt in the briefing room of Advance Troop Carrier Headquarters and was attended by wing and group commanders, and key staff officers from each unit. There were no less than a dozen speakers including Williams, Brereton, Crouch, Ridgway, Taylor,* a British representative, a naval representative and various other experts.

General Ridgway had previously told his staff that he would go in by glider but to keep his paratrooper image, he changed his mind before the briefing was called — he would jump with Col. William Ekman's 505th Parachute Infantry Regiment, the 82d Division's most experienced outfit. He told General Williams, "I want the best plane, the best pilot, the best navigator, the best crew. I want no screw-ups on this thing." Williams replied, "You will go exactly where you want to go."

During the briefing, time schedules, formations, flight routes and objectives for the six D-Day airborne missions (two by parachute and four by glider) were discussed. Operation NEPTUNE would begin at 2200 with the takeoff of eighteen planes of Colonel Crouch's IX Troop Carrier Pathfinder Group carrying paratroop teams of the 101st and 82d airborne divisions. One-half hour later, the first of 932 aircraft of the 53d and 50th wings stationed in southern England were to be in the air with paratroops of the 101st. Their mission, dubbed ALBANY, was to drop on three DZs directly east and southeast of Ste. Mère-Église — close to Utah Beach on the Cherbourg Peninsula, where the VII Corps and 4th Division of General Bradley's First U.S. Army were to go ashore.

The mission was divided into nine serials, most of which contained thirty-six or forty-five planes. The lead aircraft of the first two serials of the 438th Group would be flown by the group's commander, Lt. Col. John M. Donalson. After two serials of the 436th,

---

* Maj. Gen. Maxwell D. Taylor had replaced Maj. Gen. William C. Lee, one of the pioneers of airborne warfare, after Lee became ill in March. In addition to his clandestine incursion into Rome, Taylor had gained experience and a fine reputation in the MTO as divisional artillery commander of the 82d Airborne Division.

Lt. Col. Charles H. Young's plane (with Lt. Col. Robert L. Sink, commander of the 506th PIR, aboard) would lead the two serials of the 439th Group. General Taylor and several of his staff would fly in Col. Frank J. MacNees' plane, heading the 435th Group's serial. Brig. Gen. Anthony C. McAuliffe would be on his wing in the second plane in the formation. The last two serials were those of the 441st and 440th groups. The first drop of paratroops were scheduled for 0050 at DZ A, about four miles from Utah Beach.

For the second mission, BOSTON, paratroops of the 82d Division were to be flown in 432 planes from the 52d Wing's airfields around Grantham in the Midlands of England. Takeoffs of aircraft in each of the ten serials were scheduled so that the leader of the 316th Group's two serials, upon reaching the south coast of England, would be ten minutes behind the last serial in ALBANY. One of forty-seven planes of the third serial, 315th Group, would carry General Ridgway. Next were two serials each of the 314th, 313th, 61st, and one of the 442d. Takeoffs were scheduled to start at 2300 and the time over the first of three DZs, west of Ste. Mère-Église, was to be 0150.

At the briefing, Ridgway met his pilot, Capt. Chester A. Burke of the 315th, along with Colonel Crouch, at the table where the latest aerial reconnaissance photos were mounted. Ridgway, pointing to one, said, "Chet, I'll be happy if you drop me on that haystack there." The photo was of DZ O located about one mile northwest of Ste. Mère-Église. The story goes that Ridgway did land on a haystack.

The first reinforcements, with artillery troops and equipment, were to be delivered by two glider missions before daybreak. The first, dubbed CHICAGO, required fifty-two Waco CG-4As of the 334th Group (53d Wing) to carry 155 troops of the 101st Division with 57mm antitank weapons, jeeps with trailers, a small bulldozer, and tons of ammunition and other equipment. The objective was LZ W, centered two miles south of Ste. Mère-Église. A comparable mission, DETROIT, with 220 troops and equipment of the 82d Division, was to begin in fifty-two gliders of the 437th Group, towed to LZ O, directly north of Ste. Mère-Église.

During the briefing, some of the Troop Carrier and airborne commanders remained troubled over landing gliders at night — 0400 in this case. Since late May, when Leigh-Mallory changed the time for the glider mission's landings (originally planned for after dawn), they had protested in vain. Neither the experience from the Sicily missions — especially Operation LADBROKE — nor the restrictively small fields between hedgerows in the LZs could change his mind. Glider crashes appeared a certainty.

Among those destined for rough landings were two commanders. Before the war, Mike Murphy established quite a reputation as an experienced aviator and stunt pilot. In 1944 Lt. Col. Michael C. Murphy was the Army Air Force's highest ranking glider pilot. Earlier, during the initial training of the 82d and 101st airborne divisions at Fort Bragg, North Carolina, General Ridgway had wanted to demonstrate the practicality of gliders to the unenthusiastic glider troops in his division. With Ridgway in the right seat, Murphy put the CG-4A through a number of aerial maneuvers including slow rolls and loops. Whether or not it convinced any of the cynical glider troops, his virtuoso performance helped assure his presence over Normandy. On D-Day Colonel Murphy and his copilot, Lt. John M. Butler (Headquarters, 434th Group) were to fly the lead glider with Brig. Gen. Don F. Pratt, assistant commander of the 101st Division, and his aide, Lt. John L. May, aboard. The heavy part of the load was Pratt's jeep and command radio equipment.

At a meeting with General Montgomery and other troop carrier airborne commanders, Murphy protested against night glider landings, particularly in the small fields of Normandy. The experience in Sicily and a projected heavy loss of men and materiel made no impression at all on Montgomery. He stood up, slapped the table and said, "We'll have to suffer it!"

Two more glider missions were scheduled for D-Day, but they were to arrive in daylight about 2100, two hours before sunset (Double British Summer Time).* Both were to originate from airfields of the 53d Wing, located west of London. The KEOKUK mission was to be flown from Aldermaston for the 101st Division by thirty-two planes of the 334th Group, each towing a Horsa glider. The loads were to carry some 160 signal, medical, and staff personnel, forty vehicles, six artillery weapons and nineteen tons of ammunition. The objective was LZ E, almost four miles southeast of Ste. Mère-Église.

---

* During WWII, England advanced the time two hours instead of one hour as is done in the U.S. for daylight-savings time.

ELMIRA, to reinforce the 82d Division, would consist of two echelons: the first with twenty-six planes of the 437th Group from Ramsbury, towing eight Wacos and eighteen Horsas; the second with fifty planes of the 438th Group from Greenham Common towing fourteen Wacos and thirty-six Horsas. The second echelon of two serials was scheduled at dusk, almost two hours later. From Membury, fifty planes of the 436th Group were to bring two Wacos and forty-eight Horsas. Next and last, the 435th Group from Welford Park was to follow with twelve Wacos and thirty-eight Horsas in tow.

The amount of airborne troops and equipment to be carried to LZ W south of Ste. Mère-Église by the ELMIRA mission was impressive. The gliders of the first echelon were to be loaded with some 440 troops of Battery C, 80th Airborne AA Battalion, sixty-four vehicles (mostly jeeps), thirteen antitank guns (57mm) and twenty-five tons of ammunition and equipment. For the first serial of the second echelon, over 400 airborne troops of the 319th Field Artillery Battalion were to land with thirty-one jeeps, twelve howitzers (75mm), and over fifty tons of ammunition and equipment. The second serial was to carry the 320th Field Artillery Battalion, over 300 troops. With them would be twelve howitzers, twenty-eight jeeps and fifty-six tons of ammunition and supplies.

Two more glider missions were scheduled for D plus 1, dubbed GALVESTON and HAKENSACK. Each would involve 100 Waco and Horsa gliders with troops and artillery of the 82d and 101st airborne divisions.

*   *   *   *

In SHAEF, on 3 June, the weather forecast for the 5th was unexpectedly bad — strong winds and thick, low clouds. At 0415 on the morning of 4 June, General Eisenhower ordered the invasion postponed for twenty-four hours. Later that day, at 2115, Eisenhower and his commanders met again. The weather forecasts for 6 June indicated a certainty of heavy surf in the English Channel and a likelihood of high winds and low clouds. Rather than another delay of the Normandy invasion, it seemed better to gamble on 6 June for D-Day. Air Marshals Tedder and Leigh-Mallory, concerned about the airborne assaults, opposed the 6th. Stormy weather and low visibility could play hob with the airborne and other air support mis-

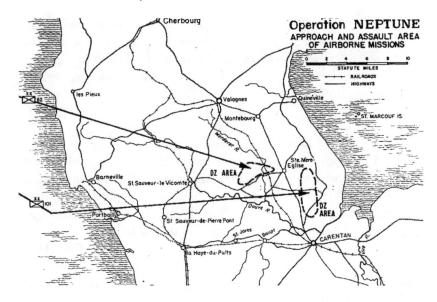

— Maps source courtesy Maxwell AFB, AL.
Warren, USAF Historical Studies, No. 97

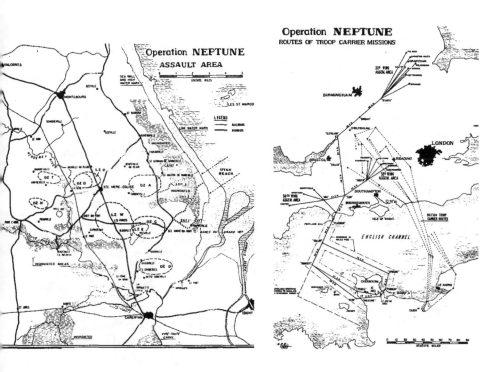

sions of the AEAF. Montgomery, who was in charge of the D-Day invasion, maintained his position of the previous night: "I would say go." The onus lay on Eisenhower, who silently deliberated for minutes. Looking up he said, "I don't like it, but I don't see how we can do anything else."

* * * *

With D-Day hours away, all Allied aircraft and their crews were ready, with the exception of one crucial process that lagged behind schedule. By the evening of 5 June, most aircraft had been painted with invasion stripes of alternating black and white bands completely encircling fuselages and wings. The striking bands identified the planes as friendly to Allied ships and troops below. This would help avoid a repeat of the tragic losses experienced by the 316th Troop Carrier Group and others during the Sicily invasion of July 1943. At some airfields invasion-stripe painting was not completed until late at night on the 5th, even as other aircraft of IX Troop Carrier Command droned toward the Continent.

Albany

First in the air at 2130 (Double British Summer Time) from the IX Troop Carrier Pathfinder Group's airfield at North Witham was Lt. Col. Joel L. Crouch's C-47. The aircraft in his three three-plane serials carried marking panels, holophane lights, Eureka beacons, and pathfinder teams of the 101st Airborne Division. Twilight still glimmered in the west as they passed the English coast. From there they flew at 500 feet or under, "on the deck," to avoid German radar.

The flight route to the Cotentin Peninsula, planned in early April by General Williams' IX Troop Carrier Command staff and Colonel Crouch, would avoid most of the antiaircraft fire by approaching the peninsula from the west, through the "back door" of the Utah Beach assault. Along the route, picket ships (named FLATBUSH, GALLOP, HOBOKEN, and RENO) were stationed in the Channel for navigational aids —using light signals only. For the return route, two others (PADUCAH and SPOKANE) were positioned east of the peninsula.

One plane from the second serial for DZ C, behind Crouch, was lost. Due to engine troubles, the pilot was forced to ditch the

C-47 in the Channel. All aboard were rescued, the first crews of many to be picked up that morning.

After passing the island of Jersy, Crouch led his three formations on a special flight course. From RENO, they turned left and headed east-northeast, relying on the Gee and dead reckoning to points two or three miles south of Montebourg where they turned right (southeasterly) to approach their respective DZs, A, C, and D. After they passed the lower cloud banks, visibility improved.

Crouch's copilot, Capt. Vito S. Pedone, quickly identified the village of St. Germain-de-Varreville from the map in his lap. It was one mile directly north of DZ A. At the same instant the navigator, Capt. William Culp, called out that his Gee scope showed they were "on target." Crouch hit the green light switch at 0015 and a green light flashed back from the C-47's astrodome to the other two planes in the flight. First to jump out into the night was Capt. Frank Lillyman, followed by a squad of sixteen men, their faces streaked with war paint. Pathfinders from the 502d Parachute Infantry Regiment were the first to land on French soil on D-Day.

The next two planes of the first serial (one had ditched in the Channel) dropped pathfinders at 0025, about a half-mile southeast of the designated spot at DZ C. The second serial was between one and two miles south for its drop at 0027. Still, the pathfinders, with their equipment, had time to relocate to LZ E where glider missions were scheduled to arrive at 0400. The last serial, with an improperly set Gee, circled back from the east coast to drop its pathfinders about a mile from DZ D at 0045.

* * * *

Late on 5 June, General Eisenhower and General Brereton had gone to Greenham Common to witness the first takeoffs of Operation NEPTUNE. Addressing the Troop Carrier air crews and 101st Division paratroopers, Ike said, "The eyes of the world are on you tonight." Before takeoff, they talked with Colonel Donalson and other flight leaders near his plane, *Birmingham Belle*. "They were grim but calm," General Brereton said.

In the moonlight, the first four serials, consisting of 171 aircraft of the 438th and 436th groups, were able to hold tight formations until they crossed the coastline at the initial point (IP), MULESHOE. Directly ahead was an unforeseen obstacle, a cloud bank with its base at 1,100 feet and its top at 2,100 feet. It extended twelve miles inland, over halfway to DZ A. In the lead aircraft, Colonel Donalson decided to hold the prescribed altitude of 1,500 feet and headed the formation directly into the cloud bank, not knowing how far it extended. With some warning, they could have flown above or beneath it, but there had been no provisions for such a warning and radio silence was mandatory. A number of the flights and individual aircraft were widely scattered during the approach. Because the pathfinder troops were delayed in activating their beacons, Donalson relied on headings given by his navigator from the Gee radar.

Through some maladjustment or misinterpretation of the Gee set, Donalson gave the paratroops the green light over the south side of DZ C. As the third and fourth serials (436th Group) began approaches some ten miles away, the pathfinder troops had the Eureka beacon in operation and ground markers placed. But they were located about two miles north of the intended DZ A. Still, the drops of the paratroops were scattered for two or three miles, some even farther away. During the approach of the four serials, enemy ground fire was mostly from small arms; eighteen planes received very minor damage.

Colonel Young led the two serials of his 439th Group and Colonel MacNees' 435th serial, totaling 126 aircraft, toward DZ C. When Young met the cloud bank covering western Cotentin, he climbed through it on instruments, descended through a hole in the clouds eleven miles inland, and headed for the drop zone using Gee and Rebecca. With the exception of the majority of his first serial, the others broke formations, climbing or diving to get out of the clouds. After passing the overcast, they encountered light flak over the last eight miles of the route. Three planes of the 439th Group were shot down.

MacNees could not help but feel an added responsibility with General Taylor and some of his staff on board — and General McAuliffe and other staff officers of the 101st Division rode in the second plane. Although the signals from the pathfinders' Eureka were strong, none of the forty-five planes of the 435th were dropped exactly over DZ C. Taylor and McAuliffe landed about one and a half miles from it. Many were dropped three miles away and some were dropped as far as ten miles from the DZ. Although Taylor, McAuliffe, and their staffs were able to assemble during the night, they did not know where they were until daylight, discovering then that they were only a short distance southeast of the DZ. However, they had had no contact from General Pratt, assistant commander of the 101st, who was due to land two miles away by glider with a jeep and communication equipment at 0400.

The last three serials of ALBANY headed for DZ D, about three miles south from where General Taylor had been dropped. The first two forty-five plane serials of the 441st Group, led by Lt. Col. Theodore G. Kershaw, broke formation when they ran into the cloud bank. They encountered intense flak on the approach to the DZ. One blew up and another crashed soon after dropping its load. A third was so damaged that it made a forced landing near Cherbourg; the crew ultimately made their way back to Allied lines. Another limped back to its Merryfield airbase, fit only for salvage.

Lt. Col. Frank X. Krebs and copilot Maj. Howard W. Cannon, heading other pilots of the 440th Group's forty-five- plane serial, were more successful in avoiding most of the clouds. They maintained a close formation to the DZ where two were shot down by intense machine-gun fire. One C-47 was seriously damaged after the drop and plunged into the Channel east of the peninsula. Among the twenty paratroops who jumped from Krebs' plane that night were a doctor, two medics, and a chaplain. One passenger was grateful that he didn't have to use his parachute. Over the Channel on the way back to Exeter, Ward Smith, special war correspondent from *News of the World*, sweat-soaked and lonely, went forward to talk with the pilots and compliment them on their skill. Colonel Krebs answered, "We had luck."

Boston

Three Pathfinder Group serials of three C-47s each left North Witham with pathfinders of the 82d Airborne Division at 2230. At 0105 the navigator of the lead plane put his Gee in operation for the ten-minute approach from the coast of the Cotentin Peninsula (PEORIA) to DZ O, located directly northwest of Ste. Mère-Église. Not all of the pathfinders landed in the drop zone. Private M. Murphy of the 505th PIR came down in the town, in Madame Angèle Levrault's garden to be precise. "At the sight of Murphy, Ma-

dame Levrault, on her way to her outhouse, stood petrified."*
Murphy freed himself from his parachute, grabbed the bag with the
Eureka beacon, and disappeared. He headed northwest toward his
drop zone a mile away.

The navigators in the next three planes believed their location
for the drop at 0138 was correct, but their pathfinder teams landed
over one mile southwest of DZ N. The last three approached their
target, DZ T, well above the prescribed 600-foot altitude and
dropped their pathfinders with precision.

* * * *

The first Eureka at DZ O was in operation at 0125, before Murphy joined up with his platoon. The 505th Parachute Infantry Regiment was scheduled to arrive between 0151 and 0208. At airfields of
the 52d Wing near Grantham, two serials of thirty-six planes from
the 316th Troop Carrier group and one with forty-seven planes
from the 315th began takeoffs at 2300. In the lead was Col. Harvey
A. Berger, who had just taken command of the 316th Group in May.
He avoided the cloud bank over western Cotentin, climbing over it
without losing the following formations. They were fired on during
the last four miles, but with the exception of one C-47 from the
315th Group, they suffered only minor damage. The C-47 was
struck by a flak burst that wounded seven paratroopers. No one
jumped.

General Ridgway was given an accurate drop by Captain Burke,
landing not far from the proverbial haystack he had chosen during
the briefing. Before daylight, his divisional CP and the 505th Regimental CP were operating in an orchard 1,200 yards west of Ste.
Mère-Église.

* * * *

The four serials of the 314th and 313th groups were less fortunate. After crossing the coast at PEORIA, they ran headlong into

---

* Cornelius Ryan, in his book *The Longest Day*, describes the account in detail. He
puts the time at 12:15 A.M., but it was actually 1:15 A.M. He also writes of the
British 6 Airborne Division assault (at 12:20 A.M.) near Caen: "Fifty miles away, at
the eastern end of the Normandy battle field, six plane loads of British pathfinders
and six R.A.F. bombers towing gliders [Horsas] swept in over the coast." He follows with an excellent account of the British mission.

the cloud bank. Most planes of the 314th, led by Lt. Col. Clayton Styles, did not emerge until they were within three miles of DZ N — and they had not yet gotten any pathfinder assistance, no signals from the Eureka. The pathfinder teams had been dropped over one mile southeast of DZ N and had found enemy forces blocking their way to the drop zone. All they could do was set up a Eureka and two amber lights at 0156. But the Rebeccas in Colonel Styles serials did not pick up the Eureka before their drops began at 0202. One plane was shot down over the DZ after dropping its 508th PIR troops on its third pass. The crew survived and reached American lines that night. The commander of the 508th, Col. Roy Lindquist, and the commander of the 82d, Brig. Gen. James M. Gavin, were dropped about two miles north of DZ N, within the territory of the 507th PIR (DZ T); subsequently, they joined forces with elements of that regiment.

The 313th Group's serials of thirty-six planes each were hit hard, mostly by accurate small-arms fire. Lt. Col. Frank J. Lumsden led eight planes from the 49th Squadron. His copilot was Col. James J. Roberts, Jr., CO of the 313th. On the approach, some ten miles away from DZ N and still in the cloud bank, navigator 2d Lt. William V. Sussner and radar technician Sgt. Seymour Greenstein worked diligently and expertly with the Rebecca. They pinpointed the drop accurately at 0220. After the jump, one plane went down in flames and all crew members were lost. Another ditched in the Channel on the return flight and its crew was rescued from their life rafts by a British torpedo boat three hours later.

The last serial of the 313th, led by Lt. Col. Quinn M. Corley of the 29th Squadron, lost one plane over Cotentin. The crew chief and radio operator parachuted. The pilot and copilot perished in the crash.

* * * *

The pathfinders of the 507th PIR had set up their Eureka exactly on DZ T at 0212. Five minutes later, a Rebecca signal response from the first serial of Col. Willis W. Mitchell's 61st Group was received by the pathfinders on DZ T. Although the lead formation with thirty-six planes held together in the cloud banks, the next arrived scattered. One plane had been hit by ground fire while in sight of the drop zone, but the crew bailed out before the plane crashed. The 61st Group dropped its paratroops between 0226 and 0245.

Col. Charles M. Smith's 442d Group, the last serial of forty-five aircraft, had more losses. The formation dispersed as it flew into the overcast; however, on emerging, the planes were hit by intense ground fire and flak. One crash-landed after dropping troops miles short of the DZ. Another was lost with all on board. A third aircraft, with both engines dead, ditched in the Channel on the way home. Most of the 442d dropped its paratroops from the 507th PIR between 0239 and 0242.

Chicago

At Aldermaston, fifty-two CG-4A gliders and C-47 tow planes from the 434th Group were marshaled on the runway before midnight of the 5th. Each was marked in chalk with its formation position number, and some bore names or logos on the sides of the nose or fuselage. Beside the big "1," the first glider had a huge "Screaming Eagle," the insignia of the 101st Division, painted on each side of its nose. After Colonel Murphy and Lieutenant Butler finished their inspections of the glider and the nylon tow rope carefully coiled behind the tow plane, General Pratt offered to ride in the copilot seat. Lieutenant May, his aide, and copilot Butler sat beside the jeep and command radio equipment in the cabin.

Murphy lifted off behind his tow plane at 0119. The formation assembled into columns of four in each echelon to the right. One of the gliders with essential communication equipment broke loose and landed four miles from the airfield. The SCR-499 radio was retrieved and placed on a later glider mission, KEOKUK. The weather was still cloudy over Cotentin but not enough to cause dispersion of the formation, although a tow plane and glider were shot down near Pont l'Abbé. Guided by the Eureka beacons at LZ E (an area overlapping the west side of the previous DZ C), the tow planes followed the same route flown by the ALBANY mission.

The landing zone, like the area around it, was flat and divided into fields between 200 and 400 yards in length. From their briefings, the glider pilots assumed the fields were divided by hedgerows, merely large hedges, not trees forty feet tall. Such hazards could not be recognized in the moonlight.

Mike Murphy released his glider at 0354, six minutes ahead of schedule, to land with full brakes on and his nose skids plowing into the ground. When the nose of the glider hit a tree at high speed, Murphy's legs were broken and Pratt was killed instantly, as was Butler, who was seated in the cabin directly behind him. Miraculously unhurt, May crawled out of the crumpled wreckage.

Some of the other fifty gliders landed with similar results, but with fewer casualties. Fourteen glider pilots and twenty-seven troops of 153 men from the 101st were reported on 1 July 1944 as dead or missing. One tow plane with a crew of four was shot down.

Detroit

Reinforcements in fifty-two gliders with jeeps, 57mm weapons, ammunition, and 220 troops of the 82d Airborne Division were flown from Ramsbury by the 437th Group. All were in the air by 0223, except one that had been disconnected from its tow plane. It was replaced and was in the air one-half hour later. The formation reached PEORIA intact where, like the preceding paratroop missions, it ran into the cloud bank. The leader and many others climbed to 1,500 feet, flew over the bank, and descended through breaks in the clouds three minutes later. Some headed into clouds that became so dense, glider pilots could not see their tow planes. Seven glider pilots released, or were released by the tow pilot, to go down in western Cotentin.

The Eureka on LZ O, directly northwest of Ste. Mère-Église, was picked up by flight leaders at a distance of fifteen miles. Thirty-seven tow planes brought gliders to the vicinity of the landing zone between 0401 and 0410. But only seventeen (possibly twenty-three) glider pilots were able to land on or near LZ O.

Fourteen glider pilots and thirty glider troops of the 209 men who landed were reported as dead or missing on 1 July 1944. One tow plane carrying a crew of four was lost. The principle cause of the many crash landings was the limited visibility at night that cloaked the unexpected trees surrounding the small fields.

Keokuk and Elmira

More reinforcements for the 101st and 82d divisions were flown by gliders on D-Day as scheduled, in daylight and before sunset. The flight route was shorter than that of the preceding missions. After a left turn at the picket ship *Gallop,* it was southeasterly, north of the Cotentin Peninsula to Spokane, thence to Padukah. From there, the final southwest approaches over Utah Beach were ten and twelve miles to LZ E and LZ W respectively.

On the first mission, KEOKUK, planes of the 434th Group towed thirty-two Horsa gliders, heavily loaded, from Aldermaston. The flight was uneventful until the glider pilots cut off at 2053, one mile away from LZ E. Although all gliders landed with no more than moderate damage, enemy fire claimed fourteen Screaming Eagle troops and wounded thirty of their comrades. Two gliders with ten troops aboard landed within German lines near les Drouries.

That was the Allies' first tactical glider operation in daylight. "It indicated that gliders, when not exposed to fire at close range, could be landed in daytime without losses." *

ELMIRA, the second mission, was larger and consisted of two echelons. In the first, twenty-six planes and gliders (eight Wacos and eighteen Horsas) of the 437th Group were followed by fifty planes and gliders (fourteen Wacos and thirty-six Horsas) of the 438th. Over the Channel they were escorted by an impressive number of P-47s, P-51s and P-38s, but no German planes appeared. It was a serene flight until they passed over Utah Beach, before reaching the release point for LZ W at 2104. Then small-arms fire and flak became uncomfortably accurate. Because of the situation at the landing zone, the Eureka, ground markers, and smoke signals were actually over three miles northwest of DZ W; believing the entire zone was in German hands, General Ridgway had decided to place the beacons and markers in the vicinity of LZ O. (His radio message never reached the IX Troop Carrier Command.) Not sure where to land, many glider pilots chose areas with small fields surrounded by tall hedgerows. Some of the designated fields turned out to be flooded and others were studded with poles of more than five inches' diameter and ten or more feet high, later to be called *"Rommel's Spargel"* — Rommel's Asparagus. Over half the Wacos landed intact while only about twenty percent of the Horsas were undamaged. Five glider pilots were killed, four were missing and seventeen were

---

* Warren, Dr. John C., *Airborne Operations in World War II, European Theater, USAF Historical Studies,* No. 97 (September 1956): 66.

wounded. Of some 437 glider troops from the 82d Division, five were killed and eighteen were wounded or injured during landings.

The second echelon of ELMIRA consisted of two serials. In the lead were fifty planes towing two Wacos and forty-eight Horsas of the 436th Group. The next serial of the 435th was reduced to twelve Wacos and thirty-six Horsas after two aborted takeoffs. It was sunset when the fighter escort departed to join the formations headed for Utah Beach and it was dusk when the transports honed onto the Eureka and visual aids set up by the 82d Division in the vicinity of LZ O near Ridgway's headquarters. As the formations approached Ste. Mère-Église directly over German positions, the ground fire intensified, increasing as the glider pilots released. The tow planes were still targeted after making 180-degree right turns for their return toward Utah Beach. Also under fire, the glider pilots had to choose landing fields at night — all surrounded by tall trees in hedgerows. Of eighty-four Horsas, only thirteen were left intact and fifty-six were totally destroyed. None of the fourteen Wacos escaped destruction or severe damage. Ten of the 196 glider pilots were killed, twenty-nine were wounded or injured, and seven were missing (as of 1 July 1944). The 82d Division's landing casualties among 737 glider troops were twenty-eight killed and 106 wounded or injured.

Galveston and Hackensack
D Plus 1

Two hundred gliders and their tow planes were marshaled at four airfields during the night of 6–7 June. All were loaded with vehicles, artillery pieces, ammunition, and almost 2,300 glider troops — more reinforcements for the 82d Airborne Division. The first mission, GALVESTON, included fifty gliders (thirty-two Wacos and eighteen Horsas) of the 437th Group and fifty Waco gliders of the 434th Group. Two Horsas were added from the 435th, those aborted during the ELMIRA mission. The second mission, HACKENSACK, consisted of fifty gliders (twenty Wacos and thirty Horsas) of the 439th Group and fifty Waco gliders of the 441st Group. Both were daylight flights and were scheduled to arrive at 0700 and 0900.

Brig. Gen. Maurice M. Beach and his staff at 53d Wing headquarters were alarmed at the reports of hazards and confusion that plagued the ELMIRA mission. They changed the landing zone for the 437th and 434th groups' mission. Instead of using LZ W, the glider pilots were briefed to land at LZ E, and the tow pilots were instructed to make left turns before heading back over Utah Beach. The change would keep them out of range of strong German forces north of Ste. Mère-Église.

The planes and gliders of the 437th came in low on the approach, some as low as 200 feet, toward LZ E, and a few gliders landed short of the LZ. Although some gliders crash landed, only twenty-two troops and some glider pilots were injured. None were killed. Gliders of the 434th were released late, causing many to land in LZ W. No troops were killed and only thirteen were injured. Again the primary obstacles were the hedgerow trees and "Rommel's Aspargus" poles.

Col. Julian M. Chappell, commander of the 50th Wing, and Lt. Col. Theodore G. Kershaw, commander of the 441st Group, decided to fly aircraft as pathfinders for HACKENSACK. Chappell led the 439th and Kershaw led the 441st glider serials to LZ W. Few gliders landed in the zone. Many landed over two miles away, some almost four miles away. Enemy fire caused numerous landing accidents, its effect compounded by small fields, high trees, flooded marshland and poles and wires erected by the Germans. In the landings, fifteen glider troops were killed and fifty-nine were injured. Two glider pilots died and eleven were injured during the landings.

Resupply Missions

Two large parachute resupply missions were to be flown on the morning of D plus 1 and were timed to arrive over the Cotentin Peninsula minutes before the glider missions already described. On the first mission, FREEPORT, the four Troop Carrier groups of the 52d Wing, each with fifty-two aircraft, were to drop over 234 tons of supplies for the 82d Division west of Ste. Mère-Église on DZ N. The 313th Group was designated to lead the 316th, 61st and 314th.

During the afternoon of 6 June, at Folkingham, Lt. Col. William A. Filer, executive officer of the 313th, reviewed the crew assignments. He would pilot the lead plane on the mission, the first of fifteen aircraft from the 49th Squadron. His copilot was Capt. Jack L. Cardwell and the navigator was 2d Lt. William V. Sussner. In addition to the crew chief and radio operator, two non-flight crew personnel would be on board. They were quartermaster assistants whose duties were to help push the supply bundles out of the aircraft over the DZ. Each of the other planes was assigned one quartermaster assistant. Lieutenant Colonel Filer was surprised that afternoon when Maj. Barney Lihn, flight surgeon of the 313th, asked to go along on the mission as an official observer. With Filer's C-47 already carrying seven men, the load limit, he was assigned to 1st Lt. Claude J. Wilson's plane, No. 7, in the first flight formation. It was a deadly choice.

There was no moonlight over the Midlands of England when the takeoffs of the 313th Group began at 0310. Layers of heavy clouds covered the sky below 1,500 feet. From the assembly point, the weather worsened during the first 120 miles toward the southern coast of England. The cloud cover was as low as 300 feet and as high as 10,000 feet. The fifteen pilots of the 49th Squadron individually made their decisions, the bold ones continuing on instruments behind Filer. One plane crashed and exploded, killing all aboard, in an attempt to land at Oxford. Four pilots of the 49th — perhaps the wise ones — turned back to Folkingham, as did forty-six others who flew back to their airfields around Grantham.

The weather was better over southern England and it was sunrise when Lieutenant Colonel Filer led some 153 planes out over the Channel, escorted by American fighter aircraft as far as the Normandy coast. On the approach to the DZ's west of Ste. Mère-Église, enemy fire took its toll. The first plane shot down by flak was Wilson's, with parapacks still loaded. After crash-landing in a flooded area, a wounded Wilson crawled out from the nose of the ship and succeeded in saving himself from enemy fire by submerging and breathing through the tube of his Mae West. The Germans took two prisoners, Lt. Evert B. Reed (copilot) and S/Sgt. Harry G. Ossman (crew chief). They left S/Sgt. Daniel M. Jennings (radio operator), who was mortally wounded, and the dead bodies of Lt. John E. Bagley (navigator) and Major Lihn. After the German troops departed, Wilson found Jennings and carried him to a dry spot of land, and then set out to find aid. At a nearby French farm house, he was refused help but was told to keep on down the road. He followed their advice and was captured and placed in a nearby German field hospital. Some thirty-six hours later, on the evening of the 8th, he was rescued by troops of the 82d Division when the Germans made a rapid retreat from their position.

Of the nine planes from the 49th Squadron that headed back toward England after the drop, only Lieutenant Colonel Filer's and one other was undamaged. Two were so severely crippled that they ditched in the Channel, but the crews were rescued.

FREEPORT was a costly mission for all the groups involved — eleven planes destroyed or missing and twenty-nine crewmen dead or missing (as of 1 July 1944) with twenty-two wounded or injured. It was not surprising that many of the returning pilots and navigators believed the mission was jinxed; too many things had gone wrong.

The MEMPHIS mission went differently in some respects although it also bore its costs. The 50th Wing assigned the 440th and the 442d groups to resupply the 101st Division on request. The division neither called for it nor expected it, therefore no Eureka beacons or ground markers were set out for guidance. Sixty-two planes from the 440th and fifty-six planes from the 442d took off between 0421 and 0430, their crews unaware of the lack of navigational aids. After sunrise, the weather over southern England was not a serious problem. The fighter cover over the Channel was appreciated but not needed. Still, without beacons or markers, the drops were scattered in and near LZ W southeast of Ste. Mère-Église, some landing behind German lines, around 0630. Three planes were destroyed or missing and two crewmen were dead or missing (as of 1 July 1944). Four were wounded or injured.

*   *   *   *

The two major airborne missions of NEPTUNE had been accomplished by the end of 7 June; however, six small parachute and glider missions followed. Each was escorted all the way to its objective by P-38 fighter aircraft. The first was requested by General Taylor — medical supplies needed by the 101st. They were dropped by a single plane of the 441st Group on the morning of the 8th. In response to General Ridgway's requests, two gliders loaded with badly needed communications equipment were landed near his 82d Division headquarters during the afternoon of 9 June. On the 10th, six gliders of the 436th with men, jeeps, and equipment arrived at 1740. Two days later, nine planes of the 436th dropped supplies by parachute at 0802. At 2021 on the same day, five gliders from that group landed with more men and jeeps. The last mission requested by Ridgway was for 13 June. The eleven planes and gliders were escorted by high- and low-flying P-38 fighters all the way to the LZ. That there were no losses among the last six resupply missions was largely accredited to the low-level fighter escorts.

Critiques

General Williams and other commanders in IX Troop Carrier Command thought the delivery of airborne troops had been an outstanding success, even though they had been handicapped by the weather at night. The number of aborts and battle losses were less than expected and mission reports indicated that all serials performed well. However, on 10 June, Brig. Gen. Elwood R. "Pete" Quesada, IX Fighter Command, Ninth Air Force, returned after a visit to Normandy. His news was highly critical of Troop Carrier — the drops had been widely scattered and General Bradley was very disappointed. It soon became a high-level issue that renewed many complex arguments between Troop Carrier and airborne commands. One important conclusion was, however, reached: there would be no more night airborne missions in the ETO.

Returning glider pilots made their complaints known, as did Colonel Murphy later on. The only aerial photographs of the LZs available for all mission briefings had been taken from 29,000 feet. There were none taken from low altitudes, photos which would have indicated the height of the trees around the designated LZs.

Aerial photography for the Normandy invasion was furnished by Col. William B. Reed's 10th Photographic Reconnaissance Group under IX Fighter Command. Before the group, with its F-5 Lightnings, was assigned the photo missions on 6 May, Reed and his staff considered all low-level photography, called "dicing" runs, to be extremely hazardous. When General Quesada visited the 10th PRG, he was told "We're ready now. Just tell us what you want and we'll get it." The results were that many low-level oblique photos were taken along the entire Normandy coastal area. But no such photos were taken of the DZs and LZs for Troop Carrier, which instead got mosaics taken from high altitudes. The hedgerows looked like bushes and haystacks, and "Rommel's Asparagus" showed up as dots.

8

Test Two: Southern France

THE INVASION OF SOUTHERN France was first named ANVIL and was originally planned in conjunction with the Normandy invasion, OVERLORD. The viability of mounting large-scale invasions in the Mediterranean while the Normandy invasion was in progress had been an issue between President Roosevelt and Prime Minister Churchill until their 5 December 1943 conference in Cairo. To Roosevelt, ANVIL was considered second to OVERLORD in priority and nothing should be done to hinder either. Vital to the success of both was the number of amphibious landing craft available. Churchill, with Roosevelt's agreement, diverted most all landing craft being produced in the U.S. and the U.K. for Admiral Lord Louis Mountbatten's operations in the Bay of Bengal to the Mediterranean Theater of Operations.

During the spring of 1944, General Sir Henry M. Wilson, allied commander in the MTO, and his American deputy, Lt. Gen. Jacob Devers, realized that any large-scale airborne mission would not be possible in June. For the airborne support mission, they could only count on the 51st Troop Carrier Wing, capable of carrying but one parachute regiment. The few RAF transports left in the Mediterranean were unsuitable for such use. Thus the invasion of southern France could not take place simultaneously with the Normandy invasions.

Although ANVIL was canceled by the combined chiefs of staff, it was still considered a viable sequel to OVERLORD by all except General Wilson, who had been influenced by Churchill to attack through Italy and push through the Balkans into southern Europe toward Germany. Due to General Devers' objections, Generals George C. Marshall and Henry H. "Hap" Arnold flew from the U.S. to the MTO in June 1944. They backed Eisenhower's objective, a southern French port deemed necessary for an Allied military build-up to help break a German stand on the Rhine.

Still Wilson resisted, in his way, by sending his chief of staff, Lt. Gen. James Gammell, to England to discuss the necessity of ANVIL with Eisenhower. On 23 June, Gammell returned with Ike's message that 15 August was the most desirable date for ANVIL. The message also ominously suggested that if the invasions of southern France were not carried out, all American and French forces in the Mediterranean would be moved to northern France. Wilson gave in and told the British and American chiefs of staff, on 24 June, that ANVIL was to be planned for 15 August. Still, Churchill opposed the southern France operation until 1 July, when he reluctantly yielded to the urging of Roosevelt. As an alternative, he "preferred a right-handed movement from the north of Italy, using the Istrian peninsula and the Ljubljana Gap, towards Vienna." *

It was not until 27 June, when the major port of Cherbourg was taken, that General Eisenhower agreed to release two wings of the IX Troop Carrier Command (Brig. Gen. Julian M. Chappel's 50th Wing and Brig. Gen. Maurice M. Beach's 53d Wing) for the operation. Two weeks later, three planes with General Williams' Headquarters detachment, twelve with Colonel Crouch's Pathfinder Group and 198 planes of each wing, were on their way to Italy via Gibraltar to Marrakech, North Africa. The pathfinder planes carried pathfinder teams from the 82d and 101st airborne divisions to serve as instructors, and also a full supply of radar and visual navigational aids. Besides equipment and cargo, there were 225 glider pilots aboard. The move was a remarkable test of Troop Carrier navigation

---

* Churchill, Winston S. *The Second World War*, Vol. 5, *Closing the Ring*, 345–346.

as well as the range of the C-47 with cabin fuel tanks added. From England to Marrakech it was 1,400 miles.

First to arrive in Italy were General Williams' and Colonel Crouch's flights on 13 July. They had a month to plan the airborne missions in conferences with Lt. Gen. Alexander Patch, CG of the U.S. Seventh Army, and Brig. Gen. Robert T. Frederick, the newly appointed commander of American and other airborne troops being activated as the 1st Airborne Task Force. The task force was made up of U.S. airborne units in the MTO; the 517th Parachute Combat Team, the 509th Parachute Infantry Battalion, the 463d Parachute Field Artillery Battalion, the 550th Glider Infantry Battalion, the 1st Battalion, 551st Parachute Infantry Regiment, and other smaller airborne units. General Wilson wanted to keep the British 2 Parachute Brigade in Italy, but at General Patch's request, it was lent to Frederick.

Shipments of crated CG-4A gliders began arriving on 15 July. By 9 August, 346 gliders had been assembled at Cercola and Brindisi. The unloading and assembly was given top priority by Lt. Gen. Ira C. Eaker, CG of the Mediterranean Allied Air Force. With the approximately 100 combat-ready gliders already in Italy, the new arrivals assured an ample supply for the mission and training.

As of the end of July there were 374 American and very few British glider pilots in the MTO. During training exercises late in July, General Wilson became aware of a growing concern among the glider troops that there would be no glider copilots — there simply were not enough to supply them. Although General Williams thought one pilot was enough, General Patch agreed with Wilson and Frederick and an urgent request was sent to USSTAF in England for 375 additional pilots. They were delivered by ATC one week later, in time for training rehearsals and exercises.

*   *   *   *

Briefings for the airborne operation, renamed DRAGOON, began on 8 August with the first meetings scheduled for wing and group commanders and some of their staffs. It was not until the 11th and 12th that squadron commanders and intelligence officers were briefed. On 14 August, D minus 1, pilots and navigators got their final briefings in tents at many of the ten groups' airfields, some with General Williams and Colonel Crouch in attendance. For

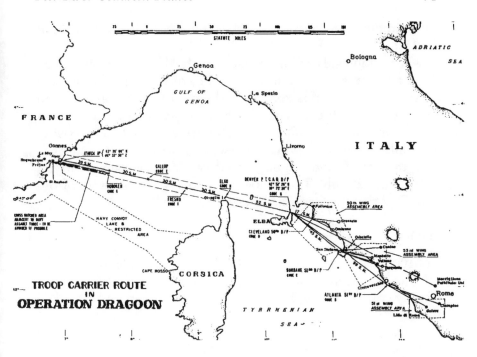

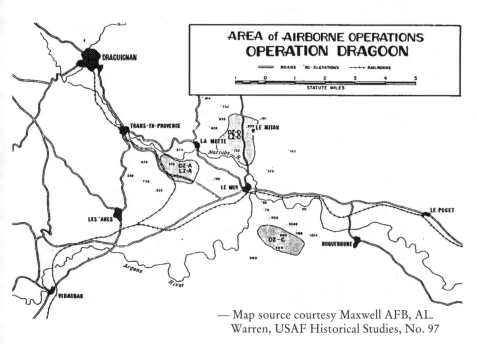

— Map source courtesy Maxwell AFB, AL.
Warren, USAF Historical Studies, No. 97

the afternoon glider mission, the glider pilots were briefed at 1300 of the 15th.

Navigation aids had been placed at the departure points along the coast northwest of Rome, the islands of Elba and Corsica, and on three beacon ships spaced at thirty-mile intervals between Corisca and the French coast. They consisted of Eureka beacons and holophane lights. The three DZs were located some twenty miles inland around Le Muy. There were plenty of excellent maps of the area, but the photographic coverage was not adequate or current, dating from 28 July. Thus the glider pilots were not aware of obstructions that the Germans had lately replaced.

D-Day

At 0100, 15 August, Colonel Crouch's nine pathfinder planes took off with 121 pathfinder paratroopers from the Marcigliana airfield directly north of Rome. The flight met clear weather until it reached the French coast. There the pilots encountered a heavy blanket of fog through which they flew by dead reckoning augmented by the vague terrain shown on the SCR-717-C scopes. At 0323, unable to pinpoint DZs (two miles south of Le Muy), the first three-plane serial turned back to the coast and made a second run. The pathfinders were dropped around 0400, but more than ten miles east of the DZ. The second serial made its drop at 0330, one mile east of Le Muy instead of at LZ A (two miles west of Le Muy). Minutes later, pathfinders jumped exactly over DZ O (two miles north of Le Muy) — a notable feat of navigation, with dawn hours away and the land for miles around thickly belted with fog.

*   *   *   *

The main paratroop mission, ALBATROSS, consisted of 396 planes carrying about 5,600 paratroop infantry and artillery with over 150 artillery pieces. The ten serials from eight Troop Carrier groups extended 100 miles from front to rear. The serials of the 442d and 441st, with forty-five planes in each, were to drop on DZ C. For the next four (forty-five-plane) serials from the 440th, 439th, 437th, and 438th groups, DZ A was the objective. The last four serials consisted of thirty-six and twenty-seven planes of the 64th and a like number of the 62d. Included in each, respectively, was a nine-plane flight lent by the 436th and 435th groups.

Scheduled to arrive an hour after the pathfinders, with allowance for formation assembly time, Col. Charles M. Smith's 442d Group was first to take off at approximately 0200. Over the Sea of Genoa a crescent moon presented good visibility. When they were just off the coast, they ran into a thick fog bank extending up to 1,000 feet. This was particularly serious for those serials headed for DZs C and A — there were no pathfinder Eureka beacons there to guide them. The drop zones were invisible and the SCR-717 in the lead ship failed. But Smith and his crew recalled the sand table model they had studied during the briefing at the Follonica airfield. Jagged hills surrounded DZ C, projecting above the heavy fog. Only a few of the 600 paratroopers landed very far off target, a remarkable achievement. Col. Theodore G. Kershaw's 441st Group went astray when it reached the clouds off the French coast. The rest of the 509th Parachute Battalion (600 men) carried by the 441st, was dropped over St. Tropez, a coastal town ten miles from the drop zone. Not only were they scattered, but two sticks of jumpers came down in the sea. Most were saved.

Col. Frank X. Krebs, with copilot Maj. Howard W. Cannon of the 440th Group, led the next four serials carrying the 517th Parachute Infantry Regiment and the 460th Field Artillery Battalion toward DZ A. Failing to get a signal from pathfinders, they had only the SCR-717 for navigation. The drop at 0431 by the 440th was widely dispersed with about a third of the paratroops landing in or near the drop zone. Lt. Col. Charles H. Young's 439th serial could not depend on its SCR-717 and dropped its paratroopers around the town of Fayence. Those in the second plane of the next serial, the 437th, mistakenly took the red warning light as the jump signal and bailed out four minutes early. They were followed by the paratroopers from the next nineteen planes. The last serial slated for DZ A, flown by the 438th Group, made its drop in a dense fog at 0453 by SCR-717 and dead reckoning. Most of its paratroops came down several miles from DZ A.

Later, Krebs described the mission to be "a breeze . . . there was nobody home." That of course was accredited to the fog; the Germans could not see the aircraft, nor could they readily discern the descending paratroopers from any distance.

The situation at DZ O was different. The Eureka beacons were in operation for almost half an hour before the two serials of the 62d

Group approached with paratroops of the British 2 Brigade. From 1,500 feet, they were dropped exactly on target and on schedule at 0454. Also aided by the Eureka, the first serial of the 64th Group was over the DZ at 0454, but four stragglers dropped as much as twenty miles away. In addition, many from the second serial were scattered for miles around.

The planes returned to land at their airfields between 0607 and 0733. After interrogations and breakfast, most of the crews hastened to catch a few hours of sleep before the afternoon glider mission, DOVE.

In the meantime the morning glider mission, BLUEBIRD, was in the air over the sea. The first serial of thirty-five Horsas, flown by British glider pilots and loaded with troops of 2 Brigade, was towed by planes of the 435th Group. When they finished the takeoffs before 0600 at Tarquinia, Col. Frank J. McNees, CO of the 435th, and his engineering officer, remained apprehensive. The grossly loaded, large glider could overtax a C-47's engines on such a long flight, and leave little fuel in reserve as well. When General Williams learned about the weather in France from the returning crews, he radioed the serial leader to turn back. Still, two C-47s had problems during the return, forcing their glider pilots to release over Corsica where the Horsas landed safely.

Col. Adriel N. Williams, CO of the 436th, also turned his serial of thirty-nine planes (towing Wacos) around. Thirty minutes later another message was received stating that his mission was to be continued if there was sufficient fuel. Colonel Williams made a second 180-degree turn and again headed for France. Two of the gliders did not make it. The wing strut on one failed and it dove into the sea — all personnel lost. The other was forced to land in the sea after the tow rope connection failed. All those aboard were rescued. When the serial passed over the coast and headed toward LZ 0, there was no sign of fog. The hour delay while circling over the sea had allowed it to burn off. There was neither flak nor any sign of Germans when the gliders released at 0926, yet four gliders landed well outside the landing zone.

One plane with glider, from the 436th, had returned to Voltone with engine trouble soon after taking off. The Waco was soon in the air again, towed by another C-47, but far behind the serial. When the tow plane pilot saw the returning Horsa glider serial, he thought the mission had been canceled and he turned back to the airfield — where he learned that his C-47 and Waco would go up again in the afternoon with the Horsa glider formation being rescheduled by General Williams and Colonel McNees. After a hasty conference with Colonel Beach (from 2 Brigade), they decided to launch the Horsa mission ahead of the large Waco glider mission, DOVE. The Horsas were to arrive over LZ O at 1800, ten minutes ahead of the first serial of DOVE.

Colonel McNees sent a C-47 to Corsica to pick up one of the Horsas that had been landed there on the first trip. The tug and glider would join the formation as it flew over the first marker boat northwest of Corsica The 435th Group, with thirty-five Horsas, began takeoffs at 1504. Navigation over the sea posed no problem and the visibility over France was about five miles, but they did not pick up signals from the Eureka at LZ 0 until they were four miles away. The gliders released at 1749 to land on target.

* * * *

CANARY was the second and last paratroop mission of the day. From the Montalto airfield, a forty-one-plane serial of the 437th Group with 736 troops and supplies of the 551st Parachute Battalion had no problem locating DZ A. The pathfinder teams had finally joined up and the signals from their Eurekas were received as far as eighty-five miles away. With the T marker clearly visible, accurate drops were made at approximately 1800.

* * * *

The last glider mission, DOVE, involved Waco gliders carrying the 550th Glider Infantry Battalion and additional artillery and support troops, about 2,250 men. It consisted of seven serials each with forty-seven or forty-eight plane and glider combinations; five of the 50th and two of the 51st troop carrier wings. (The order of formation: 442d, 438th, 439th, 440th, 441st, 62d, and 64th.) The timing for takeoffs was planned so that the lead plane of each successive serial would be eight or nine minutes behind the lead plane of the one ahead, a decision that contributed to the chaos later ensuing around LZ A and LZ O; the spacing was simply too close. To compound the problem, the serials of two groups, the 439th and 441st, were to tow gliders slated for LZ A. During the approach from the coast, the last twenty-six planes and gliders of each serial were to split away from the formation and head for LZ A. The prescribed formation, as in earlier glider missions, was to be flown in a pair of pairs echeloned to the right.

General Chappell and his copilot, Col. Charles M. Smith (CO of the 442d Group), led the mission after taking off from Follonica at 1535 in heavy dust. Some 125 miles to the southeast near Rome, the 62d and 64th groups put their planes in the air at 1510 to allow for the flight time to the command assembly point over Elba. The dust at Ombrone delayed the takeoffs of the 440th Group. Its lead plane, with Krebs and Cannon at the controls, was in the air at 1610. The last plane and glider were airborne thirty-six minutes later. Four miles out Lt. Marion L. Clem, of the 97th Squadron, was jolted by the tow rope to his glider breaking loose. He landed, and the men and equipment were hurriedly returned to Ombrone and reloaded in a standby glider. Later, Clem was on tow again behind Capt. Arthur T. Douglass of the 96th Squadron. Theirs was a solo run well behind all the other serials, the last plane and glider to reach LZ A on D-Day.

Problems for General Chappell and Colonel Smith began early on the flight, directly after passing Corsica. The glider they were towing developed a serious vibration in its tail surfaces and they turned back toward Corsica or perhaps Italy. The other forty-seven tow planes followed the leader. The glider pilot released before reaching land to ditch in the sea and all personnel were later rescued. When the serial turned again to head for France, it was well back in the formation. Not only were the groups flying too close together, they were now out of position for orderly drops at the two LZs. Before they reached landfall, three more gliders were released from the 441st Group's serial, which was in the lead of the 442d flying directly behind but trying to catch up. More problems were encountered during final approaches.

The first four serials of the 50th Wing could not pick up Eureka signals from the LZs. Flying between 1,500 and 2,000 feet, they did not locate them until the fluorescent Ts came into view less than two miles away. Chaos reigned as the 441st and 442d arrived at the same time — 1827. As previously assigned, the 442d Group split, with some tow planes heading for LZ O and the rest heading for LZ A (located less than two miles apart). To avoid the traffic jam and to head the 440th Group's serial away from the blinding afternoon sun,

Colonel Krebs passed the LZ, made a 180-degree sweep and went back over it at 1845. Lt. Howard H. Cloud did not cut his glider loose as soon as Krebs expected; not until Cloud saw a suitable field cluttered by obstacles and gliders did he release. When Colonel Young arrived with the 439th serial at 1848, with twenty-one gliders for LZ O and twenty-six for LZ A, he was surprised to see gliders from the 441st releasing at LZ O and planes and gliders from the 441st and 440th spectacularly crisscrossing over LZ A. Conversations within the aircraft could only be imagined. One minute later the 438th Group was over LZ O for the glider cutoffs.

Gliders of the 62d released over LZ O between 1854 and 1900 hours and those of the 64th cut loose over LZ A at 1905. Although relatively free from interference by serials ahead of them, both groups found that the 1,000-foot intervals between their own elements were decidedly insufficient. The rear elements climbed over the ones in front for the glider releases and several layers of gliders were in the air at the same time. Some of the 62d cut off at over 2,000 feet and some of the 64th were as high as 3,000 feet.

The tow plane crews of DOVE returned to Italy in high spirits in spite of the "air circus," as some called it. What they appreciated most was that their flak vests had turned out to be just extra baggage, unneeded. One C-47 was, however, hit by German antiaircraft fire on the way out and was forced to ditch in the sea. All aboard were rescued. Days later they learned that glider pilots came back with a far different attitude. Dodging and diving while looking for landing fields, they had barely managed to avoid midair collisions. Once closer to the ground, on the final approach, they were startled to see an unexpected foe that neither the briefings nor the photos had indicated — "Rommel's Asparagus." The poles were four to six inches in diameter, set in rows fifteen to forty feet apart. Fortunately the paratroops had had time to cut the wires stretched between them and the Germans had not had time to install the fuses on the land mines. By adroitly maneuvering, the pilots were able to set down between the rows of poles, ripping off wings in the process. Still, some gliders ended up with noses buried in hedgerows, perhaps by landing too fast in the face of the unexpected obstacles.

During the landings, eleven glider pilots were killed and more than thirty injured. Of the glider troops, about 100 were seriously injured; there was very little damage to cargo and equipment, even though only two gliders remained serviceable and only twenty-six could be salvaged.

The next morning, the scheduled supply mission EAGLE was flown by 112 planes of the 435th, 436th and 437th groups. About 246 tons of supplies, largely ammunition, were paradropped. Three more unscheduled emergency supply drops were made on the afternoon of the 17th by thirty planes from the 64th and 62d groups. By that time, enemy opposition in the drop areas had collapsed.

*   *   *   *

There were many flaws in the airborne missions of DRAGOON as was recognized by General Williams and other commanders in Troop Carrier and the airborne units. Three stand out from the planning phase. There had been no provisions made to promptly obtain the early morning weather over the target area, the seven Troop Carrier groups were scheduled too tightly for the afternoon mission DOVE, and a recollection of the German installations of "Rommel's Asparagus" in Normandy should have been reason to obtain low-level reconnaissance photographs shortly before D-Day.

Yet soon after the last gliders landed at LZ O, General Frederick reported that it had been "a wonderful operation so far." His forces had closed in on Le Muy and resistance there was "nearly neutralized." Back in Italy General Eaker summed up the official opinion of the operation when he told General Williams, "You Troop Carrier people put up a grand show." General Williams wrote his official commendation to each Troop Carrier wing: "Results . . . surpass even our most optimistic expectation. You have spearheaded another thrust at the heart of the enemy which has brought the free peoples of the world one step closer to total victory. My congratulations and appreciation to each member of your command regardless of his role, for it has required 100 percent effort to achieve today's success."

*   *   *   *

Prime Minister Churchill decided on 30 July to go to Italy to meet with his commanders and also with Marshal Tito. His visit was timed to coincide with ANVIL-DRAGOON. After two days in Naples, he was flown to Corsica on the 14th where the British destroyer *Kimberley* took him about four miles from the scene of the seaborne invasion at the Bay of St. Tropez. He took two Americans with him, Robert S. Patterson, assistant secretary of war, and General Somervell. Churchill wrote later, "I had at least done the civil to 'Anvil,' and indeed I thought it was a good thing I was near the scene to show the interest I took in it." His conclusions were that ". . . 'Dragoon' caused no diversion from the forces opposing General Eisenhower [in northern France]" and "For this a heavy price was paid. The army of Italy was deprived of its opportunity to strike a most formidable blow at the Germans, and very possibly to reach Vienna before the Russians, with all that might have followed therefrom. But once the final decision was reached I of course gave 'Dragoon' my full support, though I had done my best to contain or deflect it."

* * * *

About a week after the DRAGOON airborne missions, Brig. Gen. Paul L. Williams led the planes and crews of the 50th and 53d Troop Carrier wings and the IX Pathfinder Group back to England. During Williams' absence, Brig. Gen. Harold L. Clark, 52d Wing, had been in command of Troop Carrier resupply missions to American forces in France. Williams soon learned that his three IX Troop Carrier wings had been transferred from the Ninth Air Force to the newly formed First Allied Airborne Army.

9

First Allied Airborne Army

Almost from the day of its creation, this Allied Airborne Army showed an astonishing faculty for devising missions that were never needed.

Gen. Omar N. Bradley

THE MEN IN IX TROOP Carrier Command learned in late August that a reorganization of top commands assigned them to the First Allied Airborne Army. To most, the only effect was a change of shoulder patches. The Ninth Air Force patch was replaced by a new, larger one, with "AIRBORNE" emblazoned across the top over "TROOP CARRIER," and below that, a glider superimposed over an open parachute. Lt. Gen. Lewis H. Brereton also changed his patches. From his post as commanding general of the Ninth Air Force, he was reassigned to command the First Allied Airborne Army.

General Brereton took a dim view of the new assignment when he first learned of it over lunch with General Spaatz* at Park House on 16 July. The concept of an Allied Airborne Army had been the subject of communications between Generals Marshall, Arnold, and Eisenhower. The latter proposed Brereton to command the new organization, a combination of existing American and British airborne divisions and Troop Carrier units. At the time, Brereton was eager to continue work with General Bradley and the other ground commanders who were indicating increased respect for airborne missions in support of ground battle offensives.

---

* Lt. Gen. Carl A. Spaatz had been placed in command of the newly formed U.S. Strategic Air Forces in Europe early in 1944.

The following day General Brereton met with General Eisenhower and accepted the challenge. They agreed that there could be complications having Lt. Gen. F.A.M. "Boy" Browning as Brereton's deputy.* There had been pressure, starting before the Normandy invasion, for unification of the airborne forces and for Browning, commander of the British Airborne Corps, to be placed in top command. Browning lived up to expectations in the FAAA. He was aware that Field Marshal Montgomery was not satisfied with the appointments although he approved them.

General Bradley's disdain for the FAAA began with its inception. Bradley had been counting on Troop Carrier for gasoline resupply to support General Patton's Third Army in its drive to the Marne and beyond. The airlifts started on 23 August, but were soon discontinued by a directive from General Eisenhower, who assigned airborne forces to an operation planned by Montgomery. (Montgomery had been promoted from the rank of general in mid-August.) The field marshal's operation was to be a major airborne drop, Operation LINNET, on Tournai, Belgium, scheduled for 3 September. It was scrubbed on 2 September when General Hodges' First Army tanks reached Tournai, an advance Bradley had predicted earlier to Eisenhower. By 10 September, two more major airborne operations were planned and canceled by Montgomery. Meanwhile Bradley complained and Patton, who was running out of gasoline for his tanks, fumed.

*　*　*　*

It was on 8 August that the First Allied Airborne Army was officially created with General Brereton in command. The FAAA included the U.S. IX Troop Carrier Command, XVIII (U.S.) Corps (Airborne) with its 82d, 101st, the 17th airborne divisions, together with the British Airborne Corps consisting of the 6 Division, the Polish Brigade and the SAS Troops, plus the RAF Transport Carrier Formation if and when allocated.

The First Allied Airborne Army was established to coordinate the varied elements of air and ground forces that were essential for airborne operations on the Continent. The organization was judged

---

* During a 1987 discussion with a former British Airborne Corps glider pilot, Browning's nickname was discussed. One account has it beginning in his youthful military days; as a Grenadier Guards officer, he never outgrew it.

necessary for coordination because the parachute and glider troops used in airborne operations were a part of the ground force organization, while the troop carrying aircraft and crews, which also resupplied the airborne units, were under air force command. The complications brought about when both U.S. and British air and ground forces were involved would be alleviated and the command difficulties simplified.

The FAAA was further defined as an organization primarily with operational functions. On 18 August Supreme Headquarters (SHAEF) announced that FAAA would control its own airlifts, but the Allied Expeditionary Air Force (AEAF) would retain the responsibility for escorting and supporting air operations. The functions of General Brereton's command were further limited in early September in that it would confine itself to planning and to operational control.

As often happens in reorganizations, the FAAA had its problems. This one was predictable. From the start the most critical difficulty was the friction in leadership. During early September, Montgomery's planned operations (subsequently canceled) created friction in the FAAA. At one point, Browning put in his letter of resignation as deputy commander. Brereton persuaded him to withdraw it.

Perhaps Browning's decision was influenced by the 10 September meeting between Eisenhower and Montgomery. Browning was standing by, "waiting in the wings for the outcome of the conference." He returned to the FAAA to present Montgomery's plan for Operation MARKET, the airborne invasion of Holland. Brereton was not the only one caught unawares; General Bradley "could not have been more astonished." It certainly appeared that Montgomery had his "Boy" in the FAAA.

*   *   *   *

The resupply by air to the ground armies was an early consideration by SHAEF at the end of April. A small, obscure agency, the Combined Air Transport Operations Room (CATOR), had been created under AEAF at Stanmore on 1 June to coordinate resupply missions, and transferred to FAAA on 16 August. CATOR's communication channels went through FAAA or SHAEF. However, CATOR had no direct control over its only assigned airlift unit, IX

Troop Carrier Command. Its staff included A-2, intelligence; A-3, operations; and A-4, supply sections. When advance ground and air forces requested resupply by air through SHAEF-AIR, CATOR would plan and coordinate the air supply, which was then ordered by SHAEF-AIR. Later, during the September Holland invasion, Operation MARKET, conflicts resulted in the FAAA when heavy demands for air supply coincided with large-scale operational missions. CATOR was accused of ineffectiveness, and later SHAEF resisted proposals by the Communications Zone (formerly the Services and Supply, ETO) to transfer the function. CATOR remained as an adjunct organization of the First Allied Airborne Army for the remainder of the war, acting only as a partially effective coordinating staff, functioning as a communication channel between the battle front and IX Troop Carrier Command.

First Lieutenant Harry G. Gutherless, 92d Troop Carrier Squadron, receiving Distinguished Flying Cross for 27 December 1944 Bastogne mission, Chateaudun, France 1945.

— Courtesy: Gutherless

10

Test Three: Holland

OPERATION MARKET-GARDEN, A two-part offensive, was "one of the most daring and imaginative operations of the war. Surprisingly, MARKET-GARDEN, a combined airborne and ground offensive, was authored by one of the most cautious of all the Allied commanders, Field Marshal Bernard Law Montgomery."[*] The plan was to invade Holland with airborne forces of the First Allied Airborne Army (MARKET), to be quickly followed by armored drives of the British Second Army (GARDEN). The airborne objectives were to capture and secure the bridges along the route from Belgium to Arnhem, and the bridge over the Rhine at Arnhem crossing into Germany.

On 10 September General Brereton held a meeting at his FAAA headquarters in Sunnyhill Park with his Troop Carrier and airborne commanders and their staffs, with the exception of General Ridgway, who was in France.[**] General Browning arrived and presented Montgomery's plan for Operation MARKET, without a

---

[*] Ryan, Cornelius, *A Bridge Too Far*, 11.
[**] When Ridgway was placed in command of the new XVIII Airborne Corps headquarters in August, Brig. Gen. James M. Gavin took command of the 82d Division.

predetermined date for D-Day. Brereton named General Williams air commander for MARKET with operational control, not only of IX Troop Carrier Command, but also of the British 38 Group, 46 Group, and such bomber aircraft as might by used for resupply. For the airborne troops, General Browning was designated airborne commander.

On 11 September the commanders of the Troop Carrier wings were called in to work out flight routes, timing, and loading plans on each airborne division's selection of drop and landing zones. Brereton and his commanders expected that MARKET would go as early as the 14th. The decision was to be Montgomery's, based on when the British Second Army's XXX Corps was ready to move north from Belgium.

The First Allied Airborne Army promptly prepared to deliver airborne troops to seize and hold the river and canal crossings in eastern Holland. Montgomery's main objective, the Rhine River bridgehead, was assigned to Maj. Gen. Robert E. Urquhart's British 1 Airborne Division and the attached First Polish Parachute Brigade. Maj. Gen. Maxwell D. Taylor's 101st Airborne Division objectives were near Eindhoven, from the Willems Canal to the Wilhelmina Canal, around sixty miles south of Arnhem. The 82d Airborne Division's new commander, Brig. Gen. James M. Gavin, plotted his drops close to Nijmegen between the Maas and Waal rivers, some twenty to thirty miles south of Arnhem. Evidently, he was most concerned about Troop Carrier's abilities.

"Remembering the 82d Airborne attacks in Sicily and Italy, when his troops were scattered sometimes as far as thirty-five miles from their drop zone (the standard division joke was that we always use blind pilots), Gavin was determined to land his men almost on their targets." * This is difficult to understand in light of the Italy missions' successes. Gavin's three battalions of his 505th Parachute Infantry Regiment were dropped accurately in operation GIANT, the night of 14–15 September 1943 (as were Col. Reuben H. Tucker's 1,300 men of the 504th on the nights of 13–14 and 14–15 September). "Forty-five minutes after the last man landed, Gavin had the Regiment assembled," wrote Clay Blair in his book, *Ridgway's Paratroopers*. Perhaps the joke in the 82d Division originated with

---

* In his book, *A Bridge Too Far*, Cornelius Ryan's source was apparently from an interview with General Gavin.

the independent 509th Parachute Infantry Battalion, the U.S.
Army's oldest, which was dropped on the ill-fated Avellino mission.
But it was well known to Ridgway, though possibly not to Gavin,
that Troop Carrier aircraft on that mission were not equipped with
Rebeccas. The results of the Sicily and Italy operations demonstrated the need for reliable navigation aids for night missions. During the night airborne operations of the Normandy invasion, of all
the regiments of the 82d Division, "the 505th Parachute Infantry
Regiment probably had the best drop in the whole operation. Its
troop carrier planes too had been scattered, but many of them were
able to circle back (itself a dangerous undertaking when serials were
following closely and formations had become broken) and find the
Drop Zone which the Pathfinders had clearly marked. Unfortunately for the others, enemy troops on four of the six designated
drop zones made it impossible for Pathfinders to display their visual
signals." * Still, men of the 505th's 3d Battalion had collected and
moved in to capture Ste. Mère-Église before dawn.

*   *   *   *

Operation MARKET employed both British and American
pathfinders. To mark the British DZs and LZs west and south of
Arnhem, twelve British Sterlings (heavy bombers) of 38 Group
from Fairford, England, accurately delivered 186 British pathfinders
by parachute over the objectives at 1240, 17 September. Their navigational equipment included two types of radar transmitters: the
Gee, which most British had experience with and relied on, and the
Eureka, preferred by American crews. British aircraft of 46 and 38
groups with 130 Horsa gliders were first in, beginning at 1300. Next
came 167 tow planes of 38 Group with gliders to complete the landings of 1 Airlanding Brigade Group. Finally 143 C-47s of the 61st
and 314th Troop Carrier groups arrived over DZ X, five miles west
of Arnhem, to drop paratroops of the British 1 Parachute Brigade at
1355. While setting the final headings to the DZ, the American navigators found that their Gee sets were badly jammed, but the Rebeccas guided them well. By 1408 the brigade, almost 2,300 paratroopers, had jumped — on target.
        Aircraft and crews led by Lt. Col. Joel L. Crouch, CO of the IX

---

* Huston, James, *Out of the Blue*, 183.

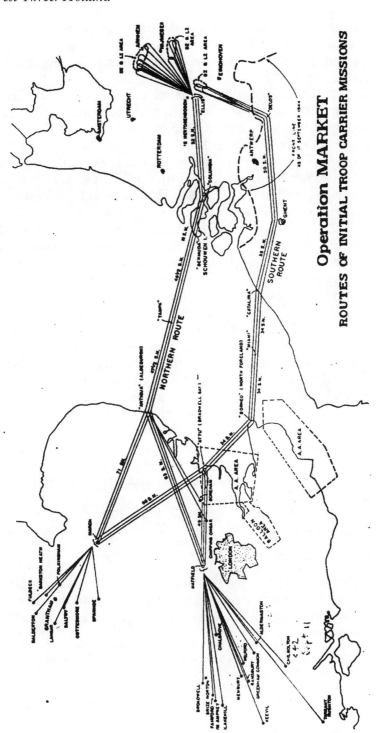

Operation MARKET

ROUTES OF INITIAL TROOP CARRIER MISSIONS

— Map source courtesy Maxwell AFB, AL. Warren, USAF Historical Studies, No. 97

Troop Carrier Pathfinder Group (Provisional)* and pathfinder teams of the 82d and 101st airborne divisions were responsible for locating and marking the American objectives at Nijmegen and Eindhoven, respectively.

After 0830 briefings of aircraft crews and paratroopers at Chalgrove, two planes with pathfinder teams of the 82d took off at 1025. Two other pairs of C-47s, with pathfinders of the 101st, followed at ten-minute intervals. The six-pathfinder-plane formation had a P-47 fighter escort over the Channel but none over the Continent. Near Grave, antiaircraft batteries began firing on the two lead planes, those carrying pathfinders of the 82d. They were under intense fire as they started their drops at 500 feet, but P-47s of the 78th Fighter Group, in the area on a flak-busting mission, dived on the guns and silenced them. After the drop at 1247, one team set up its equipment while the other stood guard against snipers, their only resistance. Within three minutes, the marker panels were in place and both radio and Eureka beacons were in operation. The first assault area for Gavin's 82d was accurately pinpointed near Nijmegen.

The four pathfinder planes with teams of the 101st were less fortunate over their approach to the Eindhoven area. The pilots of both pairs of aircraft saw the orange smoke set out near Gheel which designated the front lines. Encountering heavy fire, one of the planes was hit in the left engine and gas tank. It went down in flames.** Fortunately the team from the second plane was dropped at 1247 over the DZ near Veghel. Airborne pathfinders from the second two-plane serial jumped side by side at 1254 with great accuracy. They landed so close together that no assembly was necessary. The Eureka was in action in less than a minute, and panels and radio were ready within four minutes.

Those Who Followed

SUNDAY, 17 SEPTEMBER

Before noon on D-Day, the skies over southeastern England were thick with formations of IX Troop Carrier Command aircraft. Eleven serials totaling some 424 C-47s from groups assigned to the

---

* Transformed in name and status from IX Troop Carrier Pathfinder School by General Williams on 14 September, three days before MARKET D-Day.
** The lack of leak-proof fuel tanks in IX TCC aircraft prevailed throughout the war, a problem that was never completely corrected.

53d Wing (434th, 442d, 436th, 435th, and 438th) headed over the Channel via the southern route to fly around Antwerp and then north to the Eindhoven area. Col. Frank J. MacNees led the seventh and eighth serials of the 435th Group; in his plane were Gen. Maxwell D. Taylor and a regimental commander of the 101st. The 6,712 paratroopers (501st, 506th, and 502d PIRs) jumped onto DZ A and DZ B between 1300 and 1345. Seventeen planes were destroyed or crash-landed during the action. Following close behind were seventy tow planes with gliders in two serials of the 437th. Of those, sixty-two made it to the LZ.

During the same period, the 52d and 50th wings (313th, 316th, 315th, 439th, 441st, and 440th groups) sent 480 planes in eleven serials carrying 7,250 paratroopers of the 82d over the northern route to Holland, heading toward Nijmegen. Again they were met by effective antiaircraft fire. Ten C-47s were shot down, two from the twenty-one planes of the 49th Squadron (313th Group) in the lead serial. Less than fifteen minutes after the surviving 7,229 paratroopers were on the ground, forty-eight gliders of the 439th made it into LZ N. One of the original fifty gliders ditched in the Channel and a tow plane was shot down near Schonwen Island.

* * * *

Every survivor of MARKET Mission No. 1 had interesting accounts of his experiences. One of the more unusual episodes was about the pilot and copilot of the lead plane of the last two serials flown by the 440th Group to Nijmegen.

Flying through heavy flak, Colonel Krebs led his 440th Group's forty-two plane serial over DZ T where paratroopers of the 508th PIR began jumping at 1330. After turning back and climbing to 3,000 feet, he thought the worst was over. Not so! A direct hit in the left engine caused an explosion that blew a huge hole in the fuselage. With the controls gone and the plane in a downward spiral, the copilot, Maj. Howard W. Cannon, rang the bailout signal to the crew. Hydraulic fluid was spurting all over the pilots, and they had a slippery time trying to reach the cabin exit where they dived out at about 1,000 feet. Their ordeal had still not ended; in fact it was just beginning — they were in German-held territory and Krebs had broken his foot when he hit the ground.

Hiding in a watery ditch with their crew chief, S/Sgt. Frank

Broga (of Chester, Massachusetts), they evaded discovery by Germans who were searching for crew members. A Dutch farmer who had spotted them arrived, and, using sign language, told them to stay out of sight and wait until he came back after dark. They were fortunate; the farmer did return alone and took them to two local policemen on bicycles, both in the underground. The three followed behind the policemen, who pedaled along slowly, but it was a long walk and they had to hide three times when German patrols appeared. They finally came to a farm and were hidden in a shed where they were welcomed by many nearby farmers who brought them bread, cheese, and hot milk.

At 0200 they continued on, this time with Krebs riding on the handlebars of one policeman's bicycle. His foot was treated by a doctor in the home of an underground leader in the little town of Aubenbosch. Cannon and Broga hid in the attic of the police station for two days. The three were then given police uniforms and proceeded to ride motorcycles boldly into the city of Breda.

For three weeks they were housed in a department store that was closed to the Dutch, but open to German troops. They were joined periodically by ten others, Americans, British, and Canadian. With so many, it had become too dangerous for the Dutch who were sheltering them, as well as the soldiers themselves, to stay where they were, so they were divided into pairs and prepared to move out. Krebs and Cannon were given civilian clothes, ration books, birth certificates, and forged identification papers with their photographs, their fingerprints, and official seals. Their boots were dyed black. If they were caught now, they would be shot as spies. Their new IDs stated that one was a city clerk and the other was a schoolteacher.

During the next few weeks, they were hidden in the closets of several homes and then under the floor of a house belonging to a Dutch officer who had been a German prisoner for eighteen months. German search parties passed through several times. The Americans soon realized they were endangering their benefactors and chose to strike out for the Allied lines. They selected a day and were given new identification papers and old clothes. Krebs became a farmer shouldering a hoe. Cannon was his hired man and had a bundle of firewood to carry. Krebs could speak German and since Cannon knew only a few words, he tied a bandage around his neck indicating a sore throat, his excuse for not talking when they were stopped by Germans.

On departure day, the two "farmers" set out to meet their guides, two fourteen-year-old youths, who were to be at a certain bridge eating apples. The boys were sighted. When Cannon pulled out an apple and took a bite (the recognition signal), the boys began walking and the farmers followed at a distance. During the fifteen-mile walk, the teenage guides were replaced by a new pair every two or three miles; the Germans were always suspicious of young people who were far from their homes. Their route took them through roadblocks, around towns, and past sentry posts that could not be avoided. At day's end, they arrived at a shell-scarred farm house. The widow who lived there showed them an old silo in the yard. The bottom of it was covered by a woodpile, and when she pulled back a few pieces of wood they could see a small room under the silo. She had even fixed some food for them.

In about an hour, a battery of German 88s rolled up near the house and began firing. American shells came whizzing back. This went on for three days. The house was hit, the barn destroyed, and two sheep were killed. Consequently, fresh mutton was served by the widow to her eight children and the two Americans in the barn. During the fourth night, the Germans left and the silence seemed deafening. The Americans came out of hiding in the morning to look around and heard the sounds of a patrol approaching. As they started back toward the silo, they caught phrases of GI slang — Americans! It was the end of forty-two days behind enemy lines.

Two days later, a Dutch farmer suddenly appeared with Major Cannon in the officers' mess at the 440th Group in Fulbeck, England. Krebs and Cannon had been listed as MIAs for over a month.* Others of their crew, radar officer Lt. George T. Arnold, crew chief Frederick D. Broga, and radio operator S/Sgt. William E. Quick had returned earlier. The navigator, Lt. Edwin E. Sullivan, was less fortunate; he spent the rest of the war as a POW.

MONDAY, 18 SEPTEMBER

Due to the large number of gliders (more than 1,900) slated for

---

* A few days before Christmas, Colonel Krebs and Major Cannon loaded a C-47 with a jeep and a trailer filled with C-rations, candy, soap, and cigarettes that had been contributed by some fifty men in their outfit. When they landed near Breda, they went back over the old route, handing out tokens of gratitude to those who had befriended them. **Author's note:** Howard W. Cannon was later a U.S. Senator from Nevada, 1959–1983.

the four days of MARKET, there were practically no glider pilots available in England for copilot assignments. With few exceptions, every glider pilot was used including about 150 flown from the States by ATC only days before MARKET. Most of the new arrivals were promptly assigned to groups preparing for Mission No. 2, the largest of the four glider operations.

The 101st Division near Eindhoven was to be reinforced by a 450-glider mission flown by six groups assigned to the 53d Wing. The large flight formation was divided into two sections, A and B, totaling twelve serials. Each group would furnish two serials, one for each section. A similar formation was to be flown by the five groups of the 52d Wing and one (439th Group) of the 50th Wing on the 454-glider mission for the 82d Division at Nijmegen.

                              *   *   *   *

The 53d Wing's gliders were loaded with 2,656 troops, 156 jeeps, and 111 trailers full of supplies for the 101st Division. General McAuliffe, divisional artillery commander, chose to ride in the lead glider of the first serial — a fortunate decision.

During or soon after takeoffs, the first beginning at 1120, ten tows were aborted for mechanical reasons. Crossing the Channel via the southern route, three gliders were ditched and another crashed on Schonwen Island. At LZ W near Eindhoven, two planes of the first serial were shot down after their gliders released. Of the other eleven serials, only two tow planes were lost to enemy fire. Some gliders were cut loose prematurely during the approaches. Of the 431 that reached the LZ between 1430 and 1500, 428 landed safely.

                              *   *   *   *

Gliders of the 52d and 50th wings were loaded with 1,900 troops, mostly artillerymen, 206 jeeps, 123 trailers and sixty guns. All were critically needed by General Gavin's 82d Division in the Nijmegen sector, which was not far from Arnhem where the British airborne forces were fighting a fierce battle.*

The flight order was planned with glider loads carefully consid-

---

* Two thirty-plane serials and two twenty-seven-plane serials of the 314th and 315th groups (52d Wing) dropped some 2,000 British paratroopers and supplies over DZ Y near Arnhem between 1406 and 1420. Of the five C-47s shot down, all aboard two of them were lost and the crew of another crashed with the plane.

ered. The first serial, with twenty gliders of the 29th and twenty-two gliders of the 49th Squadron, had medics and medical supplies aboard. The pilot of 29th Squadron's lead tow plane was Col. James J. Roberts, Jr., CO of the 313th Group. The Waco glider was flown by Capt. Elgin D. Andross, group glider officer, who was designated the commander of 52d Wing glider pilots after landings. Flying to the right side of the 29th, also in pairs (echeloned right), was the 49th Squadron headed by Lt. Col. Frank Lumsden, with 1st Lt. Max Becker, squadron glider officer, on tow. The senior ranking glider pilot on the mission was Maj. Hugh J. Nevins, Headquarters, 50th Troop Carrier Wing. His glider was towed by one of the squadrons of the 439th Group in the rear of the formation, Section B. Once on the ground, glider pilots were to assemble under their particular squadron and group commanders for early evacuation if and when evacuation was deemed viable.

Andross was well recognized, and of all the glider pilots in the 52d Wing, he was accepted as the most experienced in training for ground combat. He joined the 43d Division, U.S. Army Reserve, in 1931 and was commissioned a second lieutenant and assigned to the 388th Infantry Reserves in 1936. After flight training, he received his glider pilot rating in November 1942 and joined the 313th in December. In contrast, Nevins was not known to glider pilots in the 50th Wing. In wing headquarters, he had no staff and no formal chain of command.

The weather was foggy over all the airfields around Grantham when Colonel Roberts and Captain Andross lifted off from Folkingham at 1109. The glider pilots had to accept the ordeal, a three-hour flight without copilots. Perhaps the 82d Division troopers sitting in the right seats could hold the Wacos steady for a while over the Channel. For some pilots, the feeling of loneliness was accentuated when the intercoms to their tow planes failed.

Fourteen gliders went down on the way. Two were forced to land in England, one because of structural problems. The other loss was caused by an hysterical trooper who entered the cockpit. As he leaned between the pilot and the copilot, he hit the tow release lever. Over the Channel, two gliders were disconnected from their tow planes, but all the men were rescued soon after ditching. Over Holland, five C-47s were brought down by flak before reaching the Nijmegen area and that same number were destroyed at around 1,000 feet altitude, soon after the gliders released over LZ T.

2nd Lt. Charles E. "Chuck" Yeager watched all this action while flying his P-51. Only days before, he had been promoted from the rank of flight officer. He was in the 357th Fighter Group, Eighth Air Force, based at Leiston Airfield near the English village of Yoxford, some sixty miles up the coast from London. He recalled the mission later in his book, *Yeager, An Autobiography*.[*]

> On September 18, I led two squadrons in support of airborne landings in Holland. Our assignment was to provide top cover to C-47s towing gliders filled with combat troops. German flak and small arms fire were intense, and we sat up there watching those slow-moving C-47s getting hammered. Ten of them were blown out of the sky in minutes, and the ground was littered with smashed gliders. It was a bloodbath, and a part of me ached to get down on the deck and strafe hell out of those German guns; but another part of me was damned glad that our orders were to stay at 500 feet, well above the murderous flak, and escort the surviving C-47s out of there.

The first tow plane to go down from enemy fire was flying in the number two position of the 49th Squadron's formation. Near Hertogenbosch, a direct flak burst on the right wing sent it down in a spiral with all four crew members still on board. Pilot 1st Lt. Frederick Crouse, copilot 2d Lt. Louis E. Stafford, Jr., crew chief T/Sgt. Clarence L. Olsen, and radio operator S/Sgt. Albert H. Broidy perished in the crash. Flight Officer Joseph D. Randolphs' intercom failed after takeoff, but suddenly it was no longer a concern as he watched his tow plane's right wing fold up. After cutting loose, he chose a small field between Boxtel and Schijndel — there was too much fire coming from around a larger one. His choice was a good one. Randolph and the seven medics he had on board were taken in by a Dutch family, fed, and hidden from the enemy. They soon made contact with people of the local underground who also took care of the medical supplies from the glider. Three days later, they were smuggled out to Son, which was held by the 101st Division, and were driven through the corridor, later named "Hell's Highway," to the 82d Division. From there, Randolph and other

---

[*] This quote appears on page 71.

glider pilots were driven to Brussels and then were flown by Troop Carrier to Cottesmore on the morning of the 22d. A few 313th glider pilots were flown back to Folkingham at 1400. However, most of them did not return until days later to relate their battle experiences.

Coming down through a hail of enemy ground fire, about 385 gliders landed in the 82d sector, some 240 of them in or reasonably close to the LZ. The rest were widely scattered; some were flown by the 61st Group in the eighth serial (second serial of Section B) that was carrying Battery B, 320th Glider Field Artillery. After a glider flown by one of the flight leaders released forty-five miles short of Nijmegen, its tow ship turned back. Unfortunately, the tow pilot who then took the lead had no Rebecca aboard. Followed by eight others, he flew southward and missed the LZ. The gliders released erroneously inside Germany, twelve miles east-southeast of the LZ.

The planes in the following serial were also handicapped by the failure of their Rebeccas to pick up the Eureka signals. Thirty of them made a deviation to the south, but recognized the error sooner than those who preceded them. The gliders released five miles south of LZ T in the general vicinity of Gennep. On the ground, about 160 men of the 320th and twenty-two glider pilots with ten jeeps and two guns, defended themselves until nightfall when they worked their way north to the American lines. Four glider pilots and nine airborne troopers did not return.

* * * *

At the LZ near General Gavin's headquarters, the gliders began landing under heavy enemy fire at 1430. As the siege subsided, the glider pilots helped unload vehicles and equipment. From there they headed to the predesignated assembly points to receive any additional assignments before being evacuated from the battle area. A few, those who landed too far from the assembly points and others who somehow got permission from a group or squadron leader, "set out for home." Thus freed from direct military control, they could strike out on their own, hitchhiking, maybe fighting, sometimes just sightseeing on the way to Brussels. Less than ten percent of the glider pilots who went into Holland gave all of them the reputation of "wanton unruliness." To their credit, the others performed well but not without conflict among the ranking glider officers. Major

Nevins "attempted to exercise authority but he had little to build on
... no formal chain of command ... He was from the 50th Wing
[headquarters] and the bulk of the pilots, being from the 52d Wing,
did not know him, questioned his authority and had no faith in his
competence. After all, even the most disciplined infantry do better
with officers whom they know." *

Captain Andross had no problems in organizing more than one
hundred glider pilots, seventy-three from the 313th and others,
mostly from the 61st, during the evening of the 18th. Andross
missed one he knew well, 2d Lt. John Van Sicklen, also from 313th
HQ. He had been wounded by a mortar grenade before he reached
the assembly point. John died during the night.

Early the next morning, with more glider pilots assembled,
Andross reported to General Gavin who promptly "requested" him
and his "troops" to move into the front lines near Mook to support
the 505th PIR.** They were to stay with the 505th until the 325th
Glider Infantry Regiment was landed before midday by the next
glider mission. None of the glider pilots had any idea that they
would live in foxholes for the next three nights and two days.

TUESDAY, 19 SEPTEMBER

Two large glider missions were scheduled for D plus 2. The one
for the 82d Division, consisting of 406 plane-glider combinations,
was to be flown by the 52d and 50th wings from airbases around
Grantham, in the Midlands of England. From early morning the
gliders were ready with 3,385 troops, 104 jeeps, fifty-nine loaded
trailers, and twenty-five pieces of artillery belonging to the 325th
Glider Infantry and the 80th Airborne Antiaircraft Battalion. The
heavy, low cloud cover over the entire area forced a postponement
of the mission.

The weather in southern England around Greenham Common
was better, but barely passable at midday. With 385 plane-glider
combinations, organized to fly in ten serials, the groups of the 53d

---

* Warren, John C. *USAF Historical Studies*, No. 97, 153.
** Until October 1943, Gavin had commanded the 505th PIR and it was difficult
for him to let it go to another after he was promoted to brigadier general in command of the 82d Division. Despite his new responsibilities he was seldom out of
touch with his old outfit.

Wing and the 442d Group began takeoffs at 1130. Their objective was LZ W in the 101st Division's sector, near Eindhoven. From the beginning, problems plagued the mission. First it was visibility closing in at 1,200 feet, and then worsening. Glider pilots, unable to see their tugs, had to fly by the angle of the tow rope. Many gliders broke loose, or cut loose, or were brought back to their airfields. The entire last serial was called back while it was over the Channel. Another seventeen gliders ditched in the Channel. Over Belgium, thirty-one gliders broke loose or were released by their tow pilots. Three of them crashed, killing five men and injuring four. About 225 gliders were towed through intense and accurate light flak all the way to the LZ. Seventeen tow planes were destroyed on the final approach. Of 213 gliders reaching the LZ, one was shot down and three crashed. The rest (209) made good landings. Of the 2,310 glider troops of the 101st that started on the mission, 1,341 arrived safely. The casualties were eleven dead, eleven injured, and 157 missing.

* * * *

Although the Tuesday glider mission for the 82d Division had to be canceled, a resupply paradrop was flown. Of the originally planned size of 167 C-47s, with 265 tons of supplies, only sixty were able to start the mission. One serial of twenty-five aircraft, flown by the 439th Group, ran into heavy clouds off the Belgian coast and broke up. One went on to drop its bundles in the 101st Division area. The others turned back. It was 1250 when the thirty-five-plane serial of the 61st Group left Aldermaston. They flew across the Channel through a dense haze under a 200-foot ceiling. Over Holland, the weather was good but the flak was thick and there was no fighter cover. Ground fire claimed three planes. Remembering their previous day's reception by the enemy, the serial flew over DZ O at 2,500 feet rather then 1,000 feet. Only twenty percent of the supplies dropped were recovered, a real blow to Gavin's men who were short of both food and ammunition.

WEDNESDAY, 20 SEPTEMBER

D plus 3 was a strenuous day for the 82d Division. While undertaking the capture of the Nijmegen bridge, it had to beat back the first major German counterattack. The enemy, with strong artillery support, began a drive against the 505th PIR during the afternoon. The battle raged into the night.

In England, the large glider mission by the 52d and 50th wings was again grounded by fog over the Grantham area. However, five groups (434th, 435th, 436th, 437th, and 438th) of the 53d Wing in the south were able to send off 310 planes with 441 tons of ammunition and supplies in midafternoon. Only one plane turned back. The fighter cover was good and enemy ground fire was conspicuous by its absence all the way to DZ O. Still, many of the drops, between 1648 and 1749, were scattered up to six miles north of the DZ. Glider pilots, those not in the battle lines, kept busy collecting supply bundles and transporting them to the ammo dump. That night all 185 of them were rushed to the front near Mook to be added to Captain Andross' men already there supporting the 505th PIR.

THURSDAY, 21 SEPTEMBER

On D plus 4, the weather around Grantham remained nasty and made it impossible to send the large glider mission to the 82d Division, although resupply missions were flown by the 53d Wing to the 101st and 82d divisions in the afternoon. Each carried sixteen tons of badly needed rations.

Of the thirty planes of the 437th and 438th groups that began the mission to the 101st Division's sector, six turned back due to the poor weather or to mechanical difficulties. The others made the paradrops over DZ W at 1631 and 1640. All aircraft returned undamaged.

Another thirty-one planes, of the thirty-three that started out from the 438th Group, made somewhat scattered paradrops at 1700 from 1,500 feet over DZ O. But it did not take long for the hungry troops of the 82d to find and unload the bundles.

The boldest mission of the day was flown by the 314th and 315th groups of the 52d Wing from Saltby and Spanhoe. The formation was to consist of 114 planes, two serials of twenty-seven planes each (314th) and two serials, one of twenty-seven and one of thirty-three planes (315th), all loaded with 1,115 troops and equipment of the 1st Polish Parachute Brigade. Ready since the morning of the 19th, they were to drop south of the Arnhem bridge, DZ K, in support of the British 2 Parachute Battalion. Had the Poles arrived when planned, it is conceivable that the bridge would have been saved from defeat. Although the weather was no better on Thursday, General Williams was urged by General "Boy" Browning to initiate the mission. Otherwise it would have been postponed again, just as the large glider mission had been.

After taking off at 1310, the lead serial of the 314th Group assembled at 1,500 feet, an altitude believed to be clear over the planned route. When they flew into the immense cloud banks, the formation dispersed. Twenty-five of them lost their bearings and returned to Saltby. The other two circled above the clouds until they saw a following serial, which they joined. The flight procedure for the other three serials had been revised before their takeoffs after 1405. They climbed to 10,000 feet before assembling above the clouds. Six planes lost visual contact with the serials and returned. Over the Channel, the flight leader of the 314th misinterpreted a coded message. Deciding it was a mission recall, he turned back and was followed by the other ten aircraft in his serial. The rest flew on to the Belgian coast where the clouds broke and they descended to 1,500 feet. One plane trailing the last serial was hit by flak near the mouth of the Scheldt and dropped its troops near Ghent, returning to England on one engine. The remaining seventy-two flew through high flak and small-arms fire to drop 998 Polish paratroopers between 1708 and 1715. While turning south to go back, some of the planes flew over a strong battery of German antiaircraft guns. Five of the 315th Group were quickly shot down. Casualties were eleven men dead or missing and ten wounded or injured.

The Polish brigade had arrived too late. Although they reached the Rhine River bank that evening, the Germans were in control of the opposite side and the bridge. The Poles fell back to defensive positions at Driel.

FRIDAY, 22 SEPTEMBER

Every Troop Carrier aircraft was grounded on D plus 5. Not only did fog and clouds prevail all day over England, but the weather was very bad over the Low Countries as well. Yet almost 500 Waco gliders and C-47 tow planes were marshaled along the runways at nine airfields of the 52d and 50th Wings, and one of the 53d Wing.

The only men from Troop Carrier to see battle that day were glider pilots, many of whom had been in foxholes with the 505th

PIR near Mook since Wednesday night. They were in the center of the sector, with the squadrons organized as infantry platoons, each under the control of the squadron's ranking officer. The "platoons" were organized into an infantry company under Captain Andross. On the front line from left to right, were the 49th (1st Lt. Max Becker), the 48th, the 29th (2d Lt. Clinton Corwin) and the 47th squadron glider pilots. They were flanked on the left by C and I companies, and on the right by B and A companies of the 505th Parachute Infantry Regiment.

From midnight until 0900, the entire sector received a continuous shelling by heavy mortar and 88mm fire which gave the impression that a large attack would follow. It never came, nor did the 325th Glider Infantry intended to release the glider pilots from their infantry duty. The pilots had to endure another night in foxholes with only .45-caliber pistols and .30-caliber carbines to use for their defense.

SATURDAY, 23 SEPTEMBER

General Brereton's FAAA staff planned a large airborne operation for D plus 6, a combination of three earlier missions that had been postponed on 20 September. After assembly in the air, the three separate formations flew side by side to keep the elapsed time over enemy guns to a minimum. Still the formation of the column was unusually stretched out. It consisted of 406 planes and gliders from six groups of the 52d and 50th wings for the 82d Airborne Division and another eighty-four combinations from the 53d Wing (436th and 438th groups) for the 101st Airborne Division. The formation column in the left lane totaled forty-two C-47s of the 314th Group (52d Wing). On board were the Polish paratroopers who had been returned to England two days before on 21 September. They were to be dropped on DZ O rather than at Driel. On the right side of the long glider formation were 123 aircraft of the British 38 and 46 groups, loaded with supplies for drops to 1 Airborne near Arnhem.

On Friday General Williams had named Col. James J. Roberts' 313th Group as the one to lead the unusual operation. In turn, Roberts designated Lt. Col Frank Lumsden, CO of the 49th Squadron, to fly the lead plane. The final briefing at 0800 on the 313th's airfield at Folkingham emphasized the use of a revised southern route to the objective via Leopold and Eindhoven. After three days of bad weather, this day was to be a striking contrast. Based on the early morning reports from the weather reconnaissance planes, the scheduled arrival times over Holland were set back two hours to allow the cold front to pass. In addition, the formations were to expect even better cover than Troop Carrier had experienced on the earlier missions.

*   *   *   *

The fighter cover by the Eighth Air Force and the RAF was well timed to accompany the large airborne formation. They flew many anti-flak sorties along the flight route. Some were lost to ground fire and the Luftwaffe. Near the Gelden-Wesel area, the 339th Fighter Group clashed three times with German fighter aircraft, shooting down six while losing three. Flying high south of Arnhem, as the last Troop Carrier planes were returning from the missions, the 353d Fighter Group engaged fifty German fighters. The P-47 pilots of the 353d reported shooting down nineteen enemy planes and losing three of their own.

*   *   *   *

At 1210, the first glider took off from Folkingham, flown by 2d Lt. Charles W. Hamilton and towed by Lieutenant Colonel Lumsden. By 1300 all ninety-eight tow planes and gliders were in the air to form the two leading serials; forty-nine from the 49th and 29th squadrons, and forty-nine from the 47th and 48th squadrons. In those and in the following eight glider serials were Col. Charles Billingea with his 325th Glider Infantry Regiment, Lt. Col. Raymond E. Singleton with his 80th Antiaircraft Battalion, and other, smaller units of the 82d Division, 3,378 men with 104 jeeps and twenty-five artillery pieces. Also in the formation were the four serials of the 436th and 438th, with eighty-four gliders carrying 395 troops and 100 tons of supplies which included twenty-three jeeps, trailers, and fifteen guns of the 101st Division. They were to be landed at LZ W.

The Germans along the route in the Veghel and Grave areas were prepared. The first serials received the most devastating fire and Lumsden's C-47 was one of the first to be shot down. At 1603 he crash-landed in friendly territory near LZ O. Hamilton landed his glider safely close to the LZ. One other C-47 from the 49th Squadron also crash landed, injuring some crew members.

Twelve miles from the LZ, a glider pilot in the 29th Squadron formation saw his tow plane hit by flak. Thinking the hit was severe enough to prevent the C-47 from continuing the approach, he cut his glider loose. It caused a chain reaction and eighteen other glider pilots released, landing up to twelve miles short of LZ O. Fortunately they landed along "Hell's Highway" while it was not under fire. They drove the jeeps and trailers up the highway to the LZ.

A similar situation occurred when a squadron leader in the fourth serial of the 52d Wing thought his plane was seriously damaged. He cut his glider loose near Veghel and his tow pilots followed his example. As a result, eighteen gliders landed about six miles from Veghel. Six of them were in German-held territory and all aboard were captured.

The last three serials were still over Belgium when the returning planes were advised by radio about the locations of the heaviest enemy ground fire. Although they adjusted their course, one tow plane was shot down and two gliders released early, landing in the Veghel sector. The last of the gliders carrying the 325th Glider Infantry Regiment and other 82d Division units landed by 1717, exactly on schedule.

Of the eighty-four-glider formation flown by the 53d Wing, seventy-nine flew all the way to LZ W with troops of the 101st Division aboard. Four gliders had aborted over England and one was released over Belgium. At the LZ, two gliders crash landed, killing three troopers and injuring nine.

*   *   *   *

On this last glider mission of MARKET, nine tow planes were shot down. Crew casualties totaled thirteen dead or missing and about seventeen wounded or injured. Most all of the losses were in the vicinity of Veghel and Uden. Flying over a mile on the left side of the glider column, the forty-one planes of the 315th Group delivered their loads of 560 Polish paratroops, with supplies, on DZ O at 1643 without loss of aircraft or crew members.

The RAF, with its formation of seventy-three Sterlings and fifty Dakotas flying on the right side of the glider train, had a difficult mission. They flew on to paradrop supplies to the surrounded British 1 Airborne. Two planes aborted and six were shot down at the drop zone. The area held by the British was so small (1,000 yards in diameter) that only ten percent of the resupplies were retrieved.

SUNDAY, 24 SEPTEMBER

After living in foxholes for two nights, enduring frequent bursts of mortar and gunfire, being almost without food except for the raw carrots, turnips, cabbage, and sugar beets they grubbed from surrounding fields, Captain Andross' glider pilots were elated to be relieved by units of the 325th Infantry. After a night of rest near the 82d Airborne headquarters, the first to be evacuated were those from the 52d Wing, under the command of Andross. As they headed down "Hell's Highway" from Nijmegen in a truck convoy, it seemed that the battle was over for them. Once again, appearances were deceiving. Soon after passing Veghel, they came upon a twenty-five-truck British convoy being destroyed by a German ambush. About one hundred yards ahead, a truck was burning. The glider pilots and truck drivers jumped off their trucks and took to the ditches along the road. Some fired their weapons, mostly carbines and submachine guns, toward the invisible enemy's tanks and guns.

From the rear of the leading convoy, a British officer (reportedly a colonel) strode up the center of the road. Motioning with his swagger stick while twisting his huge mustache, he pointed out Jerry positions to shoot at and said, "We'll 'ave the bastards out of here in a minute." As he walked toward the burning truck he was dropped in his tracks, killed by a German sniper.

Three British Sherman tanks moved in to counter the German artillery and machine-gun fire. Two of them were quickly knocked out along with several more trucks. The third tank withdrew. Then Captain Andross took charge and directed the glider pilots to get the trucks turned around and headed back up the road to Veghel. Under intense gunfire, they drove fifteen of them back to safety.

During the action, two glider pilots were injured by shrapnel. Lt. Max Becker, glider officer of the 49th Squadron, was wounded on the left side of his face. When he returned to Folkingham in mid-October with wounds still healing, his first action was to visit all glider pilots of the squadron in their Nissen huts to let them know he was back and still in command, as much as to say, "From now on, I'll even look as mean as I am." *

---

* When 1st Lt. Max Becker returned, he faced another worrisome personal challenge; among the newly arrived glider pilots assigned to the squadron, all fresh from the States, one was a captain. Becker was proud of his military background. He had been a B-17 crew chief before the U.S. entered World War II. During the early morning hours of 7 December 1941, his new B-17 was in one of the two six-

MONDAY, 25 SEPTEMBER

As soon as the road between Veghel and Zon became safer, glider pilots were on their way out in a truck convoy or in other vehicles headed south again. In Belgium, most of them hitchhiked to Brussels, where they caught Troop Carrier planes for return flights to England. A few found reasons to be delayed in Brussels for a day or two.

During the ground battles, General Gavin sent a long letter on 25 September 1944 to General Williams in which he included this commentary:

> In looking back over the past weeks' operations, one of the outstanding things, in my opinion, and one thing in most urgent need of correction, is the method of handling our glider pilots. I do not believe there is anyone in the combat area more eager and anxious to do the correct thing and yet so completely, individually and collectively, incapable of doing it, than glider pilots.
>
> Despite their individual willingness to help, I feel that they were a liability to me. Many arrived without blankets, some without rations and water, and a few improperly armed and equipped. They lacked organization of their own because of, they stated, frequent transfer from one Troop Carrier unit to another. Despite the instructions that were issued to them to move via command channels to Division Headquarters, they frequently became involved in small unit actions to the extent that satisfied their passing curiosity, or simply left to visit nearby towns. In an airborne operation where, if properly planned, the first few hours are the quietest, this can be very harmful, since all units tend to lose control because of the many people wandering aimlessly, improperly equipped, out of uniform, and without individual or unit responsibilities. When the enemy reaction builds up and his attack increases in violence and intensity, the necessity for every man to be on the job at the

---

plane flights approaching Hickam Field, Hawaii, when the Japanese struck Pearl Harbor. After fourteen hours in the air, the bombers were completing the first leg of their flight to Clark Field, Philippines. Becker's plane was one of those that landed before the second Japanese attack arrived around 0840.

It was not until January 1945 that Becker lost his mean look. He was promoted to captain and remained squadron glider officer.

right place, doing his assigned task, is imperative. At this time glider pilots without unit assignment and improperly trained, aimlessly wandering about cause confusion and generally get in the way and have to be taken care of.

In this division, glider pilots were used to control traffic, to recover supplies from LZs, guard prisoners, and finally were assigned a defensive role with one of the regiments at a time when they were badly needed.

I feel very keenly that the glider pilot problem at the moment is one of our greatest unsolved problems. I believe now that they should be assigned to airborne units, take training with the units and have a certain number of hours allocated periodically for flight training. I am also convinced that our airborne unit copilots should have flight training so as to be capable of flying the glider if the pilot is hit.

Neither Williams nor any other American commander went along with such ideas. Even Gavin's commander, General Ridgway, stated that the duty of glider pilots was to fly gliders and they belonged and should stay in Troop Carrier.

* * * *

The last American resupply airdrop of MARKET was a small one to the 101st Division. It was flown by thirty-four planes of the 53d Wing (434th, 435th, and 436th groups) from Ramsbury. Some forty-nine tons of howitzer ammunition was accurately dropped on DZ W at 1641. Not one plane was lost or damaged.

The Aftermath

Operation MARKET was the largest, in numbers of aircraft and troops, of all airborne offensive actions during World War II. From 17 to 25 September, the British 38 and 46 groups (RAF) effectively used 1,191 aircraft to drop 186 paratroops, and tow 621 gliders carrying 4,215 glider troops with vehicles and artillery to the Arnhem area. Fifty-five aircraft were reported destroyed or missing. In support of the Arnhem bridgehead objective, the IX Troop Carrier Command furnished 382 C-47s and crews, which carried 5,955 British paratroops to Arnhem drop zones. Eleven aircraft were listed as destroyed or missing.

During the same period, about 1,400 aircraft of the IX Troop Carrier Command delivered over 14,000 paratroopers of the 82d and 101st airborne divisions to the Nijmegen and Eindhoven assault areas. Twenty-nine were destroyed or listed as missing. Of the 1,900 gliders dispatched, 1,618 landed successfully in designated LZs with 10,374 glider troops. Forty-seven tow planes were destroyed or reported missing.

*   *   *   *

Montgomery's plan, Operation MARKET-GARDEN, ended as a failure; it did not achieve its grand objective, to drive across the Arnhem bridgehead with Allied armies into Germany through the Ruhr. It has been regarded as a costly defeat for the Allies. Yet from the airborne operations point of view, it was considered a success.

The bold decision to fly the airborne missions in daylight had proved to be relatively safe and practical. Daytime operations not only allowed more accurate navigation, they also reduced the air assembly time of airborne formations to one-third that experienced at night.

Cautious critics qualified their praise of this achievement by noting that crushing air superiority during MARKET had protected airborne missions in daylight from enemy aircraft and flak. Some 5,200 sorties had been flown to protect the Troop Carriers from the remnants of the Luftwaffe and to neutralize antiaircraft batteries. Flak suppression had proven both difficult and dangerous against well camouflaged opponents who knew when to hold their fire. Nevertheless, the guns had been silenced. As for the Luftwaffe, it was never able to break through the cordon of Allied fighters. Its only successful attacks against the Troop Carriers occurred on one occasion when arrangements for escort and cover had broken down.

As helpful as daylight was, a need for pathfinders was not eliminated. At Chalgrove, the IX Troop Carrier Pathfinder Group resumed training of aircraft crews and paratrooper teams for the next airborne operation, expected to occur in Germany.

In the meantime, the British Airborne Command had relieved General Browning of his dominating positions in General Brereton's FAAA and sent him to India to serve under Adm. F. A. Mountbatten, supreme commander, Southeast Asia Command. "His departure evoked few tears in American quarters." He was replaced by Maj.

Gen. Richard Gale, a "far more popular and capable veteran of Normandy" where he commanded the 6 Airborne Division.

In his book, *A Bridge Too Far,* Cornelius Ryan noted the many criticisms given Montgomery. The following two quotes from the book (p. 597) are most apropos:

> In my-prejudiced-view, if the operation had been properly backed from its inception, and given the aircraft, ground forces, and administrative resources necessary for the job — it would have succeeded in spite of my mistakes, or the adverse weather, or the presence of the 2nd SS Panzer Corps in the Arnhem Area. I remain MARKET-GARDEN'S unrepentant advocate.
> Field Marshal Sir Bernard Montgomery, *Memoirs: Montgomery of Alamein,* p. 267

> My country can never again afford the luxury of another Montgomery success.
> Bernhard, The Prince of the Netherlands, to the author

✻   ✻   ✻   ✻

Through October-November, IX Troop Carrier Command aircraft were heavily employed carrying resupplies (fuel, ammunition, and materiel) to airfields directly behind the armies of Bradley and Patton.

Before the end of November, the 82d and 101st airborne divisions were relieved from their battle areas and moved to rear camps for rest and refitting.

The next Allied airborne operation, outlined during 17 October – 7 November, was to be either Operation NAPLES II with two airborne divisions seizing a bridgehead between Cologne and Bonn, or Operation VARSITY with the 17th Airborne Division and British 6 Airborne Division seizing bridges over the Rhine near Wesel. During a meeting at SHAEF on 20 November, the target date for either of the operations was set for New Year's Day, 1945.

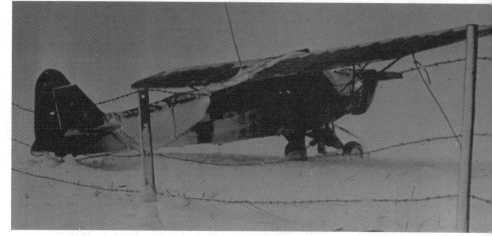

Above:
Piper L-4 Grasshopper, artillery liaison plane of 101st Airborne Division, grounded by blizzard at Bastogne, 22 December 1944.

— Courtesy: National Archives

Below:
26 December 1944. 53d Troop Carrier Wing C-47s heading back south after paradrops. Planes completed right turns north of Bastogne. Belgian Military Barracks (101st Div. Headquarters) in foreground.

— Courtesy: National Archives

PART III

Operation Repulse

To Every Member of the A.E.F.

The enemy is making his supreme effort to break out of the desperate plight into which you forced him by your brilliant victories of the summer and fall. He is fighting savagely to take back all that you have won and is using every treacherous trick to deceive and kill you. He is gambling everything, but already, in the battle, your gallantry has done much to foil his plans. In the face of your proven bravery and fortitude, he will completely fail.

But we can not be content with his mere repulse.

By rushing out from his fixed defenses the enemy may give us the chance to turn his great gamble into his worst defeat. So I call upon every man, of all the Allies, to rise now to new heights of courage, of resolution and of effort. Let everyone hold before him a single thought — to destroy the enemy on the ground, in the air, everywhere — destroy him! United in this determination and with unshakable faith in the cause for which we fight, we will, with God's help, go forward to our greatest victory.

Dwight D. Eisenhower SHAEF — Order of the Day 22 December 1944

. . . Montgomery now in fact has under his command eighteen American divisions plus his Twenty-First Army Group comprising about sixteen divisions. He is forming substantial reserves and is assuming entire charge of the battle in the area of his command. He should be able to intervene heavily. There is nothing so far to suggest that the Germans have the power to mount a full-scale offensive against the Twenty-First Army group's main front.

Matters are not by any means so clear south of the gap. The Americans are putting up stubborn resistance but there is a good deal of disorganization. Naturally an army has been gathered from the Metz region to march north under Patton. The position of the enemy does not strike me as good. As usual I am optimistic; the tortoise has thrust his head out very far.

Prime Minister Churchill to Field-Marshal Smuts. In Telegraph: 22 December 1944 From *The Second World War*, Vol. 6, 1951.

11

The Autumn Fog

A commander thinks first of his people.
James H. Doolittle

MAJ. GEN. ALAN W. JONES and his 106th Infantry Division, "Golden Lions," arrived in England in late November 1944. Jones, a fifty-year-old career army officer, had been commissioned during World War I. Ridgway knew him well as they had been classmates at the Infantry School twice during the 1920s. Jones' son, Alan, Jr. (West Point, 1943), was also in the 106th, a lieutenant in the 423d Infantry Regiment. Both would become casualties at the Ardennes front less than one month after their arrival in England.

When the division began crossing the Channel in LSTs between the 2nd and 8th of December, not all of their equipment and supplies had caught up with them. Pete House, from Jacksonville, Florida, was a machine gunner in A Battery, 590th Field Artillery Battalion, 423d Regiment. In 1991, he remembered the hasty move in trucks to the Ardennes battle front where they set up positions near the tiny German village of Oberlascheid in the Schnee Eifel (Snow Mountains) on 12 December:

> Food, ammo, and gas never seemed to catch up with us. At Oberlascheid things did not get better — never enough food and requests for fire missions greater than our supply of 105 shells. Our supply road was exposed to German view and re-

ceived constant shelling when used. So the road was only usable at night.

For survival in northern Europe in the winter, all we had was our regular issue of two blankets, overcoat or mackinaw, long johns, wool cap and gloves, and a regular wool uniform. Rumor had it that in a couple of weeks we would be rotated back for warm new winter gear.

For three days, House lived like a doughboy of World War I. His outpost was a bunker and connecting gun pit with a .50-caliber machine gun and a bazooka. With binoculars, the crew could see the Germans across the valley in their chow lines. And of course the Germans could see the Americans as well.

On Friday the 15th, House had time off to return to the battery CP where the cooks served three hot meals. He had time to heat water to bathe and shave, and to clean his carbine. That night after he returned to his outpost, the battery ran out of howitzer ammunition after firing some 100 rounds at German tanks that were being assembled. Resupply was not expected until the following night. "Other than that, the day was normal in Oberlascheid."

*   *   *   *

What was to be the most tragic American battle action in Europe involved the 106th Infantry Division and the attached 14th Cavalry Group under Col. Mark Devine. Both had been placed under General Hodges' First U.S. Army.

American successes some weeks earlier had driven the enemy from a part of the West Wall (Siegfried Line) along the Schnee Eifel which extended into Germany twelve miles east of St. Vith. The value of holding the salient through the West Wall seemed to compensate for the risk of a German counterattack to reduce it. On 11 December the 14th Cavalry Group took over positions to the north in the Losheim Gap, previously held by a cavalry unit of the 2d Infantry Division. On the same day, the 106th began relieving the 2d Division in the Schnee Eifel. During the hasty transition, the deployment of the 106th into defensive positions were those recommended by Maj. Gen. Walter M. Robertson, commander of the 2d Division, recommendations later criticized. Probably a more important question was how well the 106th was armed for defense. The nearest ammunition supply was over forty miles southwest of St. Vith, at Noville (five miles northeast of Bastogne). Resupply was slow and difficult, even under favorable conditions.

However serious the situation was, it may have been tolerable had it not been for the German Operation HERBSTNEBEL. The plan, born in the twisted mind of Adolf Hitler, was to seize Antwerp, the Allies' main supply port, and within one week cut off some twenty-five Allied divisions in Belgium and Holland. The code name HERBSTNEBEL (Autumn Fog) implied the skill of Hitler's meteorologists — for the first five days, the weather was to the Germans' advantage.

*   *   *   *

Exactly why or how the Allies misjudged the size of the German buildup remains uncertain. During the latter part of November and the first two weeks of December, rapidly mounting German activities on road and rail were reported by both air reconnaissance and ground intelligence.

Every reconnaissance mission flown on 8, 10, 11, 14 and 15 December reported numerous trains, moving or stationary, on almost all lines east and west of the Rhine River. There were many reports of "canvas-covered flat cars loaded with tanks or trucks" and, frequently, hospital trains west of the Rhine. With such increasing information on the enemy's shift of activities into the area opposite the Ardennes, it seems incredible that the Allies judged them to be only minor movements. Historians Craven and Cate summarized it thusly:

> It is clear enough that the failure was one primarily of interpretation, but the lines of responsibility are so blurred and the failure is so complete as to leave no other choice than the assumption that all organizations charged with processing the raw materials brought back by the reconnaissance pilots fell down on the job. The ultimate responsibility for interpretation lay with the ground forces, except points pertaining to enemy air potentialities, but the air force was responsible for the initial screening of the results of its own reconnaissance. Perhaps the chief fault was one of organization, for there seems to have been a twilight zone between air and ground headquarters in which the responsibility had not been sufficiently pinned down.

The First Five Days

SATURDAY, 16 DECEMBER

The 14th Cavalry Group on the north of the Schnee Eifel was holding the Losheim Gap while the 106th Infantry Division deployed its 423d Infantry Regiment at Buchet, east of Bleialf. Further south, the 424th Infantry Regiment was located in the vicinity of Grosskampenberg.

At 0400 the 5th and 6th Panzer armies began the assault into the Ardennes with St. Vith their first objective. According to schedule, the northern units of the 18th Volksgrenadier Division, LXVI Corps, soon penetrated the Losheim Gap as far as Auw, overrunning most of the American artillery positions. German armor of the 1st SS Panzer Division followed as the 14th Cavalry Group attempted to hold the northern flank of the 106th's 422d Regiment. South of the Schnee Eifel, units of the 18th Volksgrenadier Division penetrated the southern flank of the 423d Regiment, separating it from the 424th Regiment. The 106th Division had lost relatively little ground during daylight. During the night, activities in the 106th command post at St. Vith grew understandably hectic. General Jones was concerned about resupplying and reinforcing the 422d and 423d regiments — and about his son, serving in the 423d. Both regiments were ordered to withdraw back toward St. Vith if possible.

* * * *

General Bradley planned to be flown from his headquarters in Luxembourg City to attend a meeting on Saturday with General Eisenhower and the SHAEF staff at Versailles. Because of the foul and foggy weather, it was decided to make the four-hour drive in his Cadillac staff car. He arrived at SHAEF Headquarters in the Trianon Palace Hotel early in the afternoon. Ike was in a pleasant mood, since only that morning he had been notified of his promotion to general of the army. (This required the design of a new rank insignia, one with five stars.)

During the afternoon meeting, Eisenhower's chief intelligence officer, Maj. Gen. Sir Kenneth W. D. Strong, was handed a message — Germans attacking in the Ardennes along the front of Maj. Gen. Troy H. Middleton's VIII Corps. Although the magnitude of the

German offensive was not then known, a small "relieving attack" had been expected. Communications were surprisingly slow to reach SHAEF during the rest of the night.

The weather that day was better at Field Marshal Montgomery's tactical (forward) headquarters at Zonhoven, Holland. Early in the morning, Monty "felt in need of relaxation," so he was flown up to Eindhoven in his Miles light aircraft to the golf course for a few holes. His game was interrupted by a message that the Germans had launched a heavy attack that morning on the First American Army front. Monty immediately flew back to Zonhoven.

Lt. Gen. Courtney H. Hodges, commanding general of the First U.S. Army, began his day in his Spa headquarters at 0700 as the reports came in. As the German advances began, his efforts were concentrated on critical "war games" with his First Army, with Maj. Gen. J. Lawton Collins' VII Corps to reinforce Middleton's VIII Corps.

Bradley and Eisenhower spent the evening together and retired around midnight. A better and clearer picture would be available in the morning.

SUNDAY, 17 DECEMBER

Before dawn, during the 590th Field Artillery's preparations for pulling back, someone at Battery A's command post erroneously cut the phone wires to the forward outpost. At daylight on the 17th, Sergeant House ran back to the CP where he learned that the battery was getting ready to pull out. He rushed back to the bunkers to get the others in his crew. They returned with only their carbines and the machine gun: "Thus began our Battle of the Bulge." It was a most fateful day for the 106th Infantry Division.

General Jones had organized a horseshoe-shaped perimeter defense directly east of St. Vith. As Brig. Gen. Robert W. Hasbrouck's 7th Armored Division arrived from Holland (ordered in by Bradley), Jones positioned the division on the northern perimeter with the expectation that it would quickly attack to the east and relieve his 422d and 423d regiments — and his son. But he underestimated the strength of the encircling German forces.

From the north, through the Losheim Gap, the 18th Volksgrenadier Division (on its way to Schoenberg) closed the upper jaw around Col. George L. Descheneaux's 422d Regiment. The 18th's lower jaw, also headed toward Schoenberg, trapped Col. Charles C. Cavender's 423d Regiment. Both regiments were advised to withdraw toward St. Vith if possible. The only reinforcement was the return of Lt. Col. Joseph P. Pruett's 2d Battalion B to the 423d's positions. The battalion had been ordered earlier by General Jones to withdraw and protect Schoenberg. When this became impossible, the battalion was ordered back to rejoin its regiment.

Resupply by Air Requested

The first request for resupply by air was sent that morning at 1051 in a message from the 423d CP at Buchet to the 106th Division's headquarters at St. Vith:

> From 423 Inf: 2d BN 423 Inf joined with. Contact 422 Inf. Will hold perimeter. Drop amo, food, and med supplies until route open. We have no arty.

The message was not received by the division until 1445 or 1500 as recorded in the log four hours after transmission. Apparently the division was already considering the regiments' plight and had requested relief by air drops. At 1345 a message was sent to the 423d giving the map coordinates for a drop:

> Supplies to be dropped vicinity BUCHET 992828 tonight.

The division was taking action. At 1400 a similar message was sent to the 422d CP at Schlausenbach:

> Supplies to be dropped vicinity 018868 SCHLAUSENBACH tonight.

Neither of the airborne resupply drops arrived; the requests had not been sent through the right communications channels.

Sometime around midday, General Jones had called the air officer, Lt. Col. Josiah T. Towne, attached to the VIII Corps, to arrange the resupply missions. He relayed the request for food and ammunition for the 422d and 423d regimental combat teams to Colonel Myers, A-3 of IX Fighter Command, who passed it on to the IX Tactical Air Command. But there were problems with the

channels of communication, according to a later interview with
Colonel Towne by Colonel Dupuy:*

> Towne states that the message was forwarded through IX
> Fighter Command to the IX Tactical Air Command, which ap-
> parently, he alleges, ruled that the request must be handled
> through ground channels, and forwarded it to G-4, First Army.
> Then, further alleges Towne, someone in First Army G-4 office,
> ostensibly because the request had not come through "proper
> channels" — direct from G-4, VIII Corps — held it for twenty-
> four hours, telling no one of his action. When the red tape was
> straightened out weather over target and base had closed down.

No other documentation on the 106th's requests surfaced. Disposition of the requests was not clearly traceable among the various
headquarters and commands: Air Staff, SHAEF; Combined Air
Transport Operations Room (CATOR), SHAEF; IX Troop Carrier Command; IX Tactical Air Command; Communications Zone,
12th Army Group; First Army; VIII Corps. (Conspicuously missing in this roster is the First Allied Airborne Army (FAAA).)

*   *   *   *

Having had little sleep, Eisenhower and Bradley attended the
early morning SHAEF staff meeting as messages continued to arrive. The situation was more serious than had been anticipated. The
only logical decision was to first move reserve forces into the battle
area. At the time, the major reserves were the 101st and the 82d airborne divisions at Mourmelon le Grand and Snippes, about 100
miles of the Ardennes. They were hardly three weeks out of battle

---

* Royce L. Thompson in his exhaustive research for his unpublished MS, 1951,
was careful to qualify single source memories. Hugh M. Cole in his officially published *The Ardennes: Battle of the Bulge,* 1964, wrote that since he was "forced to
depend in so great degree on the human memory, unaided or unchallenged by the
written record, the scholar's old rule 'one witness, no witness' has been generally
applied." Both Thompson and Cole relied on some relaxation of the rule to provide the likeliest facts available. They took much from Col. R. Ernest Dupuy's
semiofficial history, *St. Vith: Lion in the Way, the 106th Infantry Division in World
War II,* 1949, which relied heavily on later personal interviews. Cole spent much
effort to trace the story through numerous headquarters. "Interviews with officers
involved have only compounded confusion, yielding bits and pieces of information, which lacking in written record cannot be put together in sequence."

after the Holland airborne invasions. Another division, the 17th Airborne, without combat experience, was in England.

Late in the day at his headquarters near Reims, General Gavin received orders originating in SHAEF to prepare the 82d and 101st divisions for movement "toward Bastogne" at dawn on the 19th. Gavin assembled airborne staffs and commanders at 2000 for the briefing. At 2130, another order from SHAEF directed both divisions to move "without delay in the direction of Bastogne." Gavin decided that the 82d would be the first to leave after daylight on the 18th. The 101st would depart at 1400 with independent units scheduled to go later in the day.

Meanwhile other orders emanated from SHAEF-AIR through the First Allied Airborne Army. The 17th Airborne Division in England was alerted for movement from England by the IX Troop Carrier Command to the Reims area for assembly at Camp Mourmelon le Grand. General Williams was assigned a sudden, unusual task for his IX Troop Carrier Command: to furnish available air transportation for 13,000 men and their equipment to airfields near Reims while continuing the vital resupply missions to airfields at the rear of the First and Third U.S. armies.

MONDAY, 18 DECEMBER

During the hours before dawn, there were a series of requests from the 106th Division to the IX TAC, and from the 423d Regiment to the division. At 0435, the 106th telephoned the First Army's air section and IX TAC asking that ammunition be dropped at two specific locations. Particular quantities of .30-caliber and bazooka ammunition were requested. At 0550, the 106th telephoned an additional request to IX TAC for bandages, plasma, morphine and 8,000 rations.

Within the next twenty minutes, the division received two teletyped messages from the 423d. The first at 0555 was a list of ammunition required in order of priority and quantity, 81mm, 60mm, and 105mm. At 0610 more medical supplies, bandages and Carlisle dressings were listed. In turn, at 0620, the 106th immediately telephoned corrections of the previous request to IX TAC (to a Colonel Chaffin).

Thus during those predawn hours, the 106th specifically made its requests known to the IX TAC, the air force unit attached to the

First Army. To facilitate the expected air drops, the division sent a message to both regiments with instructions to display a fifty-foot-square orange panel at the drop points.

Since IX Troop Carrier Command would provide the mission aircraft, the chain of communications must have included CATOR at SHAEF and possibly General Brereton's FAAA. How many telephone calls were made before the First Army messages reached CATOR and how many headquarters were involved was never determined.

* * * *

South of the Schnee Eifel, the 424th Regiment was able to withdraw during the night of 17–18 December, back across the Our River, and take defensive positions four or five miles south of St. Vith.

The situation of the 422d and 423d regiments in the Schnee Eifel was different. It was so critical that only an airdrop could possibly sustain resistance beyond the 18th. The regiments could not withdraw to St. Vith nor could the 7th Armored Division move out of St. Vith to reinforce them. Yet they held out all day Monday as ammunition — except what each man carried — ran out, and food, which was rationed, dwindled. They held on anticipating the Troop Carrier planes that would surely soon fly over and paradrop critical supplies — bundles from heaven. But they waited in vain.

* * * *

Soon after dawn, A Battery withdrew to firing positions just outside Oberlascheid. The communications with the division's headquarters at St. Vith had been cut off by the Germans. They were surrounded. Pete House recalls:

> We were exhausted, hungry and cold. Cooks had not prepared any meals since the morning of the 16th. There were no emergency rations. That night we moved to an open field with only four rounds left for our 105 howitzers. Then we received orders to get the vehicles running and move out. Only three of the trucks for towing howitzers would run, so one of the guns was hooked up to the ¾-ton weapons carrier I was driving. We spent the rest of the night parked on a road in a valley. It was bitter cold. Still no food.

That night those in the 590th Field Artillery Battalion were hanging on to the hope that the 7th Armored Division would arrive from St. Vith. That hope had come with the last messages from division headquarters before communications had been cut.

* * * *

On the morning of the 18th, the 82d and 101st airborne divisions moved quickly out of their camps, both short on equipment and supplies. Their actual objectives in the Ardennes were not firm until they were en route. The 82d, under Major General Gavin, was directed to the north flank of the Ardennes sector while the first elements of the 101st, under its deputy commander, Brig. Gen. Anthony C. McAuliffe, headed for the Bastogne area. A combat command of the 10th Armored Division was already at Bastogne to welcome the 101st, which was scheduled to arrive on the 19th.

TUESDAY, 19 DECEMBER

At daylight, A Battery moved its howitzers up a steep field along the edge of a woods with only four rounds left to fire. Before House could dig a foxhole, "the Germans hit us with everything." He ran into the woods to find a stream bed for protection. In his haste, he left his wool gloves, hat, and mackinaw. "This loss haunted me for the rest of my time in Europe."

After the German barrage ceased, the word was passed along that we were going to surrender. Men of the 423d walked through the woods to a clearing where they found the 590th's commander, Lt. Col. Vaden Lackey, and the commander of the 423d Infantry, Col. Charles Cavender. There was no ammunition or food; Cavender had no choice but to say they were surrendering at 1600. They were told that anyone could try to fight their way out on foot. House and about twenty others decided to do just that; they ran west for two hours until three were wounded, and then they were captured. They were among some 7,000 men who were taken prisoner that afternoon; most all of them were from 422d and 423d regiments of the 106th Infantry Division.

One of those who surrendered was 1st Lt. Alan Jones, Jr., who was on the staff of one of Cavender's battalions. The depression General Jones felt at the loss of his two infantry regiments deepened profoundly at the news of his son's capture.

Brig. Gen. Robert W. Hasbrouck's 7th Armored Division headquarters was adjacent to General Jones' CP in Vielsalm. Jones was so despondent that he requested Hasbrouck, his junior in rank, to assume the tactical command of the defense of St. Vith. Thus General Hasbrouck became *de facto* commander for the defense of St. Vith. After a quick tour and inspection of the defenses, Hasbrouck returned gravely concerned. The units were not nearly as formidable as Jones had indicated. That night he began drafting his letter to General Hodges' headquarters.

Defense of Bastogne

When the 101st had been committed to defend Bastogne, no plans for resupply by air had yet been formulated. Supply records from the earlier air missions during the Holland operations would have been helpful, but they were back at Mourmelon, about 100 miles from Bastogne. Most of the division left the camp with two days' rations for each man. The basic loads transported were ammunition as prescribed by European Theater of Operations, U.S. Army (ETOUSA) for airborne divisions. The third convoy of QM supplies and gasoline encountered an enemy attack and suffered critical losses before reaching Bastogne.

The most serious loss on the 19th was at Herbaimont, eight miles northwest of Bastogne where the division clearing station of the 326th Airborne Medical Company was set up. At about 2230, six enemy armored vehicles, supported by about 100 infantrymen, overran the company. The division surgeon, Lt. Col. David Gold, surrendered eighteen officers and 125 enlisted men. Four officers and 113 enlisted men evaded capture and moved southward along with the 426th Quartermaster and 801st Ordinance companies.

Command Decisions

The German counteroffensive wedge that had split the Allied defense was also dividing its commanders. Field Marshal Montgomery is credited with initiating a major change with his 19 December telephone call to Maj. Gen. John F. M. Whiteley, deputy chief of operations (G-3) at SHAEF. After conferring with Maj. Gen. Kenneth W. D. Strong, SHAEF chief of intelligence, the proposal was presented to Lt. Gen. Walter Bedell Smith, Eisenhower's chief of staff.

In SHAEF, it appeared that the German penetration was dividing General Bradley's two U.S. armies, the First and Third. With Bradley's advanced headquarters in the city of Luxembourg, it would be practically impossible to retain contact with the First U.S. Army in the north. The proposed solution was to give Montgomery command of the two U.S. forces north of the Ardennes. Reluctantly, Smith telephoned Bradley about the proposed shift of command. Bradley resisted and stated, "Certainly if Monty's were an American command, I would agree with you entirely. It would be a logical thing to do." But he added that if the U.S. forces were added to Montgomery's command for all operations north of the Ardennes, he might be more inclined to use the American forces against the enemy. The final decision was made by Eisenhower, causing elation for Montgomery, "Undercurrents of unhappiness" in the First Army Headquarters, and Bradley's lifelong, deep regret.

Of his decision, General Eisenhower later wrote:

> When on December 17 the XVIII Airborne Corps with its two divisions had been released to General Bradley and directed toward Bastogne, it was not in anticipation of the battle that developed in that area but merely because Bastogne was such an excellent road center. Troops directed there could later be dispatched by the commander on the spot to any region he found desirable. These troops were pushing toward the front on the eighteenth when the situation became so serious on the northern front that General Bradley diverted the leading division, the 82d, toward the left, but the 101st continued on to its original destination in Bastogne. It began closing in there on the night of December 18. During that night and on the nineteenth, while the Germans were occupying themselves with isolated detachments of the troops that manned the original defensive line, the division prepared to defend Bastogne.

In his office at Versailles on the 19th, Eisenhower made the final decision to separate the commands then under Bradley. On the battle map, he fixed a boundary running east and west through the breach in our allied lines, generally on the axis Givet-Prum, giving both places inclusively to the northern group.

Bradley's First Army, north of the line and under General Hodges, was to be temporarily assigned to Montgomery's com-

mand. The XVIII Airborne Corps with its 82d Division (at Manhay) fell under Hodges' command, while the 101st Division (at Bastogne) was placed under Maj. Gen. Troy H. Middleton's VIII
Corps. General Bradley was left with Patton's Third Army, which
included the VII Corps.

After Eisenhower made his decision, he phoned Montgomery,
who was not surprised since he had been advocating such a change in
commands for three days. There is no record of Montgomery calling
Churchill directly after talking to Eisenhower, but it seems logical
that he would. Before Ike retired that night, Churchill phoned him
"to find out how the battle was going." After the new command
organization was discussed, Churchill was delighted and said, "I assure you that British troops will always deem it an honor to enter
the same battle as their American friends."

WEDNESDAY, 20 DECEMBER

On the north flank of the German penetration, General Ridgway had set up his XVIII Airborne Corps Headquarters next to
General Gavin's 82d Airborne Division headquarters at Weromont.
Their orders from Hodges were to relieve the American 7th Armored Division then under siege at St. Vith.

General Hodges was steeped in the American military tradition
of constant and vigorous attack. He believed that anything gained in
battle with American blood should not be given up easily. When
Montgomery marched into Hodges' headquarters at Chaudfontaine, even the British officers were amused. Monty's famous pom-
posity was conspicuous as he met with Hodges and his staff. His
first opinion was to retreat, withdraw all American forces out of the
St. Vith pocket, and "tidy up the lines." It was difficult for Hodges
to believe that Montgomery was serious if the latter fully knew the
value of the St. Vith bridgehead.

The impasse between Montgomery and Hodges was alleviated
for the day when a hand-carried message arrived from General
Hasbrouck. After it was read aloud, Hodges' firm comment was,
"Ridgway's XVIII Corps will have to keep driving forward toward
St. Vith to Hasbrouck's relief."

Montgomery agreed, but he added instructions to do it his way.
As soon as the St. Vith defenders were afforded an escape route,

they would retreat to the northwest. He said, "After all, gentlemen, you can't win the big victory without a tidy show."

That night, before Patton got his Third Army attack under way from the south toward Bastogne, Montgomery delayed the companion attack from the north by Hodges' VII Corps under Lt. Gen. Joseph L. Collins. "It was not until January (twelve days later) that Montgomery completed his primping and attacked," Bradley later summarized.* The element of surprise was lost and the defenses of St. Vith were doomed to collapse the next day. From then on it was withdrawal as ordered by Montgomery.

* * * *

The town of Bastogne, sought for its road connections, lay in the southern portion of the German counteroffensive. The defenders were General McAuliffe's 101st Airborne Division and the 10th Armored Division under Col. William Roberts. In addition, there were partial units and stragglers from other divisions who came together in an improvised force under McAuliffe's command. It was quickly named Team SNAFU, the GI acronym for Situation Normal, All (politely) Fouled Up. As the stragglers arrived, many from the 28th Division, they were assigned to Team SNAFU.

Two days earlier, on the 18th, while Middleton's VIII Corps was under the First Army's command, Hodges had ordered Middleton's headquarters to move to Neufchateau, Belgium, seventeen miles southwest down the highway from Bastogne.** Middleton's headquarters was in an excellent location for communications with SHAEF, between Patton's Third Army on the south and McAuliffe's 101st at Bastogne. The embattled McAuliffe benefited from a corps radio-link vehicle, which arrived in Bastogne on the 20th. He and Middleton had two-way telephones and teletypes at their disposal throughout the siege.

---

* General Bradley also wrote later, "Although Montgomery did not commit more than a single brigade of British troops against the Bulge offensive, he backed the First Army's flank with four British divisions, while those British reserves encouraged Hodges to throw everything into the Ardennes, I afterward questioned whether this bargain was worth the misunderstanding that came with the change in Command.
** All towns have their distinctions, some through trivia. During World War I, Walt Disney spent months in Neufchateau repairing ambulance vehicles and sending cartoons home depicting his experiences.

One of the first morning teletype messages concerned supplies. It was apparent to the regimental S-4s at Bastogne and Lt. Col. Carl W. Kohls, the 101st G-4, that the supply situation was critical. Although there were approximately 100 trucks in the rear areas ready to move, ground transportation was virtually cut off by the surrounding German forces. The midmorning message from Kohls requested resupply by air, not unusual considering the recent September air support requests during MARKET-GARDEN. During the day, the town of Bastogne was foraged for medical and other supplies.

General McAuliffe decided it would be better to talk with General Middleton in person to organize for the upcoming battle. McAuliffe left Bastogne in the afternoon for Neufchateau, a twenty-five-minute drive. The conclusions of the meeting were to hold Bastogne and keep the Neufchateau-Bastogne highway open. On the way back, McAuliffe could observe the idle railroad line which paralleled the north side of the highway. There had been no rail traffic for two days. At one point, he saw the town of Sibret, located less than a mile beyond the rail line, where German forces were concentrating. Less than an hour after McAuliffe's car passed the road junction to Sibret, four miles from Bastogne, the Germans took control of the highway at that point. Bastogne was surrounded.

THURSDAY, 21 DECEMBER – SATURDAY, 23 DECEMBER

While the defenses around St. Vith were penetrated by German forces, the American commanders at Vielsalm (ten miles west, on the Salm River) had been struggling with another problem since the 19th: who was in command of and responsible for the forces defending St. Vith? Was it Maj. Gen. Alan Jones, Brig. Gen. Robert Hasbrouck or Brig. Gen. William Hoge (9th Armored Division CCB), who was senior to Hasbrouck by time in grade?

On the 21st, after the 82d Division was positioned along the Salm River, General Gavin visited Jones at his Vielsalm CP. He wrote later that Jones "was the picture of dejection . . . and was depressed by the loss of his two infantry regiments . . . I felt sorry for him." One of Jones' greatest disappointments was that the 422d and 423d regiments were not resupplied by air as he expected.

The next afternoon, on the 22d, General Ridgway arrived at Hasbrouck's headquarters for a conference with Hasbrouck and

Jones. Ridgway and Hasbrouck made a tour of the forward positions and returned to Vielsalm after dark. Then they summoned Jones for another meeting. To Ridgway, Jones' attitude was "strange." It was "casual, almost indifferent, little interested in the fact that that night we were going to bring his people out of the trap." Before the meeting ended, General Ridgway relieved General Jones of his command and placed all troops in the salient under General Hasbrouck.

The stress and the sudden relief of the burden was apparently too much for Jones. Shortly after midnight he suffered a serious heart attack. He was quickly evacuated to the hospital in Liège, Belgium.

Early on the evening of the 23d, Ridgway ordered all remaining forces to withdraw from St. Vith and regroup on his southern front near Manhay. The Battle of the Bulge was not over. To the American forces, it was just beginning.

* * * *

One question still lingers: would the resupply by air to Jones' 106th Division have made a great difference for the defense around St. Vith? Possibly not. Surely, if the 422d and 423d regiments had been resupplied, they would not have surrendered as they did. Neither Jones nor any of his men in the 106th knew why the air drops they expected never arrived. They only knew that heaven had never delivered the bundles they had awaited so desperately.

12

On the Way to St. Vith
(The Aborted Mission)

COL. FRANK J. MACNEES WAS proud of his 435th Troop Carrier Group's actions during the 15 August 1944 invasion of southern France. On 6 December, Col. Maurice M. Beach, 53d Wing commander, visited Welford Park to award decorations — Air Medals to tow plane crews and glider pilots. MacNees received the Distinguished Flying Cross. He probably missed getting another DFC due to an unusual communications foul-up causing the mission to be aborted.

On the night of 17 December, aircraft of the 435th were loaded with freight for another routine haul to the Continent. Before take-off time the next morning, Colonel MacNees was handed "Priority Orders" from IX Troop Carrier Command. Colonel Beach had chosen the 435th to make the emergency air drop resupply mission to the Ardennes near St. Vith. Over forty airplanes were to be unloaded and reloaded with parapacks and cabin bundles consisting largely of ammunition, food, and medical supplies.

The instructions were unusual; the mission was to consist of two flight segments. Only the first was defined. It was a 275-mile flight route from Welford Park to Airfield A-78, a IX Tactical Air Command fighter airfield at Florennes, Belgium. There, the Troop Carrier crews were to be briefed for the final flight route to designated DZs. To reach the location where the two regiments of the 106th Division were encircled near St. Vith would only be another seventy-five miles due east, and some thirty minutes flight time, with fighter cover there and back.

Recognizing that the orders were hastily prepared and incomplete for such a mission, Colonel MacNees decided to lead it himself. It was not unusual for Troop Carrier transports to experience operational difficulties and delays at the active fighter aircraft fields in Belgium and France. This critical operation would prove to be no exception.

✻   ✻   ✻   ✻

Maj. Gen. Elwood Quesada, commander of IX Tactical Air Command, was well aware of the serious situation as German forces drove southwest through the Losheim Gap. With his headquarters at Liege, he was in conveniently close contact with General Hodges' First U.S. Army Headquarters at Spa (they were but twenty miles from each other). The IX TAC had been assigned to furnish direct support to Hodges. Thus the urgent requests to General Quesada's command on behalf of the 106th Division began on 16 December, first for fighter aircraft support on the night of 16–17 December and then for air resupply on the 17th and 18th.

Two fighter groups of Quesada's 70th Wing, the 370th and the 474th, were based at Airfield A-78. On the 17th, the Luftwaffe was out in force with FW 190s and Me 109s. The most heavily engaged squadron was the 430th of the 474th Group, and this was its first time in aerial combat. Two P-38s were lost and another bellied in; several were severely damaged. Seven Me 109s were shot down. The airfield was busy around the clock.

The decision for the Troop Carrier resupply mission to land at A-78 for its final briefing seemed appropriate in light of the fluid battle conditions. The latest information concerning the encircled battalions was expected to be acquired by other fighter groups in the IX TAC and transmitted to A-78. It would be vital information, required by the 435th Troop Carrier Group to complete its mission.

✻   ✻   ✻   ✻

Why the operation was SNAFU'd is still an enigma. Were communications between the First Allied Airborne Army and the IX Tactical Air Command unclear? Or were the fighter aircraft groups at A-78 too busy to be bothered? Doubtless, it was a combination of the two.

* * * *

While planes of the 435th were still being loaded around noon on the 18th at Welford Park, an advance aircraft of the 75th Squadron, piloted by Maj. Thomas E. Nunn, Jr., operations officer of the 76th, took off for A-78 with two purposes: to arrange for the arrival of the 435th and for an expeditious briefing of crews soon after landing. On approaching the airfield, Nunn was advised by radio that the airfield was too busy to receive the formation.* He was told to divert to Liege, Airfield A-93, about forty-five miles northeast of Florennes.

The twenty-three-plane formation, headed by Colonel Mac-Nees, was not far behind Nunn. Eighteen aircraft of the 75th Squadron and five of the 76th Squadron had lifted off from Welford Park at 1330. (Nineteen loaded C-47s of the 77th and 78th squadrons were scheduled for departure one hour later, but the takeoffs were canceled due to the rapid deterioration of the weather.) The mission formation was in elements of two ships, echeloned right. Captain Kearnes of the 75th was in number two position on MacNees' right wing. Lt. Col. Robert C. Lewis, CO of the 76th, was in the lead of the last five planes. Each C-47 carried six parapacks mounted on the outside of the fuselage and two or three door bundles with parachutes.

When the 53d Wing headquarters received word by radio from Nunn's aircraft that he was diverted from A-78, the Wing A-3 (Lieutenant Colonel Ward) instructed him to divert all the group's aircraft to A-41, the airfield of the 50th Troop Carrier Wing's 441st Group at Druex, some fifty miles west of Paris. The weather in England had deteriorated too much for a safe return. Meanwhile, Colonel MacNees and Captain Kearns insisted on getting clearance to

---

* Airfield A-78 had two concrete runways, one of 4,500 feet approximating an E-W direction (84 degrees), the other of 5,345 feet in a NNW-SSE (164 degrees) orientation, roughly at right angles to each other. With an extremely high frequency of fighter operations that day, one runway was probably in full use. Whatever the situation was, an arriving formation of forty C-47s with subsequent uninterrupted takeoffs would have proven highly disruptive to ongoing fighter aircraft operations.

land their planes at A-78. Soon after landing, they were shocked to learn that no one at the field had any knowledge of their mission or its objectives. From there they flew their planes to A-93 to pick up the formation or prepare for the mission, which might be reinstated on the following day. The radio contact problems between Nunn and MacNees resulted in the formation splitting up. Under adverse weather conditions, MacNees and Kearns flew back to Welford Park, stunned by the fiasco.

At 2000, Major Nunn's plane and the other twenty-one C-47s, with parapacks and door bundles intended for the Ardennes, were parked on the airfield at Druex. There were no tents or cots available and it was necessary for the crews to sleep in their planes. For the next four days they were on constant alert to fly the mission as originally intended.

Meanwhile additional requests from the 106th Division, through the First Allied Airborne Army, had increased the resupply requirements to 138 aircraft loads. Because so many planes would be needed, IX Troop Carrier Command decided to plan for the mission to originate from England, when permitted by the weather. All plans for air resupply to the 106th were finally canceled on 22 December when General Patton requested that resupply of the 101st Airborne Division have first priority in all resupply missions. The confused character of the situation was reflected by the 435th Troop Carrier Group's report:

> During this period of time at A-41 conditions were most trying for the crews as the mission would be planned and briefed then postponed, then changed to a return to the UK as soon as weather permitted, then the mission would be reinstated. This type of situation continued until the arrival of Capt. Travis, a reconnaissance pilot from a unit of the XIX TAC at 0630 on 22 Dec. Subsequent to his arrival we received definite orders to unload all of our parachute supplies and return to England, if the weather permitted. Only one airplane was able to proceed on the 22d and that was the one flown by Major Nunn. All others were required to RON [remain over night] another night and early on the morning of the 23d they received orders to proceed to A-54 [Paris]. All of these ships returned to Welford during the afternoon of the 23d.

The purpose of the stop at the Paris airfield, A-54, was to pick up medical patients, wounded American soldiers, and move them to Membury. It was late in the day when the twenty-one planes arrived back at their Welford Park airbase, sometime after the first two re-supply missions of the 435th in Operation REPULSE had departed. Before 1300 of the 23d, aircraft of the 77th and 78th squadrons were in the air with resupplies destined for Bastogne, Belgium. An hour later, planes of the 76th and 78th squadrons took-off to drop resupplies at another objective, Marcouray, Belgium, where over four hundred American troops of Task Force Hogan were surrounded.

Crew of the first C-47, IX Troop Carrier Pathfinder Group, to drop 101st Airborne Division pathfinder teams in Normandy on D-Day. Lieutenant Colonel Joel L. Crouch, pilot, *standing second from left.* Captain Vito S. Pedone, copilot, *standing right,* 5 June 1944.

— Courtesy: Bancroft

13

DZ Marcouray
(Hogan's Isolated 1,000)

AFTER ORDERING THE 82D AIRBORNE Division to move up to the Salm River and to the rear of the 106th Division at St. Vith, General Ridgway anxiously awaited Maj. Gen. Maurice Rose's 3d Armored Division. It was to fill a gap between the 82d Division position and the Ourthe River. After traveling through the night, the 3d Armored Division assembled near Hotton early on 20 December. It was to control a thirteen-mile segment of the Bastogne-Liège highway north of Houffalize. At the time, Rose's direct command was one-third its prior size since General Hodges had detached two of the 3d's combat commands for other actions. One was to remain in the vicinity of Eupen in case the Germans crossed the Elsenborn Bridge and be ready for German paratroops, and the other was assigned to support the 30th Division.

Having meager information about the German drive, General Rose divided Combat Command R into three task forces for the advance from the Ourthe River. Each task force had some 400 to 500 men and consisted of a reconnaissance troop, a medium tank company, an armored field artillery battery, and a platoon of light tanks. Task Force Hogan was placed on the right flank to form the southern boundary of Ridgway's XVIII Airborne Corps.

Lt. Col. Samuel Mason Hogan was from Pharr, a small Texas

town where he grew up a hunter, fisherman, and horseman. After two years at a nearby junior college, he was appointed to West Point and graduated in 1938. Every vehicle he rode in flew the Lone Star flag of Texas.

Hogan's battalion reached La Roche, eighteen miles (fourteen air miles) northwest of Bastogne, on 20 December. After facing the strong leading units of the 116th Panzer Division there, General Rose's division headquarters ordered Task Force Hogan to move north on 21 December. During the movement, there were numerous skirmishes with lesser sized German forces until the task force reached a hill near Marcouray, where it bivouacked overnight. Every man was aware that, to hold out against the enemy, supplies and ammunition were sorely needed. Their plight for the next two days is vividly portrayed in the communications relayed by CC R, between Task Force Hogan and the 3d Armored Division headquarters.

At 1340 on the 21st, Hogan reported that he was pulling back to Marcouray ". . . to get good defending." The message was repeated at 1500 hours. Another message from Hogan at 1615 stated, "Have set up all around defenses in Marcouray. Out of gasoline." Within an hour, at 1700, CC R received the following message which included some Hogan humor:

> Request the following supplies be dropped by Liaison plane at Marcouray. Ether, surgical instruments, plaster of Paris and padding, sulfonamide powder roller bandage, iodine pantathel, alcohol, cotton, adhesive tape, sodium bicarbonate and spirit of US ferment.

It is unclear why the request was not forwarded to the division until 2022. Three hours later the message was given to the division surgeon who was assigned to assemble the supplies.

Independent of the above communications, the division G-4 was active and by message queried CC R at 1814, "What is 'Hogans' supply situation?" The 2100 reply was, "Hogan reports he is out of gas in Marcouray at 1615. He requested medical supplies by plane in msg of 1700. No other information." At 2215 a Major Griffin of the division left for Ridgway's XVIII Airborne Corps headquarters to investigate the possible dropping of medical supplies and gasoline on Hogan's force. An artillery unit of the division also became involved in the situation and planned to use artillery to actually fire medical supplies into Marcouray. A Captain Waits of G-4 contacted division artillery at 2300 to learn the identity of the unit. The information was to be called back to him.

By midnight of the 22d, Task Force Hogan's plight was well known to the division G-4, who was starting action for resupply by air.

* * * *

There were two attempts to resupply Task Force Hogan on 23 December. One was by artillery and the other by aircraft.

Little is recorded regarding the artillery effort. There are no details, nor was the firing hour specified, but during the morning of the 23d, an artillery unit of the division did fire medical supplies to Marcouray. Unsurprisingly, they were ruined, according to Task Force Hogan's report to CC R at 1950.

The airdrop mission failed in a fiasco of conflicting and inaccurate communications. The request for resupplies originated with the 3d Armored Division and was first directed to the First U.S. Army, possibly through channels. (At the time FUSA represented the ground forces in forwarding wants to SHAEF.)

The conflicting information concerned the location for the air drop. How the map readers in FUSA erred is understandable, but inexcusable. The location of Marcouray by map grid coordinates was P-438817. The coordinates for a nearby town, Marcourt, were P-426817. The following erroneous message from FUSA was received by the air staff of SHAEF at 0400:

> They want 400 gallons of gasoline, M/T 80, and medical supplies for 1000 in suitable variety. Approximately four battalions trapped, location P-439817, town of MARCOURT. Town all in our hands and drop any place in the town will be OK. There is an identifying circle which is about sixty yards in diameter, color of circle is cerise.

The stated number of men at Marcouray was also in error. Actually there were only some 480 men: the 3d Battalion (33d Armored Regiment), one company (83d Reconnaissance Battalion) and C Battery, 54th Armored Field Artillery Battalion.

One hour after SHAEF air staff received the message, it was

forwarded verbatim to IX Troop Carrier Command, at 0500. One sentence was added: "This message was received at Versailles at 230400."

The next message from First U.S. Army was to inform the IX Tactical Air Command (Ninth Air Force) directly. Received at 0500, it was worded as follows:

> Master G-4 informs that supplies will be dropped today to an outfit at P-439817. Supplies: 4000 gal. M/T fuel. Med. supplies for 1,000 men. Ident.: Circle of Cerise panel sixty yds in diameter.

"Master" was the ground (not air) code name for the First U.S. Army. Whatever role the TAC played on the 23d, if any, is missing in the records.

At IX Troop Carrier Command headquarters, the message from SHAEF air staff was perplexing. Which was correct, the town name or the coordinates? In the meantime, FUSA realized the conflicting information and sent a subsequent notice at 0525. It was a "Supplemental Copy" to SHAEF Main Air, attention CATOR. It corrected the name of the town but *not* the coordinates: "Dropping point P-439817, town of Marcouray . . ." However it was to no avail. SHAEF did not receive the correction until eight hours later, at 1337, and the information copy to 12th Army Group was not received until 1830. The belated correction never reached the IX Troop Carrier Command.

* * * *

By midmorning on 23 December, the 3d Armored Division was doing all it could to support Task Force Hogan. At 1015, Lt. Col. Eugene C. Orth (division G-4) learned that Ridgway's XVIII Airborne Corps required approval from the division's commanding general for an airdrop, "that it was a dire necessity to supply Hogan by air." During a brief meeting with General Rose, Orth was told, "It is absolutely, it is absolutely, a dire necessity!" That was quickly messaged to the corps G-4.

About that same time, however, the 3d Armored Division was informed that an afternoon airborne drop had been planned. At 1040, the division G-4 sent the following message to CC R:

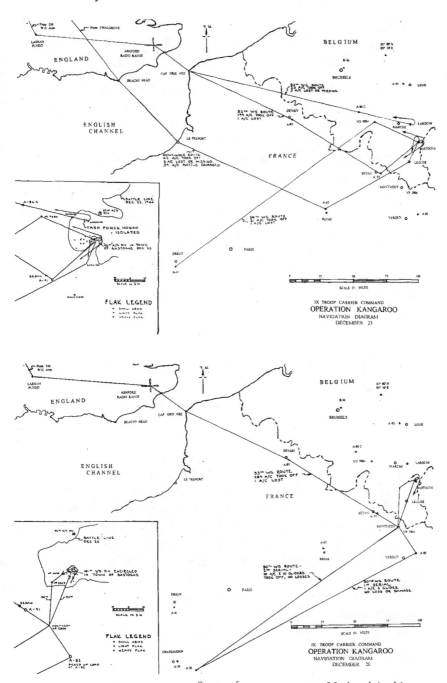

— Source for maps courtesy National Archives

Have TF Hogan display large 'T' repeat Tare with panels at 1300. Keep panels out several hours. Gasoline and medical supplies will be dropped this afternoon, weather permitting.

After further communications between CC R and the division, the instructions were radioed to Task Force Hogan at 1200. Thirty-two minutes later, as a result of FUSA instructions, Colonel Orth notified CC R that the identification should be a circle about sixty yards in diameter . . . instead of the T. Hogan received the last advice at 1330, but it was inconsequential since resupply planes had neither been sighted nor heard.

While those communications were being transmitted, Task Force Hogan sent two other requests. The first, again displaying Hogan humor, was received by CC R at 1220: "Everything quiet. Request Sitrep. Request Xmas turkey be dropped by parachute." The second request, at 1315, asked for 500 cc to 1000 cc of type O whole blood. This communication was taken seriously and was transmitted to the division twelve minutes later.

✻ ✻ ✻ ✻

In addition to resupplying the 101st Airborne Division at Bastogne, the IX Troop Carrier Command was suddenly given another assignment: resupply an isolated unit seventeen miles north-north-west of Bastogne during the afternoon of 23 December.

The 435th Troop Carrier Group at Welford Park was assigned to fly the mission which required fifty aircraft. Upon such short notice, it was decided to reallocate thirty of the group's C-47s that were then being loaded for the Bastogne mission.

The command had considered whether to drop a team of pathfinders with navigation aids in Marcouray. The decision was "that their efficiency would be reduced to ineffectiveness due to casualties from the drop and broken equipment when these men tried to land in town." At the time, it would have been impossible because there were no pathfinder parachute teams remaining at Chalgrove, the IX Troop Carrier Pathfinder Group airfield.* Thus the location of the DZ was for the 435th Group to determine. But the question re-

---

* The last available pathfinder teams, numbering twenty men, were actually in flight from Chalgrove to Bastogne during the morning of 23 December.

mained: was it at the map coordinates or was it at Marcourt? Should they look through flak for a village displaying a cerise circle on the ground, or should they look for a T?

Twenty-nine aircraft took off by 1408 to assemble in a formation led by Lt. Col. B. E. Hanson, CO of the 78th Squadron. Fifteen C-47s from the 78th, thirteen from the 76th, and one from the 75th quickly formed up en route to Ashford. At Cap Gris Nez, the route was east-southeast in a direct course to Marcouray. The route checkpoints were St. Omer, Douvai, and Charleroi, then over the sod airfield at Vitrival (A-86c), with the initial point designated at Marche. The flight time from Welford to the Marcouray DZ was expected to take about two hours, fifteen minutes.

During the final approach, before the DZ could be recognized, the formation encountered heavy concentrations of ground fire. Fighter cover had been expected in the vicinity of the DZ, but none materialized. Three planes were shot down, two from the 76th and one from the 78th.* Twenty-six aircraft of the group were able to head back out after making their paradrops at 1625. Three of them were so damaged that two made emergency landings at Denain/ Prouvy (A-83) and one at Clastres (A-71). Twenty-three C-47s landed together at Dreux (A-41) where they remained overnight. After the crews returned to Welford Park, their interrogation reports indicated some doubt as to the exact location of the drop. The results of the mission were termed "fair."

Actually, they missed the DZ at Marcouray, as evidenced by communications with Task Force Hogan. At 1619 CC R asked T F Hogan: "Have any supplies been dropped? Make every effort to retrieve any supplies dropped you." Almost an hour later, about forty

---

* The two crews of the 76th Squadron were: 1st Lt. Charles F. Jennings, pilot; 2d Lt. Thomas A. Bass, copilot; T/Sgt. Elmer J. Bailey, crew chief; Sgt. Edward L. Kraus, radio operator; and Pvt. Richard E. Chalbeck, pusher of the Quartermaster 3d Air Cargo Squadron; and Capt. William R. Wales, pilot; 2d Lt. Norman H. Beaulieu, copilot; 1st Lt. John W. Parsons, navigator; T/Sgt. Daniel J. Burke, crew chief; S/Sgt. Sebastiano P. Gattinella, radio operator; and Pvt. Arlie K. Holloway of the 3d Air Cargo Squadron. Crew members of the 78th Squadron plane shot down: 1st Lt. Calvin H. White, pilot; 2d Lt. Vincent Hagen, copilot; S/Sgt. Earl Mayo, crew chief; and S/Sgt. Andre C. Mongeau, radio operator. The name of the Quartermaster crew member was not listed in the 435th Group and 78th Squadron records.

minutes after the 1625 drop, T F Hogan responded succinctly, "No supplies received."

At 1930, when S/Sgt. Andre C. Mongeau arrived at a Task Force Hogan outpost, having parachuted from his burning C-47, the facts came to light. The supplies had been dropped near La Roche five miles south-southeast of Marcouray, after which the planes turned left and flew over Marcouray at about 1630 from the direction of La Roche. One can only imagine how elated the German troops were to receive such unexpected supplies: 2,030 gallons of gasoline and five tons of medical supplies, fourteen and one-half tons in total. Mongeau's harrowing experience, as recorded in his interrogation report:

> Our ship was hit after making the turn from the DZ. The right engine was on fire. There was no bail out bell but Lt. Hagen came back and told us to jump. The Crew Chief jumped and then I bailed out at 1645. We were about 350 feet above terrain when I jumped. My chute was slow in opening and I had to yank the rip cord four times before it finally spilled. It had no more than filled when I was at the ground. My chute caught over an evergreen tree stopping me about three feet from the ground. I slipped out of my harness and dropped to the ground. Two Germans passed within fifteen feet of where I was hiding but they did not see my chute. I tried to get my chute down from the tree but couldn't so left it there. I could hear G.I. vehicles passing on a road near by so I walked through the woods to the road. I stayed hidden which was a lucky thing as they were American trucks driven by Germans. I looked around for the other boys but saw no sign of them. There was considerable firing going on all around me but I saw no other Germans.
>
> I started out in the direction I had seen two buzz bombs headed. I was walking in the woods paralleling a road just north of Marcouray when I saw an old farmer coming along the road in a two wheeled cart. I waited until he had gotten even with me and then stepped out into the road. I speak French so I managed to convey to him who I was and what I wanted. The farmer at first refused to help me but at last he said he would tell me where the Germans and the Americans were. He said he was afraid to take me to the town where the Americans were as some of the people in the town were German sympathizers and they would

kill him. He drew a map on the ground to show me how to get to Marcouray which was held by the 3d Battalion of the 33d Regiment of the 3d Armd. Div.

I walked in the woods along side the road in a southerly direction for about ¾ of a mile. I passed a German tank burning in the road and right after that an American voice hollered "Halt." It was an outpost of the Marcouray Garrison. Again my luck had held out for they had had orders to shoot at anything that moved. This was about 1920 hours on the 23d. They took me in and questioned me very thoroughly. I had my dog tags and finally convinced them that I was an American. They fed me and gave me some warmer clothing and a new pair of shoes. They were very helpful and it was there that I learned that we had missed the DZ. None of our supplies had landed in the town and they said it had looked to them like they had all gone into La Rouche. They had enough gas at that time for their vehicles to travel ten miles and practically no medical supplies. I saw the DZ and there was a large red circle on the DZ as briefed and it was pretty evident that they had not received any of our supplies. They were supposed to receive more supplies the following day so, as they needed a Radio Operator I filled in. I repaired a liaison set in one of their damaged tanks and set up in hopes of guiding the planes in.

* * * *

After the 3d Armored Division was firmly convinced by 1950 that no airborne supplies had reached Marcouray, CC R informed the division G-4 that Task Force Hogan would expect supplies to be dropped on the next day, the 24th. Colonel Orth, G-4, called Colonel Wend, the First U.S. Army executive officer, at 2145 and informed him of the unsuccessful airdrop and asked for another attempt, with the following list of added supplies:

200 rounds of 105 M-48, 120 of 76-mm TC Gun; 15,000 of .05 cal. MG pds (in pack); 20,000 .30 cal. MG 4-1; 200 frag grenades; 300 81-mm Lt. HE; 400 7-mm HE; 1200 K rations.

Within two hours, at 2323, FUSA transmitted a request to CATOR at SHAEF for a repeat resupply mission on the 24th. Unlike FUSA's first message of the night before, the correct coordinate location for Marcouray, P-438817, was given. It also asked for immediate notice of flight time at the DZ.

Within a few minutes after Orth talked with Wend at FUSA, Orth sent instructions at 2210 to Col. Robert L. Howze, Jr., CC R's commander, to inform Colonel Hogan that every effort was being made to drop ammunition, gas, rations and medical supplies, and that the mission time for the airdrop was to be provided later. Task Force Hogan received the information at 2310. Throughout the early hours and until midday there were many communications between CC R and T F Hogan, including many repetitions. One message from CC R indicated that the task force would escape after being supplied adequately and with air support provided as needed. The division was finally advised at noon that the airdrop would be at 1345. Task Force Hogan received the belated information at 1300.

There was an airdrop that afternoon at about 1446, but not at Marcouray. It missed the town — this time to the north, and by a greater distance than the previous day's mission. Sergeant Mongeau's interrogation described the action:

> I encoded a message and sent it out for Lt. Col. Hogan (Commanding Officer of the outfit) giving an alternate route for the planes to avoid the heavy flak that we had run into the day before when the planes came in sight. I tried both channel D and B but was never able to contact the planes. The fighters heard us though and tried to herd the planes in our direction. We shot off green flares and put up smoke but they never did see us. They circled over toward La Roche and then flew several miles to the west of Marcouray and then passed to the north and looked like they were heading back out. They never did release their bundles while in sight of us.

*   *   *   *

The IX Troop Carrier Command had assigned the 438th Group to make the second Marcouray airdrop as soon as possible on the 24th. Thirty-six C-47s at the Greenham Common airfield were loading during the morning. Eight planes and crews were from each of the 87th and 89th squadrons, with six from the 88th and fourteen from the 90th. The parapacks and door bundles consisted of 14,400 pounds of gasoline, 10,200 pounds of rations, 20,350 pounds of ammunition, and 2,300 pounds of signal equipment. All planes were off the runway by 1151. For this mission, the planned flight route from Cap Gris Nez was different from that of the previous day. The formation was to fly east to a point some thirty miles beyond Brussels, then turn south, passing Liege, to the DZ. After turning back north near La Roche, the route was east of Marcouray. This northerly return trip route took the formation unfortunately close by Briscol. At 1635, Captain Waits of that section verbally notified a Colonel Figuere of VII Corps that the supplies for T F Hogan "were dropped in the approximate vicinity 470900. The supplies fell in A & B Btrys of 54 FA Bn." Inasmuch as those two batteries were located at Briscol, the drop was approximately six miles northeast of Marcouray. This time, American forces — not the enemy — received the supplies and all planes returned to England to land before 1659.

From crew members' interrogations, the 438th Group reported (Operations Flash Report) that the point of Drop was "Center of DZ Marcouray" with the remark, "All bundles delivered to the DZ." The time over the DZ was reported as 1446. Yet at 1555, the CC R received a plaintive message from T F Hogan, "No supplies. Is help coming soon?"

No one was more disappointed than Sergeant Mongeau. He had tried so hard to make contact with the Troop Carrier planes as they flew past Marcouray. More of his interrogation report follows:

> Col. Hogan had planned a break out on Xmas Day and had divided all available gas among the vehicles which would have enabled them to travel about ten miles. Word was received that there would be another attempt to resupply the Garrison by air on Xmas Day so Col. Hogan decided to hang on another day. We received little or no fire during this time from the Germans. Col. Hogan sent out a reconnaissance patrol during the day to scout the route out and they came back and reported Germans all through the area we would have to travel and considerable German vehicle travel on the roads. The Germans were evidently bringing up equipment for assault on the town.

⁑ ⁑ ⁑ ⁑

The third attempt to supply Task Force Hogan was planned for Christmas Day. This time another technique to assure precision dropping was to be employed by using "radio-planes guiding liaison," with Sergeant Mongeau on the ground radio.

Plans were developed during the night of Christmas Eve for fighter planes to guide the transports, in coordination with T F Hogan's guidance over VHF radio, and with the aid of colored smoke markings. Moreover, division artillery was to fire smoke into the town and panels were to be displayed.

The plans were formulated overnight, starting with Colonel Orth's call to Colonel Figuere of VII Corps about a resupply mission for the 25th, with the latter suggesting that the subject be taken up with the First U.S. Army. After further calls from Orth to FUSA's G-4 Section, and finally from Orth to FUSA's executive officer, Colonel Wend, the plan was summarized as follows:

> Planes could be contacted on VHF radio on channels of both the Ninth Air Force and the Ninth AF Tactical Command.
>
> The target could be marked with smoke as well as panels.
>
> He, the G-3, was coordinating with Major Martine of the Division Air Support Party to arrange for fighters to precede transport planes by ten minutes, so the former could guide the C-47s to smoked targets.

The calls between FUSA's G-4 and the division's G-4 continued until after midnight, when FUSA sent its request to CATOR. Transmitted at 0130, the message asked for a repeat mission on the 25th, and also described the air-ground radio procedure as devised by FUSA and the division. SHAEF Main received the communication at 0445.

But unexplainable, perhaps for encouragement, was the midnight message received by Task Force Hogan from CC R stating that intentions were for two resupply drops to occur on the 25th. This was ninety minutes before FUSA even asked for a repeat mission. Final instructions were sent to Hogan from CC R at 0910:

> Stand by with VHF on channel D. Ans any Instand (Division air call sign, the TF's being Instand 4) call. If you can contact planes, arrange with them when to smoke area with green. We are listening in and if planes cannot contact you, we will smoke target from here. Planes being guided by radar as well as your VHF and smoke. Keep panels in circle displayed.

Twenty minutes later, at 0930, CC R received instructions from the 3d Armored Division G-3:

> We are handling everything from here. Have Hogan stand by on channel D and listen for planes. If he can contact planes, let them decide when to smoke target. If he can't contact planes, I'll have you on the telephone and you can arrange to smoke target thru arty from your place.

Thus preparations apparently had been in particular detail by ground forces for air-ground liaison to help Troop Carrier aircraft drop accurately over Marcouray.

*   *   *   *

Undoubtedly Staff Message Control at SHAEF was saturated with incoming and outgoing communications on the morning of the 25th. One brief incoming message from General Brereton, commander of the First Allied Airborne Army, was received and recorded at 1150. It was a status report of Troop Carrier resupply missions as of the 24th and the schedule of missions for the 25th.* Brereton added his highly critical opinion of the Marcouray air drop at the end of his first paragraph:

> Report for 24 December 17 Division 540 sorties. Total sorties to date 634. Move 60% complete. 161 aircraft of 173 committed made successful resupply drop for 101 Division, 36 aircraft on emergency resupply to drop for 101 Division, 36 aircraft on emergency resupply to Troops at MARCOURAY dropped on panels and saw American troops receiving supplies. However, Army experts drop 4½ miles north of proper DZ.

---

* Not recorded were other communications between General Brereton and General Williams, IX Troop Carrier Command, and between General Williams and General Beach, 53d TCC Wing, which preceded changes in the 438th Troop Carrier Group. On 27 December, the commanding officer of the 438th, Col. John M. Donalson, was replaced by Lt. Col. Lucion E. Powell, former executive officer of the 437th Troop Carrier Group. And Maj. Richard Cathcart, also from the 437th, was assigned as Group Operations Officer.

Donalson, who had led the first airborne mission into Normandy on D-Day, flying his C-47, Birmingham Bell, returned to the United States.

Another paragraph, with Marcouray misspelled, explained the cancelation of the 25 December mission:

> 50 aircraft for resupply to troops at VARCOURAY have been requested but cannot be flown until 26 December due to short-age personnel in 490 Quartermaster Company to handle pack-aging, loading, and dropping. All available working on mission for 101 Division.

*   *   *   *

Hogan made his decision without any knowledge that there would not be an air drop on the 25th. At about 1000 he crisply messaged CC R, "Recommend supplies not be dropped." More communications passed between T F Hogan and CC R. The most noteworthy was from the task force at 1300 stating that they had one dead, fourteen wounded, three missing, and an effective strength of 467. At 1450, the task force asked CC R if Soy was in friendly hands. Forty-five minutes later the answer that it was came back. Hogan and his men began their overnight trek at about 1810. Mongeau wrote:

> We got ready Xmas Day to receive the supplies, fixed smoke on the DZ and were going to try again to make radio contact with the supply planes but then it was called off. About 1000 hours Xmas morning the Germans threw a short artillery barrage into the town causing a little damage but no casualties. Col. Hogan had decided to leave the vehicles and try to walk out through the enemy lines that night so the rest of the day we spent destroying equipment. I destroyed the radio equipment. There was nothing left that could have been of any use to the Germans. About fifteen minutes before we pulled out, Sgt. Mayo (our Crew Chief) walked into the town. His feet had been frozen pretty badly. The doctor treated his feet and he came along with us. Wounded personnel were left in the town along with the Medical Officer and a few medics to take care of them. We had gotten approximately a half mile from the town when the German artillery opened up but they were a little long and the shells started dropping close to us. We continued across country following the general direction of the River Ourthe. It was pretty rough going and several times we walked in the shadow of German guns and

missed German patrols by a narrow margin. There were 400 of us. We hoped to be able to reach our lines before dawn but daylight found us still in enemy territory. We hid the best we could and the Col. sent out a reconnaissance party. An hour or so later they appeared on a hill just ahead and started waving us on. We walked on and came to a road between Soy and Hotton. A jeep came out to meet us and right behind it came G.I. trucks which took us into Soy. This was around ten o'clock of the 26th. Sgt. Mayo was treated again by the medics and we hitched a ride to the 7th Div. Headquarters where we had a belated Xmas dinner. From there we went to Liege and caught a ride on a Troop Carrier plane. We got almost to England and had to turn back on account of the weather. We landed at Orly and spent the night. The next morning Sgt. Mayo was taken to the 1st Gen. Hospital at Orly. The weather was still bad so we spent that day and night there. I got a ride with Air Transport Command the following day (29th) and landed at Bobbington where my organization picked me up and brought me back to my home base. While at Marcouray, I checked the coordinates both grid and geographic that were given in our briefing against the locations the Garrison had, and they were right.

Mongeau's report ended with recommendations for equipping Troop Carrier crews on air drop missions, based on his experience:

When I left the ship I had no arms of any kind. It is almost impossible to jump with a carbine and if you did it would be hard to retain it. I would recommend that all members of the crew be armed with a .45, then no matter how hurried your jump was you would at least be armed. If I had been seen while hanging from the tree I would have had no means of defending myself. Suggest a pool of .45s to be weapons to be issued before combat missions.

A little more emphasis be put on the route one should take to get to friendly troops in the briefing.

All crew members should wear their flying equipment during cold weather. It can always be discarded after you reach the ground if it is not needed. Also, each member of the crew should keep one good pair of G.I. shoes for wear while on a combat mission.

* * * *

Task Force Hogan never achieved the wide notoriety accorded General McAuliffe's 101st Airborne Division and yet their situations were similar. Hogan was requested to surrender on 24 December, two days after McAuliffe issued his terse "Nuts" reply. Close to noon on Christmas Eve, a German jeep approached under a white flag with a lieutenant who, when ushered before Colonel Hogan, demanded that he surrender. The American troops were surrounded by three panzer divisions, their situation hopeless. The lieutenant said he was authorized to take an officer on tour of the German positions to verify the Americans' plight. Hogan responded that he had orders to fight to the death, and as a soldier he would obey his orders.

If only Sam Hogan, good Texan that he was, had replied with "Remember the Alamo!"

* * * *

Marcouray, at the intersection of the Liege-Houffalize north-south Highway 15 with the east-west St. Vith-LaRoche road, was given a new name by the 3d Armored Division. "Hogan's Crossroads" was the division's next primary objective, retaken during driving sleet and snow on the morning of 7 January 1945. This time Hogan and his battalion did not stay long; they headed east toward St. Vith.

14

Bastogne Expectations

As DAYLIGHT BRIGHTENED THE skies around Bastogne on 20 December, the regimental supply officers throughout the 101st Airborne Division were sending their supply problems back to division headquarters, to Lt. Col. Carl W. Kohls' G-4 staff. Before midmorning, he knew what was most urgently needed to hold each defensive position. During a hasty discussion with General McAuliffe, it was clear that the 101st Airborne Division's truck supply convoy was cut off and would not arrive. McAuliffe agreed to send a message to the division's rear base at Mourmelon le Grand. Transmitted at 1120, it asked:

> Can you arrange air resupply all types ammo, signal, gasoline, rations, in order named to point directly west Bastogne? Sup critical arty ammo.

Whether the message was relayed to either FAAA or SHAEF-AIR for transmittal to CATOR is not known. During the next twenty-four hours Colonel Kohls received no reply and he could only hope that air resupply would be forthcoming.

Since 16 December, CATOR had been fully involved in planning the movement of the 17th Airborne Division from England to France by IX Troop Carrier Command. Now the command would also be called upon to resupply the 101st at Bastogne. If CATOR (or FAAA or SHAEF-AIR) received the message, it was not acknowledged.

Colonel Kohls was understandably edgy during the morning of the 21st. At 1110 hours he again messaged the division's rear base:

> Advise on air resupply asked for. Need 105-mm, 75 pack how, mortar, cal 30 M8, and carbine. Rations second priority. Resupply wanted vic Bastogne P-454585.

Five minutes earlier, Kohls, who had decided not to depend solely on that channel of communications, had transmitted a request to General Middleton's VIII Corps at Neufchateau to be forwarded to Patton's Third Army:

> Urgently need supplies as follows: 105-mm, M3, 75 mm how; 60 mm and 81 mm mortar. Can air supply be delivered to vic Bastogne P-545585. Advise.

Less than three hours later, at 1348, VIII Corps responded:

> Army has been requested to effect supply by Air as request by you.

That was the first acknowledgment Kohls received in response to the previous day's requests for resupply by air. It was encouraging, but Kohls did not know that Third Army did not actually relay his last message to CATOR, via SHAEF, until later in the day at 1825. All radio communication channels were loaded. When Third Army did forward the request, it was "considered most urgent operational necessity." The message was explicit:

> Emergency air supply is requested for following items: 1,000 rds 105 mm How MO3; 2,500 75 mm Pck How; 3,000 rds each 60 and 81 mm Mortar; 12,000 C or K rations to be delivered at P-545585 earliest hour. XIX Tactical Air Force concurs in use of A-64 morning 22 December for marshalling operations and will provide 406 Fighter Group to escort. Third Army Air liaison will provide officer to brief pilots.

Apparently VIII Corps was confident that air supply would be provided, probably because informal conversations with Third

Army confirming the mission which went unrecorded. At 1930 VIII Corps advised the 101st Division G-4 that resupply would take place on the following day, weather permitting. The message also instructed the division to display drop zone panels.

The expectations of air resupply on 22 December were a morale booster, if nothing else. Then hope was dashed by the weather. However, it was not just a weather problem. CATOR's plan for the earliest airborne drop had been scheduled for 2200 hours on the night of 22 December. But then it was postponed until the 23d.

* * * *

At Bastogne preparations for the recovery of air drops began at dawn on the 22d. At 0730 Maj. William H. Butler and Capt. Salve H. Matheson, S-4s of the 501st and 502d parachute infantry regiments, reported to Colonel Kohls to discuss the panel laying and recovery procedures. They were joined by a Major Traver, VIII Corps G-4, who had been driven from Neufchateau to supervise the supply drop recovery.

The recovery methods had to be improvised, and at 0830 division G-4 requested major units to each have five jeeps and trailers ready. Normal operating procedures called for paradrop retrieval to be by quartermaster and ordnance companies which would segregate the scattered dropped bundles and deliver them to the division control dump. Since the quartermaster and ordnance units were unavailable, having been cut off on the night of the 19th, Colonel Kohls directed all regiments to use available vehicles to collect the paradrop bundles and transport them to unit dumps for redistribution. They were prepared and units waited as the hours dragged on.

At 1530 they were informed by VIII Corps that pathfinder teams would be dropped by Troop Carrier at 1600, and would be followed by resupply drops at 2000 hours. Some thirty-five minutes later, at 1606, corps advised Kohls of a delay until 1723, when the pathfinder teams would jump from two aircraft at Bastogne — after dark! Kohls remained hopeful. Less than a half-hour later, a disappointing message stated that the air resupply attempt for the day had been canceled. Then, twenty minutes later, Kohls' G-4 received an encouraging message, this time from the 101st Division's base at Mourmelon le Grand:

We have official info that an air lift of 60 C-47s has been committed to drop supplies to you first flyable day. No other info available.

*   *   *   *

The day of 22 December had been a disappointing one with no air resupplies delivered to the division and other units trapped with it around Bastogne. The date claimed its place in history, however, when, before it had ended, General McAuliffe answered "Nuts" to the German surrender request.

During the day, the enemy build-up opposite many of the defensive positions made McAuliffe's men frantic. They could not retaliate with effective fire — they were too low on ammunition. By midday the 463d Field Artillery Battalion, supporting the 327th Glider Infantry, had only 200 rounds. Other battalions were in a similar plight. When the division artillery commander, Col. Thomas L. Sherburne, Jr., checked them, he found that most were down to less than ten rounds of long range ammunition per gun. General McAuliffe's instructions to the artillery battalions were revealing: "If you see 400 Germans in a 100-yard area, and they have their heads up, you can fire artillery at them . . . but not more than two rounds."

The night of 22–23 December was one of hope, but also skepticism for Colonel Kohls. He had good reason to doubt the reliability of the message from VIII Corps, sent at 2130 and received at 0205:

Attempt will be made to drop portion of packages tonight. Please assist in every way you can.

He could not ignore it. Therefore, fluorescent lights were placed at the drop zones and supply units were notified of the impending event, and prepared for retrieval of paradropped supplies.

It was another night of disappointment, but with the dawn came better flying weather, and optimism again welled up around Bastogne. The only thing to do was wait and hope for early arrivals of Troop Carrier aircraft on the 23d.

From their basic training days, all U.S. soldiers, perhaps all soldiers everywhere, are well acquainted with the adage, "Hurry up and wait." Those at Bastogne repeated the words often, but with mounting despair.

PART IV

Operation Kangaroo:
The Joey of Operation Repulse

We shall then ... smash the Americans completely. ... Then we shall see what happens. I do not believe that in the long run the enemy will be able to resist forty-five German Divisions. ... We shall yet master fate!

Adolph Hitler, from a lengthy address to his commanders, 28 December 1944. From *Rise And Fall of The Third Reich*, William L. Shirer, 1959.

All of us in the northern side of the salient would like to say how much we have admired the operations that have been conducted on the southern side; if you had not held on firmly to Bastogne the whole situation might have become very awkward.

Field-Marshal Bernard L. Montgomery, 14 January 1945.
From *Memoirs of Field-Marshal Montgomery*, 1958.

A lot of people make the mistake of believing that the Battle of the Bulge was resolved at Bastogne. Actually, that was very much a side show.

Gen. James M. Gavin, 1947. From *Ridgway's Paratroopers*, 1985.

The defense of Bastogne was not only a spectacular feat of arms but had a great effect upon the outcome of the battle.

Gen. Dwight D. Eisenhower. From *Crusade in Europe*, 1948.

15

Pathfinders First

OPERATION **KANGAROO** WAS AN apt name, given by IX Troop Carrier Command, for the aerial resupply missions to General Mc-Auliffe's 101st Airborne Division surrounded at Bastogne, Belgium. Contrasted with the futile airdrop missions intended for St. Vith and Marcouray, the communications for airdrops at Bastogne were productive. The first effective message was relayed by General Patton's Third Army at 1825 on 21 December. It reached SHAEF-AIR at 0050 on the 22d. CATOR's initial planning instructions were sent to General Brereton's First Allied Airborne Army which forwarded them on to General Williams' IX Troop Carrier Command.

Midmorning on 22 December, the command hastily assigned the first airborne mission to Lt. Col. Joel L. Crouch's IX Troop Carrier Pathfinder Group. General Williams had decided that airborne pathfinder teams were essential to jump first at Bastogne. With a pathfinder team on the ground, all other planes could fly in by instruments, even during the forecasted poor weather. The drop zones would be located by the Eureka radar-radio beacon operated by a pathfinder team.

At 1130 hours, Lt. Col. John W. Oberdorf, head of Troop Carrier Command A-3, telephoned Colonel Crouch at Chalgrove to prepare for an "immediate" two-plane pathfinder mission. One hour later, Major Lightfoot called with further orders committing the Pathfinder Group to a forty-aircraft paradrop resupply mission to Bastogne, originating at Membury.

At the time, the forty pathfinder C-47s were already loaded with troops of the 17th Airborne Division, sitting on the parking ramps at Chalgrove awaiting weather reports from the Continent. They were to be flown to Dreux, France (A-41), a stopover for the movement of the 17th Airborne Division to airfields near Reims. The aircraft were quickly unloaded and flown to Membury (the 436th Group's airfield) southwest of London. There they were to be loaded for the parachute resupply mission to Bastogne.

Friday, 22 December, was one day Joel Crouch would never forget. He was afforded little time for making vital command decisions.

Recognizing the serious lack of current battle maps, he decided to head to IX Troop Carrier Command headquarters at Grantham, a half-hour's drive by jeep, to get the latest and firsthand instructions. His executive officer, Lt. Col. James T. Blair, Jr. (later to become governor of Missouri), and the XVIII Corps (Airborne) pathfinder officer, Capt. Frank Brown, were left in charge to organize the two-plane pathfinder mission until his return. He intended to fly the lead pathfinder plane to Bastogne. However, his initial plans were subverted.

While he was meeting with some of the A-3 staff members at command headquarters, he was unaware that other orders and instructions were being phoned to Colonel Blair at 1330. The DZ coordinates together with the latest, but sketchy intelligence concerning enemy locations was provided. The pathfinder teams were ordered to be airborne at 1400 hours! Time was critical; after the teams were dropped, their position had to be checked and confirmed. In addition, the operation of the Eureka beacon had to be tested before dark. Crouch considered the pathfinder testing routine to be essential before flying resupply missions into an area while under instrument flight conditions during the hours of darkness.

The Allies had converted to British Summer Time on 17 September 1944 and the Germans went back to Middle European Time on 2 October 1944. As a result, both forces used the same clock time in the Ardennes. In the Bastogne area on 22 December, sunrise was at 0832 and sunset at 1638. The brevity of daylight would prove an important tactical consideration during the Battle of the Bulge. The transitional periods of dawn and dusk — morning and evening twilight — could each add only thirty-eight minutes to the time of daylight.

After Colonel Crouch's meeting at Grantham, he returned to Chalgrove at 1455. He brought back maps of the Bastogne area with coordinate information previously unavailable in his group. The material was identical to the maps issued to units of the 101st Division around Bastogne. Crouch thought, "Now we can hit the DZ exactly."

Three minutes before he arrived at his Chalgrove headquarters office, two pathfinder C-47s had taken off with 1st Lt. Lionel E. Wood piloting the lead plane. The takeoffs had been delayed for fifty-two minutes because the 101st Airborne Division pathfinder teams lacked sufficient combat equipment, and had to be supplied from other sources.

Controlling his anger, Crouch quickly found the situation untenable. His new maps of the Bastogne area were vital for plotting the final flight approach to the exact DZ. More critical was the time of day. The flight course from Chalgrove to Bastogne at conservative air speeds would take two hours and twenty-five minutes. Going faster, the two pathfinder planes could arrive over the target by 1700, during evening twilight. That would allow an extremely short time before dark to reliably test and confirm the location of the navigational aids set up by the pathfinder teams. After reviewing the briefings given to the departed pathfinder plane crews, along with reports on the weather, and sunset and twilight hours at Bastogne, Crouch quickly radioed Wood's flight to return to Chalgrove.

During that afternoon, the forty C-47s of the Pathfinder Group had arrived at Membury to be loaded with parapacks and cabin parachute bundles for delivery over Bastogne — after the navigational aids were established. Colonel Crouch also canceled that mission and the aircraft and crews returned to their base at Chalgrove. Crouch promptly informed IX Troop Carrier Command headquarters of his decision and his reasons. During the night of 22 December, new orders came from the command: drop pathfinder teams at "first light 23 December" and "follow with forty (40) plane loads of emergency airborne resupply." Crouch replied, "We go the 23rd, Pathfinders First."

* * * *

PFC John Agnew wasn't even supposed to go on this mission. The 101st Airborne Division pathfinder team members who would participate in the mission were not permanently assigned to the IX Troop Carrier Pathfinder Group; they were there on temporary duty while attending training school for two weeks. It was a coincidence that enough of them were still available at Chalgrove for the Bastogne mission.

Agnew, of Huntington Valley, Pennsylvania, was one of the 101st Airborne Pathfinders who recorded his experiences. He was a veteran in the 101st Airborne Division, having jumped in Normandy and Holland. While at Camp Mourmelon le Grand in early December, he was one of twenty members of the 506th Parachute Infantry Regiment chosen for pathfinder training and was flown back to the school at Chalgrove. Their training had been concluded just before the 22 December mission was ordered. Although they were ready, they lacked proper clothing, equipment, and weapons. Even after the postponement of the mission until 23 December, they remained poorly equipped. As Agnew recalled they had a hodgepodge of uniforms and gear, and presented a "ragtag appearance" when they climbed aboard the two C-47s before daylight, 23 December.

* * * *

During the night and into the early hours of the 23d, the IX Troop Carrier Command headquarters A-2 forwarded intelligence by telephone to the Pathfinder Group at Chalgrove. Movement and locations of the German ground forces around Bastogne were relayed as well as possible by the 101st Division through the crammed communication channels.

The flight routes from England had been firmly established up to a point near Reims where fighter escorts were to join the two pathfinder C-47s. From there to Bastogne, the final course of some ninety miles was to be decided at a pre-takeoff briefing. The maps that Colonel Crouch brought back from command headquarters were invaluable in plotting the approach. However, information regarding the exact positions of Germans in the area was conflicting, and it was decided not to drop the pathfinder teams west-northwest of Bastogne. Instead they would be dropped directly southwest of town, where they could find cover in adjacent woods if necessary.

The plan was for the first stick, 1st Lt. Shrable D. Williams' team, to jump onto the DZ from Crouch's lead ship. The second stick, 1st Lt. Gordon O. Rothwell's team, would not jump from Wood's aircraft until the first team gave the signal, an orange smoke grenade, to indicate they were in friendly territory. In effect, two identical 101st Airborne pathfinder teams were to be flown to Bastogne as a contingency measure.*

Colonel Crouch planned that after the drops, the two pathfinder C-47s would remain and circle overhead to check and verify the reception of the Eureka beacons as soon as they were operational.

* * * *

At 0645, two hours before sunrise in Bastogne, the two pathfinder aircraft lifted off the runway at Chalgrove. In the lead plane, Colonel Crouch's navigator, 1st Lt. Robert E. De Lancy, pored over his maps. The pilot of the second ship was 1st Lt. Lionel E. Wood. The twenty paratroopers they carried would be the only members of the 101st Airborne Division to arrive at Bastogne by parachute.

The route from Chalgrove was to Beachy Head and across the English Channel to Le Treport, a distance of about 175 miles. The next leg was 125 miles to Airfield A-62, a grass auxiliary strip at Reims, where Crouch and Wood expected to be met by their fighter escort. After arriving over the empty airfield at 0820, they made two large, 360-degree turns, but no contact was made and no fighter aircraft were to be seen. Irritated, Crouch yelled to De Lancy, standing behind him, "Where's that damn fighter support?"

"Breakfast maybe?" De Lancy suggested.

Once again the fault lay in communications — either faulty ones or none at all — within the Ninth Air Force.

Before the Troop Carrier missions began on the 23d, communications had been good between IX Troop Carrier Command headquarters and Ninth Air Force headquarters near Luxembourg. Contact was to be maintained throughout each operation, giving the time each Troop Carrier serial would arrive over the Initial Point (IP). The fighters were to be dispatched by the XIX Tactical Air

---

* The pathfinder equipment to be dropped with the paratroops consisted of six Eurekas (with two extra batteries), three CRN-4s, fourteen halophane lights, fourteen AP 50s (red fluorescent), twenty AP 30s (white), and six cases of smoke grenades.

Command, Ninth Air Force, to pick up the incoming serials and provide area cover for the transports while they were in the danger area. The number of fighter aircraft assigned was decided by Ninth Air Force, heavily committed and alloting its aircraft in accordance with the priority of each mission.

In XIX TAC, the 406th Fighter Group at Mourmelon Le Grand (A-80) was directed to furnish air support to the surrounded ground forces at Bastogne, their activity limited almost exclusively to within a ten-mile radius of the town, twenty minutes from A-80. The missions began at dawn on 23 December. Three other fighter groups, the 354th at Roiseres-en Haye (A-98), 362d at Verdun (A-82), and 405th at St. Dizier (A-64), were to be alerted and provide cover for the Troop Carrier missions during the day of the 23d.

* * * *

When no fighter aircraft appeared over the Reims airstrip, Crouch decided to continue on without fighter cover. With Wood flying on his right wing, he headed to the IP at Leglise, eighteen miles southwest of Bastogne. From there they headed straight for the DZ.

Five or six miles southwest of Bastogne, they saw an enemy armored column of some ten to fourteen vehicles, half-tracks and tanks, on the highway leading to Arlon. The vehicles opened fire on the two ships and Wood's plane received several hits, all minor. Sitting on the road, exposed, the enemy armored column would surely have been destroyed had their air support been with them as promised.

John Agnew was a member of Lieutenant Williams' team aboard Crouch's lead C-47. Recently he wrote about the approach to the DZ:

> The flight from Chalgrove to Bastogne was uneventful, but as we approached the "DZ" and the red light came on for "hook-up," tension mounted and you get a lot of "funny" feelings. Suddenly there was a burst of ground fire and you could see the tracers go by. It came from a German gun emplacement, directly in front of our flight path. Quickly Col. Crouch dove the aircraft directly at the Germans (we were looking right down the barrels of their guns) who thinking they had shot us down and we were going to crash on top of them, jumped out of their gun emplacement and ran for safety. The Colonel then pulled the

aircraft back up to jump altitude, However since we were all standing (loaded with heavy pathfinder equipment) the suddenness of this maneuver caught us by surprise and most of us sank to our knees due to the "G" force exerted. Luckily we all recovered our balance just as the green light came on, and out the door we went.

Joel Crouch was still seething at the absence of his fighter escort. So for a minute he flew his C-47 like a P-47.*

The first pathfinder team jumped at 0931. Three minutes after they were on the ground, the smoke signal was set off and the Eureka and CRN-4 component placed in operation. By 0955 the second pathfinder team was on the ground (with additional navigational equipment) and contact was established with the 101st G-4. After Crouch circled to check the reliability of the Eureka (R/E) radio system, he and Wood headed back out.** Upon their return to Chalgrove, they found no damage on Crouch's plane. Wood's aircraft had several holes from small-arms fire in the fuselage. They were repaired within twenty-four hours.

*   *   *   *

Of the twenty airborne pathfinders who parachuted close to Bastogne, the six who were responsible for getting the Eureka and the CRN-4 radio into action joined up quickly. John Agnew's adventure had only begun:

> After the shock of my parachute opening, I looked around to orient myself and saw what I thought to be a German tank. I started loosening my "Tommy Gun" in anticipation of a fight. Suddenly I hit the ground in what I think was the hardest landing in my career as a paratrooper. My "Tommy Gun" slammed into my face and I became a bloody mess. A medic quickly

---

* During an interview with the author, Joel Crouch explained his abrupt maneuver. "There are times when you feel a strong need for "pissin'," and you've got to get it out. That was my time."

** Crouch's navigator, Robert De Lancy, related in an interview with the author that at first Crouch had intended to remain in the area, circling overhead, to observe the resupply drops which were to follow. When it was obvious he was attracting increasing enemy fire which would certainly be directed at incoming Troop Carrier planes, he decided to leave.

patched me up and after assembly we sought shelter in an old metal building, which the Germans quickly blasted us out of. Next we tried the basement of a damaged building, but the Germans "zeroed" in on us again. We lost some of our equipment this time and some of our people were trapped in the basement for a while, but Dewey [Cpl. John W. Dewey] and I managed to get them out. Finally we took shelter in Mrs. Massey's house and across from her place, on high ground, was a brick pile. We set up our equipment (CRN-4s) there and waited for the first sound of incoming aircraft.

Lieutenant Williams and five of his team were in full agreement that the ideal location for locating the Eureka-CRN-4 beacon was on top of the brick pile. It was over ten feet high and about twenty-five feet long with snow covering the top. No man was willing to get on top and Agnew was selected as the "volunteer." He was quickly boosted up to crawl on top and put the communication equipment in operation. At 0955, after verifying that the CRN-4 was working, he had to turn it off until the team knew that Troop Carrier planes were approaching. Otherwise, with no other American aircraft in the area, it would be possible for German planes to home in on them.

Not far away, Lieutenant Rothwell had a field telephone conversation with Lt. Col. Carl W. Kohls. Now it was definite — the first aircraft formation with resupplies was due in ninety minutes. Kohls was advised of the DZ location with the Eureka and of its size — two miles long, one mile wide, and as close to the town as possible.

Interestingly, Rothwell furnished the estimated time for the first resupply drop to the 101st Division sooner than that sent by radio. Early in the morning, as the pathfinders left Chalgrove, SHAEF-AIR received the estimated schedule for the first air drop mission from IX Troop Carrier Command. It was subsequently relayed to VIII Corps at Neufchateau. At 1045, the corps G-4 messaged the 101st that the first airborne resupply drop would be at 1143. The communication added that air resupply missions would continue throughout the afternoon. But Kohls did not receive that message until 1206, a few minutes after the first drop. The 101st Division had been continually prepared to receive the airdrops since the day before, and the message was moot.

Regimental S-4s had been alerted and panels displayed since early morning. John M. Huffman and S/Sgt. John L. Cooper of division G-4 quickly arrived at the Eureka-radar site to stand by with the pathfinders. When signals indicated aircraft were approaching, Cooper drove to division headquarters with the news. The S-4 recovery teams were waiting at the DZ. Before noon, the roar of C-47s fading, supply bundles were on the ground and others were descending with precious ammunition and rations. The first resupply mission to Bastogne had begun.

101st A.B. Division Pathfinders setting up Eureka radar beacon after parachuting at Bastogne, 23 December 1944. Private First Class John Agnew is tuning transmitter to guide subsequent Troop Carrier missions to DZ.
— Courtesy: National Archives

16

The First Resupply Missions
(23 December)

THE FIRST RESUPPLIES FLOWN into Bastogne during Operation KAN-
GAROO were not those requested by the 101st Airborne Division.
They were the ammunition, medical supplies, and rations that the
two regiments of the 106th Infantry Division east of St. Vith had
asked for five days before. After the twenty-one-plane mission of
the 435th Troop Carrier Group to St. Vith was aborted on the 18th,
the aircraft had been temporarily parked at the 441st Troop Carrier
Group airfield (A-41) at Dreux, France. Then IX Troop Carrier
Command headquarters at Grantham suddenly started planning resupply missions to Bastogne.

During the morning of the 22d, the 435th C-47s were emptied
of all parapacks and door bundles, and the planes and crews returned
to England. Early that afternoon, Brig. Gen. Julian M. Chappell's
50th Wing ordered its 441st Troop Carrier Group at Dreux to provide twenty-one planes for an air resupply mission to Bastogne.
They were loaded with the same parapacks and door bundles originally intended for the 106th Division.

After being informed by Colonel Crouch that the two-plane
pathfinder mission had been recalled late in the afternoon of 22 December, IX Troop Carrier Command promptly ordered the 50th
Wing headquarters in France to delay the 441st Group's mission

161

until the following morning. It was to be the first mission into Bastogne after the pathfinders established the DZ with navigational aids on the ground. Two other resupply missions from England were to follow, one by the Pathfinder Group and another by groups of the 53d Wing that were scheduled to arrive later in the afternoon.

Different flight routes to Bastogne were prescribed for each of two resupply mission formations. Tactically, it would be unsound to use identical final approaches over German forces near Bastogne. However, there were other reasons for the variations. During Operation KANGAROO, the 50th Wing's planning depended heavily on intelligence provided by the advanced Ninth Air Force headquarters at Luxembourg City. In England, the 53d Wing and the pathfinder group relied on advice originating from the 101st Division sent through Maj. Gen. Troy Middleton's VIII Corps at Neufchateau.

50TH Wing Mission

At Dreux, the takeoffs of the twenty-one loaded C-47s began at 0958, three minutes after the pathfinder team had set up the radar beacon at Bastogne. The course of almost 230 miles was along two headings. The first was 190 miles northeast to IP 9884, located directly south of Dinant, Belgium. From there it was southeast to the DZ.

Over the Dreux airfield, the planes assembled into normal Troop Carrier flight formations. The basic element was a flight of a three-ship V formation. Three of these made up a nine-ship formation, also in V. On this mission, there were two nine-ship formations with the last three aircraft forming the rear.

The pilots and crews had been briefed to expect a fighter escort during the approach over German forces from the IP at Dinant. At 1044, the escorts, sixteen P-47s of the 510th Fighter Squadron, 405th Fighter Group, took off from St. Dizier (A-64) to cover the Bastogne target area for the period between 1130 and 1212.

The Troop Carrier formation turned onto the final heading from the Dinant IP and met the P-47s about fifteen minutes from the DZ. At 900 feet the formation flew close to the Bastogne-Marche highway (N-4), over the advance unit of a German panzer division driving toward Rochefort, the "nose" of the German salient (twenty miles from Dinant). The P-47s remained high above the

Troop Carrier C-47s, apparently as protection against a Luftwaffe attack which never materialized. Following orders from the 405th Fighter Group, none came down to knock out or silence the German antiaircraft fire that plagued the C-47s all the way in.

Later, the report from the 510th Fighter Squadron stated:

> Two boxes, 18 and 3 C-47s were escorted. En route, flak was moderate, accurate and light at P-3565, but one C-47 was destroyed. Its equipment was jettisoned before the crash. Contact with three single C-47s was lost in the haze before reaching the target area. Drops were made on red smoke in the SE corner of Bastogne (P-5558). Ceiling and visibility were unlimited directly over target, but 9/10 from deck to 4,000 feet elsewhere.

As the Troop Carriers approached Tenneville, ten miles out from the Bastogne DZ, flak and small-arms fire from along the Bastogne-Marche highway increased in intensity and accuracy. Much of it came from the 2d Panzer Division which was moving along the highway.

Nine planes and crews of the 302d Troop Carrier Squadron were in the lead. In number two position, 1st Lt. Robert L. Anstey and his copilot, 2d Lt. Raymond G. Wiethorn, were flying the right wing of the squadron leader. Their crew members were T/Sgt. Earl D. Purgett, crew chief; S/Sgt. Morris E. Parker, radio operator; and Sgt. Joseph L. Smitrus, assistant crew chief. Their C-47 was the one destroyed as stated in the 510th Fighter Squadron report.

Since enlisting in 1941, Anstey had received considerably more varied air corps training and experience than had most of his contemporaries. He became a rear gunner in B-26s and served in Alaska for nine months before he was accepted for pilot training. He received his pilot wings in June 1943 at Ellington Army Airbase, Houston, Texas. Before enlisting, he was a premedical student at Scottsbluff Junior College, Nebraska.

Later, in his debriefing report, Lieutenant Anstey described his harrowing experience:

> I was flying the right wing of the Squadron Leader on 23 Dec 44 and we had turned from the IP and were heading towards Bastogne. Flak was encountered over the woods between Bastogne

and Marche, coming apparently from along the Bastogne-Marche Road. It was most intense from the vicinity of Tenneville. It was enemy fire from Tenneville I believe, that first hit the ship, but I do not know what caliber hit the aircraft. There was both tracer fire [and] flak. The left wing was apparently hit first. In my opinion, fumes from the punctured gas tanks spread over the parapacks and the bottom of the ship, and these fumes were subsequently ignited by tracer fire. The bundles and the center section were set afire, and the cabin and cockpit were filled with thick smoke.

Later, when I passed through the cabin on the way to the rear door, I saw that the strips on the floor, and the door load cases, as well as the seats on both sides, the top litters, and the whole left side of the center section were in flames. The forward half of the aluminum door frame had melted away.

All four members of my crew bailed out immediately after I rang the bailout bell at P-419590. This point was in enemy hands. Assuming that they all landed safely, I believe they are now prisoners of war.

I had intended to fly the ship on, but the smoke and fumes began to blind me. I made some adjustments in the controls as a precaution against explosion. Then, since I was flying the Squadron Leader's right wing, I adjusted the automatic pilot to steer the ship to the right and away from the rest of the formation. I hooked my chute to the harness that I had been wearing since takeoff, and jumped out the back door. I believe the ship at that time was at an altitude of 300–500 feet above terrain.

The chute opened and blossomed out a few seconds before I touched the ground at P-510565. (I don't remember at all drifting through the air after the chute opened, so it must have been a matter of only a few seconds before I hit the ground.) My clothing was burning and I was burned on the ears and nose. The jolt of landing knocked off one shoe, but I recovered that. I had no gun or helmet. I did have my escape kit, but no purse or maps had been issued prior to this flight. I used the food in the escape kit.

I landed on the edge of a small woods. From there I could see tracer fire from light machine guns coming from the direction of Sibret and heavier and more intense machine gun fire coming from the west. Germans on the ridge in the direction of

Sibret motioned me to come to them. I later learned that the American Third Battalion Headquarters was located in a small woods north and east of where I was, just beyond the small town of Villeroux.

A machine gun patrol from the direction of Villeroux came out and met me at the edge of the woods where I had landed. I went first to the Aid Station at Villeroux, where I got clothing. Then I proceeded to BTN HQ where I was interrogated as to the German positions in the vicinity of my landing. From there I went in a jeep to P-525565, where my ship had crashed just north of a small stream, south of a small woods, and about two miles south west of Bastogne.

It was completely destroyed but I learned that six cases of ammunition had been recovered from my load. I believe that these cases were part of the door load, since I salvoed the bundles when they started burning. The ship had hit the ground and skidded a short distance before exploding, and evidently the six cases had been thrown clear when the ship first hit.

In proceeding from there to Bastogne, I passed the remains of a burned C-47. The number on the tail was 292087. I examined the wreckage and was able to distinguish what I thought were the remains of four bodies, but there was so little remaining that I could not be sure that four or that only four had crashed with the ship. The wreckage was found at P-550565, two miles south of Bastogne.

From the scene of that crash I went to the Divisional Command Post in Bastogne, reporting at 1640. There I was assigned to the hospital located in a church in the town. I remained there from 23 December until 27 December. While in the hospital, I was carried on the morning report of the 501st Paratroop Infantry.

Unknown to Anstey at the time, the burned C-47 he examined was from the 88th Squadron of the 438th Troop Carrier Group. It was one of 199 planes of the 53d Wing which arrived in midafternoon. It had been shot down at 1544, almost four hours after Anstey jumped from his plane at 1150.

From all available information in Bastogne, he could assume that his plane was the only one of his group to be shot down, at least near Bastogne. All the other aircraft did return to Dreux, four with 1st and 2d echelon damage and two with 3d and 4th echelon damage. Although he was then unaware of it, Anstey held the dubious distinction of commanding the first Troop Carrier plane shot down during the Battle of the Bulge, and that his crew were the first to be captured. One of them soon died in captivity.

After parachuting near Amberloup, Wiethorn, Purgett, Parker, and Smitrus were immediately captured and received harsh treatment. Not only did Joseph Smitrus, from New Brunswick, New Jersey, have his dog tags taken, but his flight jacket as well. In the bitter cold weather, Smitty would have to make the long trek into Germany with only a sweater. They walked for a week along sixty miles of roadway to Prum, Germany. There Raymond Wiethorn was separated from the enlisted men on the march. Two days and another twenty-five miles later, Purgett, Parker, and Smitty were separated at Gerolstein.

Earl Purgett, from Lockport, Illinois, did not learn of Smitty's fate until after he had arrived at Stalag Luft VII A, Moosburg, on 20 January. He was told by other POWs that Smitty made the sixty miles from Gerolstein to Koblenz, where he died of pneumonia on 10 January. He was buried in a plot for foreigners at the Koblenz Main Cemetery. His grave was unmarked.*

Fighter Aircraft Support

During the period beginning 23 December, General Patton's Third Army was assigned responsibility for the Bastogne sector of the Ardennes and began moving northward to relieve the 101st Airborne Division. The XIX Tactical Air Command was assigned to the Third Army to support ground actions. Of the 451 XIX TAC sorties on the 23d, 245 were in the battlefield area, including Bastogne.

One of the complaints of returning Troop Carrier pilots was the sporadic timing of fighter escorts on the afternoon of the 23d, and also on the days to follow during Operation KANGAROO. The complaints were well-founded. The flow of communications

---

* See Epilogue for the story of his reinterment.

was convoluted and subject to delays. Many messages from Bastogne went to Middleton's VIII Corps at Neufchateau, then through Third Army for transmittal to SHAEF-AIR and CATOR, and finally on to IX Troop Carrier Command and its wings. The communications channels from Troop Carrier groups back to VIII Corps were no better. All the while, Middleton's VIII Corps staff at Neufchateau was relaying air strike requests for the division by designating targets around Bastogne for the P-47 fighter groups. In addition, the fighters were assigned to escort Troop Carrier planes, after which they returned to hammer the German ground forces around Bastogne. It is less surprising that support was "sporadic" than the fact that it even existed.

Later, on 2 January, General McAuliffe told his story about the air support to war correspondents at the Hotel Scribe in Paris:

> The first two or three days there was fog, but it cleared up about the fourth day, and that was a circus. We had a boy named Parker there — a southern cousin — "Maestro," as he called himself.
>
> But this Maestro had a group around him — it really was a circus — he really knows his stuff. I don't know where he came from, but he really knows his oats. For example, an infantryman came down here on OPs [observation post duty], then went back to his division and said: "There are 4 tanks moving around the corner." And twenty minutes later, say, six P-47s dropped bombs and blew up all these tanks. And believe me, when the infantry gets that kind of support it really helps a lot, and that is what we got all the time.

The virtuoso director of air strikes known to fighter pilots by code name "Maestro" was Capt. James E. Parker, of the Ninth Air Force liaison group attached to the 101st Division. He arrived at Bastogne on 19 December and proceeded to scrounge a high frequency radio from Colonel Robert's Combat Command B. Parker directed the first fighters, which were on the scene by 1000 on the 23d, to the northwest and west of Bastogne, in front of the positions of the 502d Parachute Infantry.

Parker's directions, however, were limited to information he was furnished by the division's forces around the Bastogne perimeter; his performance, which McAuliffe called "something tremendous," was a direct reflection of the material he got from the infantry. As for the approaching Troop Carrier planes, they were just flying ducks unless a fighter escort was present to silence the guns waiting below in German blinds.

Pathfinder Resupply Mission

A predawn briefing at Chalgrove was conducted by Colonel Crouch before his two-ship serial took off with the airborne pathfinder teams. The other forty planes of the Pathfinder Group would follow later in the morning, as soon as they were loaded at Membury. Their route to Bastogne would be the same as Crouch's serial.

Directly after Crouch and Wood (his wingman) departed at 0645, forty C-47s from the Pathfinder Group, headed by Maj. Richard K. Jacobson, group operations officer, flew to Membury for the loading. Jacobson, from Arlington, Virginia, was struck by the poor conditions surrounding the departure: "Our takeoff was from Membury after the very difficult hop from our home base. Aircraft were dispatched from there as quick as they were loaded and ready to go.... Because of the very, very bad weather at our takeoff point we dispatched by flight and not by group and thus the reason for the many, many pathfinder serials."

The planned route of some 375 miles was expected to take three hours, possibly less. The first three-ship serial took off at 0915. More three-plane formations left at sporadic intervals during the next two hours. After a takeoff accident, one was delayed and flew with the 436th Group later in the afternoon.

Soon after each serial turned toward Bastogne at the Leglise IP, German ground fire increased. There were no fighter escorts.* Because of the intervals between the three-plane formations, German gunners could reload, adjust their aim and range, and concentrate their fire. Twenty-eight of the pathfinder planes reached the DZ, or came close enough to drop their loads. One flight of three ships was so severely damaged, it turned back rather than drop resupplies over enemy territory.

---

* No record was found to indicate that fighter aircraft were ever dispatched to protect Troop Carrier missions between 1200 and 1500 on the 23d.

Only two C-47s returned to Chalgrove without damage. Four were shot down before reaching the DZ. Five were forced to make emergency landings on the way back. One, piloted by 2d Lt. Wallace C. Marley, bellied in, wheels up, with both engines and the fuselage heavily damaged by flak. Major Jacobson was one of those who landed on an emergency strip in France.

On the ground at Bastogne, the recovery teams were waiting when the first pathfinder serial arrived at 1210. For two hours, until the last of eight serials arrived at 1407, the paradrop bundles were retrieved and hauled into town. The ground teams waited for the next deliveries (by the 53d Wing) which were expected later that afternoon.

The casualties on the pathfinder resupply mission were high. A total of 252 personnel were flown into the target area. Of the aircraft crew members, four were seriously wounded, two slightly wounded, and sixteen missing in action. The QM (quartermaster) pushers counted losses of one killed, one wounded, and three missing in action.*

53d Wing Mission

The third and last resupply mission of the day was the largest, involving all five Troop Carrier groups of Brig. Gen. Maurice M. Beach's 53d Wing. The task of loading the planes began the night before and was completed by noon at each group's airfield: 434th at Aldermaston, 435th at Welford Park, 436th at Membury, 437th at Ramsbury and 438th at Greenham Common. Although the wing had requested some 220 planes for the mission, only 203 were available at the time. After four C-47s experienced mechanical failures, 199 were ready before noon to depart for the Continent.

From intelligence received during the night, the wing's A-2 and A-3 staffs designated a flight course that set the final approach to

---

* Originally trained by the 490th Quartermaster Depot Company, the 2d Quartermaster Battalion Mobile (provisional) was attached to the IX Troop Carrier Command, under control of the Command's Service Wing. Units of the battalion were trained in parachute rigging, packaging, and loading on aircraft for both air landing and paradrop operations. Small teams were further trained to accompany the plane in flight, release the parapacks fastened to the outside of the fuselage, and push the cabin bundles out the doorway over the drop zone.

Bastogne from the southwest. The route from the Ashford Radio Range in southeast England was over the Channel to Cap Gris Nez, then to Sedan IP (over Airfield A-91). From there, it was about forty miles to the DZ.

Takeoffs began at 1228 with forty-one planes from the 437th. About 1245, fifty aircraft of the 434th and forty-six of the 436th began lifting off from their respective airfields. The next takeoffs were nineteen planes from the 435th at 1250, and forty-three from the 438th at 1259. Because of the relative locations of their airfields and the time required for assembling into nine-ship formations and smaller flights, the groups joined up in sequence: 437th, 434th, 436th, 435th, and the 438th. They formed a sky train stretching some sixty miles long — three times longer than planned.

When the leading formation of the 437th Group headed toward Bastogne from the Sedan IP, the groups that followed were not uniformly organized as originally intended. From ground observations at the DZ, the formations arrived in eight serials, from 1529 until 1559, with 40, 46, 36, 14, 18, 18, 17 and 10 aircraft in each successive serial. A lone C-47 dropped over the DZ at 1606. The total of 200 aircraft, rather than 199, is explained by the report of the pathfinder group: "One ship delayed by takeoff accident flew in and dropped with 53d Troop Carrier Wing column."

Unlike the earlier Pathfinder Group resupply mission, at least two of the 53d Wing's serials were escorted by fighter aircraft. The forty-six-plane serial was guarded by sixteen P-47s from the 510th Squadron (405th Fighter Group), and eight P-47s from the 514th Squadron (406th Fighter Group) protected the thirty-six C-47 serial. Some escort was undoubtedly afforded the forty-plane serial, but the extent is unknown. The records of four fighter groups indicate their involvement with the midafternoon resupply mission:

354th Fighter Group based at Roiseres-en-Haye (A-98):
   "The 355th Squadron, 11 C-47s escorted."

362d Fighter Group based at Rouvres-Etain (A-82):
   "On its second mission of the day, 15 P-47s of the 378th Squadron escorted C-47s to Bastogne, between 1525-1557, then proceeded to its own target, and M/T [motor transport] concentration approximately 10 miles N Bastogne."

405th Fighter Group based at St. Dizier (A-64):
> "The 509th [Squadron] 16 P-47s took off at 1432, to cover the target area 1511-1559, and landed at 1710. There were no attacks upon the two boxes of C-47s, which dropped supplies on red smoke 1,000 feet."

> "The 510th [Squadron] ... 16 P-47s were dispatched at 1437, with time over target 1511-1615, and they landed at 1642. One box of 45 C-47s was escorted uneventfully, and all supplies were dropped on red smoke at NW Bastogne. Flak at P-3565 was meager, inaccurate and light, which was less serious than encountered by the earlier force at this point. Ceiling was limited."

406th Fighter Group based at Mourmelon-le-Grand (A-80):
> "Eight P-47s of the 514th Squadron's fourth mission performed area cover for 36 C-47s, then attacked M/T and houses in the battlefield area."

None of the records indicate that any fighter pilot witnessed a C-47 being shot down.

One of the forty-three planes from the 438th Troop Carrier Group did not make it to the DZ with the others at 1544. While just over a minute out, one of the transports of the 88th Squadron was virtually destroyed in the air. The group's historical report stated, "Flak was encountered near the DZ and C-47 A/C #42-92087 was hit badly and crashed on the DZ where it was observed to explode and burn." At an approach altitude of 350 feet, there would be practically no time for the crew to jump.* The crew members that went down with the plane were pilot 1st Lt. Louis M. Roberts, copilot 2d Lt. Edward R. Petzold, crew chief T/Sgt. Jim W. McDonald, and radio operator S/Sgt. Robert L. Casperson. Theirs was the last C-47 to be shot down near Bastogne on 23 December.

* * * *

Early during the drops at 1303, Colonel Phinney, of VIII Corps at Neufchateau, called Capt. John M. Huffman, assistant G-4 of the 101st, about the status of Troop Carrier supply missions. At the time, Huffman could only say that there had been two formations to

---

* From IX Troop Carrier Command Report Form 34, the approach altitudes by group were: 434th, 500 feet; 436th, 500–700 feet; 438th, 380 feet; and the 435th, 700 feet.

arrive but that much more was needed. He did not know what would arrive during the rest of the afternoon, but he had high expectations.

The 101st collected the parachuted supplies as fast as they landed during that afternoon. The waiting S-4 and unit men, directed by Captain Huffman, gathered the bundles and hauled them to the dumps for a quick inventory. All available vehicles were put into use, especially weapon carriers and 2½-ton six-by-sixes.

While Captain Huffman was retrieving supply drops, Colonel Kohls radioed VIII Corps at 1405 in regard to medical casualties and supplies. The communication adroitly described the situation:

> Be prepared for 120 urgent operation cases: 250 litter cases, 400 walking casualties. Ambulances for urgent operation cases should be brought. Penicillin should be with medical supplies brought in. Were gliders intended to bring in part of resupply.

The last sentence, in the form of a question, is the first recorded reference to the use of gliders for resupply at Bastogne.

After the last collection from the 1606 paradrop, the day's airborne resupplies reached the dumps by dark at 1700. At 1730, Colonel Kohls called VIII Corps to report receipt of the day's supplies and to request that a message be sent to IX Troop Carrier Command that the day's drop "was very satisfactory."

※   ※   ※   ※

Based on detailed IX Troop Carrier Command reports , the resupplies delivered to Bastogne by parachute on the 23d far exceeded those requested by Colonel Kohls two days earlier. Of the 264 Troop Carrier C-47s that departed on the missions, 253 arrived over the DZ to drop 334 tons of ammunition, rations, and medical supplies.

It should be noted that Colonel Kohls reported different figures at Bastogne in January 1945, when interviewed by Lt. A. Joseph Webber for 101st Airborne Division historical records.* According to Kohls, 241 planes dropped 144 tons by parachute. One cannot help but wonder how the 101st could weigh all of the supplies when so much of the ammunition was sent immediately into action.

---

* Col. S.L.A. Marshall, *Bastogne, The Story of the First Eight Days* (Infantry Journal Press, 1946).

17

Bastogne's Christmas Eve Presents

McAULIFFE WAS RELYING ON relief by the 4th Armored Division of General Patton's Third Army, but when would they arrive? Early on 24 December, Patton sent a message to McAuliffe, "Xmas Eve present coming up. Hold on." Late in the day it was obvious to McAuliffe that Patton was overconfident. That night McAuliffe talked with Middleton in Neufchateau, saying, "The finest Christmas present the hundred and first could get would be relief tomorrow."

As Middleton was aware, there was little chance of that. Indeed, with all the problems the 4th Armored was encountering, Patton was ill-advised to have sent his message, for it raised false hopes.

Colonel Kohls' G-4 staff in the 101st Division was worried about the supplies holding out for one more day. Although the paradrops on the 23d were quickly put to use, they were not enough to sustain another day's fighting. More supplies were needed as reflected in the SHAEF-AIR Staff 1944-1945 report, "further requests came in from the airborne division . . ., which indicated that further supplies would be required during the next day, and they also requested considerable equipment and heavy ammunition for 105 and 155-mm Howitzers, and 1,000 gallons of gasoline for mortar transport."

* * * *

One directive from the IX Troop Carrier Command assigned the IX Pathfinder Group to carry priority signal equipment in six C-47s for an early morning drop at Bastogne. A second mission of some 160 aircraft from the 53d Troop Carrier Wing was to follow as soon as the loading of ammunition, medical supplies and rations was completed.

In the predawn darkness, six pathfinder C-47s left Chalgrove airfield shortly before 0600. The crews had been briefed by Colonel Crouch to fly the same route as the day before, but this time at night. The ETA at Bastogne was 0855, twenty-three minutes after sunrise. As they headed northeast toward the IP at Leglise, the navigators on their Rebeccas tried to connect with the Eureka signals from the DZ.

The IX Troop Carrier Pathfinder Group's report on the mission stated:

> All pathfinder aids were working again perfectly on morning of 24 December 1944, when five aircraft of this group flew in at daylight with priority communication resupply and reported picking up R/E [Rebecca/Eureka] aids thirty-four miles out. This flight flew from French coast to IP on DR on top of overcast due to ground Gee [navigational radio aids] chain being turned off for a checking at that time. Six ships were scheduled on this mission, one of which dropped load at IP due to confused light signals. This ship was ordered to return immediately to base after dropping load by flight leader.

All planes returned to Chalgrove, three with extensive battle damage from flak and small-arms fire.

While the C-47s of the Pathfinder Group were over the channel on their way back, 157 loaded C-47s from the 53d Wing were taking off from four airfields. At their morning briefings, the crews of the 434th, 435th, 436th, and 437th groups were given a different IP from that of the wing's mission of the previous day. By locating the new IP at Montmedy, instead of Sedan (A-91), the final approach toward Bastogne would essentially follow the approach flown by the Pathfinder Group earlier in the morning.

The 437th Group, with forty-four planes assigned to lead the mission, was first off at 1025 from Ramsbury. Next came thirty-nine aircraft from the 436th at 1033. (Two returned due to mechanical failures.) Then thirty-three planes from the 435th at Welford Park, and forty-one from the 434th at Aldermaston, began takeoffs at 1039 and 1041 respectively. The 155-plane formation was not organized until it was en route, and so reached the DZ later than scheduled.

Lt. Col. Henry H. Osmer, 435th Group executive officer, led his group's formation as the pilot of a 77th Squadron aircraft. As the four formations headed for the Ashford Radio Range, the 435th was in the lead, not in the rear as prescribed by the IX Troop Carrier Command. Osmer reduced his airspeed to allow the other groups to pass, and the 437th took the lead while over England. It was not until they were over France that the 436th and the 434th moved ahead of Osmer's formation.

There is reason to believe that the manner of the group's approach toward Bastogne influenced the mission's success. The 437th made its drops from 300 feet at about 1338. Then the 436th released its bundles from 2,200 feet — unusually high for paradrops. The 434th came in moments later at 1341, 800 feet over the DZ. The final drop at 1350 by Osmer's 435th was from the usually prescribed altitude of 350 feet.

The results were far better than the Bastogne airdrops of the previous day, perhaps because of two factors: The entire formation of 155 planes passed over enemy forces within a twelve-minute period, and they came in at different altitudes. The relatively tighter formations at varying altitudes gave little time for German gunners to change their aim and range.

A third, more difficult, factor to evaluate concerned the effectiveness of American fighter cover during the mission. Crew interrogation from the 77th Squadron and the 435th Group summarized fighter support by stating, "Friendly fighters were observed north of the DZ."

Not all aircraft escaped damage from flak and small-arms fire, and one of the eleven C-47s from the 72d Squadron, 434th Group, did not return to England. The ship was forced to land at an airfield in France before running out of fuel — bullet holes in the gas tanks.

*   *   *   *

After the last paradrop, Colonel Kohls advised General Middleton's VIII Corps, "Situation under control. Air very eff. Sup drops were successful." The total delivery of supplies amounted to 159.7 tons, as complied by the IX Troop Carrier Command. A detailed description of the supplies that were dropped at Bastogne on 24 December highlights the importance of ammunition:

AMMUNITION		SIGNAL	
75-mm How.	3542	BA-Batteries:	
105-mm How. M-3	598	-37	325
60-mm Mortar	757	-38	340
81-mm Mortar	484	-40	73
Rockets, AT	182	-48	93
MG Cal. 30	228,250	-70	173
Grenade, hand frag	1,565	Wire, W-110	12
Carbine, Cal. 30	6,000	RATIONS	
Cal. 30	34,000	K Rations	9,918
57-mm	60	GASOLINE	
37-mm	270	Cans	455
Cal. 50	23,980		
75-mm Gun	140		

The G-4 staff at Bastogne spent the rest of the afternoon developing a long "want list" of supplies, ironically requested for delivery on Christmas Day. It was transmitted through channels to Patton's Third Army (TUSA) as follows:

AMMUNITION

75-mm PK How HE	3,900
105-mm How M3 HE	700
60-mm Mortar	5,000
81-mm " Lt	3,000
Bazooka Rockets	1,000
MG Belted, Cal. 30	424,000
Grenades, hand, frag.	2,200
Rifle Grenades	
Frag	600
AT	600
Carbine Cal. .30	100,000
Cal. .30 8-clip	150,000
57-mm Gun AP	900
37-mm Gun	400
Cal. 50 MG	40,000
75-mm Gun HE M54	300

76-mm Gun HE M48 AI	300
105-mm How M2 HE2 M48	800
105-mm How M2 HE2 M54	800
155-mm How Shell HE 107	1,000
Charge propelling white bags for	
155-mm How	1,000
Fuse point detonating M51A-3	900
Fuse point detonating M55A-1	100
Primer percussion marks 11 A-4	
17 grains	1,200

SIGNAL

Batteries-BA	
-37	500
-38	500
-39	100
-40	100
-42	200
-43	30
-48	50
-70	100
Wire W-110	25
Fuse 3/4 Amp 3Z 2586	10 each
6 Amp 3Z 2606	10 each

QUARTERMASTER

Rations	15,000
Gasoline M/T 80	1,000
Oil SAE #20	50 gal
Halozone Tablets	10,000 bottles

Later, at 2230, TUSA sent this message to CATOR (SHAEF-AIR) and the Communications Zone, referring to the needs of the 101st Division:

Repeat of air dropping or supply by glider at P-545585 on 25 December is requested: Items were listed, and the request concluded with the following: If quantities must be cut due to shortage of lift reduce quantities of POL, blankets and rations in amounts necessary.

For some nebulous reason, the communication was delayed and not received by SHAEF until 1030 on the 25th. Likewise the information copy to General Bradley's 12th Army Group headquarters (located across the Place de Metz from the Ninth Air Force headquarters building in Luxembourg City) was not recorded until 1030.

Of particular interest is the request in the message for supply by glider. Thus far the supplies needed by the 101st Division at Bastogne were more appropriate for delivery by C-47s than by CG-4A gliders. Gliders could land much-needed medical personnel in the small area adjacent to Bastogne, but neither the recorded request nor the want list for the 25th included medical teams.

A more likely reason to ask for gliders stems from a call by Colonel Kohls to VIII Corps at 1510. He requested "that 500 mines be air-landed." These were not included on the want list, and by the term "air-landed" Kohls may have been suggesting the use of gliders.

* * * *

During the cold, early hours of darkness on Christmas Eve, it was calm in Bastogne. A Catholic Mass was celebrated in a large room of one of the headquarters buildings at 1900. An hour and a half later the calm was shattered by the roar of aircraft engines and the crash of bombs as the Luftwaffe delivered their own Christmas Eve presents! Time and again the Junkers arrived overhead in waves — first a shrieking whistle followed by a "thunderous roar" and a "shattering blast." Several buildings were in flames or destroyed outright. The medical aid station in one of the buildings became an inferno where twenty of the wounded and a local nurse (the daughter of a Bastogne merchant) were killed. Another bomb blasted a command post, killing four junior officers.

After the shattering air raid, General McAuliffe was driven by jeep to the tiny village of Savy, about one mile northwest of his headquarters in Bastogne, to attend Midnight Mass with fellow artillerymen, the 321st Glider Field Artillery Battalion. Two other outposts beyond Savy, Hemroulle (west of Savy) and Champs (about three miles northwest of Bastogne), held similar services. Among the besieged defenders, there were others as well. It was a Christmas Eve that would be long remembered.

18

Bleak Christmas

LUFTWAFFE BOMBERS WERE OVER Bastogne again at 0300 on Christmas morning. Unlike the bombing six hours earlier, this one coincided with a planned effort by regiments of the 15th Panzergrenadier and 26th Volksgrenadier divisions to capture Bastogne. German tanks and infantry attacked at Champs and Hemroulle at about 0500. The enemy's objective was to reach Bastogne by 0800, before daybreak, when the American fighter-bombers would be expected overhead. For the first time since the start of the siege, General McAuliffe was alarmed. The danger of being overrun was high. But by 0900, McAuliffe knew his men had won the battle. Incurring heavy losses, the Germans failed to penetrate his perimeter.

The Germans' fear of airstrikes was well-founded. Directed by "Maestro" Captain Parker from his radio-equipped jeep in Bastogne's central courtyard, the XIX TAC's 406th Fighter Group mounted 115 sorties to attack them around Bastogne. The primary targets of the 406th's "Raider Group" from Mourmelon le Grand were armored vehicles, tanks, materiel and troops, and artillery. Two P-47 pilots of the 513th Fighter Squadron were hit and crashed during the attacks.*

---

* The May edition of *Starduster II*, published for the second reunion of the 406th F.G., named the two 513th Squadron pilots shot down on the 25th: Lt. Fred M. Boden and Lt. Myron A. Stone. Two P-47 fighter pilots of the 514th Squadron were also lost that day, but their names were not listed.

At 0855 Colonel Kohls telephoned VIII Corps and discussed the division's needs. He indicated some revisions to the long list of the day before, emphasizing the urgent need of four surgical teams with personnel, equipment, and supplies. He asked again about the possible use of gliders.* Kohls' next concern was to concentrate on rationing the ammunition for the day. There were meager supplies on hand and more were expected by airdrop later in the day. In a "combat interview," Kohls noted that only 455 cans of gasoline and 26,406 K rations had been received. The rations were only enough for one day. "Litters, penicillin and blankets were badly needed."

At 1100 VIII Corps called back with questions about the landing of gliders at Bastogne. Division G-4 recommended their use with the caution that the LZ should be close to the north of town, and gliders should not cut off before reaching the LZ.

Around noon the 101st Division received a disappointing message from VIII Corps: no airdrops could be undertaken that day due to bad weather in the U.K. Colonel Kohls also learned to his frustration that the list of supplies he had transmitted on the night of the 24th had been delayed through communication channels, and was not received by CATOR at SHAEF until 1030 on the morning of the 25th.

While the Bastogne defenders' want list was being revised that afternoon, Kohls was thinking of ways to send it out. Since communications were not dependable, the only other method of transmitting the division's requirements was to carry them directly to CATOR. A courier could be flown from the small grass airstrip north of Bastogne via liaison aircraft to the Third Army airfield at Verdun-Etain (A-82). The liaison pilots of the Third Army were familiar with the route, having flown to and from Bastogne at low altitudes over the German forces on previous days during the siege.

*   *   *   *

On one notable flight on Christmas Day, General Bradley was flown in a C-53 from Luxembourg City around the Bulge to St.

---

* Undoubtedly the various units — the 101st Division, VIII Corps, Third Army, 12th Army Group, CATOR, FAAA, and the IX Troop Carrier Command — considered the use of gliders to land certain munitions (such as mines), and medical teams in particular. The earliest reference to the use of gliders was in the 1405 message on the 23d, from the 101st's G-4 to VIII Corps.

Trond, northwest of Liege. Field Marshal Montgomery had invited Bradley to meet with him at his headquarters in Zonhoven. Both of them later reported that their discussions were far from amiable and their accounts of the half-hour meeting contrasted. Most disturbing to Bradley was Montgomery's view of a counteroffensive to erase the German bulge. Convinced that the Germans were still capable of another strong action, Montgomery said he had no intention of attacking until "he was certain the enemy had exhausted himself." He believed that the U.S. First Army, under his command north of the Bulge, was too weak to go on the offensive and that the U.S. Third Army would accomplish little from the south. To him the proper course for the Allies was to go on the defensive. In the south, they should withdraw to a shorter defensive line, possibly as far back as the Vosges Mountains, in order to free divisions to strengthen General Hodges' First Army. As Bradley understood him, although Montgomery subsequently denied it, he believed it would be three months before Hodges would be capable of a major offensive.

After Bradley flew back to his headquarters about sunset, he called General Patton, who found Montgomery's ideas "disgusting." If ordered to fall back, Patton stated "I will ask to be relieved." He added that Montgomery was just "a tired little fart."

* * * *

When the 24 December want list of supplies from the 101st Division reached the IX Troop Carrier Command in England on the morning of the 25th, all available C-47s of the 53d Wing's five groups were readied for the third and largest mission of Operation KANGAROO. Men of both Troop Carrier and 490th QM units rapidly loaded the planes as if they expected the weather to improve in the afternoon. However, during most of the day, the airfields in England had less than 100 yards' average visibility in heavy fog. Nevertheless the flight crews remained on alert until midafternoon, when the mission was postponed until the 26th.

Two Christmas Presents

There were two vital air deliveries to Bastogne during the afternoon. The first was by Capt. Rufus Woody, Jr. (from Forest City, Arkansas), operations officer of the 19th TAC Photo Reconnaissance

Squadron, Ninth Air Force. At 1420 he flew his P-38 in low to drop maps and aerial photographs. Many units of the 101st Division were short of the GSGS 1:50,000 scale maps which were crucial for effective coordination around Bastogne. Until Woody's delivery, there were only fifteen of the maps available among the defenders. The photographs were of enemy positions taken on the 24th. After his mission, Woody took more aerial photos over enemy positions for the following day's delivery.*

The second delivery, a different kind, was by a small liaison plane, an L-5 (Stinson Sentinel). In response to urgent requests from the division during the day, the Third Army arranged to fly a surgeon and penicillin from its Verdun-Etain airfield (A-82) to the small L-5 airstrip on the north edge of Bastogne. It was a short flight of sixty-seven miles over the customary route: twenty-five miles northwest to Montmedy, twenty-five miles north to a point beyond Neufchateau, then seventeen miles northeast to Bastogne. Maj. Howard P. Serrel, a surgeon of the Third Army, and the medical supplies were flown in after dark at about 1800. He found his skills in demand; he performed fifteen surgical procedures during the next thirty-six hours. As valuable as his efforts were, they could not compensate for the loss of the division's medical company, captured on the night of the 22d.

The Want List by Special Delivery

Capt. Roland O. Linker, assistant quartermaster officer under Lt. Col. Charles J. Rich, eagerly greeted the news that he was to fly out and personally deliver the latest want list from the 101st Division to SHAEF at Versailles. He departed by liaison aircraft, presumably the same plane that brought Major Serrel to Bastogne. How he was flown from Etain and at what time was not recorded, probably by a staff or courier flight to Orly or to Villacoublay near Versailles. It was nearly two hours after midnight when he arrived at SHAEF and met with Lieutenant Colonel Stover, CATOR G-3, and submitted

---

* On 26 December, Capt. Roger V. Wolcott (from Cleveland, Ohio) and 1st Lt. Albert Lanker (from Petaluma, California) were both lost to enemy fire. Flying P-38s of the 19th TAC Photo Reconnaissance Squadron, they were both shot down during the mission to deliver the new photographs to the defenders at Bastogne.

this requisition for supplies — and surgical teams — to be delivered on the 26th.

26 DECEMBER 1944

Air resupply to consist of the following:

75mm How, HE, M54 Fuze	3,900
105mm How, M3, HE, M54 Fuze	700
60mm Mortar, HE	5,000
81mm Mortar, HE, Light	3,000
Cal. 30 MGB	200,000
Gren. Hand Frag.	1,000
Rifle Gren. Frag	600
Rifle Gren. AT	500
Carbine, Cal. .30	100,000
Cal. .30, 8 clip	500,000
57mm AP	250
37mm AP	400
75mm Gun, HE, w/Fuze, M54	111
75mm Gun, HE, w/Fuze, M48	114
75mm Gun, APC, M61, w/BDF, M66	75
76mm Gun, HVAP-T4	400
76mm Gun, APC, w/Fuze, BD M66A1	400
Shell, HE AT, M67, w/Fuze 2BDF M62, 105 How, M2	400
Shell, HE, w/F2 M48, 105How M2	1,300,
Shell, HE, w/F2 M54, 105 How M2	1,600,
Mines AT-M1A1	500
Battery BA-37	500
Battery BA-38	500
Battery BA-39	200
Battery BA-40	300
Battery BA-48	50
Battery BA-70	100
Wire, W-110	50 Miles
Wire, W-130	30 Miles
Battery BA-42	200
Battery BA-43	30
Fuse 1/4 amp. 3Z2586	10
Fuse 6 amp. 3Z2606.3	10 each
Switchboard, BD-72	2
Telephone, EE-8	35
Litters	50

Rations	15,000
Gasoline	5,000
Oil SAE, Det. N.30	150
Radio Set, SCR-300	10
Radio Set, SCR-536	20
Radio Set, SCR-694	5
Radio Set, SCR-610	6

Four (4) Surgical Teams with personnel,
    equipment and supplies.
(This paper is the requisition of Capt. Linker of 101 Div.
who flew in with it night of 25/26 Dec.) Init. (?)
(Source: SHAEF, G-4. 471. Ammunition. 1944. Vol. IV.)

Capt. K. H. Robbins was the G-3 duty officer at CATOR the night of 25–26 December. He recorded the minutes of the meeting in his duty officer's report. Robbins and the G-4 duty officer, Lieutenant Colonel Eden, were the first to be called by Colonel Stover to join the meeting with Captain Linker. Before the discussions proceeded, Stover asked Robbins to inform the G-2 duty officer and the operations intelligence chief, (British) Col. E. J. Foord, of the purpose of the meeting. In his report, Robbins wrote that he had notified them and "Colonel Foord stated that no further action on this situation could be taken by G-2 until morning." At the meeting, Captain Linker described the critical state of the defenders of Bastogne as recorded in Robbins' G-3 officers report:

SITUATION
    101st Airborne Division is cut off in the area of Bastogne and there is a heavy concentration of enemy divisions and armour NORTH of the town. Two combat Commands of the 4th Armoured Division are endeavoring to break through to relieve the 101st, but have made no progress for about two days and are in the vicinity of RENUCHAMPAGNE and GRENTELANGE respectively.

CASUALTIES
    There are 1,000 casualties, which cannot be evacuated. Practically the entire Medical Company was captured on 22nd December with the exception of about four officers and thirty-seven men, who managed to escape. There are believed to be a few medical personnel remaining with regimental detachments.

STORES

There is no reserve of rations and the men are living from hand to mouth on food that can be obtained from civilians. Civilians are helpful and doing the best they can for the men.

Before the Division was cut off, elements were out looking for stores of rations etc. and these elements are now concentrated with stores SOUTH of RENUCHAMPAGNE and GRENTLANGE, together with the four officers and men of the Medical Company, ready to move in when the 4th Armored Division breaks through.

AMMUNITION

Providing an attack, in strength, from the NORTH, is not launched, the Division can fire a few rounds of ammunition for about two days. If an attack is launched, then it would be in a position to hold out for only a few hours. It is for consideration as to whether or not this attack will be launched, in view of our activity over that area during the past two days.

Captain Robbins then summarized Colonel Stover's comments in his report as follows:

The Division was last supplied by air on 24 December. There are 294 loaded planes in the UNITED KINGDOM, for supply of the 101st but they are unable to take off on account of fog and this condition may prevail on 26th December.

There are no supply dropping parachutes or panniers in FRANCE.

A Surgical Team is going in in Gliders today, and Lieutenant Colonel Stover will do all he can to include some stores and ammunition in these gliders. Further, he will ascertain the Glider situation, with a view to sending in further supplies by this means. The terrain is unsuitable for plane landings and even crash landings would not be possible.

Colonel Stover's statement that he would "ascertain the Glider situation" indicates that he was lacking full information — Brig. Gen. Julian M. Chappell, 50th Troop Carrier Wing, had already designated the 439th and 440th groups to tow sixty-one gliders to Bastogne on the 26th, per the wing's 25 December Field Order No. 3. (See next chapter.)

Colonel Stover was particularly concerned about the possibility of another day with bad weather in the United Kingdom. Recorded in Robbins' log, he explained that he was examining alternatives such as:

> obtaining twenty-five pilots who are prepared to take off from the UNITED KINGDOM and fly twenty-five plane loads of parachutes to FRANCE — thence drop stores at BASTOGNE from planes loaded in FRANCE. It is unlikely that any pilot could take off under existing conditions in the UNITED KINGDOM.
>
> Parachutes being brought over by sea and still saving time, if flying conditions in the UNITED KINGDOM remain bad.
>
> Colonel Stover pointed out that before either of these two operations could be carried out, Commanding General, First Allied Airborne Army would have to give authority.
>
> Lieutenant-Colonel Stover is pursuing the possibilities mentioned in paragraph above, and Lieutenant-Colonel Eden said he would contact appropriate sections of G-4 first thing in the morning. I reported to General Whiteley [Maj. Gen. J.F.M. Whiteley, British G-3 at SHAEF] prior to Captain Linker's departure. I was unable to obtain a reply at VILLEPREUX (RL 564) and a guard answered the 'phone at Colonel Hinton's quarters, who said he could not contact this officer as he (the guard) was the only person on duty there, and could not leave his post.
>
> Captain Linker left at about 0430, to return to his Division, and he stated that he was assured and grateful of the fact that all that is possible is being done to get stores and ammunition to the 101st Division, in addition to endeavoring to relieve them.

Thus ended the G-3 duty officer's report of the meeting. However, below Robbins' signature, the following statements were added:

> NOTE: At 0520 hours I received a copy of a signal from FM. MONTGOMERY, which stated that General BRADLEY hoped to get to BASTOGNE.
>
> Col. Hinton is speaking with CATOR this morning.

*   *   *   *

Captain Linker hitched a plane ride to arrive at the Verdun-Etain airfield during the morning of the 26th. No liaison plane could fly him back to Bastogne; the flight route between Montmedy and Bastogne was restricted for the large Troop Carrier Command re-supply missions all day. Later that night, he again hitched rides on Third Army trucks and jeeps to return to Bastogne early in the morning of the 27th.

He missed seeing the fruits of his labor, the resupplies dropped by parachute, and surgical teams and gasoline landed by gliders, just as requested on the want list he had carried to SHAEF.

26 December 1944. Etain, France. Jeep with medical supplies for Bastogne, backed up to Corwin's glider.

— Courtesy: Horn

19

The Plans for Gliders

THE WEATHER FORECASTS IN England for 26 December were dismal, prompting the decision to fly resupply missions to Bastogne from Troop Carrier airfields in France. Although lacking the parachutes for an airdrop, Troop Carrier groups in France had gliders available to carry in critical supplies. Ammunition proved a tougher problem; most of that requested was not readily available near the airfields.

Delivery of the surgical teams with medical equipment and supplies in a CG-4A glider required special planning and coordination. A glider would be towed empty to the airfield at Etain (A-82), where it would be loaded with medical personnel from the Third Army. From there it would be towed on a second leg to Bastogne.

By early morning on the 25th, CATOR had originated plans for three glider resupply missions. They were quickly forwarded to IX Troop Carrier Command for execution by the 50th Wing. Late in the day, the wing picked Colonel Young's and Lieutenant Colonel Krebs' groups for the glider missions. Located some seventy miles southwest of Paris, the 439th at Chateaudun (A-39) and the 440th at Bricy-Orleans (A-50) were about twenty miles apart.

Young's 439th Group was a logical choice for a fifty-glider mission since it had the largest number of airworthy CG-4A gliders on hand. Many of them were gliders that had been used in Operation

MARKET, those that were undamaged or had been repaired by the Troop Carrier Reclamation Wing at Son, Holland. They had been flown back to the Chateaudun airfield during October and November. At Bricy-Orleans, there were at least another dozen gliders also available.

The cargo was primarily gasoline and ammunition, and the initial responsibility for the logistics was with the First Allied Airborne Army. The 155mm artillery ammunition was not easily accessible in the 50th Wing area. It would have to be trucked from depots in northern France or possibly from as far away as Antwerp, where all materiel on the Continent was being stockpiled. General Chappell's wing scheduled the glider missions optimistically, without allowing for any problems in mobilization and logistics. Following many telephone conversations, the wing's Field Order No. 3, dated 25 December 1944, was the first written instructions to the 439th and 440th groups.

The first part of the field order summarized the situation in the Ardennes as it was on the evening of 24 December. The grid coordinates were from the 1:50,000 scale GSGS maps covering the battle area:

> *Enemy.* Strong forces of enemy twelve (12) armored divisions have succeeded in breaking the line *vL0536* to *vF0004* with forward armored unit striking westward to the vicinity of *CELLES (vP0585)*.
>
> American forces (101st Airborne Division) encircled in Bastogne in an area approximately four (4) miles in diameter centered on Bastogne, have successfully withstood repeated attacks from the LEHR PANSER *[sic]* (ARMORED) DIVISION and the 5th PARACHUTE DIVISION. The German Air Force, since breaking of the line has appeared over the area involved in considerable strength. Enemy Bomber activity as well as Fighter opposition has been encountered.
>
> *Friendly.* The U.S. 4TH ARMORED DIVISION is reported approximately six (6) miles south (*vP5248* of BASTOGNE) (*vP5658*) attempting to reach and support the U.S. 101ST AIRBORNE DIVISION in that town. Other elements of the U.S. 3RD ARMY are reported to have established a firm line from the East (ECHTERNACH — *vL05360*) to West (ST. HU-

BERT — *vP3161*). NINTH AIR FORCE to provide Fighter cover to aircraft of this organization.

The description of the situation at Bastogne was an appropriate beginning for the preflight briefings of aircraft crews. But surely the last sentence about fighter cover would be the one that would never be forgotten. The "Air Movement Table" (Annex No. 1 to the field order) thoroughly scheduled the three glider resupply missions to be flown on the 26th.

Serial No. 1, assigned to the 440th Group, was to be a single glider mission carrying "Special Medical Personnel and Supplies." The takeoff time from Orleans was scheduled for 0800 for a 200-mile flight to Etain (A-82). There the tow plane crew and glider pilots were to receive a forward briefing while the glider was being loaded. The second leg was scheduled so that the tow plane and glider serial would reach the Montmedy IP at 1400 where it would be met by a fighter escort for the final run to Bastogne.

The second serial, also flown by the 440th Group, would consist of ten C-47s and CG-4As loaded with gasoline — described as "Air Cargo Resupply." The takeoff time was scheduled for 1000 and the ETA for landing at the Bastogne LZ was 1202.

The third glider mission was more complex; both the 440th and the 439th groups were involved. Inasmuch as the marshaling of tow planes and gliders was to be at Chateaudun, Colonel Young was assigned the responsibilities for the operation. Fifty CG-4A gliders and thirty-seven C-47 tow planes were to be furnished by the 439th. The other thirteen C-47s were to come from the 440th. The schedule for this serial was set for an 0900 takeoff with an 1108 ETA at Bastogne.

The field order prescribed in further detail how the flights were to be conducted during the missions. The formations were to be according to standard operating procedure, "SOP." The altitude during the final course from the IP was to be 2,500 feet MSL — around 800 feet above the ground. At the LZ, the altitude for glider cutoffs was to be 600 feet above the ground. After the glider pilots released, the tow plane pilots were to turn out and climb to 5,000 feet.

The airspeeds were as closely regulated. During the tow to the IP, the airspeed was to be the normal 125 MPH. On course from the IP, it was to be 120 MPH; at the LZ, it was to be reduced to 110

MPH for glider cutoff. The tow planes were to turn out and return at 160 MPH.

Annex No. 2 to the field order was a route overlay, a diagram which depicted the flight course, with bearings and distances to Bastogne via the Montmedy IP by latitudes and longitudes. (See the following page.) The route was that proposed by the advanced headquarters, Ninth Air Force, which was reputed to be in a position to know the disposition of enemy troops accurately. Some aspects of the route overlay diagram are problematic. Although the route for the fifty-glider mission was shown originating from A-39, the route for the first missions from A-50 to the IP was missing. Yet A-82 was shown with additional information pertaining only to the single-glider mission. The omission may have resulted from error, or perhaps there was another route overlay prepared by the 440th Group.

The field order clarified command and communication channels. The command posts for ground and air operations were headed by the 50th Wing headquarters at Chartres, subordinating the 440th and the 439th groups. Further instructions stated, "Axis of communication shall be through command posts" and "Message Centers Operation will be SOP."

Last in the field order was "Specified Navigational Aids: (1) Smoke on DZ. (2) 'T' Panel on DZ. (3) MF Beacon 1558. (4) Rebecca Eureka Coded 'O'." The fourth aid listed conflicts with the note on the Route Overlay where the Eureka "EC" is indicated as "NO CODEING."

There were no indications on Field Order No. 3 as to the time of its transmittal from 50th Wing headquarters, or when it was received by either the 440th or 439th groups. It may have been sent late on the 25th, but from the two group's records of activities, it most likely accompanied the wing's Operations Order No. 361, which had been transmitted earlier.

* * * *

During the early morning hours of the 26th, the 440th Group at Bricy-Orleans got the final orders as recorded in the 50th Troop Carrier Wing Historical Report for December 1944: "This was a big day for the 440th Troop Carrier Group, as Wing Operations Order No. 361 called for a tactical resupply mission, under No. 1098, with one aircraft and glider and still another, under No. 1099, using 10 planes and 10 CG-4As."

S E C R E T

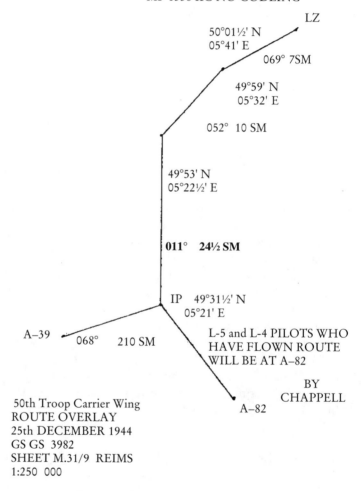

"T" INDICATING DIRECTION
OF LANDING ON L-5 STRIP
ALSO SMOKEPOTS
EUREKA "EC" NO CODEING
MF 1558 KC NO CODEING

LZ

50°01½' N
05°41' E

069° 7SM

49°59' N
05°32' E

052° 10 SM

49°53' N
05°22½' E

011°   24½ SM

IP   49°31½' N
05°21' E

A–39

068°   210 SM

L-5 and L-4 PILOTS WHO
HAVE FLOWN ROUTE
WILL BE AT A–82

BY
CHAPPELL

A–82

50th Troop Carrier Wing
ROUTE OVERLAY
25th DECEMBER 1944
GS GS 3982
SHEET M.31/9 REIMS
1:250 000

Because the critically needed ammunition could not be delivered to Chateaudun in time for the fifty-glider mission on the 26th, it was postponed until the next day. Thus the 439th and 440th groups were prepared to carry out the mission when they received wing Operation Order No. 362 during the early hours of the 27th. But intelligence concerning enemy positions had not been updated since Field Order No. 3, of 25 December. The flight route into Bastogne would be the same as the one plotted three days before.

26 December 1944. Etain, France. CG-4A glider being loaded with medical supplies for Bastogne.   — Courtesy: Horn

20

Airborne Surgeons

EXCEPT FOR THE CREWS OF THIRTY-FIVE C-47s it had been a good Christmas Day for the 440th Troop Carrier Group at Orleans. The thirty-five crews had spent the day transporting troops of the 17th Airborne Division from England to France and had missed some of the festive activities. For the rest, generally, it was a real holiday. The Christmas schedule was a welcome respite:

0900 to 1000, Breakfast.
1100, Protestant Services at Royal Theater.
1300, Catholic Mass at Royal Theater.
1400 to 1500, Dinner Menu: A turkey to every four men with dressing — potatoes — peas — carrots — two kinds of cake.
Bar in the Day Room open for the rest of the day with free drinks, and egg nog the specialty of the day.

Later that night, operations staffs in the four squadrons received new assignments. Aircraft crews and glider pilots were needed for two glider resupply missions scheduled early the next day. Throughout the night, a sergeant from the 96th Squadron sought "volunteers" for the first mission. One such "volunteer" was navigator 1st Lt. Robert S. Mauck (Columbus, Ohio), who was

194

sound asleep on his cot when he felt a nudge on his shoulder and heard, "Lieutenant, Lieutenant, I'm from operations. They want you to volunteer for a special flight this morning."

Mauck's first question was, "What time is it?" The sergeant's flashlight shining on his watch revealed that it was four in the morning. Still half asleep, Mauck mumbled, "Okay, okay, when's the flight?" All the sergeant knew was that it was scheduled for 0830 and that Mauck had to report to 96th Squadron Operations before breakfast.

Besides Mauck, Capt. Raymond H. Ottoman (Jackson, Michigan), copilot 2d Lt. Allen L. Kortkamp (Palm Springs, California) and other C-47 crew members, as well as glider pilots 2d Lt. Charlton W. "Corky" Corwin, Jr. (Normandy, Missouri) and F/O Benjamin F. "Connie" Constantino (Kansas City, Missouri) also missed a full night's sleep. Not until the preflight briefing did they realize that their CG-4A glider was to carry urgently needed surgeons and medics from Patton's Third Army to Bastogne.

They were out on the runway before 0800 and ready for take-off, but the aircraft were temporarily grounded by weather. It was another day of heavy morning frost and both the C-47 and the CG-4A were coated with ice which did not melt until after 1000. Finally at 1025, Ottoman's tow plane lifted off with Corwin and Constantino on tow, in an empty glider. It was 190 miles to Etain (A-82), easily a ninety-minute flight, and it was still possible to accomplish the Bastogne landing near the scheduled time, providing there were no delays in loading the medical team at Etain.

*   *   *   *

The morning of the 26th brought another tense period for Colonel Kohls' G-4 staff. At 0900, in a call to General Middleton's VIII Corps at Neufchateau, they stated that they were ready "for parachuting and gliders . . ." Almost four hours later, at 1357, Colonel Phiney of VIII Corps G-4 called Kohls to say that resupply could be anticipated, but the use of gliders was problematical. Three minutes later another call gave better news, that "some doctors would arrive by glider." But when? One hour and fifteen minutes later, they landed.

*   *   *   *

At midday, Corwin released his glider over the Etain airfield and landed while Ottoman dropped the tow rope and followed a landing traffic pattern to the runway. To Corwin, "It was a thrill to bring that glider down on that P-47 airstrip." Somehow the spirit of an airfield throbbing with fighter aircraft activity contrasted sharply with that of a Troop Carrier airbase.

At A-82 there was a physical difference as well — the 5,000-foot runway was surfaced with pierced steel planking (PSP). With natural turf furnishing insufficient support under the PSP, the surface could become rough during freezing weather, and even bumpier after intermittent thaws. A-82 was one of the forward fighter airfields hastily constructed as American ground forces advanced. The airfield became operational when the 362d Fighter Group, 100th Fighter Wing, moved there from A-79 (Prosnes) on 5 November. The Ninth Air Force referred to the location of A-82 as "Rouvres," the adjacent village. The IX Troop Carrier Command referred to the location as Etain, the name of a larger town nearby, about fourteen miles east of Verdun.

The surgeons and medics with their supplies were ready and waiting while the glider was parked. As they loaded the CG-4A, the tow plane crews and glider pilots received a briefing from a captain of the 362d Fighter Group in the operations office. Corwin wrote later that the briefing was an "exact repeat of the earlier one we had at Orleans." He added, "It was a relief to learn that we would have a fighter escort, made up of four P-47s."

To Mauck, navigator in Ottoman's tow plane, the briefing was inadequate. They were not furnished the exact location of the LZ, except for the photo given to the pilot, Captain Ottoman, at the last minute. "Just seconds before takeoff, somebody handed him a photograph of the drop zone." There was no extra copy for Mauck, but it was not really essential; for the approach to Bastogne, he could furnish headings and flight times for each segment from the route overlay chart he received at Orleans.

When Corwin and Constantino returned to their glider, they were met by nine volunteers from Third Army, five medical officers and four medics: Maj. Lamar Scutter, former dean, Boston University School of Medicine; Capt. Henry M. Hills, Charleston, West Virginia; Capt. Roy H. Moody, Corpus Christi, Texas; Capt. Stanley P. Weolowski, St. Paul, Minnesota; Capt. Edward N. Zinschlag,

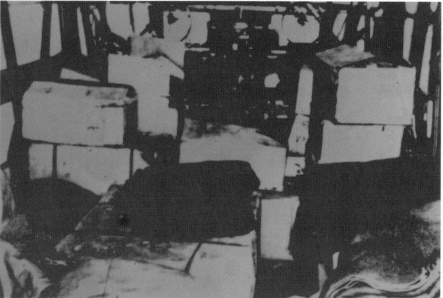

Medical supplies piled in Corwin's glider cabin on 26 December 1944, at Etain France. They were rearranged before flight to Bastogne.

— Courtesy: Horn

Five medical officers and four medics of the Third Army in front of glider that would take them to Bastogne, 26 December 1944. Etain, France.

— Courtesy: Horn

Mattoon, Illinois; T/4 John G. Knowles, St. Joseph, Missouri; T/4 Lawerence T. Rethwisch, Jersey City, New Jersey; T/3 John H. Donahue, Newark, New Jersey; and T/3 Clarence C. Matz, Chicago, Illinois. Dressed in infantry boots, trench coats, field jackets, and helmets, to all intents and purposes they looked battle ready, except that they had no weapons.

The medical supplies had been hastily piled in the middle on the floor of the glider's cabin. The passengers boarded and sat on the bench seats along both sides of the cabin, facing inward with the supplies at their feet. Inexplicably, the benches did not have the usual seat belts provided for glider infantry troops. Understandably, it would be a real "white knuckle" flight, especially during the take-off and landing. Corwin told his passengers to grip the fuselage's metal tube framing behind them to brace themselves in order to remain seated.

A new nylon tow rope, carried in the glider, was used for the final leg to Bastogne. It was carefully laid out on the runway before the hookups between the C-47 and the CG-4A, particularly to avoid possible damage from the PSP runway surface.

With Lieutenant Kortkamp assisting, Captain Ottoman eased the C-47 forward until the tow rope was taut, then went to full throttles. Crew chief S/Sgt. Joseph D. Rich (China Spring, Texas) and radio operator Sgt. Robert E. Markam (Salt Lake City, Utah) were in their places for takeoff. Lieutenant Mauck recorded the time as 1436 as he began route-time calculations based on the route overlay chart from the 50th Wing. The sixty-seven-mile flight to Bastogne would take about thirty-four minutes, allowing time to reach the first heading and altitude after takeoff. Based on the last briefing, they were apprehensive about those last seven minutes and the fourteen miles before reaching the Bastogne perimeter; they would be flying over German armored units.

While approaching Bastogne, Corky Corwin received a surprise — a gratifying one: "On the way to Bastogne I was in tow behind Ottoman when I heard prop feather on my left wing. I looked out and there was a fighter next to me for an instant. The pilot waved at me and smiled, and I waved back. Then he disappeared. It was a great relief to see him on my wing."

During the final approach, the expected antiaircraft or small-arms fire did not materialize. As the tow plane and glider flew in at

300 feet, the Germans were, in fact, caught off guard. But such a low altitude gave the tow plane crew less time to spot and recognize the ground markers on the LZ. Navigator Mauck had a quick decision to make; as he recalled, "I remember seeing the color panels on the ground, and even though my ETA wasn't up, logic said it must have been the drop zone." He flashed the green light from the C-47's astrodome at 1510, signaling the glider to cut off. It was about one minute too soon. They were still over two miles from the LZ, the airstrip used by the small L-4 aircraft of the division, located directly north of Bastogne.

Corwin and Constantino had been briefed that the LZ would have a smudge pot signal with a great deal of smoke and a T panel, and they had an aerial photo map of the area which showed the exact location of the small airfield at Bastogne. When the green light was flashed, Corwin observed a field with "plenty of smoke," but looking at the map, he felt sure they were not yet there; he could see Bastogne in the distance. Corwin took another good look at the smoke and decided it was not the LZ and opted to hang on tow until the tow plane pulled him close to the correct landing spot. When copilot Constantino yelled out that the green light had been given and emphasized that they had "passed over the field with smoke panels on it," Corwin accepted that the tow ship signal was right, and cut the glider loose. Having gone past the field, he made a 180-degree turn and glided back for a smooth landing. The glider stopped adjacent to a wooded area, about one hundred yards from B Company, 1st Battalion, 327th Glider Infantry Regiment, which was holding a part of the defensive perimeter west of Bastogne. The battalion commander, Lt. Col. Harford F. Salee, immediately called the G-4 office in Bastogne to report that "he was trying to rescue personnel and supplies" from the glider.

Corwin and Constantino soon learned of their location from a platoon leader, a lieutenant in B Company. They were but a thousand yards from the German forward lines! And they learned more about those ground panels which they had mistaken for the LZ. They had been displayed to show American fighter-bombers the front lines to keep them from bombing the Bastogne defenders. Colonel Salee's choice of the word "rescue" was an entirely appropriate one.

The two glider pilots helped unload the 600 pounds of medical supplies which were then hidden in the woods to await transportation. Three of the surgeons were immediately taken by jeep to the division hospital. The rest of the medical team and the glider pilots had to wait about an hour before a truck came for them. After loading the medical equipment, they headed for Bastogne and arrived around 1730.

* * * *

After Corwin cut his CG-4A off tow, Ottoman pushed the throttles and banked the C-47 left. As he started the climb out, turning toward the reciprocal course, the swaying tow rope was released. Mauck continued looking back from the astrodome to watch where the glider headed to land. Then something else caught his attention; he saw formations of Troop Carrier planes headed toward Bastogne by a different route, approaching from the south. "We could actually see one heck of a lot of black puffs around those aircraft." At the time, Mauck thought they were from the 440th, his group, and other groups of the 50th Wing.

Actually the formations were from the five groups of the 53d Wing that had been grounded in England the previous day. It was the largest resupply airdrop, 289 planes, of Operation KANGAROO. On this day, the 26th, they had climbed out through the fog over five airfields in England and had resolutely flown to Bastogne.

The lead formation arrived over the DZ less than five minutes after Corwin landed his glider with the medical team aboard. Although it was coincidental, the timing could not have been better planned.

There was another, more intriguing, coincidence with the timing of the large resupply mission. While navigator Mauck was observing the massive Troop Carrier formation from the astrodome of his C-47, two of General Patton's battalion commanders were watching from the ground as the long formation flew over them. The sight stirred them to change their plans for relieving Bastogne.

21

Out of the Fog

THE WEATHER FORECASTS FOR 26 December in England were accurate. During the morning, airfields of the 53d Troop Carrier Wing were afflicted with persistent fog and mist. Visibility sank to generally less than 1,000 yards all day.

More than 290 C-47s were still loaded and ready from the day before, when the mission had been postponed because of bad weather. Flight crews were placed on alert at dawn to wait for a possible break in the weather. It was not until the morning frost dissipated and the ceiling and visibility improved slightly that wing headquarters made the decision late in the morning — takeoffs at 1200.

All five airfields had marginal visibility and all pilots were on instruments until they were above the fog. There they assembled into their group formations. If the weather over England did not improve during their five-hour mission, they would return to airfields of the 50th Wing in France after the drop.

Aircraft of five Troop Carrier groups began takeoffs between 1205 and 1225 on the 26th, and after forming up over the overcast, 289 C-47s loaded with 169 tons of ammunition, signal equipment, gasoline, and other supplies headed for the Continent. Their route was the same as the one flown by the 155 planes of the 53d Wing two days earlier. The final thirty-six miles, on a 26-degree heading (19 degrees magnetic) from the Montmedy VP, took them over forward units of the Third Army, moving north to relieve Bastogne.

                              ☆   ☆   ☆   ☆

Two leading elements of the 4th Armored Division had left Neufchateau on Christmas Day to advance along the highway toward Bastogne. One was the 37th Tank Battalion under Lt. Col. Creighton W. Abrams, the other was the 53d Armored Infantry Battalion under Lt. Col. George L. Jaques. Both were in Col. Wendell Blanchard's Combat Command "R" (CCR), the division's reserve.

After taking their first objective, Vaux-les-Rosières, they were to defeat the strong German defenses at Sibret, four miles from Bastogne. From Rosières, the column left the main highway to follow a secondary road with the intention of attacking Sibret from the southeast flank.

At approximately 1500 hours, 26 December, the lead tanks reached a road junction just short of the village of Clochimont where, according to Colonel Blanchard's plan, the column was to swing northwest toward Sibret. Colonel Abrams was at that point becoming wary; he knew strong German forces were defending in Sibret, and by turning in that direction, he risked exposing a flank to other German forces beyond Clochimont in the vicinity of Assenois. A few minutes later, as Colonel Abrams and Colonel Jaques were standing at the road junction discussing their next move, they were surprised by the awesome spectacle of a large sky train of C-47s heading toward Bastogne. For twenty minutes, the stalwart transports droned overhead, a compelling symbol. It so vividly underscored the plight of the men at Bastogne that Abrams took the ever-present cigar from his lips and proposed, "Let's say to hell with Sibret and barrel-ass on to Bastogne." There was no arguing with Abrams. They took the shortest route, a secondary road from Clochimont through Assenois.

Abrams sent his operations officer, Capt. William A. Dwight, with C Team (C companies from the 37th and 53d) toward Assenois. At 1635, 1st Lt. Charles P. Boggess, from Greenville, Illinois, in the lead with six Sherman tanks, neared Assenois and requested artillery support.

The team encountered strong German resistance in its push

53d Troop Carrier Wing C-47s on northeasterly heading toward Bastogne, 26 December 1944, *foreground*, 4th Armored Division Sherman tanks shelling German positions near Clochmont, four miles from Bastogne. Photographed by a Third Army cameraman.

— Courtesy: Wide World

101st Airborne Division troops watch from Belgian Military Barracks area (101st Div. Hdqs.) as Troop Carrier planes drop supplies west of Bastogne at about 1530 hours, 26 December 1944.

— Courtesy: National Archives

through Assenois, and fighting was heavy. As it died down, Boggess saw some American troops preparing to assault an old Belgian pillbox. A quick round from the Sherman knocked out the pillbox. It was then that 2d Lt. Duane J. Webster of the 326th Airborne Engineer Battalion, 101st Division, came forward to greet Boggess, who leaned down from his open turret to shake hands. The time was 1650. The location of that historic moment was about two miles southwest of the town of Bastogne. It was dusk, twelve minutes after sunset.

* * * *

The large formation that so impressed Colonels Abrams and Jaques was headed from the Montmedy IP toward Bastogne. The 73d Squadron, leading the 434th Group's sixty-five C-47s, had descended to the drop altitude of 300 feet before reaching Clochimont, four miles from the DZ. The 437th Group's fifty-six-plane formation followed at the same altitude. The third formation, fifty-six planes of the 435th Group, was at 350 feet for the drop. The seventy-one C-47s of the 436th Group followed at 2,000 feet. In "tail-end-Charlie" position, the 438th Group's forty-one aircraft came in at 400 feet.

At first the German ground forces were unprepared for the approaching troop carriers. The aircraft of the 434th Group were unhit and there was little damage to the planes of the 437th. But as the 435th Group approached, many of the enemy weapons were positioned and ready.

Lt. Col. Gordon W. Lambert, operations officer of the 435th, flew the lead ship of his group. Later, back at Welford Park, he summarized the battle he had observed. Because there were no clouds and visibility was between ten and fifteen miles, he had a clear view of both the ground and sky. During the descent, "Sibert, Clochiment, and Assenois appeared to be burning." Lambert saw American tanks a few miles south of Bastogne. From three miles to one mile out from the DZ, "machine gun fire was directed at the formation on both sides of the approach." In the air, "fighter cover was observed from the IP to the DZ . . . Straight ahead of the DZ, on the approach, there was an enemy flak barrage up to 4,000 feet. This was apparently directed at friendly fighters, one of which was seen to go down." There was even more aerial action in sight. "Fighter dog fights were in progress north and northeast of the DZ." Instead of the usual left turn after the drop, the formations made a sharp turn to the right, around Bastogne, and climbed out back over the approach route.

It was after that turn that a C-47 of the 75th Squadron, 435th Group, was shot down. Capt. Paul W. Dahl had managed to drop his bundles over the DZ in spite of wounded crew members and critical damage to his plane. With Dahl were 2d Lt. William L. Murtaugh, copilot; 1st Lt. Zeno H. Rose, navigator; T/Sgt. George T. Gazarian, crew chief; S/Sgt. David Lifschultz, radio operator; and Sergeant Walsh, 3d QM Air Cargo. Dahl's was the only aircraft lost to enemy fire on the mission. The account is vividly described in navigator Zeno Rose's interrogation report of 30 December 1944, after his return to Welford Park:

> We took off from Station 472 about 1211 BST on 26 Dec. 1944 and flew as the lead ship of the right element of the 75th TC Squadron in the 435th formation. About two and one half minutes before we reached the DZ at Bastogne, Belgium, we were subjected to enemy fire from both light machine gun and light flak. Both types of fire were effectively hitting our airplane knocking out the instrument panel on the right side, and at that time, the Copilot, Lt. Murtaugh, was hit by both MG and AA fire that broke his right shoulder or collar bone. This caused profuse bleeding and severe pain, however, Lt. Murtaugh remained at his position and carried on his duties. At this same time, the flak burst hit me, although the injury was slight.
>
> Our bundles both in the parapacks and the cabin were ejected over the DZ about 1525 BST, we made a sharp right turn and were in formation on the run out when about 2½ minutes from the DZ light flak burst in the cockpit, most probably severing the fuel lines, knocking out the instruments, wounding Capt. Dahl and starting fires in the forward part of the airplane. Capt. Dahl rolled the trim tab back, checked the power which was already on full, and gave the order and signal for bailing out.
>
> I quickly proceeded to the cabin door and saw that the enlisted men had not yet jumped; they seemed to be hesitant possibly because of our altitude. There was no hesitancy on my part so without further thought I jumped and was followed by the

enlisted men. (I later learned that the enlisted men were followed by Lt. Murtaugh and then Capt. Dahl.) It seemed that we were about three hundred and fifty feet above the ground at that time and my parachute opened instantly. During my descent to the ground I could hear enemy bullets whizzing past. I landed near some woods southwest of Bastogne and north of Assenois at approximately P535545, which at that time was between our lines and those of the enemy. There was a great deal of fire coming toward me so I feinted dead until I could become oriented.

After lying prone for a very few moments someone rushed forward to me and threw himself prone along side. At first I thought that it was the enemy, however, fortunately it was an American infantry officer who asked if I was able to run; I replied in the affirmative so we made a break for the woods in our lines where I was later turned over to the medics for aid. This area was at that time held by Company H, 318th Inf Regt of the 80th Division.

Capt. Dahl, Lt. Murtaugh and Sgt. Walsh landed at a position about 100 yards southeast of my landing near or in the woods and they were picked up by the same organization that joined me. Capt. Dahl had a broken arm, some wounds and lacerations from flak and burns about the nape of his neck; Lt. Murtaugh had the broken shoulder, several flak wounds about the face and a sprained ankle, and Sgt. Walsh had a broken leg. All three as well as myself were given medical aid at the Aid Station, then sent to a Clearance station, then to a Field Hospital and then to the 103rd Hospital about forty miles south of Bastogne.

Before departing from the area in which we landed, we were told that the parachute of one of the men had not opened and that in the case of the sixth man, that he had landed closer to the enemy lines and that he had been taken prisoner or had been killed by the enemy.

I remained at the 103d Hospital until the 28th of December when with permission I was discharged. Received a ride on an ambulance to A-82 (Verdun) where I remained overnight. Returned to Membury, England on the 29th with a plane from the 314th to Group arriving there in the early afternoon. The distance from there to Welford was covered by jeep with arrival about 1545 BST.

Twenty-eight planes of the 435th Group received Category A battle damage and three were forced to make emergency landings at airfield A-83, Denain, France. One, a C-53D of the 77th Squadron, piloted by 1st Lt. Harry Clausen, was hit by flak at or near the DZ and the copilot, Second Lieutenant Trout, was wounded. The following is an account by Pvt. Garnett R. Woolwine, 3d QM Air Cargo crew member on board.

Going into the DZ the plane was hit twice by flak. During the turn away from the DZ another burst of flak hit the fuselage just opposite the rear door, throwing me off my feet. Very shortly afterward I heard an explosion in the pilot's compartment. Lt. Trout had been hit badly, so he came back to the cabin where the crew chief [S/Sgt. Christie D. Truitt] and I helped him remove his jacket, cut away his sleeve and apply first aid to his wounds. A tourniquet was applied to his arm, which had been bleeding profusely.

Along the return route, airfield A-83 lay less than an hour away. It was the closest one designated for emergency landings where medical facilities were available and Trout could receive immediate attention. The stricken C53D headed toward it.

The 436th Group, the fourth formation, fared better with five planes slightly damaged by small-arms fire. Its planes turned and flew back without changing their altitude of 2,000 feet.

The last formation, the 438th Group, was equally fortunate, but paired their luck with courage as exemplified by a crew member of the 90th Squadron, the last over the DZ. T/Sgt. Jesse W. Aycock, from Sumiton, Alabama, enlisted in October 1942. As a crew chief, he earned Air Medals for the Normandy and Holland airborne operations. After the drop at Bastogne, Aycock's plane began to lag behind the formation. An inspection revealed that the number six pararack chute, left front, was open and was hanging on to the middle rack. The bundle was swinging against the tail of the plane, threatening to damage it and, because of the drag it produced, cutting the plane's speed. Putting on his parachute, Aycock hung his upper body out the open doorway. The radio operator, Sgt. Charles N. Steed, clung to his legs while Aycock tried to blast the burden loose, but to no avail. Next, after lashing a parachute knife to a metal

pole, Aycock inched his way further out the door. This time the
navigator, First Lieutenant Weiser, helped Steed and Woolwine hold
him by his chute harness and his legs. With his improvised tool, he
managed to cut the shroud lines and the open parachute and the
bundle dropped away. None of the crew cared where the bundle of
resupplies landed — they headed back to England.

Aircraft of the 438th Group had been the last of the four
groups to take off from England and were the last to return to their
Greenham Common airbase between 1748 and 1825. Poor visibility
prevailed as the planes returned, but they succeeded in landing without incident.

✵   ✵   ✵   ✵

Airfield A-83, close to Denain, was used by the Luftwaffe before the invasion. With a single concrete runway 5,076 feet long, it
became a P-47 fighter airfield, but for a few dramatic moments on
the day after Christmas, 1944, it belonged to a lone Troop Carrier
transport. Flying a damaged aircraft with wounded aboard, Harry
Clausen was given a priority to land. Garnett Woolwine recalls that

> when it was found that the hydraulic system was shot the crew
> chief tried to refill the system, but was unsuccessful. Upon
> reaching A-83 the pilot, Lt. Clausen, tried to shake the gear
> down so we could land. He finally succeeded in doing so. We
> landed with full flaps, and had to make two complete turns at
> the end of the runway to stop. An ambulance was waiting and
> took Lts. Trout and Clausen with them. Lt. Clausen said he
> would be back shortly.

After seeing that Trout had been hospitalized, Clausen returned to his plane. He and his remaining crew members, Christie
D. Truitt (crew chief) and S/Sgt. Walter C. Cassidy (radio operator), remained over night after deciding they could repair the damage sufficiently to fly the plane back to England.

They were out early the next morning making emergency repairs for the 230-mile flight to Welford Park. About 1400 hours,
Clausen took off with Truitt in the copilot seat and Cassidy functioning as radio operator. The takeoff time was not verified and is
questionable because it was reported that they contacted the Ashford VHF station at 1740 for weather at Welford using the code

Errand C Charlie. The weather was given, but when the station asked C Charlie for his position, it was reported as uncertain. The VHF station advised him to divert to Hawking Field for better weather conditions, but contact with him was lost. Later the VHF station at Ford made contact with C Charlie and learned that he had only forty gallons of fuel. As the plane was over water, Ford advised C Charlie to fly a heading of eighty degrees. The next reports said the left engine, then the right engine was out and they were bailing out. At 1755, radar located the aircraft approximately ten miles south of Portsmouth. An Air-Sea rescue launch searched until midnight. A trawler took up the search until daylight when another launch searched until 1320, 28 December. No trace of the aircraft or crew was ever found.

101st Airborne Division G-4 retrieval team members drag parapacks of precious supplies dropped at Bastogne by Troop Carrier aircraft.
— Courtesy: National Archives

22

Gasoline in Gliders

"If you look up 'Intelligence' in the new volumes of the Encyclopaedia Britannica," he had said, "you'll find it classified under the following three heads: Intelligence, Human; Intelligence, Animal; Intelligence, Military. My stepfather's a perfect specimen of Intelligence, Military."
— Aldous Huxley *(Point Counter Point)*

THE 50TH WING FIELD ORDER No. 3 of 25 December designated the ten-glider mission as "Air Cargo, Resupply." The subsequent wing Order No. 361 that reached the 440th Troop Carrier Group at Orleans during the early hours of the 26th was explicit — the cargo was gasoline. Each CG-4A glider was to carry 300 gallons of 80 octane gasoline in five-gallon jerrycans tied down to the wooden floor of the cabin, directly behind the pilots. As one glider pilot later remarked, "We had gasoline lashed to our backs." The typical load was fifty-nine or sixty jerrycans.

Col. Frank X. Krebs, CO of the 440th, committed all four squadrons to the mission with Lt. Col. Irvin G. Anderson, CO of the 95th, leading the formation. Anderson had other squadron concerns as well that morning. Nine of his C-47s were dispatched to England to pick up 17th Airborne Division troops for transportation to France, and later that morning eight other planes were assigned to the 439th Group at Chateaudun to take part in a fifty-glider mission to Bastogne. As Anderson put it, "I was so busy with

210

getting other phases organized that the mission I was to lead was just another job."

At the time, Anderson was possibly the youngest Troop Carrier squadron commander in the ETO. After earning his pilot wings at Kelly Field in December 1940, he was assigned to the 5th Transport Squadron at Patterson Field. He was given the responsibility of forming a new Troop Carrier squadron in June 1943 and was promoted to captain at age twenty-three. Eight months later his squadron, along with the 440th Group, flew to England via the South Atlantic route. Major Anderson led his 95th Squadron on the Normandy airborne invasion and subsequent resupply missions, and at twenty-four, he was promoted to lieutenant colonel.

* * * *

On such short notice, the marshaling and loading of the ten gliders and assigning of crews could not be completed in time to meet the original 1000 takeoff scheduled by 50th Wing Headquarters, and departure was delayed until afternoon.

The final pre-flight briefing at 1300 in the group war room was attended by all pilots, copilots, and navigators assigned to the mission. Maj. Howard W. Cannon, group operations officer, 1st Lt. William P. Crawford, A-2, and the group weather officer conducted the meeting. The crews were briefed on an enemy situation that was admittedly forty-eight hours old. They were told that "you find it this way or you may be deep in enemy territory!"

Why intelligence reports had not been updated is unclear, possibly because of communications delays. Headquarters, 50th Wing, relied solely on battle information originating from the advanced headquarters of the Ninth Air Force at Luxembourg City. The wing depended on this intelligence as it formulated resupply flight routes, and none evidently had been received in wing headquarters on the 26th.

The 95th Squadron navigator, 1st Lt. George F. Wasson, was assigned to Colonel Anderson's plane as the lead navigator. To Wasson, the most disturbing aspect of the briefing was the lack of flight route plans. "We were given the location of the landing site for the gliders but no flight plans."

The formation was to fly in two glider-tow elements. In No. 2 position of the 95th Squadron element, 1st Lt. William S. John was assigned two navigators. One was Charles D. Skelton, who had been promoted from flight officer to 2d lieutenant on Christmas Day. In Colonel Anderson's crew were 2d Lt. Jens P. Lind, copilot; 1st Lt. George F. Wasson, navigator; T/Sgt. Douglas W. Goodrich, crew chief; and S/Sgt. Walter E. Hubmaier, radio operator. In Lieutenant John's crew were 2d Lt. Richard E. Haller, copilot; 2d Lt. Charles H. Miller, navigator, assisted by Lieutenant Skelton; T/Sgt. Homer G. Forshee, crew chief; and Cpl. Robert E. Massey, radio operator. The mission would also provide training for one of the newest navigators in the squadron, instructed by Miller — it would be training by experience.

The loading of the gliders was completed during the briefing. Ten C-47s had been marshaled in pairs at the end of the runway. The CG-4As were parked close to the outside edge of the pavement, each near the rear of its tow plane.

By 1430 the crews were all out on the runway to inspect their particular aircraft and to test the tow rope connections and release mechanisms. As glider pilots entered the rear door of their gliders, they cast leery glances on the cans labeled 80 octane as they walked between them toward the cockpit. It would be no "milk run."

In the lead glider on the left side of the runway, 2d Lt. Thomas P. Longo and F/O Royal H. Taylor signaled their readiness to the ground crew. On the runway's right side in No. 2 position, F/O Warren de Beauclair and F/O Lowell E. Dashow signaled they were also ready. As the tow planes' engines idled, the "ready" signals were passed up from the rows of gliders, five on each side.

* * * *

De Beauclair and Dashow were two of the most recent glider pilots to arrive in the 95th Squadron. They had been in glider pilot training together, graduating at Lubbock, Texas, 15 June 1944. After the Advanced Glider Pilot Course at Laurinburg-Maxton A.F.B., they were among over 300 glider pilots shipped to the United Kingdom in early September — ostensibly for the Holland invasion, Operation MARKET. They arrived too late for the operation.

When Warren de Beauclair entered the glider program at Bowman Field, Kentucky, in December 1943, he doubtless had personal regrets. He and his identical twin brother, Wayne, had applied together for training which had opened to pilots who had already

logged flight time in powered aircraft. Wayne was not accepted because he did not have the minimum of 125 hours. He became a gun-
nery instructor and was in a B-17 bomber group at Sudberry, England, while Warren was at Orleans, France. Some of the glider
pilots who were with Warren in training and in the 95th Squadron
often joked about the confusion the two could have created, had
they stayed together! Warren had devised a plan to catch a flight to
England for a get-together with his brother. For the time being the
reunion had to be postponed.

※   ※   ※   ※

Anderson's tow plane and Longo's glider climbed away from
the Orleans' runway at 1510. Within five minutes, the others were
off and had begun closing up the formation en route to Montmedy.
The ETA at the LZ was 1715, almost forty minutes after sunset.

As the formation approached the Montmedy IP, at about 1650,
a fighter plane escort joined up and accompanied the glider formation as far as the Meuse River, where the fighters dropped their belly
tanks and took off in another direction. The Troop Carrier pilots
were left to fly the last seventeen miles at low altitudes to the Bastogne perimeter, over strong German forces, alone.

After turning from the IP, three miles south of Libramont,
they were seventeen miles from Bastogne. In the lead plane, Wasson
was at the Rebecca radar scope trying without success to pick up the
Eureka beacon. In John's plane, the Rebecca was constantly moni-
tored by one of the navigators; they could not pick up the beacon
either — obviously it was not working.

For seven minutes they encountered ground fire, north of
Morhet and Sibret — both 20mm and machine-gun fire to Sibret,
then machine-gun fire the rest of the way. Anderson's C-47 took a
20mm round through the left side of the fuselage and machine-gun
bullets through the left wing and cabin floor. John's plane, in the
right position of the element, was not hit at all.

It was six miles from Morhet and three miles from Sibret to
Bastogne. Irvin Anderson won't ever forget those last three miles: "I
can recall heavy flak from the left side for quite a time, I think coming from railroad flat cars for the last ten miles."

George Wasson was busy with navigation problems from the
IP south of Libramont to Bastogne. A single-track rail line ran be-

tween the two towns. After the turn, they crossed the railroad. In 1986, Wasson recalled:

> We flew with the track on our right side. About half way [to Bastogne] we came upon a huge tank battle. Many small fires could be seen on the ground below us. Suddenly we began to draw considerable ground fire and had to take evasive action. [By then, the railroad was too far south for visual navigation reference.] We returned to our original compass heading. The sun had set behind us, it was dark and the area was sparsely populated so we couldn't identify any land marks. We came upon a wide road and we could see a town in front and off to the right. In a very short time we identified the landing area and gave the glider pilot the first warning light. In a few seconds we were adjacent to the field and gave the second light. The glider cut loose. We made a sharp 180 turn to the right, hit the deck and headed home to Orleans.

During the approach, Anderson and Lind could recognize Bastogne ahead, but the first possible indication of the LZ was five red lights northwest of the town. With snow on the ground, they could not see the white T they had been briefed to expect. Lind shouted, "There's an American liaison plane parked in that field." They were sure it was on the LZ or very near it. The light signals to cut were flashed back to the two gliders. Longo and de Beauclair landed their gliders almost in formation at 1712 in the LZ just to the north of the Belgian military barracks which were now being used by the 101st Division. The field was the airstrip used by the division's L-4 liaison planes.

Glider pilots 2d Lt. Robert H. Price and F/O John H. Wesley, 96th Squadron, were in the No. 3 position of the formation. When Price saw the flak and the tracers streaking up toward Anderson's C-47 and Longo's CG-4A directly ahead, he wondered why he had volunteered. Only six hours earlier, another glider pilot in the squadron, F/O Harold W. Morgan, had come into Price's room announcing, "Hey, guess what? Corwin went to Bastogne. Now they want more glider pilots for this afternoon. We can volunteer."

As Price and Wesley watched their tow plane being peppered with machine-gun fire, they expected the same for their glider. When the green light came on, Price's instinct told him to get on the ground quickly by using a high speed approach — unlike that practiced during training. He had an added sense of security in making a fast landing because his glider had a Griswold nose, offering the pilots better protection. (The Griswold nose was a steel frame structure which was mounted in front of the fragile cockpit of the CG-4A glider. A number of the bolt-on nose kits were in the ETO in December, but relatively few had been installed.) After slowing from 120 MPH to 100 MPH, Price made a 90-degree turn to the right and headed for a field northwest of the town. The snow cover over the field was deceptive: hidden beneath the snow were deep ruts made by tanks and other vehicles before the ground had frozen. The landing gear was wiped out. As the pilots headed for the rear exit, Price smelled gasoline. If the jerrycans weren't punctured, the caps must have been loose, he thought.

F/O John T. Corpening and F/O Joseph D. Dubbe, in No. 4 position, cut their glider seconds after Price. With a slower glide approach, Corpening made a right turn and landed on the designated LZ without any damage.

In the fifth and sixth places within the formation, Capt. John E. Yeates and 1st Lt. Victor O. Reinemer were towing glider pilots from their 97th Squadron. As they approached Bastogne through the ground fire, they anticipated a critical decision: the exact moment when the gliders should be given the green light to release. They could see hits scored on the gliders in front of them and they could hear the .50-caliber bullets pierce their C-47s, but they had no way of knowing whether the gliders they were towing had been damaged. As long as they stayed on tow, there was always optimism. Over the LZ, the gliders were given the cut signals simultaneously. Yeates, followed by Reinemer, hit left rudder and started a climb to 5,000 feet on the return heading. During the turn, they were unable to observe the landings of the gliders.

The glider on tow behind Yeates was flown by 2d Lt. Joseph A. Purcell with copilot F/O L. Decker, a good pairing — Decker was one of those who arrived too late for the Holland missions and Purcell was a veteran. About two miles from the LZ, their glider was hit by small-arms fire. Seeing smoke from smudge pots, Purcell cut off and landed in a field directly west of the Belgian military barracks. Some of the jerrycans had been punctured.

Glider pilots F/O William W. Burnett and F/O James C.

Crowder, on tow behind Reinemer, had problems before they turned at the IP. The tie rods bracing on the empennage between the fin and horizontal stabilizer came loose. With a twisting tail section — fin and rudder — it took both Burnett and Crowder to fly the glider the rest of the way through the barrage of enemy fire. As they approached the cutoff point northwest of Bastogne, Burnett did not hesitate to hit the tow release lever when the green signal flashed. Even after the airspeed bled off to around 80 MPH, Burnett required Crowder's help on the right turn in to the landing strip. Although the strip was 450 feet wide, they landed alongside of it to avoid the three gliders at the far end, already being unloaded by the division's cargo retrieval teams.

Capt. Wallace F. Hammargren and 2d Lt. Nathaniel J. Shoenfeldt were in the lead glider of the 98th Squadron, the fourth element in the formation. On their right, in No. 8 position, were 2d Lt. Richard E. Baly and F/O Vernon E. Carter. Both gliders were hit from ground fire, but Baly's took the most punishment — a four-foot section was knocked out of the left wing and his left elevator was damaged. Although his steering column was only grazed, the panel over his head was blown off. Before they arrived over the cut-off point, a piece of flak cut through Hammargren's tow rope one foot in front of the glider's nose. He was in a position to make a 360-degree glide pattern and land. Hammargren and Baly did not land their gliders on the designated LZ airfield, but in a field well within the 101st Division's perimeter northwest of Bastogne.

As the formation headed into the hail of ground fire, the view from the last two gliders was ominous. After F/O Harold W. Morgan and F/O Russell L. Eppelheimer were given the one minute white warning light from their 96th Squadron's tow ship, they watched Hammargren's glider directly ahead for an indication of the cutoff point. They were understandably impatient to get off tow and down onto the ground. Although Bastogne was visible about a mile ahead, when Morgan saw Hammargren's glider release, and then Baly's, he followed suit and cut off tow before he was given the green light. He followed Hammargren's landing pattern to touch down in a field covered with deep snow.

F/O Charles F. Sutton was 2d Lt. O. B. Blessing's copilot in No. 10 position, the tail-end Charlies of the 98th Squadron. As they flew toward Bastogne, Sutton "was reminded of a popcorn machine by the sound of small arms fire piercing the fabric of the glider." Blessing, influenced by the release of the three preceding gliders, also cut off early and landed northwest of Bastogne within the 101st Division's positions. None of the glider pilots were sure just where they were. After landing, Blessing and Sutton quickly got away from the glider. They ran about thirty yards and jumped a fence and were challenged by a trooper of the 101st Division. It was a welcomed "capture."

To Charles Sutton, the crews were fortunate. "I think that the timing of our arrival was good. We were between five and six hundred feet. The sun had already set and the moon had not yet risen. Therefore, the enemy had difficulty in getting our range."

The mission was termed one hundred percent effective; every glider landed with nearly all the gasoline intact. Although some of the cans of gasoline had been pierced by small-arms fire, none, fortunately, had been hit by incendiary bullets. All tow planes returned safely to Orleans, many with damage. Remarkably, not one man had been injured on the mission.

*   *   *   *

About 1730, Colonel Kohls was called in Bastogne and told that ten gliders with gasoline aboard had landed safely. He was pleased but perplexed. The message he had received from VIII Corps at 1600 stated "expect 50 gliders at 1700." After the ten gliders were unloaded and towed away, other retrieval teams remained ready and waiting for forty more. It was well after dark when Kohls finally concluded that there would be no more gliders that night. The inventory of gasoline and minor amounts of ammunition and rations from the gliders was quickly taken.

That evening, communications from Bastogne, through General Middleton's VIII Corps at Neufchateau, then through Third Army headquarters to CATOR at SHAEF, moved more quickly than ever before. At 1825, Third Army headquarters at Luxembourg City sent a message to CATOR indicating that the surgical teams had arrived but many supplies requested at 2028 of the 25th had not been delivered.

All items, except Auxiliary Surgical Teams with their equipment, listed in cable this Headquarters GNMCD 38-A (that of

252028) requested for supply, by air to P-545585 on 27 December. This request is additional to any amounts previously requested and possibly delivered. Delivery of back logged items also requested at earliest possible date.

The list referred to as "(that of the 252028)" was the one flown out of Bastogne by Captain Linker on the night of 25 December and carried to SHAEF.

*   *   *   *

Twenty-two glider pilots spent the night of 26 December at Bastogne, quartered in the Belgian military barracks on the north edge of town. K rations and sleeping bags were two much-appreciated items recovered from their gliders, as Charles Sutton later described: "It was the coldest night I have ever experienced. We were sent to a building whose windows and doors had been knocked out and it had a concrete floor on which we were expected to sleep. The temperature was close to zero. Our sleeping bags were just a bit better than nothing."

Before they settled in for the night, they heard some good news that was spreading among the men of the 101st Division: "Patton's tanks broke through, they're here!" One glider pilot sounded off, "So are we!" The next morning, when news of the breakthrough had spread throughout the town, some of the glider pilots complained that the weapons firing was keeping them awake.

*   *   *   *

It was an hour after midnight before Colonel Jaques' 53d Armored Infantry Battalion cleared Assenois and the woods behind the village, ensuring a fairly secure route into Bastogne. They took 428 German prisoners in the process.

The 26th Infantry Division soon advanced north along the highway on the right side of the 4th Armored Division. Maj. Gen. John Millikin's III Corps entered Bastogne with forty trucks loaded with medical supplies, ammunition, and food. Still under the cover of darkness, 260 of the most seriously wounded men in Bastogne were taken out in twenty-two ambulances and ten trucks that III Corps brought in.

*   *   *   *

It was obvious to commanders in the 101st Airborne Division that the approach route flown by the 440th Group's glider mission was a perilous one. The final approach used by the 53d Wing for their midafternoon paradrop was less vulnerable — over the 4th Armored Division, which subsequently established the ground corridor to Bastogne.

During the evening and through the night, the 101st Division sent messages to VIII Corps at Neufchateau with information about the breakthrough. Because more gliders were expected on the 27th, advisories were frequently added to the messages, instructions for IX Troop Carrier Command to route resupply flights over the newly established corridor, southeast of the Neufchateau-Bastogne highway.

✻ ✻ ✻ ✻

The ten tow planes returned to the 440th Group's airfield at Orleans and landed between 1840 and 1910 as planned. The crews were eager to inspect their aircraft and count the holes. One C-47 had taken seventy hits.

Pilots and navigators were soon interrogated by their squadron intelligence officers. After Colonel Anderson supplied the routine information on the mission report form, the interrogator wrote an additional comment under "Remarks": "Navigator suggests a Rt course from IP Montmedy into Bastogne and stay right of original course. Stay away from *Morhet* & *Sibret*."

When Anderson learned that the fifty-glider mission from Chateaudun had been postponed until the 27th, he headed for the 440th Group headquarters. His advice was "to get the wing to change our entry into Bastogne." He was sure that if the next "morning's flights were to be made on the same IP to LZ legs the visibility would be better and the AA could surely get a better target." The Germans would certainly be more alert and prepared with more antiaircraft batteries. In effect, Anderson's recommendations were disregarded and the 50th Wing continued to rely for changes only on advice originating from the Ninth Air Force.

As early as 23 December, when Operation REPULSE began, General Chappell's 50th Wing headquarters planned to obtain intelligence directly from CATOR rather than depend on communications forwarded through First Allied Airborne Army or IX Troop

Carrier Command. Therefore 50th Wing Special Orders No. 108 assigned Maj. David G. Moss, wing assistant A-2, "to proceed on or about 26 December 1944, to Versailles, France, for the purpose of obtaining Intelligence information in connection with tactical operations performed by this Wing's units to Bastogne, Belgium."

Since the fifty-glider mission had been postponed until the 27th, timely intelligence reports on enemy dispositions around Bastogne should have been closely considered. Perhaps the previously planned flight route should have been changed to the safer approach to Bastogne, over the newly opened corridor from the south.

Above:
Lieutenant Colonel Irvin G. Anderson's C-47 at Orleans, France, after belly-landing on return from airborne mission.
— Courtesy: Anderson

Left:
Lieutenant Colonel Irvin G. An-derson, commander of the 95th Troop Carrier Squadron, England, July 1944.
— Courtesy: Anderson

23

Ammunition Sky Train

Mobilization

RETURNING TO ORLEANS AFTER the ten-glider mission, George Wasson was looking forward to swapping tales with his three roommates about his "gasoline-milk run" and their larger mission of the afternoon. But during his interrogation, he learned they were still at Chateaudun because the fifty-glider mission had been postponed until the next day. Wasson and 1st Lts. Michael A. Whitfill, Richard P. Umhoeffer and 2d Lt. Wilmer S. Weber had gone through navigator training together and had been assigned together to the 95th Squadron.

Late in the morning of the 26th, Whitfill learned of the larger glider mission without great interest; Capt. Donald M. Orcutt was away on an air evacuation mission transporting wounded to England. Normally, Whitfill flew as Orcutt's navigator, and he had been with him on every one of the squadron's combat missions. Believing he would not be needed, he recalled that he decided to "get out of the way" and visit a friend in the 96th Squadron down the hall. When someone came looking for navigators, Whitfill and another lieutenant "were dragged, kicking and screaming back to the briefing room in the 95th." There he and his two roommates were as-

signed to three of eight 95th Squadron C-47s scheduled to fly to
Chateaudun that afternoon ahead of three C-47s from the 96th
Squadron, two shy of the number of tow planes the 96th was slated
to furnish.

It was afternoon when they made the short, eighteen-mile hop
to the 439th Troop Carrier Group's airfield at Chateaudun (A-39).
After they were positioned on the runway at the rear of the 439th
Group's formation, the mission was postponed until the next day. It
was not a pleasant night for crews from the 440th. To Whitfill, "It
was a very cold day and night and sleeping in the plane that night was
a miserable experience."

                            *   *   *   *

The 439th Troop Carrier Group at Chateaudun was struggling
to meet a challenge presented on short notice by 50th Wing headquarters. It came up with thirty-seven C-47s and crews, and fifty
CG-4A gliders. But locating one hundred glider pilots posed a problem. Many were away on passes and leaves for the holidays.

The problem was relayed to the 50th Wing headquarters and
the 441st Group at Dreux (Airfield A-41) was alerted. The 441st,
located forty-five miles north of the 439th, could be expected to
move glider pilots there quickly.

On the morning of the 26th, Capt. Merrell R. Kirkpatrick,
glider operations officer of the 100th Squadron, 441st Group, was
called by Lt. Col. Willie Pate to come to his office at once. Pate,
group operations officer, instructed Kirkpatrick "to set up a six-
glider, twelve-pilot list for a resupply to Bastogne." Back in the tent
area, Kirkpatrick had eleven glider pilots lined up when the telephone rang. It was Colonel Pate again. "The wing has just scrubbed
the mission [for the 441st] and is going to use another squadron."

The glider pilot shortage at Chateaudun had been resolved with
the decision that gliders would be flown without copilots. At that
time, the four squadron glider officers of the 439th Group had made
a science of assigning pilots and copilots in balanced combinations.
Reversion to solo pilots presented a new, onerous challenge. A
guideline was that rookie pilots with less than two previous combat
missions were to be selected only as volunteers. Although many of
the glider pilots were newcomers, there were a number of veterans
on the roster.

F/O Thomas J. Berry was one pilot taken off the mission by Capt. John A. Neary because there were others in the 91st Squadron with *fewer* missions. Likewise, in the 93d Squadron, F/O Waverly M. Jarvis, who was to fly with F/O Paul Hower, was put on the reserve list at the last moment.

To Capt. John L. Patterson, glider officer of the 94th Squadron, "The mission came up so fast that all four squadrons of the 439th had a tough time coming up with enough glider pilots for the mission. Group Headquarters told me to pick any new men or anyone with only one mission for the so called 'Milk Run.'" Of the twelve glider pilots he assigned, six he knew very well. One was a roommate, 2d Lt. Raymond D. Schott, who was assigned to Chalk No. 42 position in the formation. At the time, Patterson could not imagine the misfortunes his twelve glider pilots would encounter.

* * * *

According to the 439th Group Headquarters Diary, there was scant time indeed to mount a fifty glider mission on the 26th:

After lunch, we learned of a proposed fifty-glider mission to re-supply the 101st Airborne Division, which is fighting valiantly in the Bastogne pocket, cut off from all but aerial support. Briefing was held for Squadron Commanders, Intelligence Officers, Operations Officers, Navigators and Glider Operation Officers. Colonel Young explained the general situation, Captain La Forest briefed on operational details, Captain Smith on the course and times, and Major Martin on radio procedure and navigational aids. Eleven of the fifty tug ships are to be borrowed from the 440th — and two pilots of that group were represented at the briefing. Supplies did not arrive in time to be loaded for takeoff by 1515, so the mission was postponed, with a scheduled 0815 takeoff tomorrow.

Aside from flak information which Colonel Young brought back from the 440th, the only thing we had was the route and destination.

The commanding officer of the 439th Troop Carrier Group, Col. Charles H. Young, was particularly concerned about the lack of current intelligence along the route prescribed by the 50th Wing headquarters. After learning that the 440th Group's tow planes (the ten-glider mission) could be expected to return around 1900, he traveled that evening to Orleans by auto to obtain the latest information from crew interrogations.

After Young returned with information acquired at Orleans, a briefing was held at 0230 in the group's combined operations-intelligence office. In attendance from each of the four squadrons were the S-2 (intelligence) officers, the S-3 (operations) officers and the 93d Squadron commander, Lt. Col. Robert A. Barrere. The actual briefing was presented by Capt. La Forest, operations; Capt. Patrick Maloney, intelligence; and Capt. Smith, group navigator.

Crews were furnished copies of the route overlay (from wing headquarters) which gave the flight route in segments with headings and distances to the LZ at Bastogne. The last seventeen miles from the IP (four miles northeast of Neufchateau, three miles south of Libramont) was a dogleg course, one that would take them three miles north of the enemy concentrations in Morhet and Sibret. The route, however, was based on intelligence from the advanced headquarters, Ninth Air Force, and was over forty-eight hours old.

1st Lt. William M. Brady, weather officer, forecast favorable ceilings and visibility at A-39 and in the battle area. The quick briefing was summarized in copies of the "Route Forecast, A-39 to DZ" which Brady distributed. It also gave advice, "NOTE TO GLIDER PILOTS: Worst visibility will be encountered within 500 ft of ground. Landings made *down sun* will probably have best visibility." The surface winds would be, "Light and variable but chiefly from NE and less than 5 mph." The Route Forecast ended with "MINIMUM TEMPERATURE THIS MORNING: 16 Deg. F. Watch out for Frost."

Francis L. "Bud" Carroll, a native of Salem, Massachusetts, was one of the glider pilots from the 94th Squadron to attend the early morning briefing. He heard that "there was a third, or a quarter of the perimeter surrounding Bastogne that was opened, and that the glider missions of 26 December had no problem, only some scattered small arms fire."

In the 91st Squadron, F/O Duke F. Jarvis, from Yakima, Washington, was assigned to chalk position No. 2 in the formation. Later he recalled, "On 26 December an afternoon briefing in the mess hall indicated we were to follow close to the railroad track into Bastogne. Re-Con reported a railroad-mounted 88mm antiaircraft rifle on the way in, but about five miles west of Bastogne." To Jarvis, "The early morning briefing revealed nothing new, but that we were to fly in at about 400 feet, so low that if that 88 was still there they couldn't fire without peeling the barrel."

The delivery of ammunition to Chateaudun was the first critical problem facing the mission. Maj. Bernard G. Parks, 439th glider officer, summarized it: "The mission was obviously put together in a hurry. We were given very little time to assemble the gliders and the C-47s and then had to wait for the arrival of the 155mm ammunition which was our load. We called on whoever was available to come out and help us load the gliders and then we waited. After loading, everyone was helping to clean the snow and frost off the glider wings."

※   ※   ※   ※

During the night of the 26th, only forty-eight tow planes were marshaled on the Chateaudun runway, thirty-seven from the 439th Group and eleven from the 440th Group. At dawn five more C-47s from the 96th Squadron arrived from Orleans, two to complete the fifty-plane mission requirements and three as alternates.

In some Troop Carrier groups of the 50th Wing, glider pilots had been given navigator training. One in the 96th Squadron was F/O Roderick D. MacDougall, from Lubbock, Texas. On the night of the 24th, he had been on a flight to England with pilot 1st Lt. Kent Maynard. They returned to Orleans on the 26th, after the weather cleared, and early on the 27th they were quickly sent to Chateaudun. "No briefing, just line up on the end of the A-39 runway as the first alternate, Number 51 in formation," he recalled.

Ironically, written in chalk on one of the gliders was, "IS THIS TRIP NECESSARY?" In hindsight, an appropriate question.

On the Runway

The weather forecast at Chateaudun for the morning of the 27th had been accurate. At sunrise, about one-half hour before the scheduled 0815 takeoff, the sky was clear and the temperature was 16 degrees. The tow planes and gliders were covered with heavy frost.

They marshaled at the southeast end of the longer of two concrete runways. (At 7,375 feet, this was the second longest runway on the Continent, exceeded only by the 7,788-foot strip at Orleans. As the glider pilots located their CG-4As by the chalked numbers on the fuselages, they realized it would be another of those typical "hurry up and wait" operations. Only time and the sun's rays could clear the frost off the windshields and wings. The mission was rescheduled for 0915 and then again for 1015.

F/O Paul O. Hower, from El Dorado, Kansas, found his 93d Squadron glider, Chalk No. 31, already fully loaded on the runway. He had been concerned about the mission since the previous afternoon. "The mission was scrubbed and rescheduled for early A.M. of the 27th, and there would be no copilots. I had a bad feeling about this mission (my 2nd) and was awake all night long. Our scheduled takeoff was delayed because of frost on our windshields. Mechanics tried to scrape it off, but it came back on. Brake fluid was tried but it didn't help. We had to wait until the sun came up and melted the frost."

F/O Verbon E. "Pete" Houck, from Wenatchee, Washington, was another glider pilot who arrived too late for the September Holland missions. Of the CG-4As assigned to the twelve glider pilots of the 94th Squadron, Chalk No. 49 was Houck's and was the last one in the right row of gliders. He glumly thought he was the Tail-end Charlie, but he was actually next to last. Because the first serial consisted of thirteen tow planes and gliders of the 91st Squadron, the leader of the second serial, 92d Squadron, was positioned as number fourteen on the left. All subsequent elements were designated by even numbers on the left and odd numbers on the right.

When Houck reached his glider, 155mm ammunition was still being tied down on the cabin floor. He was anxious over the location of the fuses. "I vividly remember loading the detonators myself. I placed them very carefully in the V parts of the fuselage's tubing to better protect them from ground fire."

Glider No. 36 was to carry more than ammunition, as 2d Lt. Albert S. Barton learned when four surgeons were delivered to his glider. At the time, the Iowan incorrectly assumed that some others of his 93d Squadron had similar loads. Because bench seats were mounted on one side of the cabin, the ammunition had not been tied down to his satisfaction. Taking advantage of the delayed takeoff, he decided to make adjustments: "I took one look and the sight of those 155mm shells lashed to the floor mounts sent me scurrying for more ropes. By the time I had tied and retied them it was too late

Above: Tow planes and gliders marshaled on A-39 Runway, Chateaudun, France, 27 December 1944. F/O John W. Burnett's 91st Squadron CG-4A in foreground; 2d Lt. John D. Hill's beyond. 2d Lt. Joseph Fry's C-47 (Hill's tow plane) on far right. Capt. Thomas Corrigan's C-47, 92d Squadron, on far left.
    — Courtesy: Corrigan

Right: 1st Lt. Philip C. Hecker, 94th Troop Carrier Squadron, under his C-47's left aileron after the 27 December glider mission to Bastogne. — Courtesy: Hecker

Below: Capt. Ernest Turner's C-47, *Ain't Miss-behavin*, 94th Squadron, 439th Troop Carrier Group, after wheels-up belly-landing near Savy, 27 December 1944.   — Courtesy: National Archives

to run and talk to the tug crew." He hardly had time to talk to his passengers who were staring at the ammunition that was interfering with their leg room. His only advice to them was, "Keep your seat belts fastened at all times."

*   *   *   *

In 439th Group headquarters at Chateaudun on the morning of the 27th, 1st Lt. Arthur Kaplan was manning the A-2 desk. He was a glider pilot and, at the time, an assistant group intelligence officer. He was also the group historian assigned to keeping the diary and records. At 0925 he received an unusual telephone call from wing headquarters, Maj. Roy E. Weinzettel's intelligence section (A-2), informing him that a ground corridor south of Bastogne had been opened by the 4th Armored Division of General Patton's Third Army. In addition, the latest known locations of German antiaircraft guns along the corridor were furnished. A change in the flight route was suggested, one that would approach Bastogne from the south. Kaplan immediately relayed the message to Capt. Patrick Maloney, assistant group A-2, in the control tower, for their information. (The authority to revise flight routes and take-off times had been delegated only to operations (A-3) at both wing and group levels.

Colonel Young was out on the runway in a jeep checking last minute details of the marshaling and the frost on the glider's windshields before the takeoffs. While he was checking one glider, a jeep slid to a stop with an unpleasant problem. A copilot of one of the 91st Squadron's C-47 was ill. When Young arrived at the plane he found the man vomiting. He sent his driver, Cpl. Collen R. Connell, for his (Young's) flight gear; he would replace the sick copilot. He continued on foot inspecting other gliders when Captain Maloney pulled up in a jeep with the suggested change telephoned from Wing A-2. Young asked Maloney, "Why would I want to consider a change in route?" Maloney replied, "I don't know, they didn't say." Then Maloney repeated the message aloud word for word and emphasized that it was from the wing's A-2, not A-3.

Charles Young summarized the situation forty-one years later:

> The crews were already in their airplanes and gliders, it was almost engine start time, there was no time to rebrief the pilots, and most important in my estimation was that a delay could

Lieutenant Gutherless' C-47, 92d Troop Carrier Squadron, received extensive damage on the 27 December 1944 Bastogne mission. Photo *top* shows flak damage to elevator and fin. Photo in middle shows flak damage to elevator. Photo *bottom* shows hole in lower rear of fuselage by unexploded 88mm shell.
— Courtesy: Gutherless

make us miss our fighter protection. This was not expected to be a difficult mission, however, as we knew that another group had gone into Bastogne the day before on the same route we were briefed to fly, and they had experienced no enemy action of consequence. We discussed the situation briefly and I said "We'll go as planned."

When Young arrived at the C-47 with the sick copilot, a standby copilot from the 91st Squadron was already in his seat. Colonel Young was not needed.

At 1010 1st Lt. Paul Foynes, operations, received a call from Lt. Col. Jack Neale's A-3 section, wing headquarters. He was given the same information and advice that Kaplan had received earlier. The new flight route toward Bastogne was described with grid coordinates on the 1:50,000 scale map, but the crews had different, larger scale maps without grids. Foynes forwarded the instructions to the control tower at once. There was not enough time to convert the grid coordinates to geographic coordinates and also brief the crews on a new flight route without delaying the mission for at least two more hours. Just as the new course was being plotted amid the roar of a hundred Pratt & Whitney engines, the first tug and glider lifted off. At the far end of the runway, Colonel Young and Father John M. Whelan, the group chaplain, stood side by side watching the aircraft climb out. As each element flew over, Father Whelan made the sign of the cross.

Why the 50th Wing headquarters' A-2 and A-3 sections transmitted the route change data to the 439th Group at different times is inexplicable. The wing's resume and diary for December 1944 makes no mention of it. The following is from the resume:

> The increased action of the enemy on the Western Front caused reactions of paramount importance in all phases of intelligence work. The tactical missions accomplished during the month in support of the 101st Airborne Division necessitated a keener observation of the enemy's progress and concentrated fire in the great counterattack, as well as his *anticipated* moves and flak positions. The priority of such information held precedence over all other functions during the period the missions were run. Another unanswered question is why 50th Wing headquarters did not delay the mission until the new flight route could be established.

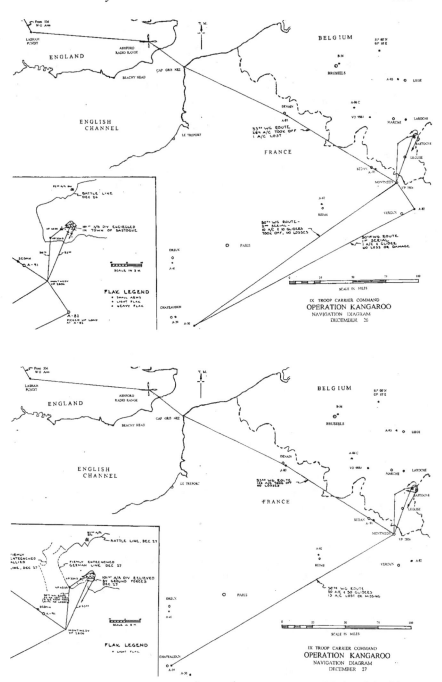

— Source for maps courtesy National Archives

*   *   *   *

The 101st Airborne Division was getting its messages promptly the morning of the 27th, but those pertaining to the Troop Carrier mission caused some confusion. At Neufchateau, Colonel Phinney (VIII Corps G-4) called Colonel Kohls at 0923 stating that the glider mission was canceled. Seven minutes later Phinney called again to declare that it was still on schedule. The division's G-4 responded that the 101st was set up to receive whatever came.

Regardless of the corridor established into Bastogne by the 4th Armored Division, and the resupplies brought in by the 26th Infantry Division during the night and morning, the 101st Division was eager for more ammunition, and on the morning of the 27th, Colonel Kohls' retrieval units were again on alert at the landing zone and at the drop zone.

Takeoff

Engine starts began at 1015 and the ground crews inserted the tow ropes' ring-plugs in tugs and gliders while the pilots tested their tow release mechanisms. Ten minutes later the radio clearance for take-offs was given and the first element of two C-47s received a green light from the control tower. The "go light" signals would be flashed to subsequent elements at about thirty-second intervals.

In the lead of the 91st Squadron's thirteen planes, Capt. William M. Sammons, with copilot 1st Lt. Boleslaw Sienkiewicz, eased the throttles forward until the tow rope was taut, then plunged them full forward. In the glider, gathering speed, Capt. Richard K. Fort allowed the tail to raise and guided the CG-4A toward the center of the runway to line up directly behind Sammons' C-47. A low rumble resonated up from the wheels through the landing gear struts to the drum-like glider cabin. As the wheels spun faster, the bumps from the concrete pavement joints became a staccato until Fort eased the control column back to lift off at about 75 MPH indicated airspeed.*

---

* Takeoff airspeed for the CG-4A was prescribed as 15 MPH indicated airspeed (IAS) higher than the stalling speed, estimated for the glider at its particular gross weight. At the design gross weight of 7,500 pounds, the stalling speed was approximately 60 MPH. On this mission, the glider gross weights averaged over 7,000 pounds (empty weight of 3,750 pounds plus one pilot and equipment at 250 pounds and about 3,100 pounds of ammunition).

Above: The crew of *Ain't Miss-behavin,* 94th Troop Carrier Squadron, shot down on Bastogne glider mission, 27 December 1944. *From left* pilot Capt. Ernest Turner, copilot 2d Lt. Keistitis J. Narbutas and radio operator S/Sgt. Richard C. Whitehurst. Crew chief T/Sgt. John E. Douglas (not in photo) was in aid station for treatment of wounds.

— Courtesy: Hoskins/Young

Below: CG-4A glider landed by 2d Lt. Mack Striplin, 93d Squadron, 439th Troop Carrier Group, 27 December 1944. Ammunition being unloaded by 101st Division troops and soldiers from all black 969th Field Artillery Battalion of Maj. Gen. Troy H. Middleton's VIII Corps. His units arrived early hours of 27th.

— Courtesy: US Army (from Devlin)

Then the only sound came from the slipstream. Fort held the glider at about twenty feet over the runway until the tow plane lifted off at 120 MPH. While climbing, Sammons made a gentle turn to a 60 degree heading toward the first IP at Montmedy, 210 miles away. After reaching 2,500 feet, he set his airspeed at 125 MPH. The ETA at the Bastogne LZ was 1230.

Capt. Thomas Corrigan, operations officer of the 92d Squadron, began his takeoff at 1030 with glider pilot 1st Lt. Herbert B. Bailey, Jr., on tow. The eight planes and gliders of the 92d were off within three minutes and climbing.

The next to take off were the twelve C-47s of the 93d Squadron with Capt. Fred O. Brauer, acting operations officer, in the lead. The first four towed glider pilots of the 92d, in formation positions 22 to 25. The next eight glider pilots were from the 93d Squadron.

With engines running, the four C-47s of the 94th Squadron were ready when Capt. Jake Cratty, in formation position No. 34, and 1st Lt. Phillip C. Hecker, No. 35, were flashed the green light at 1039. One minute later, 1st Lt. Ernest Turner lifted off with 2d Lt. Albert S. Barton on tow. Turner was not aware that the glider carried four surgeons as well as ammunition. Barton's glider was chalk-marked No. 36 as was Turner's C-47, which also had painted on each side of its nose *"Ain't Miss-behavin."* The four tow planes of the 94th Squadron were off the runway and climbing at 1043.

The thirteen tow planes from the 440th Group were positioned last in line for takeoffs. The first eight were from the 95th Squadron with Capt. Wilton C. Smith in the lead aircraft. His copilot was 2d Lt. A. A. Calderwood and his navigator was Michael A. Whitfill. F/O Richard W. Blake, from the 93d Squadron, satisfied that he and his glider (Chalk No. 38) were ready, wondered why his tow plane did not move. Captain Smith delayed his takeoff for almost ten minutes until it was determined whether or not some of the last twelve gliders were loaded properly. When the gliders were ready to roll, Smith eased his throttles forward at 1052. He was immediately followed by the other seven planes of his squadron.

The departure of the 96th Squadron, led by 1st Lt. Ernest O. Foster, was also delayed. The C-47 slated to fly in right echelon (47th position) to Foster developed engine problems. The pilot, 1st Lt. Albert S. Jalkut, taxied the plane off the right side of the runway. Its glider, to be flown by F/O Clifton H. Kiser, had to be towed onto the right shoulder of the runway.

Waiting on the entrance taxiway in the first alternate tow plane, 1st Lt. Kent Maynard was waved onto the runway. Kiser's glider was towed back and hooked up to Maynard's C-47 some five minutes after Foster's flight of four planes and gliders were on their way. Maynard's takeoff was at 1057, thirty-two minutes after the first plane of the 91st Squadron left the runway and five minutes after his flight leader. Like those well ahead of him, his navigator, F/O Roderick MacDougall, set the flight course on an ENE heading (68 degrees). Cliff Kiser was Tail-end Charlie.

En Route

Because the planes headed directly toward the Montmedy IP after taking off, rather than forming up in a close formation around Chateaudun before proceeding, the sky train was stretched out for sixty miles. Closing up to standard separation distances, the train would shrink to a still-impressive length of nearly eight miles. The catch-up was a challenge for tow plane pilots, progressively more difficult toward the rear of the formation. As the first serial, the 91st Squadron, set off at 125 MPH, the trailing aircraft would have to fly at airspeeds up to 150 MPH to move up in formation, provided that closure rates were orderly. Such airspeeds were not a problem for the glider pilots because at a gross weight of 7,500 pounds, the permissible airspeed for the CG-4A was 150 MPH. But C-47 pilots were always concerned about their engines when a loaded glider was on tow, and each engine had its limits.

When Captain Sammons turned north at the Montmedy IP at 1206, his thirteen C-47s had closed up their formation. Captain Corrigan, leading his 92d Squadron, was about two miles (one minute) behind Sammons. The first eight of Captain Brauer's 93d Squadron had closed up to Brauer, who was over three miles back in line. But the flight leader of his last four planes, Capt. Edward Nachowitz, was lagging behind, worried that engine problems could develop if he increased his airspeed. Also, elements of the 95th and 96th squadrons had not closed up from the rear.

It was still a long, irregularly spaced-out formation behind Sammons at the IP beyond Neufchateau, when he began the turn to the northeast heading (52 degrees) toward Bastogne at 1220. As each of the two-plane elements passed west of Neufchateau, the ten-minute red warning lights flashed from the tugs to their respective gliders.

"The flight was smooth and uneventful until the Neufchateau IP" was a typical comment made by glider pilots in their debriefings. However some in the 92d and 93d squadrons had more to report. As they neared Neufchateau, about three miles to the right, they had a good view of the town from 1,500 feet. Suddenly they saw "tremendous explosions in the town with fires raging afterwards." (Later at Bastogne, the glider pilots had their curiosity satisfied. Neufchateau, they were told, had been dive bombed by jet-propelled planes.)

Glider pilot 2d Lt. Albert S. Pacetta was anticipating the ten-minute signal when he saw the explosions in Neufchateau. He was in 24th formation position, on tow behind 1st Lt. Crawford D. Kinney, from Hampden, Maine, and copilot 2d Lt. Harrel R. Sullivan. Without a navigator, Kinney was obliged to trail directly behind the 93d Squadron leader, Captain Brauer, who was guided by his navigator, 2d Lt. Michael Zubritsky. Nearing Neufchateau, Kinney pulled his folded route overlay chart from his pocket to verify when to tell his crew chief, T/Sgt. John Young, to flash the red light to Pacetta. He had written the instructions on the chart during the briefing, "Red — 10 min, White — 1 min, Green — cut." Later, after Kinney returned to Chateaudun, he wrote the following about the 27 December mission in his diary:

> After a two hour delay we got off with our gliders at 10:30 A.M. It's a beautiful day and smooth. We were supposed to pick up our fighter cover on the IP at Montmedy. They never showed. As we turned for the final run in I knew we were in for it! I looked at Sullivan and he looked at me. Ahead there was a solid wall of flak bursting. They had our altitude cold.

What they saw was antiaircraft fire from 88mm and 20mm guns located five miles ahead in woods east of Ramagne. The German batteries, slightly left of the flight path, had yet to zero in as the leading elements of the 91st Squadron flew by, although they had started firing at the formation from almost a head on position. Beyond the range of those batteries, it was nine miles to the Bastogne LZ, over more German gunners who were ready and waiting!

The Approaches

The location intended for glider releases was near the small village of Savy, about one mile northwest of the 101st Airborne Division headquarters (in the Belgian military barracks at Bastogne). At the time, a schoolhouse in Savy was the headquarters of the 321st Glider Field Artillery Battalion. Capt. Joseph K. Perkins, from Homosassa, Florida, battalion S-2 officer, was in a good position to watch the action, which he recalled forty-one years later:

> The day is remembered as if it were yesterday, as no "show" I have seen, or ever will see, compares to this spectacle, and this includes the armada off the beaches on D-Day. Nothing compares to seeing those fellows march headlong through that intense flak . . . I picked them up when they were about four miles away (20-20 vision), and could see the flak like sparklers around the formations. Several tows were hit and went down along with their gliders.

91st Squadron

The thirteen tugs and gliders of the 91st Squadron flew through the first barrage of flak without serious damage and headed directly for the LZ located north of Bastogne. Instead of descending to 600 feet, as prescribed by the 50th Wing (Field Order No. 3), Sammons continued on at 1,500 feet with Fort on tow. The last two miles of the approach to the cutoff point near Savy were directly over terrain held by the 101st Division. However, at their altitude, the tow planes and gliders were still targets for the German batteries located outside the defensive perimeter.

Glider pilot Dick Fort did not fully realize how fortunate he was to be in the lead of the formation until after he landed. As he approached Savy, he saw no panel or smoke markers to designate the LZ. But he recognized Bastogne, which he verified with his GSGS map. He saw gliders from the previous day's mission still in the LZ, and decided to land in an adjacent field. He cut off at 1228 before seeing the green light and made a 90-degree turn right, while reducing his speed, toward Bastogne. Over the town, he turned left on a base leg pattern and then left again onto his final approach. He settled in fast and landed on the frozen snow-covered field. His brakes and nose skids had little effect in the snow.

After jumping out of the glider, he paused to look west. "The sky was thick with air bursts" — it reminded him of "a black summer storm." He soon learned that he had landed directly west of Savy, an excellent location for unloading the ammunition without moving the glider.

As F/O Duke F. Jarvis watched his tow plane for the green light, he saw Fort's glider cut loose. About the same time there were two flak bursts, one on the right of Jarvis' tow plane and the other to his own immediate left. Without hesitation, he released and followed Fort, as did 2d Lt. Morris A. Gans who described it in his debriefing report:

> Saw gliders in field and same time saw lead glider cut make steep right turn, number two glider cut almost immediately. I received green light and allowed No. 2 glider to get past me, then I cut, made a steep right turn. Visibility poor as sun was then straight ahead. Followed gliders 1 & 2 in. Noticed airspeed about 85 MPH landed, hit low wire fence, tore off right wheel.

F/O Claude A. "Chuck" Berry, from San Antonio, Texas, was flying on Gans' right wing as he saw the first two gliders cut loose from their tow ropes and make sharp right turns. Berry released his glider only a moment after Gans' cutoff so that his "spacing would be so as not to collide with any other gliders in the air at the time." There was reason for his concern over that first sharp turn at high speed. In the next glider, fifth in position, 2d Lt. Howard M. Loomis was spared serious damage. He reported later that his "glider was hit by another glider, damaging tail section, but made successful landing." F/O Eric B. "Case" Rafter followed in his undamaged glider.

It continued to be "follow the leader" to the landings directly northwest of Bastogne, near Savy. F/O Robert R. Bisch landed close to the village cemetery. Next to land were F/O Charles A. Balfour, 2d Lt. Delford T. Summers, F/O Ivan Burton, 2d Lt. Roy W. Sample, and F/O John W. Burnett. Their gliders had all been hit by small-arms fire but Burnett's, in twelfth position, was also hit by flak, which went through his tail section. Burnett could still control the glider, but there were some nervous moments immediately after he cut loose as he heard machine-gun bullets piercing his right wing. After making a quick dive, he glided in for a safe landing.

In No. 13 position, 2d Lt. Joseph Fry's C-47 flew directly into the black puff that had damaged Burnett's glider. At the time, radio operator S/Sgt. William M. Connarn had his head in the astrodome viewing the formation fore and aft, and saw the close flak bursts. Just seconds later he and others of the crews fully realized how badly their plane had been crippled. Flak had penetrated the underside of the fuselage causing a fire that was sweeping along the bottom of the plane. The fire and smoke began breaking through the floor near the cargo door and then spread forward. Fry gave the order to bail out while he locked the plane on automatic pilot set for straight ahead. He decided not to release the glider and left the cutoff option up to the glider pilot.

The smoke was thick at the rear door when Connarn and crew chief S/Sgt. Alex Jakush jumped. Copilot 2d Lt. George N. Weisfeld raced back through the flames and bailed out on the run. After Fry adjusted his parachute, he looked back from the cockpit and realized the flames in the cabin were too intense to get through, and he chose to exit by the hatch on the nose of the plane. Out of the hatch, he crawled on top of the fuselage past the astrodome to a position even with the wing's trailing edge. Afraid the plane would blow up any moment, Fry jumped head first off the fuselage, hitting the rudder and hanging there momentarily. He was so dazed for the next few seconds that he did not remember pulling the rip cord on his parachute. When the plane broke in two, he managed to slip off the rudder and float down. He had to jiggle his chute to keep from landing on the burning plane. He came down ¾ of a mile north of the LZ.

Glider pilot 2d Lt. John D. Hill, from Abilene, Texas, on the end of the 350-foot tow rope behind Fry, watched in awe as smoke and flames billowed back around his tug ship. He stayed on tow even after he saw three parachutes drift under his glider. The optimism he had felt when he had "volunteered" for the mission, and had managed to maintain when he was assigned to glider No. 13, was vaporizing as he followed his burning tug, waiting to see the pilot jump before cutting his glider loose. He was still two miles from the LZ when the tow plane seemed ready to explode. He hit the release lever. At 1,500 feet, he was able to pick out a landing field. After veering 45 degrees right, he turned 90 degrees left and landed safely west of Bastogne.

92d Squadron

Capt. Thomas Corrigan, from Kansas City, Kansas, in the lead of the 92d Squadron, was less than one-half mile directly behind Fry's plane when it was hit. On tow behind him was 1st Lt. Herbert Bailey, Jr. When Corrigan began making turns to the left and then to the right, Bailey, who might have missed Fry's inferno, thought it was "as if the formation leader was lost."

Bailey hastily made his cutoff well before reaching Savy and made a 90-degree right turn as small-arms fire continued to hit his glider. Over Bastogne, he banked left and turned 180 degrees toward the northwest, into the wind. He landed directly south and within 500 yards of Savy.

Seeing the smoke pots which marked the LZ about one-half mile on his right, 2d Lt. Frank J. Hynes released his glider and followed a glide pattern similar to Bailey's. But to land nearer to the smoke signals, he dived the glider and landed too fast. His landing gear was wiped out on the frozen, plowed field just west of Bastogne.

F/O Joseph V. Monks was also anxious to get down. After cutting loose, he made a diving turn to the right and then a full circle to the left. He landed toward the southeast, downwind, on a ridge south of Bastogne.

On his first mission, F/O Edward T. Carrell was disturbed about the approach altitude of 1,500 feet. It was "too high above the 600 feet we were briefed for." He set a left hand glide pattern of turns and landed downwind about one mile northwest of Bastogne, near Savy.

The 92d Squadron formation's arrival was neither orderly nor routine. As Corrigan varied his headings during the final approach to avoid the intense flak which continued after Fry's C-47 was hit, succeeding elements did not follow. The third element flew left, north of the designated (70–80-degree heading) approach. Glider pilot 2d Lt. Bless R. Rusk was towed toward the LZ at 100 degrees. He cut his glider about one mile west of Bastogne and made a diving turn to the right. He circled around the town, making left turns, and flew a base leg over the southeast side of town. He landed at 1230, directly southwest of Bastogne.

F/O Frank S. Armi, Jr., was on his first mission. His tow plane flew through the heavy flak until they were over the tram railway directly west of Bastogne, and then he cut off. After a right turn, he glided over the town making left 180-degree turns and headed northwest. Rather than continue beyond the LZ, he turned right and made a crosswind landing directly south of Savy.

The last element of the 92d Squadron was not as fortunate. New to the squadron, F/O Kenneth W. Avery was unacquainted with his tow pilot, 1st Lt. Harry G. Gutherless, flying in position No. 20. On their right wing, in echelon, 1st Lt. Martin H. Skolnick was towing F/O Jack D. Hancock, also a squadron newcomer.

At the turn around the IP, Avery could see the nineteen C-47s and CG-4As ahead, a formation three miles long. Near Remagne, many got obscured by flak bursts. The accuracy of the German AA batteries improved and Avery was horrified to see his tow plane's tail section hit by flak, but relieved when the tug continued on course past Remagne. Two minutes later the next flak barrage struck more intensely and suddenly the C-47's left aileron had a large hole in it. The tow plane dived and immediately pulled back up to level flight as smoke from the left engine ominously poured back. Avery's body tensed as he expected to be cut loose at any moment — before reaching the LZ. Gutherless descended to about 600 feet before Avery saw the LZ smoke signals ahead on the right. He could make it if he flew on without sharp turns. He landed "downwind about one and one-half miles from the edge of town," safely but not as close to the LZ as he intended.

Gutherless' C-47, sporting the name "*Gazette 'R'*" on its nose, was severely damaged. Yet Gutherless was able to make a sharp left turn and follow his comrades back out by holding a lower altitude all the way to Chateaudun. Forty-two years later, Harry Gutherless, from North Platte, Nebraska, wrote about the damage to his plane and his experience. His regular crew members were on leave and he did not recall the makeup crew.

> We ran into heavy flak and small arms fire. My Crew Chief said he counted over 1,000 holes in the C-47 and quit counting. We had a control cable shot in two, aileron half off, elevator with a hole two guys could stand up in, a cylinder head shot away, one 88 through the tail cone (that didn't explode), and all kinds of smaller hits. One burst came through the pilot's side, hit the

rudder pedal, another hit my chest pack parachute — my radio operator said at one time he couldn't see our glider for flak between us and him. Why he [the glider pilot] didn't cut the tow rope I'll never know.

Avery wrote in his debriefing report, "I want to acknowledge the highest praise and valor to my tow pilot, Lt. Gutherless, for continuing to tow me into the LZ when his ship was at a point of crashing."

When Jack Hancock saw that his tow plane was critically damaged about two minutes out from the LZ, he prepared for the worst. The C-47 began a rapid descent, but he did not get alarmed until it pulled up in a nose-high attitude, apparently out of control. Recognizing that his glider, staying on tow, could only add to the problem, Hancock released at about 1,200 feet.

Skolnick lost full control of his C-47 when flak exploded through the tail section and severed the elevator cables. He could not keep the plane in level flight even with the help of copilot Second Lieutenant Fredrickson adjusting the trim tabs. As they descended, Skolnick ordered the crew, "Everyone back, to the rear of the ship." Fredrickson ran back close behind crew chief Sergeant Gonzales and radio operator Sergeant Vaughn to the rear of the cabin. The weight shift helped Skolnick control the descent of the plane with the throttles. Heading for a clear area, after passing directly over Savy, he came in faster than intended. The C-47 hit the ground and bounced thirty feet in the air, hit down again and spun around. It rested at the south edge of the LZ, north of Bastogne. Martin Skolnick was the only crew member injured, and only slightly at that.

To reach the LZ over two miles away, Hancock glided straight ahead behind the descending tow plane. To avoid the C-47 during its crash landing, Hancock veered right and landed downwind about a thousand feet away.

Meanwhile tow planes of the 91st and 92d squadrons were climbing back out of the foray after making 180-degree left turns. Not all could keep to the exact formation they had followed on the approach. In twelfth position, 1st Lt. James F. Hurley made an evasive turn to avoid Fry's flaming plane close behind on his left. Corrigan, following Fry, quickly made a sharp turn and climbed out fast on the reverse heading.

Above: The rear of Capt. Wilton C. Smith's C-47, 95th Squadron, shot down 27 December while towing a C-47 glider toward Bastogne. Only one of five crew members survived, navigator 1st Lt. Michael A. Whitfill, who parachuted and was captured.

— Courtesy: Imperial War Museum, London (from Benfield)

Below: Glider LZ north of Bastogne, 27 December 1944. Village of Savy is at lower left. At least 33 gliders can be seen. Those showing definite landing marks in the snow arrived on the 27th. Those without probably landed on the 26th. Parallel crash landing tracks (lower center) were made by 1st Lt. Martin H. Skolnick's C-47, 92d Squadron.

— Courtesy: Smithsonian Institution

Recalling the flight thirty-nine years later, Thomas Corrigan wrote from Colorado Springs, Colorado, "on the way out a C-47 cut across the flight path, right ahead of me filling my windshield." As he watched the plane fly on, it appeared that "a bevy of 88mm flak bursts blew him out of the sky." He saw parachutes but could not watch long enough to verify how many jumped, or if their chutes opened.

All four of the crew bailed out: radio operator S/Sgt. Harry A. Kortas, crew chief S/Sgt. Marion B. McCarter, copilot 2d Lt. Lester J. Epstein and Lieutenant Hurley last. Unfortunately they came down in German-held territory.

Other 91st Squadron planes were not spared from flak damage either on the way in or out. But only one, in tenth position, returned with crew members injured. Copilot 2d Lt. Robert F. Schillinger was hit in the foot (he lost three toes) and crew chief T/Sgt. Harry T. Cullen received "minor" shrapnel wounds in the back and head.

93d Squadron

Capt. Fred O. Brauer was troubled by the formation he was leading. It consisted of three flights with four tow planes and gliders in each. When he reached the IP, near Neufchateau, not all of the flights in his formation had moved up behind him. Back in chalk position No. 30, Capt. Edward Nachowitz, flight leader of the last two elements, was intensely concerned about overtaxing his engines and was varying his airspeeds. Therefore he had not closed up in the formation, even though Brauer had held his airspeeds lower than he had wanted to. When Brauer turned toward Bastogne, he was about one mile behind the 92d Squadron formation, knowing that his own formation was still inordinately stretched out.

It was about 1225 when Brauer saw the intense Remagne flak barrage ahead that pounded the 92d Squadron. And in the distance, the sky around the 91st Squadron was black with antiaircraft bursts. Later, in 1986, he wrote from Missoula, Montana, "We were briefed to fly right up the railroad to Bastogne. Also, we were briefed to go in at 600 to 900 feet, depending on the surface fog conditions." Therefore, rather than trail the first two squadrons, and avoid the fire they were flying through, Brauer veered right directly toward Bastogne.*

Brauer led the 93d Squadron at about a 70-degree magnetic heading on a route which passed but one mile north of Morhet and Sibret. The 88mm, 20mm, and machine-gun fire from around the two towns, inaccurate at first, increased. Brauer recalled his view of the action after he passed Sibret. About a mile away to the left, he saw an 88 fire a clip and score a direct hit on a P-47 flying high cover for the airborne mission. Next they were firing at his formation. As he approached Bastogne, he saw the last C-47 of the 92d (Skolnick's) "come in from my left and really going like hell and crash land at the far end of the LZ."

Before giving the one-minute signal for the glider to cut off, Brauer made turns to head easterly toward Bastogne at 1500 feet above the ground. Glider pilot F/O Hollis W. Jones (92d Squadron) was hit as they passed north of Sibret. A 20mm round zipped through the floor in front of his pilot seat, through his flak suit, and out the top of the glider's nose compartment. Only slightly injured, he headed east toward Bastogne, cut loose and dived at high speed to make a 360-degree turn and land in the LZ about one-half mile northwest of town.

F/O David H. Sill, from Mobile, Alabama, flying the glider in right echelon next to Jones, was encouraged when the "foggy and hazy conditions cleared considerably at the LZ" — and the antiaircraft fire was behind him. Like Jones, after the release, his glide pattern was a 360-degree turn to lose altitude, and finally he turned "180 degrees to the left and landed to the west about a quarter mile from the Div. C.P." **

---

* Not every preflight briefing on the morning of the 27th conveyed identical information. Some made use of 440th Group pilot reports from the 26 December missions advising an approach closer to the railroad than to the route shown on the 50th Wing's route overlay. The railroad referred to was actually the tram railway which, for over eight miles, was an east-west line through Chenogne and Senonchamps, not the railroad between Libramont and Bastogne. A flight route along the tram railway would approach Bastogne from the west, more than one mile south of Savy.

** The glider pilots expected approaches to be between 600 and 900 feet, subject to ceiling and visibility conditions. Why they came in much higher is both understandable and debatable. Tow plane pilots and crews were inclined to prefer high approaches which would allow more time for maneuvering and parachuting if the

In 1986, Crawford Kinney recalled his experience by quoting from his diary. He was flying directly behind Fred Brauer: "Soon we were in the middle of it. With my flak suit, helmet, and chute on, I was sweating. I turned the radio up so I couldn't hear the noise. [The] BBC was playing 'Spring Will Be A Little Late This Year.' How true, I thought."

At the end of Kinney's tow rope was 2d Lt. Albert S. Pacetta who reported later, "About 10 miles from the LZ I began to see very intense and accurate AA fire from directly below and also from the right." F/O Elisha B. Page, also from the 92d Squadron, was about a fourth of a mile behind Pacetta. It was obvious to Page that the German gunners had found the 1,500-foot altitude of their targets. In a 1985 letter from Lynnwood, Washington, E. B. Page described how close the flak was. "I was number 25 in a formation of 50 when I went through the flak, it was all at the right elevation (right off the wing tips, it seemed), they hadn't cross bracketed yet and I got through."

It was two miles to the LZ when Pacetta and Page passed out of the enemy's range. Pacetta cut his glider "over the LZ at 1229 hours, made two 180 degree turns and landed right on the NW edge of town in a good field." Page "cut loose right over the NW edge of Bastogne, made a big 360 degree turn and landed in a field directly below my point of release." Actually he landed at the west edge of town, along the north side of the Bastogne-Marche highway. His glider was across the road and about one hundred yards from the brick pile where the pathfinders had their Eureka radar beacon set up.

*   *   *   *

The second flight of the 93d Squadron did not follow directly behind Brauer's flight from the IP. Capt. James B. Murrow, Jr., led his flight north to Libramont before turning northeast. Murrow, his copilot 2d Lt. Robert A. Nelson, and navigator 1st Lt. William E.

---

plane was critically damaged. The glider pilots objected to the high approach as evidenced by comments many made in debriefing reports. The glider, without an automatic pilot, was not easy to exit even after it had been trimmed for a glide. The glider pilots considered their parachutes as better protection from small-arms fire, even flak, and as cushions on those hard plywood seats. In fact the Waco CG-4A pilots' seats were designed for a parachute as the cushion.

Alexander, plotted their route left of the Libramont-Bastogne railroad with both Morhet and Sibret also on their right. Two minutes after setting their heading, German batteries on their left came into action. On tow behind Murrow's C-47, 2d Lt. Charles R. Brema saw the AA fire coming "from the railroad junction south of Bras" and from the "woods ½ mile east of Remagne." In right echelon tow position, 1st Lt. Lloyd G. Clark, from Belleville, Illinois, located the German guns at "2–3 mi north of RR running from Libramont to Bastogne." The enemy fire was both "intense and accurate." They flew through it as did the element that followed, but soon they all learned that they were still within the range of German batteries around Morhet and Sibret.

In 28th position, copilot 1st Lt. Robert L. Sakrison had a good view of Morhet ahead, over a mile south of their projected flight path. It was the route they were briefed to take, and he wrote about it in a 1986 letter from Waunakee, Wisconsin: "The briefing on December 27th stated that the previous day's mission had run into heavy flak from the north of that route and therefore, we were to fly a direct path from IP 3345 to Bastogne with the expectation of avoiding that fire." He recalled that they were "flying over an open area with woods to the north and a wooded ridge to the south. I could clearly see several AA batteries operating along that ridge. We were looking at them at an angle of about 45 degrees from level." With 1st Lt. Byron Myers piloting, Sakrison had time to spot the guns from Morhet to Sibret.

In right echelon to Myers and Sakrison, 1st Lt. Oscar B. Pedersen and his copilot, 2d Lt. Robert G. O'Keeffe, encountered another sight — in addition to flak — that captured their attention. For glider pilot 2d Lt. Mack Striplin, the sight momentarily distracted him from the flak. As he described in his interrogation report, "During the run in I noticed about 5 or 6 phenomena, which I had never seen before and which I cannot explain. They looked like silvery balls of tin foil, in the shape of a star and were about a foot wide. They seemed to float through the air. I did not see them rising from the ground, nor did I see any bursts. They just suddenly appeared before me. They did not dissipate; they passed out of my sight and I do not know what eventually happened to them. All of them were quite close to our flight. The nearest passed about 12 feet from my glider." *

* * * *

The four gliders of Captain Murrow's flight (Chalk Nos. 26–29) landed close to Bastogne with ammunition intact. Brema saw the smoke signals on the LZ before Murrow's tow plane gave him the green light. His glide pattern was a "270 degrees approach to the left," to land directly west of Bastogne along the Bastogne-Marche highway and tram railway. The glider's right wing was damaged by a tree and the outer panel of the left wing was sheared off by a telephone pole adjacent to the railway. Unhurt, Brema and his load of ammunition lay three-fourths of a mile west of the pathfinder's radar beacon on the brick pile.

On tow in right echelon, Clark did not notice any light signals from 1st Lt. James D. Beebe's tow ship, but the smoke signals on the ground marked his LZ. He flew a "360 degree approach to the left" and landed in a field close to ten or twelve other gliders. When F/O Frank W. Andux saw smoke pots on the LZ, he saw no reason to wait for light signals from Myers' tow plane. His glider pattern was similar to Brema's, with the exception of the latter's encounter with trees and poles. Striplin made a 360-degree approach to the left downwind. He foresaw no problem. "From the air the field looked good, but as soon as I put wheels down I saw a large ditch, which I hopped over. I also plowed through a barbed wire fence with iron posts and found it necessary to dig the left wing to stop, due to snow on the ground. [An] Artillery unit unloaded [the] glider." His performance was described as a "Special Delivery" in *Stars and Stripes*, 1 February 1945:

Flying a CG-4A glider loaded with 155mm. shells, 2/Lt. Mack

---

* Such a tactic was employed during the Normandy invasion. On the night of 5–6 June, some RAF Stirling bombers directly preceded the first IX Troop Carrier Command's formations which carried paratroops of the 101st Airborne Division. At a point over the English Channel, west of the Cherbourg Peninsula, the bombers flew on south while the troop carriers turned east toward the DZs near Ste. Mère-Église. The bombers dropped large quantities of "window" foil strips, which appeared on radar much as a formation of aircraft would, confusing the enemy. Why "windows" were dropped over this formation, and who did so, has not been ascertained.

Striplin, 439th Troop Carrier pilot from McKinney, Tex., cut loose from his C-47 tow ship over besieged Bastogne to deliver the howitzer ammo in the nick of time.

With flak bursting on all sides and one wing and the tail hit, there wasn't time to find the perfect spot. The brakes didn't hold on the snow-covered slope and a 15-foot drop-off loomed ahead.

Striplin had sufficient speed and soared right off the embankment, landed again, plowed through a steel fence and came to [a] stop ten yards from the Command Post, where he learned shells were being rationed and only 20 rounds remained.

* * * *

The gliders in the third and last flight of the 93d Squadron did not reach Bastogne. Flight leader Capt. Edward Nachowitz was still worried about his engines after turning on the approach from the IP, and was still lagging behind the formation. During the entire flight from Chateaudun, Nachowitz had intently watched the engine instruments, frequently adjusting the throttles and propeller pitch. In his crew were copilot 1st Lt. Edward L. Williams, navigator 1st Lt. Robert W. Nelson, crew chief T/Sgt. Vernon J. Brasch and radio operator Sgt. John M. McCann.

From the IP, Nachowitz set his heading toward Bastogne at 68 degrees. While passing Morhet, glider pilot F/O Harold K. Russell followed Nachowitz's C-47 as it began a gentle right turn. Russell assumed that it was to avoid the increasing flak directly ahead. Soon into the turn, he saw the severe damage to the left midsection of the fuselage and the left wing of his tow plane. Seconds later, the left center of the fuselage and the wing blossomed into flames. Russell hit his tow release at the same instant the tow rope was cut loose from the tail of the C-47. While trimming the glider as the airspeed decreased, he saw two of the C-47 crew bail out and their parachutes float back under his glider. Distracted while going into a right turn, he did not see any others jump. Just then machine fire pierced the glider's nose compartment and one of the bullets passed through his right thigh. He dove the glider steeply and turned eastward, then reduced his speed and headed toward a field just beyond Sibret, still in German territory. Only a minute before he landed (at 1230), two more of Nachowitz's crew parachuted onto the outskirts of Sibret.

The last one out of the plane was navigator Nelson, whose parachute failed to open, a "streamer." Nachowitz stayed with the plane as it descended in a gradual right turn to crash and burn south of the railroad at Sibret.

In the squadron, "Nack" was well known for his pragmatism and foresight. On this mission to Bastogne, his thoughtful preparations likely helped save the lives of three of his crew. His careful approach began before the Normandy invasion, when the 439th Troop Carrier Group carried paratroopers of the 101st Airborne Division during the night of June 5–6. He was just as thorough prior to the September Operation MARKET mission into Holland. Again, for the Bastogne mission, Nachowitz personally supervised additions to his C-47's interior. He had installed a series of grab ropes which would help crew members quickly reach the rear door exit to bail out, despite the airplane's attitude. He spent considerable time and effort drilling his crew in jump procedures, taking a personal interest in their safety.

On this mission to Bastogne, it is not known if Nachowitz left his pilot's seat. If he did, it was probably after the last crew member jumped, and by the time he would have reached the rear door, the plane could have been too low, or the fire in the cabin too intense for his escape. Even the pilots who flew close behind did not know what happened.

The pilots of the other three tow planes in Nachowitz's flight were maintaining a proper formation at 120 MPH and 900 feet behind him as they approached Morhet. Heading directly toward Bastogne (at 68 degrees magnetic, 61 degrees true) they "saw no indication of the plane being hit." On Nachowitz's right wing, 1st Lt. David L. Reidy and copilot 2d Lt. Earle R. Stimson saw their flight leader's C-47 start "what seemed to be a normal, slow turn to the right." In the C-47 directly behind Nachowitz were Capt. Randell E. Ladd and his copilot 1st Lt. Robert G. Ramsey. Ramsey's interrogations stated:

> Our flight of four planes was approximately three fourths of a mile behind the column at the time the accident occurred. The flak puffs were extremely numerous and the column ahead disappeared into them. Captain Nachowitz started a twenty degree turn to the right and I assumed that he was attempting to avoid the bursts ahead. The turn increased and three chutes came out

together and shortly afterwards a fourth one. About the same time the tow plane cut the glider. The plane was making a rather skidding and jerking turn. I noticed a flash and smoke from the right engine. The plane was still turning to the right, but was diving at about forty degrees when it hit the ground and exploded, just south of the railroad at Sibret.

Flying the fourth tow plane position in the flight, 1st Lt. Max F. Stripling also assumed that Nachowitz "was attempting to avoid intensive flak immediately ahead." Then he saw the tow rope drop from the C-47, "three chutes came out together, followed by a fourth. . . . the first three chutes opened properly and I saw them land in and on the outskirts of the town of Sibret. I saw the parachute of the fourth jumper come out of its pack but it did not blossom out. It merely trailed a streamer. I saw the body of the jumper strike the ground near Sibret."

Stripling's copilot, 1st Lt. Robert E. Stout, had become a close friend of Nachowitz earlier in England when they lived together in the same Nissen hut. Knowing how meticulously "Nack" planned ahead for a mission, it was an agonizing disappointment for Stout when a fifth parachute failed to appear.

* * * *

Before glider pilot Russell was cut loose from Nachowitz's tow plane, F/O Paul O. Hower, on tow behind Reidy, thought that the flight leader's right turn was appropriate — better than flying straight ahead through that heavy flak. His approval vanished when he saw Russell's glider release and his tow rope drop loose from his tow plane. Reflexively he hit his release lever and climbed over the twisting tow rope as it fell back under his glider. Reidy banked his C-47 steeper on a right turn and headed back out. Hower wrote about his experience forty-two years later:

> I wanted to land as fast as possible to get away from that flak. I didn't understand why I couldn't land until I looked at my airspeed which was 150 miles per hour. I finally landed OK with my right wing tip on the ground. I saw two other gliders land about 400 yards away. A big gun (88?) started shooting at them while they were still rolling. The first two rounds missed but there were direct hits after that. I saw both glider pilots blown

out of their gliders and was surprised to learn later that they weren't killed or seriously wounded. While I was pinned down by small arms fire for about 30 minutes, a half-track came out of the woods and captured them. I considered going to them and surrender because my position was untenable. While I was trying to make up my mind the half track left. A few minutes later I was captured. The glider pilots I saw from a distance were George Juneau and Frank Hobart.

Flight Officers George W. Juneau, Frank W. Hobart, and Hower had been classmates during glider pilot training, were together in the 93d Squadron, and together became prisoners of the Germans.

In a letter from Everett, Washington, Juneau vividly recalled those moments before the gliders were released. He saw two damaged C-47s returning from Bastogne. The first "was hit about where Nachowitz was hit. He pulled up in a half roll and went in almost straight, which wasn't more than 300 feet off of our left wing. Close behind (300-400 feet) was another C-47 with its left engine smoking badly." Undoubtedly the first plane was Lieutenant Hurley's in the 91st Squadron, well after all of the crew had parachuted. The second one was that flown by Lieutenant Gutherless in the 92d Squadron.

Now, with the wall of flak before them, came a moment of decision in the second element of Nachowitz's flight. After seeing Russell's and Hower's gliders cut off by their tow planes, they weighed the better decision — to go through that deadly flak or release the gliders? Juneau's glider was released by Ladd's tow plane and Hobart's glider was cut off by Stripling's ship, one after the other. Freed of their gliders, the C-47s turned sharply right and headed back toward Chateaudun, surely regretting the possible capture of the pilots they had released.

✻   ✻   ✻   ✻

94th Squadron

The 94th Troop Carrier Squadron had only one flight of four C-47s (Chalk Nos. 34–37) on the mission towing glider pilots from the 93d Squadron. Flight leader Capt. Jacob "Jake" W. Cratty, from Los Altos Hills, California, had named his plane *"PIEDISH 'D',"* D for dog. His navigator was 1st Lt. Joseph P. Sullivan who had been promoted on Christmas, two days before. As they passed Neufchateau, Sullivan signaled crew chief T/Sgt. Robert F. Foote when to flash the ten-minute red light to glider pilot F/O Narcisco M. Monje. After they turned at the IP toward Bastogne, it was soon clear that to follow Nachowitz's flight would be disastrous. Cratty decided to fly a heading shown on the 50th Wing's route overlay chart, well north of the one taken by the 93d Squadron. He would follow the route used by the 91st and 92d squadrons which were then over three miles ahead.

On Cratty's right wing, 1st Lt. Philip C. Hecker was flying a C-47 named *"Gruesome"* (1st Lt. William Grieb's plane until this mission) with F/O Herbert W. Ballinger flying the glider on tow. The crew chief was S/Sgt. Staley T. Trzaska and the radio operator was Sgt. George M. Haug. It was the third combat mission for Hecker and his copilot, 2d Lt. Allen B. Simmons. He recalled in a 1986 letter from Minnetonka, Minnesota, that this one was unlike either of the other two. In his log book, he wrote later in reference to Cratty not following Nachowitz's flight, "Really used evasive action for once." Still they were targets of German guns on their left. Ballinger wrote from Wichita, Kansas, in 1990, that he clearly remembered the flak around his tow ship and "praying that they would not hit it." But they did. Another burst put holes in the nose of his glider. Yet another round hit the rear of the glider but did not damage the controls. A four-foot section of *Gruesome*'s left aileron was ripped out by flak but the damage was not serious; he could still control the craft.

Cratty and Hecker towed their gliders directly toward the LZ near Savy, when both Monje and Ballinger were given the white light, and a minute later, the green. To Ballinger, the terrain did not match his map and he held on a little longer, but released before being cut off. Monje made a 270-degree approach to the left and landed without incident. Ballinger's glide pattern was a 360-degree approach to the left to land in the LZ, a field already crowded with fifteen other gliders. He made a good landing, but because of obstacles — fences, other gliders, and the snow — he hit a sturdy fence post which promptly stopped the glider and tore the fabric off its nose.

The third C-47 in Cratty's flight was Capt. Ernest Turner's *Ain't Miss-behavin.* Flying in the second element directly behind Cratty, Turner began a gradual letdown from the 1,500-foot altitude about seven miles before the LZ. A minute or so later a hail of .50-caliber machine-gun fire from a wooded area east of Remagne hit the descending plane. He remembered it later in a letter from Colonia, New Jersey: "I was hit and hit good in the left engine. I lost power in the left engine. The fire [bullets] then proceeded into the right engine. I then lost the right engine and was forced to release the glider at this time. I was able to glide and land wheels up on a farm in the Bastogne area. I don't know what happened to my glider but I figured that if I was able to glide into the area that he would have also." At the time, Turner was unaware that his glider, piloted by 2d Lt. Albert S. Barton, carried a team of four surgeons — undoubtedly the most vital "cargo" needed by the 101st Division at Bastogne. With Turner were copilot 2d Lt. Keistutis "Casey" J. Narbutas, crew chief T/Sgt. John E. Douglas and radio operator Sgt. Richard C. Whitehurst.

When Turner's right engine began convulsing, he shouted to Casey and the crew members behind him, "Bail out and quick!" It was evident that they had little altitude and for the crew to jump, Turner had to hold the plane as high as possible during the descent. Casey ignored the order, "Hell no, I'm staying." It was an excellent wheels-up landing, considering the vicious bouncing and uncontrollable skidding over the frozen, snow-covered ground. Turner and Narbutas quickly climbed out of their seats and headed back to the cabin, and were surprised to see Douglas and Whitehurst unfastening their seat belts — they too had elected to stay. Ernie Turner wrote, "I was mad but happy. If they had jumped they might have been captured. When I asked them why they hadn't obeyed my orders to jump, their explanation was that if I was going to stay with the ship that they were going to stay with me. Some crew! The best!"

Ain't Miss-behavin came to rest on its belly about 2,000 feet west of Savy, one and a half miles northwest of Bastogne, near the Bastogne-Hemroulle road. It was not long after Turner and his crew were out of the plane that Capt. Joseph Perkins and others from the 321st Glider Field Artillery Battalion headquarters arrived from Savy to greet them.

Since this was his first combat mission, Albert Barton was determined to stay on tow as long as possible, even after they met the 20mm and small-arms fire between Libramont and Remagne. After passing the woods east of Remagne, he saw heavy black smoke trailing from the tow plane's left engine. As they continued on through flak bursts, the tow pilot decreased the airspeed to 120 MPH and began descending. When the airspeed dropped to under 100 MPH, his tow rope dropped loose and he hit the release lever. He noted the time to be 1234, and glanced back at his passengers who were unaware of the seriousness of the situation. Barton needed distance; he cranked the elevator trim for 80 MPH and headed straight out. He saw that the two gliders ahead were lower but he could not locate the LZ. He decided he could reach a field, although smaller than he liked, which would require a slight S turn for a straight-in approach. When he was about 500 feet above the ground, he slowed the glider to 60 MPH and made an easily controlled smooth landing and rolled up to stop near some trees. The field was almost two miles west of Bastogne, just south of the Bastogne-Flamierge road, and less than a mile inside the 101st Division's perimeter.

Six men of the 101st Airborne Division quickly met the glider and moments later escorted the four surgeons to the closest field aid station, but not until the passengers shook Barton's hand and thanked him for a good ride!

Next to arrive was Colonel Kohls, who pulled up in a jeep to see what was in the glider and thank Barton for the much needed 155mm ammunition. It was decided that the glider was too close to enemy positions and the jeep was used to pull it about three-quarters of a mile closer to Bastogne before it was unloaded.

Years later, through correspondence with the author, Barton learned who his tow pilot was that day. From Dallas Center, Iowa, he wrote to Ernest Turner, "If you had cut me off ten seconds earlier I wouldn't have been able to fly out of that black curtain of AA. It's been 42 years later now, but Ernie, I surely want to thank you for those ten seconds." Turner was elated to learn that the glider reached Bastogne safely.

＊　＊　＊　＊

Flying on Turner's right were 1st Lt. Ray Leonard with copilot 2d Lt. Carl E. George. The crew chief was S/Sgt. O. C. Knapp, and the radio operator was Sgt. Frank Mendola. Leonard wrote from Casper, Wyoming, in 1986, "I was following the map too closely — just following others in the formation." It was apparent that Turner's C-47 was seriously damaged, with both engines smoking, before the tow rope was released. Leonard, with F/O J. B. Hardin on tow, continued on the heading behind Hecker. Hardin saw the ground smoke at the LZ before he was given the green light from his tug. After the cut, it was a fast 270-degree approach to the left to land in a field near many other gliders. He landed fast, hitting two fences and a ditch which wiped out his landing gear. It was a good landing in that there was no injury or damage to pilot or ammunition. The time was 1234 hours.

Elisha Page had landed his glider only four minutes earlier along the Bastogne-Marche highway. Leaving his glider, he had only a 100-yard walk to the brick pile where the Eureka transmitter was in operation. There a captain of the 101st Airborne Division was making notes and counting the gliders. As they watched Hardin's glider land, the captain said, "Well, thirty-three . . . I guess that's all."

Page objected, "There must be a mistake, we had fifty gliders." The captain's confidence in his count wasn't shaken. He was positive. And he was correct. Hardin was the last glider pilot to land within the defensive perimeter of the 101st Airborne Division.

✻ ✻ ✻ ✻

95th Squadron

The last thirteen tow planes and gliders did not get near the 101st Airborne's perimeter around Bastogne. When the leader of the 440th Group, Capt. Wilton C. Smith, with F/O Richard W. Blake (93d Squadron) on tow, turned around the Neufchateau IP, he was almost two miles behind Captain Cratty's flight of four tugs and gliders. After flying through the heavy flak near Remagne and Nimbermont, Smith followed Cratty's flight around the VP for the final approach toward the LZ. Navigator 1st Lt. Michael A. Whitfill was standing behind Smith and copilot 2d Lt. A. A. Calderwood when they saw flak clouds virtually obscure the planes ahead. Smith said he was going to turn left before the final approach to avoid being zeroed in on, as would surely happen if he continued to follow the formation ahead.

He headed northeast, intending to later swing back to a southeasterly direction toward the LZ at Savy. A minute later there was a flak burst close to the nose of the aircraft, so close that Whitfill saw "a flash of flame in the cockpit area" which burned his hand slightly. He could not tell if the pilot or copilot were injured. Recognizing that the plane's controls were damaged, Smith instructed Whitfill to go back and tell crew chief T/Sgt. Floyd E. McConnel and radio operator S/Sgt. Anthony T. Piriano to get their parachutes on "in case we have to get out." As Whitfill put on his parachute, he looked beyond the two crew members and saw a bedroll lying in the aisle between them and the rear door. He ran back, picked it up and tossed it out of the way to the rear of the cabin. Then another explosion, with "a flash of flame again," knocked him to the cabin floor. In the fall, his left hand was pinned under him by the heavy metal staves of his flak jacket, which was very painful. He lost no time in ripping off the jacket. Lying on the floor, he could not see into the cockpit because the door was almost closed. The plane was pitched into a high position and seemed to be nearing a stalling attitude when Whitfill yelled at McConnel and Piriano to come back and get out of the plane. He got up and grabbed the door frame with his left hand and the rip cord with his right and swung outside the door, keeping one foot on the bottom of the door and placing his other foot against the side of the fuselage to kick himself away from the plane, still in a nose high position. His descent seemed to take an eternity as the tracer bullets flew past him. He saw other planes flying overhead, but he did not see the demise of his plane. After the stall, it dove to the ground before any of the other crew members could jump out. It crashed directly south of the intersection of two roads about one and one-half miles west-northwest of Flamierge.

When glider pilot "Dick" Blake, from Belvidere, Illinois, saw his tow plane hit around the nose, he prepared to release his glider, but he was cut loose before he could hit the lever. At almost 1,500 feet with Bastogne nowhere in sight, he could only continue straight ahead and land in a field about one and one-half miles northwest of Flamierge, among German ground forces. As they fired at the glider, he ran away from it and "hit the dirt" before it exploded. He had no choice but to surrender.

Flying in right echelon to Smith, 1st Lt. Stanley J. Zdun was towing 2d Lt. Raymond D. Schott of the 94th Squadron. Northwest of Flamierge, Zdun's C-47 was mortally damaged. Before the plane went down, crew chief S/Sgt. Telio A. Puccio and radio operator Sgt. William F. Spearing were able to parachute out of the plane, only to be captured quickly after they hit the ground. Zdun and his copilot, F/O Seymour R. Belinky, were lost in their burning plane that crashed directly north of Salle, one and a half miles north of Flamierge.

Schott landed his glider some 600 yards west of where his tow plane crashed. Nothing was recorded officially about his experience — he was reported as killed in action.

* * * *

In the second element, trailing Smith was 1st Lt. Robert J. Webb, who had also been promoted on Christmas Day. His new silver bar and a pay raise were farthest from his mind as he listened to the radio intercom. Zdun advised Webb to alter the course and altitude and to prepare his crew for bailout. Soon after that, Zdun's burning C-47 dropped from the formation. Webb took the advice in time and veered his plane right to an easterly heading before his ship was critically damaged. He followed his crew out the rear door behind radio operator S/Sgt. Tony F. Ferrucci, crew chief T/Sgt. Lawerence P. Marsh, and copilot 2d Lt. Wilson W. Scott, Jr. The glider had been released by Scott when Webb gave the order for the crew to jump. F/OHenry H. Nowell quickly cut the tow rope loose from his glider and looked ahead for a field.

* * * *

Henry Nowell was an "old-timer" in gliders who also had previous military experience. At age eighteen, his flight training began while he was a sophomore at North Carolina State University. With a private pilot license, he enlisted in the Army Air Corps on 7 November 1940. Not eligible for pilot training, he completed Air Mechanics School in the fall of 1941 and was assigned at Langley Field, Virginia, to a B-25 medium bomb group which was transferred to Westover Field, Massachusetts, for submarine patrol duties in December 1941. Early in 1942 when the glider pilot program was offered to those with pilot licenses, Nowell was one of the first to enlist. After completing the earliest training class at 29 Palms, California, and a subsequent assignment as an instructor at Fort Sumner, New Mexico, he became one of the first to receive the new rank of flight officer (Serial No. T-275), on 7 December 1942. Nowell arrived in England in May 1944 and was assigned to the 94th Troop

Carrier Squadron. The mission to Bastogne bore little resemblance to the one he flew as a copilot on the morning of 6 June 1944, when his glider carried troops to an LZ near Ste. Mère-Église, Normandy.

Years later, in 1975, Nowell wrote about his unique experiences near Bastogne: "The tracers of machine gun fire were like screen wire, and 35mm phosphorus flak got my tow ship on the 2nd shot. . . . After the tow plane started down I pulled up to gain as much altitude as possible, to land as far away from the source of fire as I could. The fire became so intense, however, that I put the glider into the steepest glide hoping to feign a hit, and pulled out at 175 miles per hour, 25 miles above 'red-line' speed, pushing the glider into the snow of a plowed field at 125 MPH. As a result of a hit on one brake cable, I crashed into the only Belgian telephone pole in the field made of concrete." He hid in the woods southeast of Frenet to avoid capture. Late the next day he arrived on foot at an outpost of the 101st Division.

* * * *

Pilot 2d Lt. Luther J. "Rock" Lizana and copilot 2d Lt. George E. Morrow barely had time to cringe as the first three C-47s of their flight were shot down in front of them. In his interrogation report, Lizana wrote that their plane was hit while following the flight on a course of about 40 degrees. When he felt his glider cut loose, he assumed the tow rope had been severed by flak. Lizana noted in his report that the time was 1230. As he made a climbing left turn, he saw that the oil pressure was down and the temperature was up in his left engine. On the return heading, he flew toward flak and descended while cutting off the left engine and feathering the propeller. By then the plane was too low for the crew to jump safely and he tried to climb, but it was difficult to even fly level on one engine. The fuel gauges were out and they could not guess how much gasoline was left in the tanks.

In the vicinity of Verdun as radio operator Private First Class Berkowitz tuned in on the Paris Range, they were able to get their bearings and set a heading. Then the right engine stopped. Morrow restarted it by switching to a different fuel tank but that cost them altitude. Lizana found he could not clear the surrounding hills and decided to make a forced landing near the town of Varness. Although there was no fire, he told crew chief Sgt. Hunter F. Lohr to watch for it. The field was small and Lizana stopped by holding one brake and letting the plane make a ninety-degree turn up a little hill before stopping. They were safely back in friendly territory, unlike the glider pilot they had towed.

Near Flamierge, F/O Pershing Y. Carlson was preparing to hit the tow release to cut his glider from Lizana's C-47 as he saw the left engine hit by flak. Just then an explosion ripped the bottom of the glider's nose section out from under his feet and a piece of shrapnel wounded him in the right ankle. Carlson reached up and cut the glider free from his damaged tug. Then there was another flak burst above the glider. It shattered the steel cross bar over his head, sending slivers of metal into his neck, shoulders and back. A third burst set the rear of the glider on fire. He was then too low to consider parachuting, so he decided to "ride her on in and hope for the best." After the glider crash-landed, the wooden floorboards caught fire and the entire fuselage filled with smoke. Carlson got out of the glider, but in his haste he forgot to unfasten his parachute. When he hit the ground, it spilled out all around him. He unhooked the harness and started running away from the smoking glider toward a wooded area when caution told him to drop down and crawl before the 105mm shells in his glider exploded — and explode they did, just after he dropped to the ground. Carlson avoided capture until 3 January 1945.

*   *   *   *

The second four-tow plane-glider flight of the 95th Squadron was headed by Capt. David G. Morton (Chalk No. 42) who held a close position behind Smith's flight. When Morton realized his plane was so badly damaged by flak that there was no chance for a crash landing, he gave the order to copilot F/O Virgil W. Anderson and navigator 2d Lt. Wilmer S. Weber to bail out along with radio operator S/Sgt. Robert I. Fine and crew chief T/Sgt. Worth B. White. They all followed the order except White, who was unable to jump out of the burning C-47 as it plunged to the ground with Morton still in the pilot's seat. The plane crashed within 300 yards south of where Smith's aircraft had crashed some moments earlier. Glider pilot 2d Lt. George S. Freeman was injured during his landing near Flamierge, and was quickly captured.

To 1st Lt. James P. Harper and copilot 2d Lt. Donald M. Smaltz, flying right echelon to Morton, the enemy's antiaircraft fire was too dense and accurate to fly through. After seeing three C-47s and CG-4As being shot down directly ahead, Harper decided that it would be folly to follow Morton. He told Smaltz to cut off the glider's tow rope and then he made a left turn and headed back out. Crew chief Sgt. Lafette J. Nerren and radio operator S/Sgt. Joseph R. Buckner were partially relieved when they felt their plane lurch forward as the glider was released. During Harper's steep climbing left turn, the sounds of flak bursts and shrapnel piercing the aircraft stopped. It was not until after they landed back at Chateaudun, about 1430, that Nerren and Buckner learned, to their surprise, that their glider had not been released over the Bastogne LZ!

F/O Velton J. Brewer's glider was cut off from Harper's tow ship after they had passed Nimbermont and Remagne, over the north edge of the large Bois des Hales de Magery forest. From 1,500 feet, he had sufficient time to pick a place to land south of Tillet about eight miles west of Bastogne. When he was captured, he was furious with the Germans, who took his two bottles of Scotch. For a pilot, losing both liberty *and* good liquor on the same day must have been a hard blow.

1st Lt. Harvey D. Rideout was another pilot in the 95th Squadron (with Webb and Harper) who had been promoted on 25 December. Flying less than a mile directly behind flight leader Captain Morton, Rideout concluded that it was almost suicidal for them to continue through the flak barrage and told his copilot, 2d Lt. Robert C. Mauck, "Cut off the glider, now."

To the rear of the pilot's cockpit, crew chief Cpl. John R. Boyes and radio operator S/Sgt. Benjamin M. Layton were alerted to watch for any critical damage to their plane. Rideout quickly banked left through the initial flak and headed back on a fast climb.

After suddenly being cut off from Rideout's tow plane, 2d Lt. Douglas C. Bloomfield surely knew he could not glide beyond the forest east of Remagne. He turned his glider to the left and after a 270-degree pattern, landed near Nimbermont. In the next glider, F/O Emmett M. Avery, from Richmond, Virginia, was not far behind and landed in a cornfield close to Bloomfield. (They were recent arrivals in the 94th Squadron and had been tent mates with Velton Brewer.) Avery and Bloomfield joined up on the ground and under enemy fire ran for a hay stack and began firing back with their rifles for over two hours. Then they decided to run to a large forest about 400 yards away where they were separated.

As copilot 2d Lt. Earl E. Putnam released Avery's glider, 1st Lt. William H. Lewis was struggling to control his C-47 as he watched the four planes well up ahead of him go down. His plane's hydraulic system had been knocked out, severing the flight controls, and the plane was on fire. He gave the bailout order before the uncontrollable aircraft began a slow left turn. First out were radio operator Sgt. George D. Mehling, Jr., and crew chief S/Sgt. Wilmeth H. Harvey. Next to jump, at intervals, were navigator 1st Lt. Richard P. Umhoeffer, Putnam, and Lewis. All were promptly captured.

96th Squadron

The last five tow planes, from the 96th Squadron, followed the route of the 95th, and at the IP began a descent from 1,000 feet. F/O Francis L. "Bud" Carroll's glider was behind the lead plane piloted by 1st Lt. Ernest O. Foster and 2d Lt. Lewis F. Green. In Foster's C-47 were navigator 1st Lt. Michael H. Brady, crew chief T/Sgt. Theodore W. Mrenosco and radio operator S/Sgt. Robert E. Thompson.

Carroll wrote from Las Vegas, Nevada, about this, his one mission. Near the last IP, they began a slow descent when the formation ahead entered what appeared to be a "thick black cloud." He was "momentarily stunned" by what he saw — "Four C-47s shot down out of the preceding eight-plane formation!" According to his midnight briefing, twelve hours earlier, this had not been expected. The glider missions on the 26th had not encountered such enemy fire over the same route. "They had no problems except only some scattered small arms fire." Now, on this mission, "I realized what a difference a day makes." The German guns concentrated on his tow ship, Foster's C-47. "I saw the vertical stabilizer hit with a flash before I heard the blast from the flak shell which exploded only 350 feet ahead. At the moment, my tug was taking evasive action by making a slight turn to the left." After the C-47 was hit in the empennage, it immediately made a sharp 90-degree turn left. Unable to know how seriously the tow ship was damaged, Carroll continued on tow and followed it out of the flak, and then hit the release lever. The C-47 flew on but Carroll was too concerned with looking for a place to land to notice whether or not any parachutes emerged from his tow plane.

In the C-47, Thompson was standing up in the astrodome

ready to give the glider the cutoff light when he saw his plane's rudder blown away. Next came a flak burst in the cockpit. When Mrenosco saw Brady fall to the floor dead, he rushed forward and found that Foster and Green, still in their seats, were also dead. He quickly grabbed two parachutes from the stretcher racks, one for Thompson and one for himself. They ran back through the cabin as blue flames licked up through the cracks in the floor, got to the door and jumped. As Thompson hit the ground, he caught a glimpse of his plane as it disappeared over a ridge. After Carroll cut loose, he saw two other gliders landing close together in formation (Bloomfield's and Avery's). His first thought was to follow them, but at his low altitude, he decided to find his own landing field. He saw a farm house with a clear field next to it and after setting his glide pattern, he came under fire, the first machine-gun tracers passing in front of him. Then they came up through the glider and one burst completely destroyed the empty copilot seat. Spotting the enemy gunner's position, which was camouflaged with hay and snow, he turned and pulled up quickly, barely clearing some high tension lines. When he nosed down to increase his airspeed, the next bullets creased his leg, pierced his hip and tore into his thigh. He leveled the glider for landing before he passed out. Some Germans pulled him out of the wrecked CG-4A as he momentarily gained consciousness. When he came to the second time, he was in an open truck on a stretcher.

The formation in Foster's flight was not in elements of two, echeloned, as originally planned back in Chateaudun. There was no tug-glider flying in right echelon (Chalk No. 47) to Foster. Cliff Kizer's glider, towed by Kent Maynard's C-47, was now in last position well back of the flight formation. Directly behind Foster, the second element, led by 1st Lt. Billy J. Green and copilot 2d Lt. John S. Bachman, was experiencing engine problems and began dropping back while F/O Gerald "Jerry" D. Knott remained on tow.

At the time, crew chief T/Sgt. Albert J. Sabon was in the cockpit standing behind Green and Bachman. Sabon recalled, "At the loss of the engine, I raced back into the cargo area and looked out to see if there was any smoke or fire. Seeing none, I thought the gas tank must have been hit. Green decided to feather the propeller rather than risk switching the fuel tanks."

After Knott's glider was cut off, Green put the C-47 into a dive to put out the fire he thought was in his right engine. He turned the plane around and headed out at a low altitude. Nine days later, on 5

January 1945, Green wrote his buddy, 2d Lt. Lester A. May, from a field hospital near Sedan, France: "Everything was going fine until I caught another burst in my rear setting me on fire again and at the same time caught one in my left engine which knocked it out. I feathered it and cut all my switches and started to set it down."

When an unusual sound came from the rear of the plane, Sabon turned to look back and saw an explosion. He ran up to Green, shouting, "We're on fire!" Green barked, "Bail out!" They were too low to parachute and the fire in the rear deterred passage to the door, but Sabon went through the flames and jumped out the rear door. Falling upside down, he pulled the rip cord and the chute came up between his legs and opened just before he hit the trees. He did not remember falling through the trees or how he hit the ground.

Radio operator Sgt. Robert J. Slaughter decided not to jump through the fire and joined Green and Bachman in the cockpit to get out through the front escape hatch. When Bachman bailed out, they were too low for his parachute to open. He was critically injured with a fractured skull and a broken leg. Green continued to glide his C-47 over the densely forested areas, about four miles northeast of Libramont. He had no choice but to come down in the woods. He remembered the noise of the tree tops slapping the nose of his plane and when he came to, he was pinned in the front wreckage of the plane. The rear of the aircraft was still burning. His left foot was tightly wedged under the rudder pedal. With Slaughter's help, he got his foot out of his shoe and flying boot. The boot had saved his ankle. After Green and Slaughter crawled out of the wreckage, the fire continued to devour the fuselage. The wings had been ripped off by the trees as he landed. Green suffered a broken back and cuts on his head.

The next tow plane and glider (Chalk No. 49) were shot down by the AA batteries before reaching Nimbermont and Remagne. Crew chief T/Sgt. Robert Londo was standing just behind 1st Lt. Alan J. Maeder and 2d Lt. Lee W. Dahman when they were hit by flak at almost the same time the flight leader Foster's C-47 was set on fire over two miles ahead. Dahman released the glider. A high explosive shell hit the fire extinguisher box between the pilot and copilot, knocking Sergeant Londo back against the door. A fraction of a second later, a burst of .30-caliber bullets came up through the floor exactly where he had been standing before the explosion. With the cockpit aflame, Maeder yelled, "All bail out." Londo kicked out the cargo door and jumped. Radio operator Cpl. Robert L. Holste was the second and last of the crew to bail out. Both Londo and Holste parachuted into an area held by American forces southwest of Nimbermont, near Ste. Marie. Before he bailed out, Holste was injured and seriously burned. Londo was luckier, as he was the first tow plane crew member of the 440th Group to return to his 96th Squadron.

On tow behind Maeder's C-47, Pete Houck watched in amazement as they followed the leading flights of the 95th Squadron heading into what "looked like a black curtain." Some tow planes "dropped like golden balls of fire." Houck knew that Jerry Knott, a classmate during glider pilot training days, was in the glider on his left (behind Green). As he was towed past Knott's tug at about 1,000 feet altitude, the C-47 appeared to be going down as the right propeller slowed to a halt.

Houck's CG-4A was also hit by ground fire before he was cut off from Maeder's C-47. Flak exploded under the glider's nose and Houck was burned and shaken. His flight controls were undamaged and he managed to release the tow rope and make a landing on a slope next to some farm buildings, some distance from Flamierge. Before he was captured, he saw American fighter planes fly overhead strafing German AA batteries. In pain, he sadly pondered how different it could have been if fighter escort planes had been there when the Troop Carrier formation needed them.

In his debriefing report, 1st Lt. Frederic W. Wheeler wrote about the approach after turning at the IP. "We were flying the #4 position in the glider formation, and Billy J. Green was piloting ship #42-100977 in the #3 position on Wednesday, 27 December 1944. Lt. Green was having trouble keeping his ship in formation. At 1225 hours, we passed him almost five miles from the LZ. In passing I did not notice that there was anything wrong with his plane." It was in the vicinity of Remagne where Wheeler's plane and its glider overtook Green's while flying on a 40-degree heading toward Flamierge.

Wheeler continued to follow the flight courses set by the 95th Squadron, thinking he was headed toward the Bastogne LZ. In the flak, navigation took second place to survival, and there was little time available to make course corrections while trying to avoid obliteration. In Wheeler's crew were copilot 2d Lt. Wendell Ebright, navigator F/O Charles Long (also a glider pilot), crew chief T/Sgt. William F. Byrd, and radio operator Sergeant Eliason. Wendell Ebright wrote about their experiences forty-two years later from Lyons, Kansas. "We thought we had reached the LZ or at least 'safe' territory." He recalled that after the glider released, Wheeler made a diving turn to the right toward a wooded area, when a severe jerk reminded him that he had not dropped the tow rope. As they were skimming over the tree tops, a blast from German artillery jolted the plane but there was no serious damage. They returned intact to their airfield at Orleans.

Glider pilot F/O Meyer "Mike" Sheff could see the "antiaircraft fire and smoke in the far distance" as his tow plane (Wheeler's) "headed straight for it." In letters from New York City in 1985 and 1986, Sheff recalled, "I thought to myself — 'Oh God I'm not going to make it!'" He debated whether to release his glider before they reached the flak clouds. He thought about the blood plasma in the glider as well as the ammunition. But as soon as they "reached the outer rim" of AA fire, his tow plane "released the tow rope" while banking sharply to the right. He scanned the snow-covered landscape for a landing field, which was difficult to find because the area was heavily wooded. After he spotted an open area, he concentrated on his landing pattern. Although he heard the "popping sounds tearing through the fabric" of his glider, he did not notice that a bullet, or flak fragment, had pierced his left forearm. After he landed, he raced back and jumped out the door to have a look around and decide what he should do. Bullets shot past him, kicking up the snow at a lively rate. He raised his right arm in surrender. Sheff wrote, "I suspect the tow pilot did me a favor by releasing me where he did, or was it luck — or fate?"

No one was more Tail-end Charlie than Kent Maynard, flying the last tow plane on the mission. So late in taking off, Maynard never caught up to close the formation. After turning at the Neufchateau IP, he and his glider were almost two miles behind Wheeler's C-47 and Sheff's CG-4A. Following the leaders, Maynard flew on a heading of about 50 degrees. Nearly three miles beyond Remagne, Cliff Kizer's glider was released near the winding tram railway, six miles directly west of Bastogne and four miles southwest of Flamierge. F/O Roderick MacDougall, navigator on Maynard's C-47, recalled later that the glider was cut off before they reached the railway. Maynard turned back after crossing the railway and MacDougall wrote, "Never did see anything that looked like Bastogne during our right hand turn."

While flying over the northern area of the large forest, Bois des Hales de Magery, Kizer was gripped with apprehension — there was no apparent landing site should his plane be hit. His glider was released directly after they cleared the forest. Although the snow-covered terrain ahead was not wooded, his choices of landing fields were limited because of obstructions, pole lines, fences, and the railroad. During his landing, he was severely injured, primarily in his back and legs, and was easily taken prisoner. His captors carried him away on a stretcher.

❖　❖　❖　❖

Losses

Thirty-six tow planes returned to their airfields in France: thirty-two from the 439th Group at Chateaudun and four from the 440th Group at Orleans. Among the crew reports, accounts of the mission within some squadrons were inconsistent with others, particularly in regard to flight routes they followed on the approaches toward Bastogne.

Captain Sammons' C-47 was the first of the eleven planes from the 91st Squadron that returned to Chateaudun. Although some of the crew members reported Fry's crash landing at the LZ, none could accurately describe where Hurley's plane crashed.

Gutherless' C-47 was the first from the 92d Squadron to arrive back at the Chateaudun airfield, and of all those from the 439th Group that returned, it sustained the heaviest damage. But it was classified in Category B condition — salvageable. Squadron leader Capt. Thomas Corrigan and glider pilot F/O Kenneth Avery recommended him for the Distinguished Flying Cross for towing his glider all the way to Bastogne even though his plane was severely damaged. He accepted the DFC but turned down the Purple Heart, which he later regretted.

1st Lt. Harry G. Gutherless, 92d Troop Carrier Squadron, receiving Distinguished Flying Cross for 27 December 1944 Bastogne mission, Chateaudun, France 1945.

— Courtesy: Gutherless

After eleven of Captain Brauer's flight of twelve planes from the 93d Squadron returned to Chateaudun, the crews were interrogated and their reports were quickly incorporated into the "FLASH REPORT NO. 1 FOR 27 December." It was sent from the commanding officer, 93d Troop Carrier Squadron, to the commanding officer, 439th Troop Carrier Group. The following is an excerpt:

> Eight C-47s towed their glider to the LZ area and they were properly released. One C-47 was apparently hit by flak and was seen to crash and explode south of the railroad tracks near the town of Sibret. The glider was cut there, but no observation was made as to where it landed. The altitude at release was 2,600 Ft. [900 feet over terrain] and the indicated air speed approximated 125 miles per hour. The other three gliders in the element of four, the destroyed C-47 being the leader, apparently mistook the situation and released at the same time. There was no observation of where they landed.

It should be noted that the most sensitive issue between tow plane pilots and glider pilots was the degree of emergency in a situation where the tow pilot is justified to release the glider. During combat, under heavy enemy fire, the tow pilots were certainly in a better position to decide whether both the tow ship and the glider would be in danger if the glider was not released. Another issue dealt with reporting which pilot actually hit the tow release first. The 93d Squadron's account of the glider releases was ostensively from interrogations of only the tow plane crews who returned immediately to their airfield. However, from letters written years later to the author by three glider pilots who were captured, the account differs. They all say they were cut off by their tow planes. MacDougall, Maynard's navigator, expected that theirs would be the last plane to return to the 440th airfield at Orleans. In 1987, he wrote the author that on the flight back, they overtook a C-47, on a course toward Reims, which they thought was seriously damaged because of its low airspeed. It was Wheeler's plane, but his copilot Ebright explained later to MacDougall that the damage to the plane was not serious enough to land at Reims; it was the last plane to return to Orleans.

From the time the tow planes from the 95th and 96th squadrons began returning to Orleans at 1430, almost all air and ground crews were on the airfield to greet them. They were dismayed to see only four of their thirteen planes return. The extent of damage to the surviving planes told the story. Don Orcutt, a flight leader in the 95th Squadron, described it in a letter from Seattle, Washington, in 1989: "Harper's aircraft was a flying wreck. Both main tires had been shot off and he landed on the bare wheels, losing one completely during the roll out. The fuselage and wings had been shredded by twenty millimeter and small arms fire. Rudder and elevator fabric was almost nonexistent. Fuel was leaking from the tanks. There were even holes in the propeller blades. It was a miracle that both engines continued to run. Rideout's aircraft was in much the same condition. Harper's airplane was relegated to the bone yard for salvage and Rideout's was repaired and returned to service."

The aircraft losses, by percentages, were the highest of any Troop Carrier mission in the ETO. Of the thirteen C-47s shot down, five were from the 439th Group and eight were from the 440th Group — a twenty-six percent loss. Seventeen CG-4A gliders, or thirty-four percent, did not reach the 101st Division's defensive perimeter at Bastogne.

From left on 8 February 1945 at airfield A-50, Orléans, France, 1st Lt. Armand D. Venezia, navigator, 98th Squadron; Sgt. Bob Bacon and another dog team handler, unidentified; S/Sgt. Hulen S. Dean (back to camera), unload dog sled teams from one of two C-47s, 98th Squadron, 440th Troop Carrier Group, that flew them from AY-14, Marseilles, France. Destined for the Ardennes, six teams arrived at AY-14 earlier in the day by Air Transport Command from Newfoundland.   — Courtesy: Lowden

24

The Quick and the Dead

IT WAS SOON AFTER MIDNIGHT on 27 December when a barely secure
ground route was established into Bastogne by the 4th Armored
Division. Immediately 260 of the most seriously wounded were sent
out by ambulances and trucks. During the rest of the morning, other
wounded were evacuated.

One of the wounded was a seven-year-old boy, André R. Meurisse, who had been injured on the morning of the 23d. Along with
other civilians, he and his parents had found refuge in the home of a
resident in Mande-Saint-Etienne, a town some three miles west of
Bastogne. Although the 327th Glider Infantry Regiment was deployed around the town, recognition panels had not been placed on
the ground. A flight of P-47s from the IX Fighter Command decided the area was another German "field target of opportunity" and
bombed the town. One bomb fragment came through the roof and
pierced André's right shoulder. He ran out of the house in a panic
but didn't realize he had been hit until he felt the pain and looked at
his bleeding shoulder. It was a serious wound, one that could cause
the loss of his right arm. A 327th medic arrived, stopped the bleeding and sent him to the 101st Division's aid station in Bastogne for
X-rays. From there, he was sent to the 501st Parachute Infantry
Regiment's aid station. For the next three days, André's father took

him back for antibiotic treatments (no penicillin was to be had) to ward off gangrene infection. On the morning of the 27th, André was evacuated along with the wounded from the 101st Division. The surgeons at the 107th Evacuation Hospital, Sedan, France, saved his right arm — and that he never forgot.

*   *   *   *

During the morning of the 27th, optimism reigned in Bastogne as units of Patton's Third Army rolled in from the south with resupplies. Even so, Lieutenant Colonel Kohls' G-4 retrieval teams were eagerly awaiting a glider train bringing in still more supplies. After the week-long siege, they wanted all the supplies they could get, whether they needed them or not. Kohls saw no reason to cancel the glider mission; they could always use more ammunition.

At 1225, the formation with gliders was spotted flying toward Savy through heavy flak and Lt. Col. H. W. O. Kinnard, McAuliffe's G-3, was puzzled. He had expected the formation to come from the southwest over the corridor which had been opened the night before.

Colonel Kinnard and members of his staff were out at the LZ to meet the glider pilots, asking them why they had come in from the west. The pilots knew only that from the west was where they had been told to come. Only then, at Bastogne, did they learn that a better approach had been advised by the 101st Airborne Division.

Lloyd Clark was told by a transportation corps major of the 101st Division, "You should have approached Bastogne as we suggested after those other gliders came in yesterday." And Colonel Kinnard told Frank Andux, "I sent word last night that the next resupply missions should come in by the southern route, not from the east." A captain of the 4th Armored Division, 704th Tank Destroyer Battalion, described to Narcisco Monje how his unit had cleared the route from the southwest all the way to Bastogne before 2300 of the 26th, and the favorable situation was immediately radioed back to his division.

*   *   *   *

Kenneth Avery had landed his glider west of Bastogne where Joseph Fry had parachuted close to his crashed C-47. Avery ran to the wreck as a jeep arrived and the two were driven to the division's aid station in Bastogne where Fry was treated for burns, as was his copilot, George Weisfeld, who arrived minutes later. William Connarn's parachute landing was near Alex Jakush, who had hurt his back when he hit the ground. They were taken directly to the aid station and it was determined that the back injury was minor. Martin Skolnick, who crash-landed his C-47 in the LZ, was treated for a wrenched back, head injuries, and possible internal injuries. The last to arrive at the station was John Douglas, who suffered a leg wound. He was from Ernie Turner's C-47. With the exception of Skolnick and Jakush, all were released for evacuation; some on the afternoon of the 27th and others on the morning of the 28th.

*   *   *   *

In the afternoon at 1315, Colonel Kohls instructed his units to send glider pilots to the 101st Airborne Division command post for assignment as guards over the evacuation of German prisoners. Most of the captured Germans were the 428 taken by the 53d Armored Infantry Division during the night. Also slated for evacuation were C-47 crews and remnants of other ground units that had been trapped with the 101st Airborne Division. There were sixty-seven on the Troop Carrier roster, twelve C-47 crew members and fifty-five glider pilots, twenty-two of which had landed on the 26th.

*   *   *   *

Mack Striplin was one of those who did not land directly in the LZ. At 1231, his glider was some thirty yards from a gun battery of the all black 969th Field Artillery Battalion of Maj. Gen. Troy H. Middleton's VIII Corps that had arrived during the early morning hours. (The 969th was the first segregated unit to take part in the Battle of the Bulge.) The 155mm ammunition carried on Striplin's glider was exactly what the battery needed and there was no delay in unloading it. He watched, satisfied, as the battery resumed firing on a German target.

When Striplin reported to the division command post, Colonel Kohls asked him to go with an artillery officer to the gliders that had not landed directly in the LZ to make sure that all of the primers had been recovered. It had been learned that some glider pilots had stashed them in what they considered to be the "safest" places in their CG-4As. After checking all the gliders, they were on the way back to Bastogne when their jeep was held up for one and a half hours while the Germans shelled the bridge. There were P-47s in the air, bombing and strafing enemy positions, and during one attack Striplin cringed as he watched one P-47 strafe an American battery. By the time they returned to Bastogne, the first convoys of trucks with glider pilots and German prisoners had departed.

It was about 1500 when the glider pilots were furnished weapons at the CP and taken to the stockade where the first twelve trucks were loaded with captured Germans. The truck convoys drove to Neufchateau, VIII Corps headquarters, where the glider pilots were relieved of their prisoners. It was fifteen more miles to Florenville where some of the men spent the night at the railroad station or in a hotel lobby. A few of them, together with C-47 crews, were quartered overnight at Neufchateau and driven to Florenville the next morning in time to board the 0900 train to Paris.

There was little sleep for those who spent another night at Bastogne, in either the Belgian Military Barracks or in a barn, as William Connarn did with the injured and medics from the 101st Airborne Division. The Luftwaffe was out in its usual force, bombing and strafing. Five German aircraft were destroyed that night by Northrop P-61 "Black Widows" of the 422d Night Fighter Squadron, 70th Fighter Wing of IX Tactical Air Command.

At 1230 on the 28th, another convoy left Bastogne with German prisoners guarded by evacuated American troops, including C-47 crew members and glider pilot Striplin. Radio operator Connarn was impressed by the battle debris along the road to Neufchateau. "I saw large numbers of German dead that had been killed when the 4th Armored Division broke through to relieve the pressure on Bastogne. The dead were either quite young or very old and didn't resemble first line troops." At Florenville, the Troop Carrier personnel were furnished with jeeps to take them fifty miles southeast to Luxembourg City where they were scheduled for a flight back to Chateaudun or Paris. After their arrival in Luxembourg City, about 1800, they were quartered for the night and were interrogated by the intelligence section of XII Tactical Air Command, Ninth Air Force. One G-2 lieutenant colonel was curious about the flight route and asked Striplin about it. He told Striplin, "I would like to know who passed out the information that flak was south of the railroad, because the fact of the matter was exactly the reverse." He was referring to the Libremont-Bastogne Railroad.

Early the next morning, Capt. Harold W. King, operations officer, and Capt. Russell Orthman, from the 94th Squadron, flew to Airfield A-97 near Luxembourg City to pick up the members of the 439th Group. Connarn, 91st Squadron; Fredrickson, Gonzales, and Vaughn, 92d Squadron; Turner, Narbutas, and Whitehurst, 94th Squadron. Striplin, 93d Squadron, was the only glider pilot there. They were flown to Le Bourget, Paris (Airfield A-54), and landed at 1600. After a stopover, they were flown to Chateaudun later on the 29th. Striplin missed the flight and did not return to the 439th Group until 1100 on 31 December.

Meanwhile some fifty-four glider pilots and three C-47 crew members (Fry, Douglas, and Weisfeld) were on a thirty-hour train ride to Paris via Metz, sixty miles southeast of Florenville, a trip of about 260 miles. After arriving in Paris on the 29th at 1230, some of the glider pilots demonstrated their individuality . . . or frequently alleged lack of discipline, depending on the observer. Some managed to find flights back to their airfields on the 29th. Others experienced fanciful problems finding flights from Le Bourget until the 30th and the 31st of December. On the 30th, a few took a train to Chartres, 50th Wing headquarters, where they were driven by jeeps to Chateaudun and Orleans. There were also the hitchhikers who returned at 1700, 31 December, in time for champagne at their squadron's New Year's Eve parties.

On the first day of January, the squadrons of the 439th and 440th groups began preparing a tentative list of names of MIAs. Through daily communications, they had been informed of the names of the C-47 crew members and glider pilots who were known to have survived the mission. By deduction, the others became Missing In Action. During the first week of January a few messages arrived with good news, but the long lists of the missing were hard to accept.

＊　　＊　　＊　　＊

It was on the way out from the Bastogne LZ that James Hurley's plane, from the 91st Squadron, was shot down. Hurley, Lester Epstein, Marion McCarter, and Harry Kortas bailed out over enemy territory. After hitting the ground, Hurley saw Kortas running and disappearing over the crest of a hill. All were captured except Epstein. Later in January, his body was found in a shallow grave not far from where the crew parachuted before the plane crashed.

Edward Nachowitz, 93d Squadron, perished in his plane when it crashed near Sibret. Three of his crew, Edward Williams, Vernon Brasch, and John McCann were captured after parachuting northwest of Sibret. Robert Nelson was killed when his parachute failed to open.

* * * *

Harold Russell, who had cut his glider off from Nachowitz's C-47, landed well beyond Sibret with a wound from small-arms fire in his right thigh. He limped out of the glider and realized he could not walk very far. With his holstered pistol and a carbine, he stood his ground while two men in undershirts and pants approached. Although they were armed, he thought at first they were civilians — until others in German uniforms came up behind them. Russell, who could understand German, was told that they would go to the command post before he could be taken to the aid station. During a courteous "name, rank and serial number" routine, his questioners were surprised when Russell took a can from his musette bag and sprinkled sulfa in his wound. They didn't seem to know what it was.

The aid station was in a farm house some 500 yards away. One-half of the house served as a communications office. When Russell arrived for treatment, he was relieved of his helmet, bedroll, trench knife, and musette bag. There were no other wounded there and the German doctors treated him at once. They told him that his wound was not serious. At about 1400 he was left alone, lying on the straw-covered floor, where he could overhear conversations among the medics and the communications staff. Their morale was high and they were confident that the Ardennes offensive would drive the Allies back into the sea. They also voiced great expectations from their V weapons and jet-propelled aircraft. However, they were very bitter about the Allied bombing of German cities, such as Berlin and Cologne. All the while Russell was offered tea, coffee, and cigarettes. At about 1800 the Germans seemed tense and began looking out of the windows as they hastily made preparations to vacate the house. Russell was left unguarded long enough for him to hide in a potato bin in another room. By the time he was missed, the Germans were so anxious to get out, they made only a token search for him before leaving. After a safe interval, ex-prisoner Russell crawled into the hayloft to get some rest, although sleep was hard to come by with the continuous firing throughout the night, and his uncertainty over what to do next.

About 0800 the next morning, the owner of the house found him and after the two identified themselves, he told Russell that there were American forces nearby. The farmer left and returned ten minutes later in a jeep with an American lieutenant who took Russell to a battalion aid station. From there he was taken to a clearing station and then to the 103d Evacuation Hospital at Longuyon, France, about fifty miles south of Bastogne. On the 29th, he went by train to Paris to the general hospital where he was treated until 2 January 1945. Then he was flown to England. He was released from the Hospital Plant 4103 on 10 February. On 15 February, he hopped an ATC flight to Paris and there at Le Bourget, he found a plane from his 93d Squadron for a flight to Chateaudun. Of those who returned to their Troop Carrier units after the Bastogne resupply mission, he was the last.

*   *   *   *

Paul Hower, George Juneau, and Frank Hobart landed their gliders on the north side of Sibret within strong German positions. They were not far from where Edward Williams, Vernon Brasch, and John McCann had parachuted from Nachowitz's C-47. After their capture, the six were marched westerly together, away from Bastogne toward Chenet and Nimbermont. About four days later during their trek, Hobart, Juneau, and Williams were walking close together. With nothing else to grouse about, the two glider pilots taunted Williams about why he and Nachowitz had flown so far back in the formation, which made the planes and gliders easier targets. Williams explained, "Nach didn't want to damage our engines." Hower snapped, "Where in the hell are your engines now?"

After being held at Chenet during the early days of January, the captives were moved out and Juneau was amazed to see two CG-4A gliders in the snow near Nimbermont. He did not know they were Douglas Bloomfield's and Emmett Avery's gliders from the 94th Squadron. Without a map, Juneau could not know they were nine miles west of Bastogne.

*   *   *   *

Michael Whitfill, the only survivor from Wilton Smith's lead plane of the 95th Squadron, landed by parachute two miles west of Flamierge. A German soldier was waiting for him and was disappointed that the lieutenant did not have a weapon, but he settled for his flight jacket as a souvenir. Whitfill was left to lie on the ground between two German dug-in gun positions for over an hour while American P-51s and P-47s strafed enemy guns located a mile away. From a forward command post, he was taken to another CP in a small village as darkness came. While there, Wilmer Weber and Robert Fine, from David Morton's C-47, were brought in. They were all fed stew, the same meal the Germans were having. A German lieutenant was curious about why Whitfill was flying without a flight jacket. When he learned the answer, he bristled and told Whitfill he should not have surrendered his jacket, but that it would be returned to him. They gave him a blanket to use until the jacket was returned, but he never saw his jacket again.

After black bread and tea at 0900, the prisoners were sent a block away for an examination by the doctor. Whitfill had a small wound, slightly bloody, on the top of his head and a bruise on the side. The bandage that was wrapped around his head was excessive in Whitfill's opinion, but it earned him rides in trucks with some twenty other injured prisoners while Weber and Fine walked with the healthy ones. It was the first time Whitfill ever considered himself to be a "goldbricker." After they crossed the Rhine into Germany, the traffic changed. It became a long, slow trek for the prisoners because they were often pulled to the roadside as miles and miles of two- and four-wheeled horse-drawn vehicles loaded with ammunition headed west toward the battle front. After internments along the way (one at Nurnberg), the prisoners eventually arrived at Stalag Luft VII A in Moosburg, Germany.

Glider pilot Dick Blake, who had been captured a mile away, was among those who were marched into Germany and ended up in Stalag Luft I, Barth, Germany.

* * * *

Raymond Schott landed his glider less than half a mile from where his tow plane (Stanley Zdun's) crashed. Two days later, a local farmer, Rodolphe Flock, discovered his body on the snow-covered ground. It was apparent that he had been shot while running away from his glider. If he had carried a carbine or pistol, which he surely did, it had been taken by the Germans.[*]

Henry Nowell and Pershing Carlson landed their gliders in separate, isolated fields near the forests beyond Flamierge. Although they were not near one another, their evasive actions on the ground were similar — at first. One was captured while the other eluded capture.

Carlson hid for six days in the dense forest nearby. He improvised shelter from tree branches. With no food, he finally headed out of the woods to a road he hoped would take him to American forces. A half-hour later he was captured. It was 3 January 1945. After a month of walking and train rides in boxcars, he arrived at Stalag Luft I, Barth, Germany.

While German troops were searching for downed air crews, Nowell hid in the forest until near dark and then moved to the edge of the woods and peered out. Not far away there were only civilians to be seen at a farm house, apparently gathered together there to weather the German artillery barrages nearby. Nowell approached them cautiously, identifying himself as American. This sent the lady of the house into a rage that let him know in no uncertain terms that he was not welcome. He retreated to hide among some large boulders he had seen earlier and wait out the very cold night. As he kept moving to keep from freezing, he could hear music from the German artillery unit which was bivouacked less than 400 yards away.

At dawn, after a sleepless night, Nowell spotted another farm house, smaller than the first. He knocked on the door and this time got a cordial reception. The man who opened the door appeared to be in his late twenties. Not recognizing Nowell as an American, his first question was *"Café?"* The response was *"Oui."* Inside were the man's wife and two small children, one about five years old and an infant in a crib. As Nowell stood as close to the red-hot stove as possible, he made it known that he was an American and needed shelter for the night. The couple nervously tried to explain that Ger-

---

[*] André R. Meurisse, who was wounded as a lad, now lives in Büllingen, Belgium. After corresponding with the author in 1991, he found that Rodolphe Flock still lives on a part of the farm his parents had in the hamlet of Trois Monts, very near the village of Salle. Flock vividly recalled the tragic scene.

Raymond G. Schott, Jr., 2d Lt., 01998159, was interred in the Henri-Chapelle American Cemetery, Belgium.

mans were all around and could be expected to show up any time. He could not spend the night in the house. More animated conversation followed and surprisingly, they asked Nowell if he was hungry. He hadn't really thought about eating, but it would keep him there and also keep him warm a while longer, so he said he was hungry. The couple opened a trunk, took out the tray, and feeling around among the clothes, pulled out two fresh eggs — a treat Nowell had almost forgotten existed. They fried the eggs in butter and he ate them with a slice of bread as slowly as he dared. Then he was offered a place to sleep, an offer he could not refuse. Taken upstairs to a bedroom, he fell exhausted on the bed, still fully clothed.

About 1100, he was awakened by a knock on his door. A young man told Nowell in broken English that he should leave because Germans were moving toward them. He went downstairs and looked outside. It was foggy and it was snowing. Which way should he go? With a wave of an arm and in more broken English, he was advised to head southward.

                              *   *   *   *

In October 1991, forty-seven years later, André Meurisse discovered more information surrounding Henry Nowell's experience on the morning of the 28th. After writing to the *Ardennes Magazine*, his letter of inquiry brought results. He drove to interview the residents of the two lonely farm houses at "La Ferme du Grand Vivier," located about one and a half miles east-northeast of Flamierge. Meurisse was elated by what he learned there from Antoine Pierson and Félix Debarsy.

Nowell had been taken in by Mr. and Mrs. Pierson-Juseret. Antoine, the eldest of their two sons, was fourteen at the time. He recalled the "tall and slim" American airman standing outside their opened door and how his parents fed him and led him upstairs where "he fell asleep in full dress on the bed."

In the nearby farm house some 120 yards away, Mr. and Mrs. Debarsy's twelve-year-old son, Félix, was Antoine's close friend. On the day before, the two of them had watched "a lot of planes and gliders flying at low altitudes just to the south of Grand Vivier." They recalled seeing one tow plane and glider go down not far away, to the south of them. Later in the evening, or early in the morning, they knew that "two or three American airmen" had taken refuge in the barn adjacent to Debarsy's house. They both remembered that there was a very dense ground fog all morning.

About noon, they saw a German column coming out of the woods and heading toward the house Nowell was in. The two boys and another young refugee dashed to the house and awakened him. "He stood up immediately, ready to leave. We waved for him to walk southeast in the direction of the American lines." As he faded into the fog, the Germans were entering the other house. The boys heard a few gun shots, but if Nowell was their target, the heavy fog was to his advantage. The boys headed back to the other house and found that German troops, some twenty to thirty of them, were occupying the entire ground floor of the Debarsy home. The boys worried about whether they would discover the Americans hiding in the barn. "We knew that if they did, we would all be shot on the spot." The Americans stayed hidden in the hay until they realized that the German platoon had not posted a sentry outside. They were all inside the house eating and getting warm and showed no intention of leaving. By now the boys knew that the Americans had already slipped out of the barn. "But we were not content with that 'verdigris' infection all over the house, we knew about the German brutality. They could always be expected to become wild for some reason, or no reason."

One of the Americans was caught after he left the barn and was taken back to the house by a "bunch of Germans." The boys never forgot the shock of watching the scene that followed. "Some of the German soldiers in the house took charge of the prisoner and rapidly questioned him." The boys were still afraid that Germans would find out that he had been hiding in one of their barns. "Then all of a sudden two or three Germans literally fell on him with their fists, punching the poor American flat down to the floor while another one was still barking question after question at him." The boys did not know what the American said, or if he was even replying as "the interrogators began kicking him again and again, over all of his body . . . especially to his stomach and groin.

"Suddenly, we the civilians, were all chased out of our houses by the damned Germans and we had to take refuge among the cows and manure in the adjacent stables where we lived for several days until the crude and brute 'Boche' troopers left for somewhere else . . . 'into hell' we all wished. They were obviously forced out by approaching American forces."

* * * *

After Henry Nowell slipped out the back door of the farm house, he headed south, through the fog, across fields and through woods. He did not know that he was less than a mile from the most western point of 101st Airborne Division's defensive perimeter, near the village of Flamizoulle. Occasionally he heard small-arms fire and he would drop down. For almost four hours, he headed south, never knowing where he was. When a gunshot came very close, he hit the ground and listened. Someone yelled, "What the hell you shootin' at?" The response, "Nothin' in particular." He had come upon an outpost of the 101st Airborne Division but they had not yet spotted him. In order not to surprise them, he walked around in a direction that put him in front of them. Walking straight toward them, he stopped in midfield, raised his hand and called "Hold your fire." A GI from the outpost walked to Nowell and established his identification and he was taken by jeep to division headquarters at Bastogne where he was interrogated by Lt. Col. Paul A. Danahay, McAuliffe's G-2. The intelligence section was extremely interested in Nowell's information. Later, on the 28th, after all other Troop Carrier personnel had been evacuated, he was put on a resupply truck that was returning to Neufchateau.

Nowell spent two nights there with the 26th Infantry Division and then hitchhiked to Sedan, arriving on the 30th at about 1400. He contacted the rail transportation officer and was seated on a train that left for Paris at 1500. Without heat, light, food, or toilets, the train made comfort stops along the way. It arrived in Paris at 0600 on the morning of 31 December 1944.

* * * *

Although Velton Brewer had been close behind George Freeman while they were on tow, they landed their gliders almost five miles apart. Brewer was cut off first and was captured south of Tillet. Freeman was injured and easily taken prisoner near Flamierge. They were reunited weeks later at Stalag Luft VII A, Moosburg, Germany.

The last time Emmett Avery saw Douglas Bloomfield was when he ducked into a small woods of scrub pine north of Nimbermont. Avery ran on by and into the large Bois des Hales de Magery forest. He wandered about the rest of the day and night, and all of the next day and night, often hearing German patrols moving around. On the 29th, he decided to strike out in a direction he thought to be toward Bastogne. After climbing over a fence, two soldiers called out for him to approach them. He was glad to oblige until he got closer to them. They were in American uniforms but they were Germans!

At the CP, which was a farm house, the commanding officer came out smiling and asked Avery if he was English. It seemed that the CO and other officers were curious about the flak suit Avery was still wearing; it was something new to them. After about a five-mile drive in a new automobile, the prisoner was taken to another farm house and placed alone in an upstairs room. Soon he was visited by an interrogator who got only his name, rank, and serial number, and then retaliated with a surprise. He showed Avery a plastic ID card with the name, 2d Lt. Douglas C. Bloomfield on it and subtly asked if he knew him. His reaction made it obvious that he did. The German said nothing more than that Bloomfield had been killed. Avery was among others from the mission who were later imprisoned at Stalag Luft VII A. After the war, at the direction of the next of kin, the remains of Douglas Bloomfield were repatriated for permanent interment in a private cemetery in Michigan.

The entire crew of Avery's tow plane (Lewis, Putnam and Umhoeffer, Harvey and Mehling) had parachuted close together west of Nimbermont, practically on top of German ground forces. Following the first days of capture, some of them were separated during the trek across the Rhine and ended up in different stalags in Germany.

✻   ✻   ✻   ✻

The two survivors from Ernest Foster's lead plane of the 96th Squadron, Robert Thompson and Theodore Mrenosco, parachuted northeast of Nimbermont. Before the mission, Thompson was wearing his class A uniform to go on leave to England. When he was assigned to the mission, he decided to wear the low cut shoes that he had kept after he had been eliminated from cadet training. Although they stayed on his feet when he hit the ground, he soon wished that he had dressed for combat.

Landing about a hundred yards apart, Thompson and Mrenosco ran to nearby haystacks for cover. It was then that Thompson found the cause of the pain on the back of his neck; he reached back and peeled off a three-inch strip of melted aluminum. Months later he learned that his back pains were from injuries to two spinal discs. Mrenosco's only injury was a sprained ankle. It was a very painful march into Germany for both men. Thompson's feet were constantly wet and seriously frostbitten.

Francis Carroll was transported in a semiconscious state from his glider to a German aid station which had been set up in a barn. Later another seriously injured glider pilot, Clifton Kiser, was also brought in on a stretcher. Their reunion was a surprise indeed. Among other prisoners brought in was a Troop Carrier navigator. When asked how far they were from Bastogne, he answered, "Four minutes." The navigator, Richard Umhoeffer from the 95th Squadron, knew where they were. It was not his first time to abandon a C-47 during a mission.* From the area of Nimbermont it was about eight miles to the Bastogne LZ via the route on the chart he was using before his C-47 was shot down.

Carroll was operated on and interrogated simultaneously by the German doctor and an assistant who removed a bullet from his leg. After he came out of the ether, the doctor questioned him again. The prisoners were moved out two days later having shifted to a diet of black bread. Carroll and Kiser were held for weeks with other injured and wounded in southern Germany near Limburg, before being moved to Stalag Luft VII A.

The two survivors from Alan Maeder's C-47 were lucky because they parachuted before they were directly over German forces, that were pushing southwest from Nimbermont. Robert Londo did not know whether the others, Robert Holste, Alan Maeder or Lee Dahman, were able to bail out. While recovering from a hard landing, Londo thought he should join up with crew mates — if there were survivors — and he headed toward the sound of the plane crash and explosion. Londo walked until he found the still burning wreckage of his plane. There was no one in sight. After that futile effort, he headed back in a southwesterly direction. The next day, near Ste. Marie, he was met by American soldiers who directed him

---

* On 7 June, Umhoeffer's plane was hit over a Normandy DZ. Four were killed instantly and he was injured. After the plane was ditched in the Channel, he and the pilots were rescued by a PT boat.

back to safe territory. There he found transportation by truck, train, and plane, and arrived at Orleans late on the night of the 29th.

Holste was in critical condition when he was found by an American patrol in the evening of the 28th. Besides the burns he had received before parachuting, he had a sprained ankle and his feet were severely frostbitten. From Ste. Marie, he was moved to the evacuation hospital at Saint-Hubert. There he stayed until 9 January when he was flown to England.

The only fortunate aspect of Billy Green's crash-landing on the way back was that it was in American territory. The location, in the forest about four miles northeast of Libremont, was unavoidable. Crew chief Albert Sabon was the only crew member who parachuted. He thought he was within American lines but, still in shock, he used his hand compass to walk due east through the woods until he came to a dirt road. Sabon hid for a moment when he saw two men in the distance walking along the road toward him. They were obviously in need of help and he went on to meet them. They were his pilot, Green, and radio operator Robert Slaughter. All they knew about copilot John Bachman was that he had bailed out before the crash. The local villagers who came out to help had found Bachman in the woods. American medics, from an armored division, sent the three to an aid station by ambulance and then to the field hospital at Sedan later that night. Bachman died of wounds from a skull fracture on 30 December. Slaughter was released to duty on 3 January 1945. The war was over for the other two. Green's back injuries required a cast, and Sabon's spinal disc injuries were serious enough to have them both flown back to England and subsequently to hospitals in the United States. They were discharged months later.

Pete Houck, who was flying the glider on Jerry Knott's right wing, was so busy maintaining his tow position through the flak that he did not see how Knott went down, whether he crashed or landed his glider. The only records found stated that F/O Gerald D. Knott was killed in action and was interred at the American Cemetery at Henri-Chapelle, Belgium.

When Houck was captured, he considered his only injury minor, burns on his posterior from flak. His captors took him to a farm house CP where some young German soldiers prepared to give him a beating, but an older soldier stepped in and stopped it. He was driven to the interrogation center which was in a barn not far from

Flamierge, and the atmosphere was dismal as captured Americans sat on the ground along the walls awaiting questioning. Houck recalled meeting another glider pilot there, Dick Blake, and learned that they had been in the same flight training classes in Texas and North Carolina. The next day the *Kriegsgefangenen* (prisoners of war) began the walk to Germany. Through the Rhineland, they were given little to eat and scrounging became routine. Near a German camp, they ate a few handfuls of potato peelings that had been left near the road. After walking for one week (over 170 miles), they were interned at the stalag at Limburg for more interrogation. The next leg of their journey was in boxcars with an overnight in the Berlin railroad yards. Three weeks after their capture, Houck's contingent of prisoners arrived at Stalag Luft I, near Barth, where many American bomber crew members were also interned. The newcomers soon learned to call themselves "Kriegies."

Mike Sheff had a serious flak wound on his left forearm but it was ignored by his captors when he surrendered near his glider. They took him quickly to a farm house where he was questioned by a pleasant German officer who spoke like an American. He took Sheff's Colt .45 pistol and six packages of cigarettes that had been stashed in his flight suit. The questioning became conversational when the German said he had once lived in Ohio where he had been a Coca-Cola salesman. Sheff was taken to a nearby village where his arm was treated and he was once again questioned. Following three days in a hospital, he spent another short internment at Stalag Luft IV F. Again he was moved, this time to the stalag at Nurnberg and then he was transferred to Stalag Luft VII A at Moosburg, not long before VE Day.

✻ ✻ ✻ ✻

Henry Nowell was the last one on the mission to return to his unit uninjured. From 31 December, the morning he arrived at the railway station in Paris, his experience was almost as unusual as were his exploits evading capture. It began after doughnuts and coffee had been furnished by the ever present Red Cross. The rail transportation officer's questions led to Nowell being taken to a hotel that was primarily used for "crashed crews," particularly for airmen who had evaded capture with the help of local civilians. It was military policy for these airmen to be transferred to another theater of operation to eliminate any chance of civilians being identified should the airmen be captured on a subsequent mission.

At the hotel, he was assured more than once that his unit, the 94th Squadron, had been notified of his status. His primary concern was for his parents not to be sent a "Missing In Action" telegram. But his squadron was not informed except for a communication from Paris that stated he had drawn a partial pay. Evidently that single message was sufficient for the squadron not to include his name on the official Missing In Action Report of 7 January 1945.

The captain who interrogated Nowell in Paris told him he would be sent home for a public relations tour before reassignment to the Pacific Theater. He was glad to learn that he was under orders directly from SHAEF. Next he was given a physical by a flight surgeon and then made a trip to the PX for new clothes. While waiting for his orders to be cut, he was given a pass for all areas in Paris — which he put to good use. On 10 January, his SHAEF orders to send him to London and then to the ZI, came through.

In London, he was listed for a low priority flight home to the United States, to his hometown, Raleigh, North Carolina. While waiting, he was requested to accompany an injured airman, also slated to return to the United States, on a special trip back to France.

The injured airman, radio operator Cpl. Robert Holste (from the 96th Squadron) had been convincing at the hospital in London, about his need to return to his airfield at Orleans for personal financial reasons and to pick up valuable personal possessions before going home. He needed an escort and Nowell agreed to accompany him on 20 January 1945. After a train trip to Winchester, they were able to find rides on a courier flight of the 439th Troop Carrier Group to Chateaudun where Holste found other transportation to Orleans. He was soon flown back to England and subsequently returned to the United States.

At Chateaudun, Henry Nowell was not surprised to see his foot locker packed with all his effects, ready to be sent home. He was amazed to learn that the 94th Squadron's only word about him had come as a result of his partial pay transactions in Paris and London. He was further shocked to learn that the squadron commander, Maj. Ward W. Martindale, had papers prepared for his general court-martial! He was saved from that ordeal when he produced the SHAEF orders he had received in Paris and London. Nowell was

André R. Meurisse, age five, Senanchamps, Belgium, during German Occupation 1942. Two years later, he was wounded during bombing attack by P-47s at Mande-Saint-Etienne.

— Courtesy: Meurisse

2d Lt. Mack Striplin, glider pilot, 93d Troop Carrier Squadron, in cockpit of CG-4A glider during training Lubbock, TX, December 1943.

— Courtesy: Polly Striplin

F/O Henry H. Nowell, glider pilot, 94th Troop Carrier Squadron. Nowell evaded capture after the 27 December 1944 mission.

— Courtesy: King/McCullough

never granted an interview with Ward Martindale but the squadron adjutant, Capt. James A. Bradley, relayed a request from Martindale for Nowell to remain in the squadron because there was a shortage of glider pilots. That was particulary true in the 94th Squadron where eleven were listed as Missing In Action. Nowell was the only glider pilot to return to the 94th Squadron. He remained with the unit and flew a glider on another combat mission, Operation VARSITY, on 24 March 1945.

*   *   *   *

Casualties

Two hundred eighteen crew members flew in the fifty C-47 tow planes on the 27 December glider mission. Thirty-nine did not return, seventeen were killed in action (KIA), one died of wounds (DOW), and twenty-one were taken prisoners; an eighteen percent loss. Of those who returned from the mission, twelve were wounded or injured. Fourteen C-47s — 28 percent — were shot down.

The highest number of tow plane crew casualties were from the 440th Troop Carrier Group. From the fifty-eight crew members of the group's thirteen C-47s, there were thirteen KIA, one DOW, and seventeen POWs — 53 percent.

Glider pilot casualties were three KIA and fourteen POWs, or thirty-four percent. The highest loss of any squadron was that of the 94th, which suffered three KIA and eight POWs — 92 percent.

*   *   *   *

To put the high casualty rate of the 27 December 1944 Bastogne glider mission in perspective, it should be compared to the previous two American glider operations.

In Operation NEPTUNE, the airborne invasion of Normandy, 517 tow planes and gliders were dispatched. Of 2,197 tow plane crew men, nine were KIA or MIA, and of 1,034 glider pilots, fifty-seven were KIA or MIA.

In Operation MARKET, the airborne invasion of Holland, 1,899 gliders were dispatched and were towed by an equal number of tow ships. Of about 8,085 crew men, ninety-seven were KIA or MIA, and of 1,899 glider pilots, seventy-seven were KIA or MIA.

25

The Last Drop

FIFTY-FOUR ARMED GLIDER PILOTS assembled at the 101st Division's command post in Bastogne on the afternoon of 27 December. They were assigned to guard the German captives waiting to be trucked to Neufchateau. Before being driven to the prisoner stockade, they heard the familiar sound of C-47s approaching from the south at 1425. For half an hour they watched 129 planes drop parapacks on the DZ, directly west of the town, then turn right, around the town and head back south. From some of the thirty-two pilots who had landed two hours earlier, the word had spread quickly. Their excited discussions either started or ended with "That's the way we should have come in."

What the ground observers did not know was what losses, if any, the formation had suffered, either on the approach or on the way out. Nor did they know what Troop Carrier units were involved. They incorrectly assumed that the planes were from groups of the 50th Wing in France.

* * * *

Originally, for the last airdrop mission, a total of 238 C-47s from the five groups of Brig. Gen. Maurice M. Beach's 53d Wing, based in England, had been committed. Their first foe was the

289

weather in England. At Aldermaston, only forty-nine assigned planes of the 434th Group took off, but soon aborted due to weather. All forty-eight loaded C-47s of the 438th Group at Greenham Common were grounded.* The weather at the other three airfields was also marginal, but adequate. Of the forty-eight planes of the 437th Group at Ramsbury, nine were grounded for mechanical reasons before mission time. The others took off between 1140 and 1151. One returned quickly with several mechanical problems, and had to make a belly landing. At Membury, all forty-nine loaded C-47s of the 436th Group were off the runway between 1142 and 1153 with no problems. The third group on the mission was the 435th. It had prepared and loaded forty-five planes. Three of the aircraft experienced mechanical problems. The other forty-two took off from Welford Park between 1212 and 1224.

The route from England was the same as that taken for the airdrops of 24 and 26 December. The final approach to Bastogne was north-northeasterly, some thirty-seven miles from the Montmedy IP. It was directly over the corridor newly established by the 4th Armored Division and held by other divisions of Patton's Third Army. The Troop Carrier planes were subjected to "meager and inaccurate" enemy small-arms fire. One plane of the 78th Squadron, 435th Group, released its parapacks prematurely and turned back. First opinions from other Troop Carrier crews were that the supplies landed in enemy territory, but it was later learned that they were secured by the 101st. Nine aircraft sustained minor damage: five from the 437th Group, three from the 436th, and one from the 435th.

After the airdrops, flown at 300 to 350 feet, the three serials made climbing right turns around the north side of Bastogne to head back toward the Montmedy IP. As they continued climbing at 150 MPH, they passed out of range of the small-arms fire they had encountered on the way in.

On the way back, the pilots were not surprised to hear by radio that a weather front had spread over England and the Channel, and

---

* The uncertain situation at Greenham Common, headquarters for the 53d Wing as well as the 438th Group, was compounded that day. Both Col. John M. Donalson, CO of the 438th, and his group operations officer were replaced. (See Chapter 13.)

they diverted their flights to Troop Carrier airfields in France. It was a cold night for the crews from the 435th, who slept in their planes at A-39, Chateaudun, and for those from the 436th and 437th at A-41, Dreux. Some flew their planes back to their airfields the next day, the 28th, and the rest returned on the 29th.

＊　＊　＊　＊

The supply drops on the 27th contained only 118½ tons of ammunition and eight and one-quarter tons of gasoline; no K-rations this time. On the previous missions, sizeable amounts of quartermaster, medical, and signal supplies had been included.

The greatest difference between the last airdrop on the 27th and those of the other three days was that no planes were lost, nor was any crew member injured. Damage to aircraft was relatively light.

The 101st Division was pleased, as indicated by the G-4's message at 1715 to VIII Corps at Neufchateau, that 130 planes had arrived and the drop pattern was very good.

The 27th, a day which had brought Troop Carrier blood and fire, ended a highly successful day for three groups of its 53d Wing.

27 December 1944. CG-4A glider landed near Bastogne by 2d Lt. Charles R. Brema, 93d Troop Carrier Squadron.　— Courtesy: Perkins

PART V

Troop Carrier Airlines,
Operation Repulse

Paris, 31 December 1944
The 17th Airborne Division yesterday relieved the 11th Armored Division in the zone between Givet and Verdun.

Maj. Gen. Lewis H. Brereton / "The Brereton Diaries." 1946

Ardennes, 21 January 1945
A severe blizzard during the night blocked most of the roads and delayed the jump-off. At 0800 General Ridgway and I met General Hasbrouck, commander of the 7th Armored, and we accompanied the 7th Armored's advance to the vicinity of enemy-held Boran . . . The principle difficulty was moving through the deep snow drifts. In midafternoon left for General Miley's 17 Division Hdqs. Travel was exceedingly difficult, but we arrived at 1900 hours. The weather dropped to zero during the night.

Maj. Gen. Lewis H. Brereton / "The Brereton Diaries." 1946

A curious cargo went winging across the Atlantic during the past month aboard four huge C-54 transport planes of the U.S.A.A.F. Air Transport Command. To save the lives of soldiers wounded on the snowbound Western Front, ATC has flown a total of 209 yelping, sloe-eyed Eskimo Husky dogs, together with the sled-drivers and Arctic equipment, over the ocean to France.

Today, 23 dog teams, the cream of the Arctic canine corps, are ready to haul wounded men from the front to advance medical stations of the First and Third Armies. In many instances they may provide the only efficient means of transportation through snow drifts that had been bogging down human stretcher-bearers.

From the 1 March 1945 Press Release
Air Transport Command, USAAF

293

26

The 17th Airborne Division
into Battle

IT WAS A JOB FOR Troop Carrier!

During the 20 December meeting at SHAEF-AIR, Lt. Gen. Lewis H. Brereton, commanding general of the First Allied Airborne Army, received orders to move the 17th Airborne Division from England to airfields on the Continent in the vicinity of Reims. The troops were then to be mobilized nearby at Camp Mourmelon le Grand, which had been vacated by the 101st Airborne Division two days before when it had been sent into the Ardennes.

Early on the 21st, Brereton notified General Williams at his IX Troop Carrier Command headquarters near Uxbridge, and Brig. Gen. William M. Miley's 17th Division at Camp Barton Stacey, of the upcoming move. The division's operations officer attended a brief conference at command headquarters for formulating the logistics and schedules. Based upon the available aircraft and favorable weather, the operation was expected to require four or five days.

Seven airfields, located thirty to fifty miles west of London, were designated for marshaling and embarkation. Five were airfields occupied by groups of the 53d Troop Carrier Wing: Ramsbury, Welford Park, Greenham Common, Membury, and Aldermaston. Another at Chalgrove was the IX Troop Carrier Pathfinder Group's airbase. The seventh was at Chilbolton, having the best proximity to the 17th Division at Barton Stacey. The airfield at Chilbolton had been occupied by P-47s from the 368th Fighter Group (71st Fighter Wing) of the Ninth Air Force until 23 August 1944 when it was relocated to Chartres (A-40), France. Chilbolton became a IX Troop Carrier Command airfield when the 442d Troop Carrier Group moved in on 11 September and it was attached to the 53d Wing for Operation MARKET. After the Holland airborne invasions, the 442d was moved to St. Andre-de-l'Eure (B-24), France, and was reassigned to the 50th Wing. Chilbolton remained primarily as the wing's support airfield in the U.K.

Four forward airfields near Reims in France were earmarked for airlanding the troops and equipment of the 17th Division. Three airfields of the 50th Wing, southwest of Paris, were chosen as alternates in case of adverse weather, or as en route stops for other reasons. The alternates were at Chartres (A-40), Dreux (A-41), and Chateaudun (A-39).

At the time, groups of the 53d Wing were committed to the task of flying resupply missions to the rear of the U.S. Third and First armies. As first priority, the 53d Wing had been assigned to fly airborne resupply missions to encircled ground forces in the Ardennes. Therefore, the movement of the 17th Division was initially delegated to groups of the 50th and 52d Troop Carrier wings and the IX Pathfinder Group. The operation, not at all formidable in its size, was challenging in its urgency.

Brig. Gen. Julian M. Chappell, 50th Troop Carrier Wing commander at Chartres, was the first to be called by General Williams on 21 December. In effect, Chappell was told to get an airline operation in action to transport passengers and cargo of the 17th Airborne Division from England to France. Chappell's first wing Operation Order, No. 356, to his four groups was to assign 224 aircraft to fly to three airfields in England and to begin the airlift early on the 23d.

At daybreak on the 23d, 224 C-47s lifted off on schedule from four airfields in France and headed for England to pick up the first contingents of the 17th Airborne Division. A total of 112 aircraft from the four groups were sent to Chilbolton (thirty-five from the 439th, seventeen from the 440th, thirty-five from the 441st, and twenty-five from the 442d). Another 112 were dispatched to other airfields for subsequent ferrying of 17th Division forces.

Loading of troops and equipment began as soon as the planes parked. During the morning, eighty-four planes from Chilbolton and ten planes from Aldermaston were off and en route to airfield A-70 at Laon/Couvran, located about twenty-five miles northwest of Reims. From there it was forty miles by road to Camp Mourmelon le Grand.

The Airways

The REPULSE missions developed so quickly that it was impossible to install the usual thorough Troop Carrier route navigational aids. The status of the missions was so uncertain, the commitments and the routes so changeable, that IX Troop Carrier Command considered it impractical to establish new fixed route aids on the Continent.

IX Troop Carrier Command decided to use the existing MIDNITE Airway aids to transport a part of the 17th Division at night. The MIDNITE system provided two air traffic corridors over the English Channel, one with a radio range station on the English coast and an M/F Eureka beacon on the French coast, and the other corridor had the aids reversed on the two coasts. The result was dual direction airways over the Channel. A third radio range station and M/F was in operation at Dreux (A-41), the 441st Troop Carrier Group airfield west of Paris. The other airfields of the 50th Wing, southwest of Paris, also had M/F beacons: Chateaudun (A-39), 439th Group; Bricy-Orleans (A-50), 440th Group; St. Andre-de-l'Eure (B-24), 442d Group; and Chartres (A-40), 50th Wing Headquarters. Along the airways, flashing light beacons were located at up to fifteen-mile intervals. Eastward, toward the front, the flashing beacons had been installed for about 125 miles from Dreux, the hub of the airways, to the Villeneuve/Vertus airfield (A-63) south of Reims, and Prosnes airfield (A-79) southeast of Reims.

The primary purpose of the MIDNITE aids was for the diversion of England-based aircraft to the 50th Wing airfields in France when the weather in England fell below landing minimums at night. Also the east-west lighted airway was to facilitate night flights between the Paris area and the rear of the Third Army. The airways were a brilliant application of American civil air traffic control facilities for military purposes.

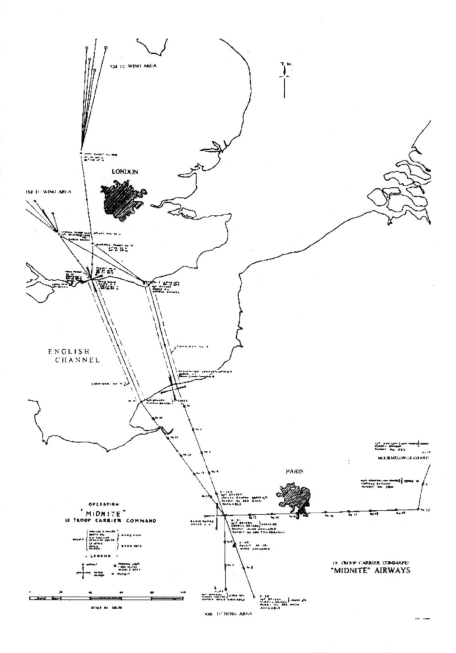

— Source for map courtesy National Archives

On 22 December, the Pathfinder Group was called on to place an M/F beacon and Eureka beacon at the Laon/Couvron airfield (A-70) northwest of Reims. It was the first time lighted airways were to be used to transport airborne troops to within seventy-five miles of enemy lines.

The Passengers

Parachute infantry regiments were first formed at Fort Benning, Georgia, in August 1942 when the 82d and 101st airborne divisions were activated. The 17th Airborne Division, with its 507th and 513th PIRs, was not activated until 15 April 1943.* The first large-scale airborne training exercises with the 17th Division were from Camp Mackall, North Carolina, in May. Next came the Tennessee maneuvers during June and July, where the division took part in the Second Army maneuvers.

It was in Tennessee that the men of the 17th were first exposed to taunts from contemporary rivals in other organizations. A remark that would surely provoke a fist fight was one referring to the Golden Eagle Claw insignia, the 17th Division shoulder patch, as a "chicken foot." Men of the 513th PIR were just as proud of their maxim, "Thunder From Heaven." However, the division's first entry into combat would be by land.

The 507th PIR was the first unit of the 17th shipped to the U.K., arriving in Belfast, Northern Ireland, in December 1943. There it was attached to the 82d Airborne Division. After fighting in the Normandy airborne invasion, the 507th was withdrawn from the 82d Division and returned to England in August 1944.

The rest of the 17th Airborne Division arrived in England in August 1944. It consisted of the 513th Parachute Infantry Regiment, 193d and 194th glider infantry regiments, 680th and 681st glider field artillery battalions, 466th Parachute Field Artillery Battalion and the 155th AAA (Antiaircraft Artillery) AW Battalion. Soon the 507th moved into a tent camp next to the 513th at Wind-

---

* From its inception, the 17th Airborne was commanded by Maj. Gen. William M. "Bud" Miley. He followed in his father's and brother's footsteps as a professional soldier upon graduation from West Point in June 1918. Carrying on the tradition, his son "Buzz," Col. William M. Miley, Jr., now also retired, was in the 11th Airborne Division.

mill Hill, near Ludgershall, on the Salisbury Plain in southwest England. There the two regiments were given a practice jump exercise before being moved to Camp Barton Stacey, about six miles north of the Chilbolton airfield.

When the 82d and 101st divisions went into Holland in late September, the troops of the 17th felt rejected at being left behind and were frequently ridiculed in the English pubs. Fights were not uncommon.

Units of the division routinely underwent various training exercises while at Barton Stacey. Before mid-December it was the 2d Battalion's (513th Regiment) turn to be sent to the Tillshead Artillery Range to practice the directing of field artillery fire. Unexpectedly, on the afternoon of the 16th, the battalion was told to return to Camp Barton Stacey. Orders on the next day were provocative. Units at the camp were told to draw all their basic loads of ammunition and other supplies — and pack for combat.

For 2d Lt. Samuel Calhoun, from Fresno, California, the time for action had come at last, but he was upset; he would enter combat without the promotion he had been expecting during the past year. He had been assigned to the same platoon for twenty-three months, the Second Platoon of F Company, 2d Battalion. Conflicts between the previous F Company commander and the battalion commander had delayed the promotion. Capt. Marshall M. "Bud" Reynolds (from Berryville, Virginia, VMI, class of 1940) took over F Company in September, not long before the practice jump at Windmill Hill. He had less than three months to acquaint himself with his men and platoon leaders before they were ordered to prepare for actual combat.

The 513th and 507th parachute infantry regiments were the first to move to tent camps adjacent to the Chilbolton airfield on 18 December. The men still did not know where they were headed. Every morning they would get up and move to the parked C-47s on the fogged-in airfields, put on their parachutes and relax under an aircraft wing. When they learned how serious the German counteroffensive was in the Ardennes, and that the 101st Airborne Division was being attacked at Bastogne, the rumors proliferated. The scuttlebutt was that the 17th Division was to jump at Bastogne. That rumor disappeared on 21 December when all parachutes were taken from the paratroopers and the parapack bundles were unpacked. Finally, after the hurry-up-and-wait routine, definite orders from General Miley reached his troops encamped at Chilbolton.

At dawn on the 23d, the officers of the 17th Division were gathered together for a briefing to learn of their itinerary — at least the first stage. Because of possible foggy conditions in France, they were told that the planes might not land at the designated airfield. Each officer was given the telephone number of Oise Base command to call from wherever they landed. That would get them transportation to Camp Mourmelon le Grand.

*   *   *   *

Moving over 13,000 men to France was only one task of the IX Troop Carrier Command. Its aircraft were also assigned to bring back high-priority passengers, wounded soldiers. Some were able to sit on the bench seats of the C-47s, but many were loaded in litters mounted along the sides of the cabin or tied to the floor. On the 23d alone, 878 patients were flown to England.*

On 24 December aircraft from all three wings of IX Troop Carrier Command were active in the movement of the 17th Division. A total of 540 airplanes were involved (232 of the 50th, 295 of the 52d, and 13 from the 53d). Five hundred thirty-one wounded soldiers were airlifted to England simultaneously.

*   *   *   *

The paratroopers of the 513th and 507th parachute infantry regiments and the 466th Parachute Field Artillery Battalion were the first to land in France from Chilbolton on the 23d and 24th. The glider troops from the 193d and 194th glider infantry regiments, 680th and 681st glider field artillery battalions, 139th Airborne Engineer Battalion and the 155th AAA AW Battalion were next from other airfields. They arrived less spectacularly than they trained. The paratroopers rode in the familiar C-47s, but without parachutes on

---

* For the first time during World War II, hospital facilities and staffs in England were overloaded. After the Normandy invasions, to some extent, hospitals in the ETO began retaining patients for treatment when they should have been returned to the U.S. as originally planned. By the time of the Battle of the Bulge, most hospitals were full. Since there was no room for more casualties, many of those who were airlifted from forward areas arrived at Mitchel Field, New York, within seventy-two hours from the time they were wounded, with the original battle dressings still in place.

their laps, and they climbed down from the rear exit instead of jumping out. The glider troopers were in an aircraft with engines and there was no rush to get out after landing.

Still, apprehension gripped the men of the 17th Division as they were trucked to Camp Mourmelon-le-Grand. Sam Calhoun wrote the author about his experiences in the 2d Battalion, 513th PIR:

> About 8 PM on Christmas Eve, large open vans, having the appearance of cattle trucks and trailers, pulled in to Camp Mourmelon-le-Grand. As each unit assembled, we marched into the large open trailers, and as soon as they had it full the tail gate went up. They gave us, "At Ease." There was no way to sit down, the open sides of the open trailer came up to our arm pits. It was also snowing and we did not have any winter clothing. None of us had been briefed on where we were going. About 10 PM the trucks started moving out. We traveled until about 7 AM. We unloaded, and then found out we were in Stenay, France, on the Meuse River.

They were at the tip of the Bulge, less than fifty miles from Bastogne. As other units of the 17th Division were transported to positions along the Meuse River, south of Givet, they were ordered to hold all bridges against German crossings. The German counteroffensive never reached the Meuse and the challenge on Christmas Day was not the enemy, it was trying to find food — at least that was the experience of the 2d Battalion of the 513th PIR. Calhoun wrote about the lack of food rations, which had not been supplied when they left Camp Mourmelon-le-Grand. "It had not been issued to us. We borrowed from Armored Units and from MP Units marching prisoners to the railway at Stenay for evacuation."

At the time, only 60 percent of the movement to Camp Mourmelon-le-Grand had been completed. There were combat and support units, as well as the bulk of supplies and rations, still in England.

* * * *

General Brereton's First Allied Airborne Army staff prepared its 25 December morning report for SHAEF main headquarters at 0950. Before noon, the SHAEF-AIR staff read the message. The parts pertaining to moving the 17th Airborne stated:

Report for 24 December 17 Division 540 sorties. Total sorties to date 634. Move 60% complete . . . Schedule for 25 December 452 sorties to complete move of 17 Division . . . 25 sorties to move personnel and equipment XVIII Corps to A79.

The message was optimistic, apparently without taking the weather into account. However, it was consistent with the schedules as set by the FAAA and IX Troop Carrier Command.

On Christmas Day the weather in England was socked in and curtailed the planned missions. The official weather description stated that the "53d Wing was affected by melting frost and deteriorating visibility in the afternoon and although no more clouds existed in the dry upper air over the Wing area, the sharp inversion and calm winds maintained the very foggy conditions."

At Chilbolton, in the 53d Wing area, five C-47s from the 439th Group (50th Wing) had been loaded with troops since early Christmas morning but could not depart until the weather permitted. The visibility improved at the air base and along the route to the Channel sufficiently for takeoffs at midday. They were able to deliver their troops northwest of Reims, at airfield A-70, that afternoon.

Some seventy planes of the 439th also delivered troops and equipment to A-70 on the 25th. They had left England too late on the day before to complete their daylight missions, and therefore overnighted at their Chateaudun airfield. The early morning takeoffs were marred by tragedy. One aircraft of the 91st Squadron, piloted by Lt. Warren L. Schuman, was in the takeoff pattern at 500 feet when it apparently stalled, nosed in, and crashed. The pilot of the following plane, Lieutenant Harris, believed the crash was due to icing on the wings. The four crew members and six airborne troops were lost. With Schuman, the crew members were F/O Harold L. Boggs, copilot; T/Sgt. Robert M. Kelly, crew chief and Sgt. Roy L. Harker, radio operator.

The weather was no problem on 26 December. The 50th and 52d wings dispatched 214 planes with airborne personnel and equipment from airfields in England to airfields around Reims. The 53d Wing provided twenty-three planes to transport troops and equipment of the 490 Quartermaster Company and XVIII Corps Headquarters.

Again on the 27th, 114 Troop Carrier aircraft, consisting of 107 from the 52d Wing and seven from the Pathfinder Group, airlifted 17th Division personnel. Four C-47s from the 53d Wing carried 490 Quartermaster Company troops and materiel.

The planned airlift could have been completed on 28 December, but again the weather was the deterrent; no flights were possible. Therefore on the 29th, the last of the troop movements was fully realized with all three wings' involvement, employing 145 aircraft.

On each of the last three days of troop movements, the Troop Carrier planes continued to return with higher numbers of wounded soldiers than before. Nine hundred fifty-four came back on 26 December, followed by 908 on 27 December and 1,993 on 29 December, totaling 5,264 casualties carried during the 23-29 December period. The IX Troop Carrier Command continued the evacuation of wounded, as it had done before Operation REPULSE, through the end of the war.

The movement of the 17th Airborne Division and other units involved about 1,340 sorties carrying 13,397 troops of the division, eighty-nine personnel of the 490th Quartermaster Depot Company, and thirty members of XVIII Corps (Airborne). According to available loading manifests, over 350 jeeps and trailers, and about 1,750 tons of weapons, mines and explosives, ammunition, combat equipment, supplies, and rations were airlifted to airfields near Reims.

The Terminus

While General Patton's Third Army divisions were fighting fiercely to widen the corridor to Bastogne and drive further north, General Hodges' First Army was attacking toward the south. The objective was to cut off the German forces in the western part of the Bulge; surrounding thousands of Hitler's favorite troops. Getting its shot at the action, the 17th Airborne Division was assigned to head north on Patton's left flank toward Flamierge.

*   *   *   *

By 25 December, the 507th and 513th regiments held positions along seventy miles of the Meuse River. Captain Reynolds' F Company was located at the bridge at Stenay, France, with a large factory building as the company command post. When the Germans, who were six miles away, began to withdraw, the 513th was sent east to

join the Third Army. On New Year's Eve, F Company was at Luneville, France. Sam Calhoun never forgot the dinner that night with
the town dignitaries. In his speech, the mayor welcomed them and
added, "If any of your company had been killed, we would erect a
monument at Luneville just as the one you have seen, the one for the
eight Americans who died here in World War I." After Bud Reynolds thanked him for the welcome, he added, "A monument is
proper for the dead, but not one of us wants to die for one."

*   *   *   *

The 507th and the 513th regiments did not cross the Meuse and
enter the Ardennes until 2 January. About midday they were moved
by trucks into the south side of the Ardennes and the next day they
were trucked closer to the battle lines. In the village of Chenogne,
about twelve miles southwest of Bastogne, Captain Reynolds' company helped unload supplies. They then marched north and crossed
the Bastogne-Marche highway to Mande-Saint-Etienne as the artillery fire became louder. They were in the combat area, one where
troops of the 10th Armored Division had been fighting a bloody
battle for two days with heavy casualties on both sides. F Company
was assigned to support a unit of the 41st Armored Infantry Regiment, a company which was down to about forty men with one half-
track in operation.

Lieutenant Calhoun's 2d Platoon was assigned to set up a perimeter defense on the northwestern edge of the village and began
digging in — in full view of German soldiers visible in the trees,
some 150 yards away. Calhoun was told, "As long as you don't fire
at them, they won't fire at you." He was called to battalion headquarters, which was located in a house at the north edge of the village, for an officers' briefing. There the plans for an 0800 attack on
the next morning were presented. Before the meeting ended, the
sound of *Nebelwerfers* (rockets) and rifle fire were heard from the 2d
Platoon. Lt. Col. Allen C. Miller, the 2d Battalion commander, ordered the officers back to their units.* Running back through *Nebel-
werfer* explosions to his platoon's position, Calhoun saw some of his

---

* Colonel Miller was sometimes referred to as "Ace" by his officers but many of
the enlisted men called him "Boots and Helmet." He was hardly five feet, five
inches tall and his helmet covered his forehead while the tops of his jump boots
almost reached his knees.

men running near a wooded area about a hundred yards in front of the defensive perimeter. Platoon Sergeant Milton C. Smith was wounded but died before he could be taken to the aid station. He had wanted to capture some of the Germans while they were relaxed and smoking at the edge of the woods. Smith was the first battle casualty of the 513th PIR, and perhaps of the 17th Division.

* * * *

Artillery fire into the woods began at 0745 on the 4th. Lieutenant Calhoun's 2d Platoon was ready to attack before 0800, but E Company had not yet joined on the right flank and F Company's 1st Platoon was nowhere in sight on the left flank. Captain Reynolds agreed that it would be suicidal for one platoon of thirty-eight men to attack across the open field. He told Calhoun to hold while he went to locate the other units. Lieutenant Colonel Miller came out of his observation post, the northernmost house of Mande-Saint-Etienne, and asked Calhoun, "Why aren't you attacking?" After listening to his explanation, Miller said he had information that the Germans had withdrawn from the woods. Just then a call came in on the radio from Reynolds who told Calhoun that he had found Lieutenant Gilles' platoon headed in the wrong direction and directed Calhoun to wait for it. Lieutenant Colonel Miller then took the radio and said, "I'm ordering Lieutenant Calhoun to attack before the artillery barrage is lifted." Calhoun got back on the radio and Reynolds ended their talk with, "Good Luck, Sam."

Two minutes later, the men of the 2d Platoon were advancing over a gently rising snow-covered field without any sort of cover. The Germans opened up with all types of automatic weapons. Calhoun hit the snow as did three men who were near him, with tracers hitting all around them. He could tell they were dead, and he played dead for thirty minutes after the firing stopped. He noticed a small beet pile some seventy-five yards to his rear and made a mad dash for it as more bullets peppered the snow around him. He leaped over the pile and dropped flat. He was just thirty-five yards from the defensive perimeter when a voice called out, "Lieutenant, can I help you?" It was a mortarman and a forward observer from his unit. And help he did.

Calhoun thought about what they had been told at the briefing. The battalion was down to its last smoke shells — only sixteen left, and they were ordered not to use them. Some of the men in the snow were calling for help, and without smoke, Calhoun knew he could not bring them back. He asked for smoke. Six rounds were placed directly in front of the Germans. The men who had gotten safely back to the defensive perimeter began carrying the wounded from the battleground. Lieutenant Colonel Miller called for Calhoun to report to the observation post where he was chewed out for using smoke. He was told to round up his men and get ready to attack again.

Calhoun assembled fourteen of his platoon (twenty had been killed or wounded) and noted that the 1st Platoon was still not at its attack position along the road embankment on his left flank. Since he could not locate Reynolds, he took his men to the 1st Platoon's line of departure and ordered them to fix bayonets and spread out in a skirmish line behind the embankment. They charged across the snow-covered ground towards the woods. Among the trees, they killed about twelve Germans and captured fifteen. At the same time, Lt. Richard Manning's platoon, from E Company, was clearing German troops out of log-covered bunkers in the eastern side of the woods.

Two hours later, after Sam Calhoun and his men had reached their first phase line, about a mile southeast of Flamizoulle, Bud Reynolds arrived in a jeep. He said that Gilles and his 1st Platoon would arrive soon. As they watched the Germans digging in some 300 yards to their left front, Reynolds pulled out maps to plan their route to the next objective, Flamierge. A sniper's bullet went through the map. "He's close enough. Let's get out of here." A second shot cracked, and that one hit Calhoun in the arm. "Captain, I've been shot!" Looking at him, Reynolds spit out "No shit!" While Reynolds took off in the direction the shots came from, Calhoun ran for cover behind a snow bank along a fence. Soon the 1st Platoon arrived and the wounded lieutenant was evacuated that night. Two days later, Calhoun was flown by Troop Carrier to England.

General Patton had ordered General Miley to take Flamierge at all costs. And it was costly. By the time the village was firmly secured on 8 January, the 17th Division had lost about 3,000 men, dead or wounded. The German losses were even greater, with many prisoners taken. During the next four weeks, the division moved eastward. By 6 February, St. Vith had been retaken and the 17th Division battled to cross the Our River into Germany. First to establish a foothold on the east bank of the Our were E and F companies of the 513th. On 10 February, the 6th Armored Division relieved the 17th Division which moved back by truck and rail to an encampment at Châlons-sur-Marne, France. There it would be brought back to full strength, with new men as well as those released from hospitalization. The casualties totaled 564 dead and 3,000 wounded. Of the 17th's regiments, the 513th suffered most, with 229 KIA/DOW and over 1,200 WIA/ILA.*

The next movement of units of General Miley's Golden Talon Division from Châlons began before mid-March when they were sent to Troop Carrier airfields in France for Operation VARSITY. On this last airborne invasion of World War II, over the Rhine, the 17th Division would at last enter battle by parachutes and gliders, not by trucks.

---

* William C. Mitchell (513th PIR, B Company), Eugene, Oregon.

23 December 1944. 73d Squadron, 434th Troop Carrier Group C-47 over DZ directly west of Bastogne at about 1538 hours.

— Courtesy: Smithsonian Institution

27

Operation WOOF-WOOF
(Parapups Destined for Battle)

LATE IN 1943, WHILE Col. Elliot Roosevelt was in command of the North African Photo Reconnaissance Unit during the Sicily invasion, Operation TORCH, he made a return flight to the United States from England on an Air Transport Command aircraft. It would have probably gone unnoticed had not his companion been a large English bull mastiff dog. The press played it up about a dog taking a serviceman's seat. As a result, air force orders were issued: Under no circumstances shall dogs be carried with passengers on ATC or military aircraft.

The orders were worded to exempt the North Atlantic Division of Maj. Gen. Harold George's Air Transport Command in the performance of its duties. Its Arctic Search and Rescue Unit, with headquarters at Presque Isle, Maine, employed many dog sled teams and drivers. They were based at airfields in Canada from Manitoba east to Labrador and Newfoundland, and in Greenland, along the flight routes to Great Britain. Often aircraft encountered icing conditions, or simply got lost, and crash-landed in remote areas. Dog sled teams were the only way of reaching crash sites in the winter.

Lt. Col. Norman D. Vaughan, from Hamilton, Massachusetts, had organized the Search and Rescue Service in 1942 and was its director. He and four of his top enlisted men, M/Sgts. Richard S.

Moulton, Louis P. Columbo, Joseph D. Healy, and S/Sgt. Edward L. Moody, were veterans of the Byrd Antarctic Expeditions of 1928- -1930. The service had a good record of rescuing downed airmen, but there were problems.

For the unit based at Presque Isle, one of its more difficult assignments took place in 1943, in Labrador. After the drivers, dogs, and sleds were landed at the airstrip nearest to a downed plane, it took them three days and nights to cover the thirty-seven air miles to the crash site because of the rough, rocky terrain. To save time, a proposed solution was to drop dog sled teams by parachute at locations that were difficult to reach.

Before the unit ever dropped a dog, they practiced with a block of wood. The first dog to "jump" was Suzee, a sled dog obtained from Eskimos in Baffinland. The harness was then perfected for two dogs per parachute, hitched together nose to tail — to keep them from fighting on the way down. A twenty-pound sand bag, on the end of a twenty-five-foot rope attached to the dogs' harness, was thrown out of the plane. After the dogs were pulled out, the ripcord attached to the airplane pulled the parachute open just like it did for paratroopers. The dogs were soon dubbed "Parapups" of the Air Transport Command. From then on, dog sled teams and drivers could be dropped into the most remote regions soon after an SOS was received.

No one conceived that any dog sled teams would be wanted or even sent to battle areas in Europe. But they were, during the last days of the Battle of the Bulge, although not as Parapups.

※　※　※　※

In early January 1945, after the liberation of Bastogne, General Bradley's 12th Army Group turned eastward in the Ardennes. North of it was Field Marshal Montgomery's 21st Army Group, and to the south, General Devers' 6th Army Group. The primary objective was beyond the Siegfried Line — all the way to the Rhine. Bradley's group consisted of General Hodges' First Army, on the left, and General Patton's Third Army on the right. Units belonging to one or both armies would pass beyond Losheim into the Schnee Eifel (Snow Mountains) which extended more than twelve miles into Germany, east of St. Vith.

On 13 January, General Patton was driven from his headquarters in Luxembourg to Bastogne where he picked up General Middleton and went to St. Vith. He described the town as "the most completely destroyed I had seen since the First World War." On the way back, they visited the 87th and 4th infantry division positions in the Third Army's northern flank. Patton was disturbed by the many cases of "frozen and trench feet" and, at the time, was "very fearful" that there would be more. There was reason for his concern.

Every day since early January the snow had become deeper. Trucks and tanks stalled in it and on the packed ice. Two miles a day was accepted as a major advance. One of the critical problems was the slowed removal of wounded, and many developed severe frostbite. Stretcher bearers were often bogged down and isolated in the snow, and the problem was expected to worsen for those units of the Third and First armies which entered the Eifel.

The experience of the 90th Infantry Division of Patton's Third Army is but one example of the problem. Before mid-January, the division headed northeast from Bastogne toward the Our River, south of St. Vith. The medical records of the 358th Infantry Regiment for two days, 16–17 January, indicate that twenty-two men were treated in the aid station: two for illness, nine for wounds, one for battle exhaustion, and ten for frozen feet.

It was a difficult time for the stretcher bearers. Frozen ground, covered with a foot or more of snow, was encountered all the way to the Our, which was frozen solid and was blanketed with a foot of snow. On 29 January, the edge of the river was located by a scout of the 2d Battalion. He found it while sweeping the snow away with his hands.

It was not determined who first came up with the thought that dog sled teams could supplement the stretcher bearers in heavy snow areas. However, the suggestion was passed forward from General Patton's headquarters, through SHAEF, to Washington where it was soon accepted. The authorization for airlifting dog sled teams to France was then given to Maj. Gen. Harold George's Air Transport Command.

At 1745 on 27 January 1945, General George received the call to provide the dog teams, related personnel and equipment, as well as aircraft, for the priority movement to France. In Boston that night, Brig. Gen. Lawrence G. Fritz, CG of the ATC North Atlantic Division, called Colonel Vaughan at Presque Isle, Maine, with instructions to mobilize the teams and equipment for the movement. A total of twenty-three dog teams (usually nine huskies in a team) and drivers were to be flown in C-47s from their remote stations to the major airfields in Labrador, Newfoundland, and Greenland. At first, Vaughan was highly disturbed; the temperment of the dogs was not suited for battle front duties. But as some of the drivers knew, he was always interested in more publicity about his service as well as himself.

Vaughan and a distinguished team were to be flown to Europe: Capt. Peter H. Hostmark of Seattle, Washington, past president of the Pacific Northwest Ski Association; Capt. William L. Shearer of Sherborn, Massachusetts, three-time winner of the New England Sled Dog Club championship; Capt. Willie Knutsen of Providence, Rhode Island, Greenland explorer and well-known sketch artist of Eskimo life; and 1st Lt. Don A. Shaw of Concord, New Hampshire, another former New England Sled Dog Club championship winner. The enlisted men, all sportsmen, trappers, and traders, were: S/Sgt. Leroy W. Billings, of Newport, New Hampshire; S/Sgt. Hulen S. Dean, of Conway, Arkansas; Sgt. Donald Adams, of Eureka, California; Sgt. Willard E. Gregg, Wynet, Nebraska: Sgt. Ralph W. McClintock, of Philadelphia, Pennsylvania; Sgt. Truman C. Watson, of Oklahoma City, Oklahoma; Sgt. Clement Mahoney, Philadelphia, Pennsylvania; Sgt. Hazzard Ruland, of Minnesota; Sgt. Bob Bacon, of Seattle, Washington; Cpl. George Esslinger, International Falls, Minnesota; and Pvt. Merlin E. Parker, of Brainerd, Minnesota.

Four Air Transport Command C-54s were slated to carry the teams to Prestwick, Scotland. Unaccustomed as the huskies were to such long flights, the aircraft were to fly at 11,000 feet altitude, to reduce the risk of problems; at that height, while chained to the bucket seats, the dogs would be kept drowsy from lack of oxygen. At Prestwick, the teams were to be promptly reloaded on C-54s from the European Division of ATC and flown to Orly Airfield, Paris, where Brig. Gen. Earl S. Hoag (ATC) would be responsible for arranging the transfer to aircraft of IX Troop Carrier Command. After that, the confused canines would endure another hour and a half confined in C-47s, before arriving in the Ardennes.

* * * *

On 30 January, Colonel Vaughan, along with key staff members and equipment from Presque Isle, was flown to Goose Bay, La-brador. With Vaughan were Captains Hostmark and Shearer, and Sergeant Moulton. The next day, after five dog sled teams were loaded, the C-54 headed over the North Atlantic. About the same time, another plane with a similar load left from Stevenville, New-foundland. The plan was for secrecy at Prestwick, where the cargos were to be transferred to other C-54s and flown to Orly. However, the secrecy turned into an embarrassment for ATC when there was a misunderstanding of communications.

The message received by ATC at Prestwick stated, "Expect Woof-Woof and attendents on Mess House Dog." It was passed on to the airbase commander who concluded that such a cryptic mes-sage could only mean that President Roosevelt was on the plane. At that time, Roosevelt and the presidential party were actually aboard the USS *Quincy,* headed toward Malta from North Africa to meet with Prime Minister Churchill.

When the C-54 taxied onto the parking apron at Orange Field, Prestwick, Scotland, there were MPs in white helmets and gloves lined up at attention near the airbase commander and his staff. The surprise came a minute later as the loading ramp was rolled up to the plane and the door opened. Yelping dogs came running out of the door and down onto the ramp with their handlers close behind. It was an embarrassing moment for both the airbase commander and Colonel Vaughan.

On 2 February a third plane flew to airfield Bluie West One (BW1), Greenland, to pick up seven dog teams. However, the C-54 did not have space for all of them and their equipment, and one team was left behind. Conveniently, there was space available on another plane, one that had made an unexpected landing in Greenland. The copilot was Willis Patterson, from Wooster, Ohio, and in 1989 he recalled that mechanical problems were the reason his plane landed at Greenland: "At BW1, we landed shortly after the plane left for Prestwick with the dog teams. Since we had room for this extra team and driver we loaded them and they became part of our manifest. We did have to delay a day and a half to replace a loom harness."

After landing at Prestwick on 4 February, it was not long until the handler and his huskies were loaded on another ATC aircraft and flown to Orly. Colonel Vaughan, still expecting another plane-load of dog teams to arrive from Canada, was naturally impatient.

Weather over the North Atlantic delayed the last plane, which finally left Newfoundland on the evening of 7 February, loaded with six dog sled teams. Because of the exigency, the planned route to Orly was by way of the Azores. Weather forced the C-54 to veer from its final course, and with a fuel shortage and mechanical problems, it made an unscheduled landing at AY-14, one of the airfields near Marseilles in southern France. The high priority "passengers" would have to be delayed en route before reaching Orly, or so it seemed at first.

For one week, Lt. Col. Bascome L. Neal, commander of the 98th Squadron, 440th Troop Carrier Group, and ten of his C-47s and their crews were on detached service at AY-14. While stationed there they had flown some 973 French military personnel between Algiers and Marseilles. On this Thursday, 8 February, they began returning to their home airfield at Orleans, located some sixty miles south-southwest of Orly. The pilots of the last two planes to leave were in the operations office when they were asked to carry the loads of unusual passengers to Orleans. The pilots, Capt. John C. Sealy, from Spokane, Washington, and 1st Lt. Dan P. Tibbot from Alliance, Nebraska, were hesitant until the purpose of the dog teams was explained. In a 1989 letter, crew chief S/Sgt. Walter F. Wilson, from Davis, Oklahoma, recalled being told by the dog handlers that they were from Canada. All they knew was that they were "to evacuate wounded out of snow areas to First Aid Stations." After they landed at Orleans, the teams were driven by truck to Orly where they joined the others. But from there, where were they to go — and when?

* * * *

General Hodges returned to Spa, Belgium, on 28 January, to reestablish his First Army headquarters in the Hôtel Britannique. Six weeks earlier, at 2200 on the night of 18 December 1944, Hodges and his staff were the last to leave Spa and move back to the First Army's rear headquarters at Chaudfontaine, near Liège. Chaudfontaine was known for its mineral springs, but it never became as famous as Spa, with its mineral waters and bath.

On 1 February, General Bradley ordered General Patton to be in Spa the next day for a conference. There the attack plans were formulated for the First and Third armies of Bradley's 12th Army

Group. It was also learned that Eisenhower had approved the transfer of the U.S. Ninth Army from Bradley's 12th Army Group to Montgomery's 21st Army Group. The objective for Bradley's forces was to secure a large stretch of the Rhine between Cologne and Koblenz. Although their attack was already under way in the Ardennes, Montgomery would not move his armies to attack until 10 February and Patton "was very bitter" about that.

Since units of both the First and Third armies were expected to encounter snow as they battled eastward, one question was "What should we do with those dog sled teams that are on the way?" It was quickly agreed that they would be based there at Spa until they were reassigned.

The meeting in Spa left another impression on Patton. It was in the same room that Field Marshal Paul von Hindenburg had his headquarters in 1918. "From the windows of this office one could see the lake around which the Kaiser walked while waiting for Hindenburg to decide whether or not the war should be continued."

During the first week of February, the battle lines in the Ardennes extended south through three contrasting areas. The first was in the Haute Fagnes (High Marshes) with elevations over 2,500 feet, about twenty miles east of Spa. The second was southeast of the Haute Fagnes and was a lowland, the Hürtgen Forest. Farther south was the Schnee Eifel (Snow Mountains), which was directly east of St. Vith.

*   *   *   *

On 9 February, nine C-47s of the 441st Troop Carrier Group, based at Chartres, arrived at Orly Airfield. Soon Colonel Vaughan's men and dogs were loaded and on their way to A-93, an airfield directly west of Liege. Its single runway of 5,000 feet was being reconstructed with (PSP) pierced steel planking, a difficult project during freezing and thawing temperatures. Vaughan and his staff were told, "We will go but we may have to return if we can't land there." But they did land and unload. After being quartered in a slaughterhouse overnight, they were hauled by trucks for twenty-eight miles the next day to Spa, southeast of Liege.

At Spa, Vaughan, Hostmark, Shearer, and Moulton explored the area and found excellent facilities for both men and dogs on the property of the Château d'Alsa, about one mile south of Spa. The

Bastogne, Belgium, 5 February 1945. Generals Eisenhower, Bradley, and Patton. — Courtesy: *Stars and Stripes*

Dependency Building, Château d'Alsa, Spa, Belgium. From 30 September to 18 December 1944, it was occupied by 654th Engineer Topographic Battalion, U.S. First Army. From 10 February to mid-March 1945, it was the quarters for men and dog teams from the Arctic Search and Rescue Unit.

— Courtesy: Mr. & Mrs. Demeret, Spa, Belgium (current owners)

dogs were assigned to the dependency building — a fancy barn. The officers and men were quartered in the Château d' Alsa. It was more luxurious than anything they had seen for months. Colonel Vaughan was assigned headquarters in the Hôtel Britannique, adjoining General Hodges' headquarters.

Two days later, the teams were divided into three groups: one was sent to the First Army, the second to the Third Army, while the third, with Colonel Vaughan and his staff, remained in Spa as reserves.

Staff Sergeant Dean was with the last six teams to arrive on the ATC flight that landed 8 February at AY-14 near Marseilles, France. They were assigned to the 87th Infantry Division of Patton's Third Army. In 1990, Hulen Dean recalled that at times they were positioned behind the infantry engaged in battle, directly in front of the artillery. The loud noise from the gunfire was too much for the sensitive ears of the huskies. During periods of heavy bursts, they howled constantly. Even while the large guns were being repositioned and it was relatively quiet, the dogs whined and barked in protest. After a few days, most of them quieted down. But not enough snow fell for them to be needed.

Staff Sergeant Moody, with other sled teams from Greenland, was sent to the 82d Airborne Division which was on the southern (right) flank of the First Army. He recalled that there was snow, but it fell on a muddy battlefield, not getting deep enough for dog sled teams. They were never called on for rescue actions.

Meanwhile in Spa, Colonel Vaughan's reserve sled dog teams were kept ready by Captain Hostmark and Master Sergeant Moulton. Although there was snow on the ground in and around the town, it was not nearly deep enough to accommodate the sleds. Therefore, the huskies were kept in training by pulling empty jeeps through the streets. The residents assumed the American vehicles were having numerous mechanical failures. The training exercises had not been publicized enough, but the children thought they were great fun to watch.

In early March, after General Hodges' First Army and General Patton's Third Army had fought their way beyond Losheim and St. Vith through the Schnee Eifel to the Rhine, there was no more need for dog sled teams. They had yet to rescue a single casualty.

*   *   *   *

The dog sled teams' return to the United States was not given the high travel priority received six weeks earlier. In mid-March, they were reassembled near St. Vith and then waited days for trucks that would take them all the way back to Le Havre, France. The next leg of their journey was aboard the SS *Robin Locksey*, in a ship convoy to New York, arriving in April. From there, many were returned to their previous stations in Maine, Canada, and Greenland. Air traffic over the North Atlantic route was busier than ever, and their services were required.

Thus ended the saga of WOOF-WOOF.

Château d'Alsa, Spa, Belgium, built in 1870. This and three other buildings on a forty-six-acre estate around a small lake were owned by Count Van Den Burg. The buildings were taken over in early 1942 and used by Nazis as a school for Hitler Youth.
— Courtesy: Mr. & Mrs. Demeret, Spa, Belgium (current owners)

C-47 flown by Lt. Rideout, 95th Troop Carrier Squadron, 27 December 1944 Bastogne Mission. Maj. Abe E. Smick, 440th Group Engineering Officer (L) and Capt. Samuel L. Higginbottom, 95th Squadron Engineering Officer (R). Flak damage: forward fuselage, engine nacelle, wing, aileron, and right landing gear-wheel.
— Courtesy: Rideout

Top photo: 1st Lt. Philip C. Hecker, 94th Troop Carrier Squadron, in cockpit of his C-47, Chateaudun, France, 1944.   — Courtesy: Hecker

Middle photo: Left to right: Sgt. Bob Bacon; 2d Lt. Howell R. Lindsey, glider pilot/navigator, 98th Squadron; S/Sgt. Hulen S. Dean; Sgt. Willard E. Gregg. (Bacon, Dean, and Gregg: dog team handlers from Canada.) 8 February 1945 at Orléans, unloading dog sled teams destined for the Ardennes.   — Courtesy: Lowden

Bottom photo: Airfield A-50, Orléans. Foreground, 1st Lt. Armand D. Venezia, navigator, 98th Squadron. Background near plane, S/Sgt. Renato Raimondi, radio operator.   — Courtesy: Lowden

PART VI

The Last Invasion:
Over the Rhine

I would dearly love to have one big airborne operation before
the war ended . . . it would really be fun to do.

> Dwight D. Eisenhower. In notes of a conference
> at SHAEF Forward HW. 12 March 1945. From
> *Out of the Blue*, 1957.

I am with Field Marshal Montgomery at his H.Q. He has just
ordered the launching of the main battle to force the Rhine on a
broad front with Wesel at the centre. The operation will be supported by about two thousand guns and by the landing of an airborne corps.

> In a letter by Prime Minister Churchill to Marshal Stalin.
> 23 March 1945. From *The Second World War*, Vol. 6, 1951.

I had flown up to Hodges' CP that morning and we loitered in
the air as the long train of C-47s and a few fat-bellied C-46s
swarmed by.

> Omar N. Bradley. From *A Soldier's Story*, 1951.

Never having viewed an airborne operation, I flew up from
Sissonne in a . . . Troop Carrier transport. It was an awesome spectacle.

> James M. Gavin. From *On To Berlin*, 1978.

319

28

Invasion Plans, Over the Rhine

BY 20 MARCH 1945, thirteen airfields of the IX Troop Carrier Command in France were surrounded by tent encampments of Maj. Gen. William Miley's 17th Airborne Division. At the same time in England, the British 6 Airborne Division was being located at eleven RAF airfields. They were preparing for the largest single day airborne operation of World War II, conceived to facilitate Operation PLUNDER, the amphibious crossing of the Rhine by Lt. Gen. Sir Miles C. Dempsey's British Second Army and Lt. Gen. William H. Simpson's Ninth U.S. Army, under Field Marshal Montgomery.

The date for PLUNDER, 23–24 March 1945, was not made firm by SHAEF until the 14th. At General Dempsey's urging, the objective for the airborne forces, Operation VARSITY, was placed around the Diersfordter Wald, the woods between three and five miles east of the Rhine and directly northwest of Wesel, rather than closer to the river as originally planned. This would place it out of range of artillery supporting the amphibious assault. Generals Brereton and Ridgway were in full agreement that they would go in by daylight after the night assault was under way across the Rhine. There was no doubt that the Germans positioned at least ten of their divisions east of the Rhine to oppose the expected invasion. The airborne attack on their rear and on their flanks would cut them off.

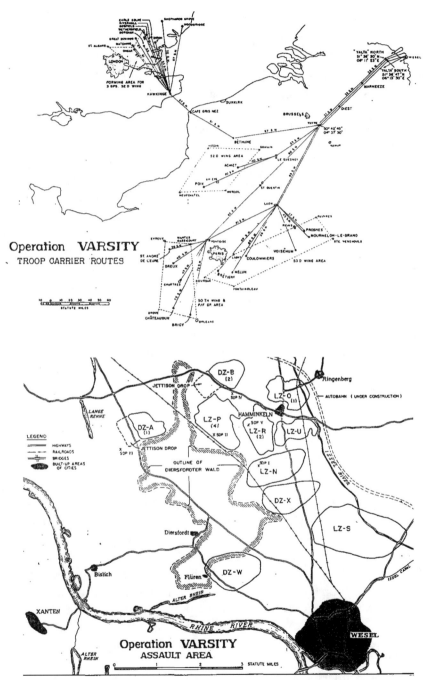

— Source for maps courtesy Maxwell AFB, AL.
Warren, USAF Historical Studies, No. 97

*   *   *   *

Operation VARSITY was one of two airborne operations proposed at SHAEF on 2 November, before the Battle of the Bulge. It
was targeted for New Year's Day. But it was not until 2 February
that VARSITY was reconsidered and approved by General Eisenhower's combined chiefs of staff. At the time, the 50th Troop Carrier Wing was the only Troop Carrier wing in France with its four
groups based at airfields southwest of Paris. On 12 February the five
groups of the 53d Wing began moving to airfields scattered over a
wide area east and southeast of Paris. The bomb-damaged French
airfields around Amiens, more than forty miles north of Paris, were
undergoing extensive repairs. Only two were usable in late February
and early March, providing bases for two groups of the 52d Wing,
the 313th and 314th. The other three groups (61st, 315th and 316th)
remained in England, assigned to carry British paratroops from U.S.
Eighth Air Force airfields in East Anglia.

During the planning, the need for an advance airdrop by pathfinder teams was questioned. Since the airborne objectives were so
close to the Allied ground forces holding the west bank of the
Rhine, dropping a small number of pathfinders in the midst of
strong German positions was considered unnecessary — even suicidal. However, the IX Troop Carrier Pathfinder Group was still
needed to fly paratroops of the 17th Division. On 27 February,
Lieutenant Colonel Crouch was ordered to move his Pathfinder
Group from Chalgrove, England, to the airfield at Chartres, France,
the location of the 50th Troop Carrier Wing headquarters.

*   *   *   *

By the end of February, plans for the exercise of command and
control of VARSITY were firm. Under General Brereton's First Allied Airborne Army were General Williams, heading its Troop Carrier component, and General Ridgway, in command of its airborne.
Brereton and Ridgway would be in France; therefore operational
control of Troop Carrier missions from England was assigned to the
British 38 Group AOC (Air Officer Commanding). Air Marshal Sir
Arthur Coningham, AOC of the Second Tactical Air Force, RAF,
was to command all Allied air forces in support of the assault, except
for Brereton's.

One primary concern of both Brereton and Ridgway was the

new Curtiss C-46 Commandos that General Williams assigned to one Troop Carrier group for Operation VARSITY. None of their paratroopers were familiar with it.

The Commandos

Since January, groups of IX Troop Carrier Command were ready for Operation VARSITY — all except one — the 313th Troop Carrier group of the 52d Wing, based at Folkingham, England. It was selected to replace its C-47s with the larger C-46 aircraft and its CG-4A gliders with larger CG-13A gliders. It was the first Troop Carrier group in the ETO to be so equipped.

The new aircraft began arriving in mid-January and the group's first priority was transition training of flight and ground crews in the C-46. On every good weather day during February, all air crews were kept busy. After transition, there was practice in formation flying. They were flying a much different aircraft and some likened it to a whale in comparison to the old gooneybird. Then routine training as such was stopped.

In late February, Col. James J. Roberts, Jr., was told to move his 313th Group to B-54, Achiet, France. By 10 March, the air echelon was relocated. The flights over the English Channel allowed for more transition training — even for towing CG-4A gliders, loaded with vehicles and personal effects such as footlockers.

However, on Friday, 2 March, and during the next week, fifty-six C-46s were sent to Airfield A-63 near Reims; not far from where the 17th, 82d and 101st airborne divisions were encamped. In addition to ground instructions, the training exercises included some 125 lifts in which 3,246 paratroopers made practice jumps. Most of them were from Col. James W. Coutts' 513th PIR, 17th Airborne Division, encamped at Châlons-sur-Marne.

In contrast with the C-47, the C-46 could carry double the number of paratroopers. Because it had two doors at the rear of the cabin, one on each side, the exit time was the same as for the C-47 with only one door on the left side of the cabin. However, the training emphasis at Airfield A-63 concerned the physical coordination for jumping from either door of an unfamiliar aircraft. One of the jokes among the paratroopers at the time was "the left door is the *right* one and the right door is the *wrong* one."

The men in the 513th correctly concluded that their regiment would be the only one of the 17th Airborne Division to make their first jump into battle from the new Commandos. Yet there were paratroopers from the 82d Airborne Division at A-63, one that Ken M. Kasse (from Perryville, Ohio) still remembered years later.

With others from I Company, Private Kasse was aboard the C-46 for the practice jump. Seated on the left side next to the jump door, he would be the first one out. Then another paratrooper climbed aboard. He had two stars on his helmet and an 82d Airborne patch on his sleeve. Kasse recognized Maj. Gen. James M. Gavin immediately. The general asked the private if he could take his seat so that he could be first out the left door on the practice jump. Ken quickly agreed, and he still remembers that jump! Out of the door, he was almost on the general's back. Yet, after the landing, he never saw General Gavin again.

Still more pilot flight time in the C-46 was wanted before undertaking a major airborne combat mission. One of the senior pilots in the 49th Squadron, Capt. Robert W. "Blick" Blickensderfer from Conneaut, Ohio, had acquired only sixty-two hours in the C-46 before Operation VARSITY. And that included the very special practice mission called TOKEN, from Achiet on 17 March. It involved only six C-46s flown by veteran pilots and crews — those who would lead formations in VARSITY. From takeoff to landing, TOKEN lasted three hours and forty minutes. It was a simulation of the upcoming mission in every aspect, including preflight briefings. The flight route was to an LZ near Montlaucon and back.

Two top commanders were there to witness the mission: Lt. Gen. Lewis Brereton, CG of the First Allied Airborne Army, and Brig. Gen. Harold "Hal" Clark, CO of the 52d Troop Carrier Wing. They wanted to observe, firsthand, how effective the larger C-46s could be, with double the load of the C-47s.

That night, General Clark and his staff remained for a farewell party given for Colonel Roberts, who was being reassigned back to the United States. The next day, Lt. Col. William A. Filer took command of the 313th Troop Carrier Group.

*   *   *   *

The move of the 17th Airborne Division from Châlons-Sur-

Marne was classified secret. Before their assignments, paratroops and glider troops of the division removed the insignia (the Eagle Claw) from their clothing. The troops were to be moved to Troop Carrier airfields with as little notice as possible. All they knew was that they were going into battle somewhere — this time by air.

Two hours after sunset, on 19 March, some 2,000 men of the 513th PIR climbed aboard huge semitrailers and were driven to a railroad siding where they were loaded in boxcars, not unlike the "40 and 8" boxcars used in World War I. Even with the doors closed, the train trip was uncomfortably cold, but there was a steady flow of heated conversation. Many of the men were recent replacements for those wounded or killed during the battles in the Ardennes and at the Our River.

A few hours before boarding the train, 1st Lt. Samuel Calhoun arrived at Châlons directly after his release from the hospital. Upon reporting to Capt. Marshall M. "Bud" Reynolds, F Company commander, they had much to talk about. Reynolds had been wounded during the crossing of the Our River. However, he returned to the regiment after less than two weeks in the hospital. He said he was AWOL. Calhoun had missed the ceremony at Châlons when General Miley decorated a number of paratroopers for gallant action in the Ardennes and during the crossing of the Our River. Of F Company, only Reynolds was awarded the Bronze Star for the battle at the Our.

At 0400 the train arrived at a station that had its identifying signs covered. The men of the 513th PIR were not to know they were being unloaded at Bapaume in northern France. Admittedly, it was a good example of the extent that secrecy was attempted during pre-mission movements. It was still dark when trucks hauled the paratroopers the last eight miles to Airfield B-54, where the 313th Troop Carrier Group, with its new C-46 Commandos, was based after moving from England just three weeks earlier.

On 19 March, General Clark and some of his staff returned to brief the 313th Group's headquarters staff on details about the upcoming mission. During the next day, Maj. Gen. Paul Williams, CG of IX Troop Carrier Command, visited the airfield, "presumably to determine the combat efficiency of the C-46." Earlier, he had made the final decision that C-46s would be employed for VARSITY, but not the CG-13A gliders. The big gliders had not been tested enough to be used on a combat mission.

Williams' visit was on the same day that the 513th PIR arrived. The War Diary of the 313th Group noted, "So carefully were they bivouacked, and so quietly, that few knew of their presence."

As of 21 March, the airfield was closed and no one was allowed to enter or leave except on official business. Among those allowed on and off the airfield were a number of accredited journalists and photographers, among them Robert Capa from *Life* magazine. He and a number of journalists requested permission to go on the mission.

The four squadrons' S-2s spent the day working with the Group S-2 on the intelligence phase of the operation. They were furnished maps and overlays of the flight route to DZ X, located east of the Rhine River, about two and one-half miles northwest of Wesel. That and the tentative date (24 March) were "Top Secret."

During the afternoon of the 22d the squadron commanders and operations officers were briefed at group headquarters. Also in attendance were Col. James W. Coutts, CO of the 513th PIR, and his G-2, Capt. Gates Ivy. The 49th Squadron was to lead the formation of seventy-two C-46s, eighteen from each squadron. After returning from the briefing that evening, both Maj. George A. Smith and Capt. Jack L. Cardwell of the 49th Squadron studied the mission thoroughly in preparation for the next day's briefing.

* * * *

Late in the afternoon of the 22d, the last C-46 ferry flight returned from Folkingham with personnel and baggage. One of the crew members, navigator 1st Lt. David Hardy, from Chicago, Illinois, was well known in his 49th Squadron as a radio buff — always turning the dial and listening. On this day he could hardly wait to tell his barracks mates (mostly glider pilots) what he heard. "I caught Axis Sally on the radio two hours ago. Guess what! She said, 'We know that part of the 17th Airborne Division is at Achiet. We'll be waiting for you and other bad boys at the Rhine.'" He added, "And she named other Troop Carrier airfields where units of the 17th Division were encamped, too!"

Hardy's audience stopped laughing after he said, "There's more! . . . I saw the crew assignments posted in the Op's office. The 49th is to lead the mission with eighteen C-46s. And Colonel Filer is

Major Smith's copilot in the lead plane." After placing his hand on his prematurely bald head, he smiled and said, "I'm in Blick's plane, Chalk Number 10; we head the second flight of the 49th."

A glider pilot asked, "Well, when's the mission?"

Dave thought for a moment. Then, "Don't know. She didn't say."

* * * *

During the morning of 23 March, each squadron briefed its pilots, copilots, and navigators, along with officers of the 513th PIR battalion that it was to carry. At 0900, the 49th Squadron meeting was headed by Lt. Col. William A. Filer. Present were Lt. Col. Allen Miller and his 2d Battalion company commanders. One was Captain Reynolds of F Company. He and his three platoons were assigned to the second flight, in a three-plane element headed by 1st Lt. Gilbert A. Whiteside, in Chalk No. 13 position. Not being superstitious, Bud Reynolds gave his platoon leaders their plane assignments later that night.

The formation, in two thirty-six-plane serials, was assigned to drop paratroops at DZ X. The serials, numbered five and six, were to follow four others from France: the Pathfinder Group, the 438th Group (2 serials) and the 434th, destined for DZ W, with paratroops of the 507th PIR. The timing for joining the formation would be critical, due to varying airspeeds between the C-46s and the C-47s.

The Flight Routes

To place nearly 17,000 well equipped paratroopers and glider troops from both France and England at four DZs and six LZs in Germany within a two-hour period before midday on the 24th required the most intricate scheduling and routing. All Troop Carrier aircraft were to be funneled to a command assembly point, located at Wavre, southeast of Brussels. Those from England, after crossing the Channel to Cap Gris Nez, had before them another 138 miles via Béthune to Wavre. The flight courses for each of the IX Troop Carrier wings in France were designated to avoid crossing each other's assembly areas or their routes to Wavre. Navigational aids were placed at seventeen locations, including all turning points. From Wavre, the course for all aircraft was northeast for ninety-two miles to Weeze, a village on the Nierse River, about twelve miles west of the Rhine. The location was given the code name YALTA and designated as the IP for the final approach. Three traffic lanes, spaced one and one-half miles apart, were provided for the flights between Wavre and YALTA. The north lane was to be taken to YALTA NORTH by the British airborne contingent from England, with both paratroops and glider troops of 6 Airborne Division. The center lane was allocated solely to the IX Troop Carrier Command glider tow serials carrying troops of the 17th Airborne Division. Troop Carrier planes carrying paratroops of the 17th were to follow the southern lane to the IP, YALTA SOUTH.

Two different altitudes were specified for the northern lane. The British RAF 38 and 46 groups, towing 440 Horsa and Hamilcar gliders, were to fly at 2,500 feet. The slower Dakota (C-47) tug-glider serials, flying at 115 miles per hour, were scheduled sufficiently ahead of the Halifax and Stirling-towed glider formations which could manage 135 MPH or more. Thus from the IP, YALTA NORTH, there would be a continuous arrival of British glider troops at the LZs. The American C-47s with British paratroops were to fly a lower altitude of 1,500 feet until they neared the IP. The paradrops on the DZs were to coincide with the glider landings.

In the center lane, American glider tows, with 906 Wacos, were to fly in pairs of pairs echeloned to the right, with 1,500 feet between successive elements. They were from all three IX Troop Carrier Command wings. The first contingent was to be flown by the 437th, 436th, 435th and the 439th Troop Carrier groups with gliders on double tow. This would be the first time in World War II that the double tow would be used, other than in training. The formation of eight serials, two from each group, would consist of 296 C-47s and 592 Wacos. The gliders were to carry some 3,600 troops, 654 tons of supplies, 208 jeeps, 101 trailers, and forty artillery pieces. From their respective airfields (Coulommiers, Brétigny, Melun, and Chateaudun) they would carry the 194th Glider Infantry Regiment, the 680th and 681st field artillery battalions and four batteries of the 155th Antiaircraft Battalion to LZ S directly north of Wesel.

The last flight contingent, with 314 gliders on single tow, was to be flown in seven serials by four Troop Carrier groups to LZ N, located on the east edge of the Diersfordter Wald, four miles north of Wesel. The first two serials, each with forty-five gliders in tow, were from the 440th at Bricy. The next two serials, each with forty-eight gliders, were from the 441st at Dreux and the 442d at St. André de l'Eure. The fifth and sixth serials, with twenty-four gliders in each, were also to be flown by the 441st and 442d, from Chartres. The last two forty-glider serials were assigned to the 314th at Poix. The glider loads would consist of over 1,320 troops of the 139th Engineer Battalion and others, including medics, signalmen and staff personnel. Additional supplies and equipment included 143 jeeps, ninety-seven trailers, and twenty guns and mortars. Unprepared for first line battle actions, these specialists would be dependent on the 513th Parachute Infantry Regiment and 464th Parachute Field Artillery Battalion, which would be dropped earlier at DZ X, located immediately south of LZ N.

Almost 5,000 paratroops and their equipment were to be flown by 298 aircraft, in seven serials, to DZ W and DZ X by the southern route. The IX Pathfinder Group, with forty-six of its C-47s located at Chartres, was assigned by General Williams to head the first four serials to DZ W, with the 507th Parachute Infantry Regiment aboard. Lieutenant Colonel Crouch would pilot the lead plane. Next to follow were two serials with eighty-six planes from the 438th Group from Prosnes. The fourth, with forty-nine aircraft from the 434th Group from Mourmelon-le-Grande, was to carry paratroops from the 464th Parachute Field Artillery Battalion. A total 2,479 paratroopers with equipment were to be dropped at DZ W. The last three serials were slated for DZ X, with 2,071 paratroopers of the 513th PIR and 387 paratroopers plus twelve howitzers, of the 466th Parachute Field Artillery Battalion. The 466th would arrive last in forty-five conventional C-47s from the 434th Group. In the two thirty-six-plane serials ahead of them, paratroops of the 513th would exit by two doors, one on each side of the C-46s flown by the 313th Group from Achiet. This would be the only airborne combat mission in the ETO in which C-46 Curtiss Commandos were used.

29

Varsity Team in Action

GENERAL MONTGOMERY SCHEDULED PLUNDER, his amphibious assault across the Rhine, for the night of 23 March, subject to VARSITY's punctual execution on the morning of the 24th. The final decision to launch the transports was made by Brereton and Coningham on 23 March at 1600. Their meteorologists forecasted good weather for the next day. Thick haze was expected during early morning around Wesel, but it would clear before the Troop Carrier aircraft were scheduled to arrive. At least two miles of visibility was predicted. Montgomery was given the "go ahead" message.

The first assault boats with four battalions of the British 51 Division moved out into the Rhine at 2100. Their objective was Rees, twelve miles downstream from Wesel. At 2200, the Commando Brigade began its crossing about two miles west of Wesel. The assault by the Ninth U.S. Army began at 0200, south of the Lippe River's confluence with the Rhine. Unexpectedly, at most of the British crossings, the opposite bank was thinly held by the Germans. During all that morning, however, most of the British forces remained pinned close to the river by enemy artillery and mortar fire, particularly at Rees. It became more difficult for succeeding Rhine crossings after daylight. When the airborne assault began, the situation changed. Still, the German stronghold in and around Wesel held on stubbornly throughout the day.

The Witnesses

General Eisenhower arrived at Lt. Gen. William H. Simpson's Ninth Army headquarters on the 23d. The next morning he accompanied Simpson to a convenient hill, south of Xanten, to observe the airborne operations from a church tower overlooking the Rhine. In his book, *Crusade in Europe,* Eisenhower did not mention that Churchill and Montgomery were also present. He wrote:

> Fog and the smoke of the battlefield prevented a complete view of the airborne operation but I was able to see some of the action. A number of our planes were hit by antiaircraft, generally, however, only after they had dropped their loads of paratroopers. As they swung away from the battle area they seemed to come over a spot where anti-aircraft fire was particularly accurate. Those that were struck fell inside our own lines, and in nearly every case the crews succeeded in saving themselves by taking to their parachutes.

In *The Second World War,* Vol. 6, *Triumph and Tragedy,* Churchill in turn neglected to mention that Eisenhower and Simpson were also there. He wrote:

> In the morning Montgomery had arranged for me to witness from a hilltop amid rolling downland the great fly-in. It was full daylight before the subdued but intense roar and rumbling of swarms of aircraft stole upon us. After that in the course of half an hour over 2000 aircraft streamed overhead in their formations. My view-point had been well chosen. The light was clear enough to enable one to see where the descent on the enemy took place. The aircraft faded from sight, and then almost immediately afterwards returned towards us at a different level. The parachutists were invisible even to the best fieldglasses. But now there was a double murmur and roar of reinforcements arriving and of those who had delivered their attacks returning. Soon one saw with a sense of tragedy aircraft in twos and threes coming back askew, asmoke, of even in flames. Also at this time tiny specks came floating to earth. Imagination built on a good deal of experience told a hard and painful tale. It seemed however that nineteen out of every twenty of the aircraft that had

started came back in good order, having discharged their mission. This was confirmed by what we heard an hour later when we got back to headquarters.

Churchill may have lost track of time. Almost two hours elapsed while more than 2,500 transports and some 1,200 gliders passed "overhead." If his statement that "nineteen out of every twenty of the aircraft that started came back in good order . . ." is assumed to mean that 5 percent of *all* planes on VARSITY were destroyed or missing, the percentage for some Troop Carrier units were less favorable.

Paratroops from England

British paratroops were flown by American Troop Carriers of the 61st, 315th, and 316th groups from Chipping Ongar, Boreham, and Wethersfield, England. Between 1709 and 0745, 242 C-47s, loaded with about 3,900 paratroopers of 6 Airborne Division, took off. There was a brief delay in embarking at Boreham while the British finished their tea. The planes soon assembled into elements of three, those elements into flights of nine, and the flights into serials for the first formation's departure for Hawkinge, the departure point for the Channel crossing.

Everything went well all the way to the Rhine. There were no navigation problems. The sky was clear and visibility was excellent. After crossing the Channel, aircraft of the RAF Fighter Command flew cover and no enemy aircraft were to be sighted near the route that day. However, the transports encountered unexpected, poor visibility east of the Rhine. It was from the extensive smoke screen that Montgomery had ordered to camouflage the amphibious operations along nearly fifty miles of the Rhine.

The arrival of the first three serials from England over DZ A began at 0951 with eighty planes of the 61st Group and thirty-nine of the 316th. Two had turned back for mechanical reasons. After dropping 1,920 men of 3 Parachute Brigade, enemy flak brought down three C-47s and damaged thirty others.

The next three serials, with forty planes of the 316th and eighty-one planes of the 315th Group, arrived over DZ B (located beyond DZ-A) at 1003. Within fifteen minutes, 1,917 men of 5

Parachute Brigade jumped from altitudes between 700 and 1,000 feet. It was after the left turn to head back that the ten C-47s Eisenhower referred to were shot down while still east of the Rhine. Many were damaged and seven soon crash-landed in friendly territory.

Glider Troops from England

At airfields in England, 440 heavy Horsa and Hamilcar gliders were loaded with almost 3,400 troops with over 300 jeeps and trailers, and sixty-six artillery pieces of 6 Airlanding Brigade. The tow planes were converted Stirling and Halifax bombers from 38 and 46 groups. Because of the time required for climb out and formation assembly, the takeoffs began at 0600. One tug failed to take off and thirty-five gliders broke loose after takeoff, two ditching in the Channel. All aboard were quickly rescued. The rest, 402 tugs and gliders, approached the Rhine at 1000.

They followed the parachute serials, but at higher altitudes, ranging from the planned 2,500 feet to 3,500 feet. The objectives in the British sector were around Hamminkeln, almost five miles north of Wesel. The four landing zones were designated O, R, U, and P. In addition, seventy gliders were to land at DZs A and B with reinforcements for the paratroops.

Over haze and smoke from combat, visibility was between 1,000 and 3,000 yards. Glider releases began at 1011 and about 90 percent of them landed on or very near their LZs. The high-altitude releases gave the German gunners considerable time to fire on the formation. Seven tow planes were destroyed or subsequently reported missing. There was even more time to fire on the descending gliders. Ten were shot down and 284 were damaged by flak. Of the British glider pilots, thirty-eight were killed, thirty-seven were wounded and 135 were reported missing, for a 28 percent casualty rate.

By nightfall, organized enemy resistance in the British sector was broken with heavy German casualties and over 600 taken prisoners. The cost to 6 Airborne was far from light: 347 dead, 731 wounded, and 319 missing. Many of the missing, however, were soon found and rejoined their units.

Paratroops from France

In France, a total of 298 planes were assigned in seven serials to carry almost 5,000 paratroops of the 17th Airborne Division to two DZs over the Rhine. First off at 0725 from Chartres was Colonel Crouch with his forty-six-plane serial. In his plane was Col. Edson D. Raff, commander of the 507th PIR. (Raff had commanded the paratroops in Operation TORCH, the invasion of North Africa.) Within ten minutes after the last aircraft left the ground, the serial assembled in formation and headed for Wavre. With prompt takeoffs and assemblies from Prosnes, eighty-six planes of the 438th Group proceeded toward Wavre to take second and third serial positions behind Crouch. From Mourmelon-le-Grand, forty-nine C-47s of the 434th Group joined the formation as the fourth serial. With 2,479 paratroopers of the 507th PIR and the 464th Parachute Field Artillery Battalion, 181 C-47s headed toward their objective, DZ W, three miles northwest of Wesel. After encountering heavy smoke from battle, the airdrop began about 0950 on the west side of the DZ. The fourth serial arrived about 1005 with the 464th Parachute Field Artillery Battalion. One plane was shot down during the turn back from the DZ.

Some of the 507th were dropped in the woods directly north of the DZ. Maj. Gen. William M. Miley, CG, 17th Airborne Division, jumped with the 464th, "but was little more than an observer during the initial stages of the battle. High-level coordination of the innumerable small-unit actions was neither possible or necessary." By 1100, the 3d Battalion had taken about 150 prisoners. German resistance almost disappeared by early afternoon, after the 1st Battalion attacked a fortress castle near Flüren. Relieved by the 3d Battalion around noon, the 1st Battalion had cost the enemy five tanks and about 500 soldiers taken prisoners.

Before 1400, the 507th had taken its objectives. Prisoners were taken too quickly to count and interrogate precisely. It was estimated that approximately 1,000 surrendered from three regiments of the German 84th Division. It took the 507th the rest of the day to link up with ground forces and other airborne units.

The Commandos

Early in the morning at Achiet, seventy-two C-46s of the 313th Group were loaded with paratroopers of the 513th PIR and their equipment before many of the aircraft crews arrived. The aircraft were parked on individual PSP hardstands along the sides of the taxiways around the airfield. In addition, eight aircraft and crews, two from each squadron, were parked as spares.

After Colonel Filer, Major Smith, and war correspondent Robert Wilson were driven by staff car to their C-46, they posed for photographs before boarding. Wilson certainly felt privileged when he was assigned to the lead plane of the 49th Squadron (Chalk No. 1). There would be other correspondents in each of the three squadrons to follow, but Wilson could write that he was in the first Commando over the Rhine along with Lt. Col. Allen C. "Boots and Helmet" Miller and some of the staff of his 2d Battalion. He intended to summarize his notes for early publication, during the return flight to Achiet.

Captain Reynolds' F Company boarded the three C-46s of the second flight of the 49th Squadron, Chalk Numbers 13, 14, and 15. The company's executive officer, 1st Lt. Sam Dean, from Gaffney, South Carolina, platoon leader 1st Lt. Isham Sann, S/Sgt. Joseph Kitson, from Ridgewood, New Jersey, and others in the 2d Platoon would fly in Number 13 position. Reynolds and F Company's 1st sergeant, Royal Donovan, loaded with the 1st Platoon in Number 15, and 1st Lieutenant Calhoun and his 3d Platoon climbed aboard Number 14. Before boarding, Reynolds' final guidance to his platoon leaders was, "Our first objective on the ground is to get together, and then give 'em Hell."

✻ ✻ ✻ ✻

Exactly at 0800, Major Smith turned his C-46 onto the primary south-southwest runway for takeoff. He and all the pilots to follow were well aware of the 20- to 25-MPH prevailing crosswinds from the right, not unusual for March. The shorter secondary runway that matched the wind direction had not yet been repaired. It still had many bomb craters in it. The fat-bodied C-46, with its large fin and rudder, was susceptible to crosswinds. Therefore, Smith began his takeoff run near the runway's right edge, as did those who followed.

The first flight of nine Commandos lifted off in order, as did the first three of the second flight, led by Capt. Robert W. "Blick" Blickensderfer. Thirteenth for takeoff, 1st Lt. Gilbert A. Whiteside's plane drifted too far left before lift off. After riding the left edge of the runway, it veered off the pavement, over the grass shoulder, plowed into and ran over a crash truck, a fire truck, a six-by-six truck, seven jeeps, and a motorcycle. Whiteside had the presence of mind to cut the exterior parapacks (full of explosives) before his C-46 neared the parked vehicles.

Three six-by-six trucks arrived quickly and loaded the 2d Platoon as they climbed out of the crashed Commando. Visibly shaken and confused, they were hauled to the 49th Squadron's first spare plane still parked on its hardstand. This would be the fourth airborne combat mission for pilot Capt. Robert F. "Scotty" Scott, from New Braunfels, Texas. Now he would be the 313th Group's Tail-end Charlie. His crew chief, T/Sgt. Frank J. Joda, and radio operator, S/Sgt. Vincent Russo, were veterans of Operation MARKET. It was the first combat mission for Scott's copilot, 2d Lt. Frederick C. Davis and navigator 2d Lt. Charles D. McCall.

* * * *

As the C-46 Commandos began assembling into their formation positions east of Achiet, Colonel Miller rose from his bucket seat and walked back to the rear of the plane. With an unlit cigar clamped between his teeth, he looked out from the left exit door for a few moments and then again from the right door. Apparently satisfied that his battalion was airborne he popped a dramamine pill into his mouth and strode forward to navigator 1st Lt. William Sussner's seat behind the cockpit. "When will we reach the DZ?" he asked. Bill answered, "1016 hours as scheduled." Miller returned to his seat and seemed to doze off, unaware that one of his platoons would arrive late. Facing him across the aisle, Robert Wilson was busily writing his notes.

Radio silence between aircraft was mandatory, and Captain Blickensderfer was not aware that one of the planes of his second flight was not in the formation — Number 13. At the last briefing, he was instructed to follow Major Smith's first flight all the way to the DZ. He also remembered Lt. Col. William Filer's parting words at the 23 March briefing, "Follow me and you'll get out quick." Thus

Hardy, Blick's navigator, had spare time between logging locations, headings, and times en route. Periodically, he tuned in Radio Berlin, only to learn that a large Allied airborne mission was under way.

* * * *

Ingenious as they seemed, the flight routes and schedules left too little margin for error over Wavre. Essentially, the plan was for the Commandos and the glider formation to cross flight paths at Wavre. From there, the glider serials were to fly the center lane, at 1,000 feet, to the YALTA checkpoint before crossing the Rhine. From Warve, the two Commando serials, also at 1,000 feet, were to fly the left lane, which would then be temporarily free of British aircraft. After outpacing the glider train, the Commandos were to shift to the right-hand lane and head northeast toward the YALTA SOUTH checkpoint.

As Major Smith approached Wavre at 0934, the C-47s, with gliders on double tow, were actually crossing his flight path from his right side. He veered left and made a considerable detour before he headed on a northeast heading, presumably in the right-hand lane toward YALTA SOUTH. Following close behind Smith's 49th Squadron was the 29th Squadron with its operations officer, Maj. Robert F. Laird, flying the lead plane. Their airspeeds were over 180 MPH the entire 104 miles to the Rhine.

Leading the following serial, Maj. William G. Oliver, Jr., operations officer of the 48th Squadron, had more time for his decision. Instead of turning left behind the leading serial, he climbed to 2,000 feet and passed over the glider train. The 47th Squadron, with Maj. Maynard T. Swartz piloting its lead C-46, followed. Some fifteen minutes later, the 48th and 47th squadrons were back in formation behind the 49th and 29th squadrons. They followed the leader all the way to the DZ, which was thought to be DZ X.[*]

The seventh and last parachute serial with forty-five C-47s of the 434th Group from Mourmelon-le-Grande fell in behind the 313th at Wavre. The serial was carrying the 466th Parachute Field Artillery Battalion. Because it flew at airspeeds under 150 MPH, it crossed the Rhine some fifteen minutes after the Commandos.

---

[*] Major Smith, Colonel Filer, and navigator Lieutenant Sussner were killed in action on the mission. What passed between them regarding the decision will never be known.

Close behind the C-47s were two C-46s. The two stragglers were from the 48th and 47th squadrons of the 313th Group at Achiet. As standbys, they had been loaded with paratroops from planes unable to take off, one with engine problems and the other with a flat tire.

Captain Scott never caught up with the others. The loading of his C-46 required considerable time; both paratroops and parapacks had to be hauled from the crash site of the C-46, Chalk Number 13, near the far end of the Achiet runway. When he began his takeoff at 0930, his 49th Squadron was approaching Wavre. He was ninety miles behind it and accepted the fact that even flying at over 200 MPH, he would never catch up.

* * * *

At the YALTA IP, twelve miles from the Rhine, the Commandos began the final approach. Although they were over a mile north of their designated route, Major Smith, Colonel Filer, and their navigator, Lieutenant Sussner, must have thought they were on course when they crossed the Rhine at 1005. They dropped down to 700 feet. The battle smoke remained a hindrance, but the configuration of the forest (Diersforder Wald) they saw ahead convinced them that DZ X was just beyond on the east side of the forest, as shown on their maps. Actually, they were heading toward LZ R and LZ U, the British glider landing zones directly south of Hamminkeln.

Approaching the forest, Smith abruptly chopped his throttles back to decrease his airspeed to 110 MPH to prepare for the jump. At that moment, his serial was raked by intense and accurate light flak and small-arms fire from the left and heavier flak from the right. At 1008, Colonel Miller and his paratroops began jumping. Crew chief T/Sgt. Alvin F. Rehse, on this, his fourth combat mission, was at the left door, pulling in the static lines when he felt the flak explosion. After running forward to get radio operator S/Sgt. William L. Magruder and radar technician Sgt. Seymore Greenstein to help, he ran back to the right door and pulled in the static lines. As he started forward again, he saw flames streaking back from the left engine. Then heavy smoke from burning hydraulic fluid swept into the cabin.

Still carrying the static lines, Rehse saw flames sweeping over the wing from the right engine. As more smoke entered the cabin, he decided that he and his crew should parachute while they still had sufficient altitude. Later he wrote in his interrogation report, "I figured the quickest way to get the men clear was to lead them out instead of trying to force them out first. The radio and radar operators were standing around rather spellbound. I ripped off my flak suit, which came off easily, and jumped out." The others followed.

Rehse did not mention correspondent Robert Wilson, the last man known to jump, but Wilson reported later that someone pushed him out. His savior was probably William Sussner, who remained in the Commando with George Smith and William Filer as it went down and crashed in flames.

In Number 2 position, on Smith's right wing, Capt. Charles F. Cochran and his copilot, 2d Lt. Phil H. Fortie, went unscathed until they were climbing to the right after leaving the DZ. Their plane was hit between the left engine and the fuselage. Navigator 1st Lt. William R. Pully, from Richmond, Virginia, told Cochran that flames were entering the fuselage. The fire was near the hydraulic fluid reservoir and was spreading. Pully raced back to where crew chief Cpl. Barney J. Viviano and radio operator S/Sgt. Kingdon Taylor were trying to kill the fire with the extinguisher. As the plane began losing altitude in a left turn, Viviano and Taylor jumped out, followed by Pully who later wrote in his interrogation report:

> When I reached the ground I was taken prisoner by a group of German soldiers who took me, and the crew chief who had landed near by, to a flour mill near the village of Hamminkeln. We were treated quite well but we did not understand German and they did not speak English. We were with them in the mill from about 1030 hours until 1430 hours. They took my lighter, escape kit and purse but did not see my wrist watch which was pushed far up my wrist. At about 1430 the British had the place surrounded and the Germans pushed me out toward them and then followed me themselves. The British troopers went inside and got the rest of those who did not come out.

Flying in Number 3 position, on Smith's left wing, were 1st Lt. Crockette B. Goerner and his copilot, F/O Thomas P. Kelly; crew chief T/Sgt. Philip N. Linn, and radio operator S/Sgt. Joseph B. Langlois. Nothing is known about the last moments of Goerner and his crew after the paratroops jumped; their plane crashed in flames with the crew aboard.

✻   ✻   ✻   ✻

In the first flight's Number 9 position, 2d Lt. Gordon R. "Gordy" Wood had a good view of the planes ahead. In 1987, referring to a copy of his interrogation report, he wrote about it again from Dublin, California:

All looked good as we approached the IP with planes coming in from the right and left of us which we could see in the distance. About the time we hit the IP we could see planes coming out of the first drop zone all in formation and it looked like a piece of cake. The picture soon changed with the second serial coming out. They were all over the sky and I can remember at least two going down in fire.

We were coming in pretty hot about 170 [MPH] and as we hit the first drop zone, Major Smith started his slow down. We hit the second drop zone and were picking up very heavy fire. We were still going too fast and the Major chopped the power way back. This caused us all to ride up partly high. When I chopped back hard, I thought I heard a back fire on my left engine. It was a hit and I did not know it.

About three miles out I saw Major Smith get hit with an engine on fire. About 30 seconds later the No. 3 plane got hit with an engine on fire too. I was up so high that I just about lost my flight leader and I was walking the rudder trying to slow down as we were gliding in at 600 feet. Out came the 17th [Division's paratroopers] out of Major Smith's plane right through the flames of the engine fire then No. 2 and No. 3 dropped. I made my drop, hit the fire wall with the throttles and started my right turn. The problem was I was not going anywhere. I looked out the left window and there was the big prop just windmilling away. Major Smith and No. 3 were winged over to the left and headed toward the ground. About that time I got hit hard, something hit the seat plate and I lunged forward. When I straightened up I could only see black flak, no other planes, nothing. We got the engine feathered, the gear dropped ½ way down. The stick had about two inches of play and I headed for the deck. I could see a couple of big holes in the left wing, there was a big hole in the back and the damn ship was shaking and lunging like a centipede walks.

After crossing back over the Rhine, crew chief T/Sgt. William F. Greenwood went into the cockpit. Leaning between Wood and copilot F/O Boyd E. Card, he told them the right engine and one fuel tank were undamaged. Wood slowly climbed to 3,000 feet, leveled off, and set a southwest heading at 130 MPH. With about fifty gallons of fuel in the usable tank, they spotted a runway up ahead. Perhaps it was serendipity; the crew members all thought they had been pretty lucky to get out of the battle area uninjured. Now they could land on a runway instead of making a crash landing.

The runway, 3,600 feet in length, was surfaced with steel matting. Located near Charleroi, Belgium, about thirty miles south of Brussels, it was designated Airfield A-87. Although squadrons of the 67th Tactical Reconnaissance Group were based there, radio operator Cpl. John S. Young did not have time to get them on the radio before Wood was on final approach. Greenwood had to crank down the landing gear. Without any hydraulic pressure, Wood made the approach without flaps. After a three-point landing and some braking, the C-46 rolled about ten feet beyond the far end of the runway.

They lost no time in getting out of the plane which "smelled worse than a gas station, inside and out." Gordy Wood delayed lighting a cigarette until he was quite a distance away — and upwind.

✳ ✳ ✳ ✳

Two of the eighteen Commandos of the 29th Squadron went down in the battle area east of the Rhine. The first was Major Laird's lead plane in Number 19 position. The other was piloted by Capt. Joseph R. Kreiser in Number 22.

Maj. Jerome F. Cobbs, squadron adjutant, was in Laird's C-46 as observer (Public Relations). The following is from his account in the 1990 publication, *We Are The 29th!*

> Going in, the paratroopers were in various moods. Some smoked, others indulged in harmless horseplay, while one or two stretched out on the floor and dozed. The drop zone ahead looked like an ideal picnic ground. The green light was flashed back to the troops to jump and, simultaneously, the air around the plane became criss-crossed with tracer bullets accompanied by white and black puffs of flak smoke. As the last trooper left the plane, Laird applied full power and began a sharp climbing

turn. As we reached the top of our turn, an explosion jarred the ship. A glance out of a side window showed the whole right wing to be a mass of flame. We were ordered to hit the silk. All but Laird gathered at the left door and waited for the power to be reduced. I got into a squatting position and rolled out. I pulled my ripcord and the chute opened with a half hearted pop. I discovered the shroud lines to be twisted and the canopy only partially opened. I soon had the lines in proper order but fire from the ground was adding a bit of interest to the proceedings. With bullets whistling by my head and body, I began to pull my shrouds in order to make myself oscillate. Though I was not hit, there were three sizeable tears made in my canopy. The next thing I knew, my two hundred pounds hit the ground like a ton of lead and I did two complete back flips.

While unbuckling my chute I saw a German soldier running away from me. Just then two bullets hit the dirt not three feet from my head. I did a hundred and fifty yards on my stomach to a nearby mortar crater in nothing at all. A burp gun opened up on me as I rolled in and hit bottom in a shower of stones and dirt. I cautiously raised my head to look out and was treated again to a burst from the burp gun fired from a farmhouse 50 yards away. Rifle fire from the opposite direction began throwing dirt around my hole. Everytime I raised my head I received burp fire from the other. I stayed put for an hour or so when I heard feet running towards my position. They were going to get me. Imagine my surprise and relief when a British Tommy showed. "Oh, a Yank. We thought you were a Jerry." To which I replied, "I don't know what you thought, but you're about to be kissed."

Major Laird was the only one of his crew to be wounded. His account, also from the 1990 publication:

Filer and George Smith were in front of us when they did a wing over and came at us with both their engines and their fuselage on fire. We were on our run, having already given the green light, too late to take any evasive action. We just sat there and crawled into our flak suits. We got hit when we were in about the same position as was Filer when he got hit. Our right wing tank was opened up and on fire. We tried to get back over the river, but when the skin of our wing started to peel, I said "Get Out!" I trimmed the plane as much as possible so I too could get out. All you can do at a time like this is get up out of your seat and run like hell for the door. I hit the flak suit release, grabbed my parachute, and clamped it on. As soon as I got out of the plane I pulled the ripcord. It seemed like I swung once and hit the ground. Though I was doing everything right, flexing my knees and all, I hit the ground hard and bounced back into the air about 10 feet. The next time I landed, it was flat on my belly in an open field. They were shooting at me with rifle fire from the second floor of a farmhouse. I looked for a tree or a ditch to hide in. As I rolled over to release my chest strap, "Kwarp," that's when they hit me. The bullet went in right under my right arm and hit my spinal cord.

I lay there for a little while. Overhead I could see a cub [aircraft] flying around. I could not walk, I knew something was wrong. Pretty soon there were noises and three Germans approached, their Lugers pointed at me. To me they looked like three inch cannons. The Germans could see that I was not in a position to do them harm. My 45 was left in the aircraft, didn't even have a pocket knife. In English, I was asked where I was from, and said "USA." "What city, San Francisco, New Orleans, Los Angeles, New York?" He knew all the big cities. I again said "I'm from the United States." He didn't like my answer and kicked me in the ribs. They jabbered in German and apparently decided to take me out of there. I was rolled over on my back, one guy getting hold of my legs, the other under my arms and carried me toward the farmhouse. About halfway there we heard new sounding machinegun fire. They again jabbered to each other in German, then dropped me. That's right, just dropped me. Away they went, split for Berlin. German civilians came out of the house, one with a blanket to cover me. I was dubious. On earlier missions we were told not to surrender to German civilians; that they were known to come at Allied crews with pitch forks. These civilians seemed to want to help. The guy just started to lean over me when all of a sudden he jumped up, with hands raised over his head, yelling, "Comrade!"

British Commandos came up. The sergeant in charge had seen me bail out, come down, even knew where I was, but could not arrive any sooner. I began to feel pain. It was now about two hours after bailout. The sergeant offered me a drink of Scotch from a bottle he had wrapped (tied) around his neck. I took a big slug of that Scotch and thought I was shot all over again. That was horrible stuff. After awhile it warmed me up. Four British stretcher bearers placed me on a litter and dog trotted, carrying me about three miles to the river. There they had an aid station. I remember the doctor taking a look and saying, "We can't do anything with this." He gave me a shot of morphine. I was then marked with a lipstick letter "M" on my forehead. They put me on a DUK [boat] and took me across the river. It was now about three in the afternoon.

Captain Kreiser, in the lead of the three-plane element flying to the right and rear of Laird, was holding his ship steady as the paratroopers began jumping. The instruments showed the right engine was losing power and crew chief T/Sgt. Theodore Crall rushed up to tell Kreiser and his copilot, 2d Lt. John Harris, that the engine was on fire. After ordering the crew to bail out when the paratroops finished jumping, Joe Kreiser had his hands full just holding the plane straight and level. He had to drop the nose to increase the airspeed to obtain better control. When Harris left the cockpit, he thought Kreiser was preparing to follow.

After parachuting, the crew members were captured. Navigator 1st Lt. Walter Connors was taken prisoner and placed under guard in an air raid shelter. Several hours later when the British troops approached, his German captors surrendered to him. Subsequently, he turned them over to the British.

The appeal the C-46 held for radio operator S/Sgt. Eugene Brashear quickly vanished. Compared to the C-47, the Commando was not "more solid and very stable," as he had been told, and the roomy space for the radio operator seemed now insignificant. A part of his experience is from the 29th history publication:

I was the last to bail out. Everything happened so quickly, it seemed like we jumped out with the paratroopers. On the way down I busied myself spilling the chute to throw off enemy fire. There was a lot of that. Contact with the ground was unexpected. We were still being shot at. One bullet struck my left wrist, almost severing it. I began to lose blood rapidly. Ted Crall put a tourniquet on my arm. The Germans put down a blanket for me so I could lie down. There were several German soldiers involved in our capture. There seemed to be a discussion between two groups about who was to stay with us and who was to leave. Those who stayed, later gave themselves up to us.

Before long the British popped into the doorway with machineguns at ready. It's hard to know what really happened, but the British took the Germans outside (I think to shoot them). When Ted went out and told the British we could look after them until the P.O.W. detail picked them up, the Germans were left with us. In departing, the British told me that they would send back a medic and the stretcher bearers. In a short time the medics arrived and took me off.

The 29th Squadron records listed Captain Kreiser as MIA until mid-May, after V-E Day, when it was learned that he was at Stalag Luft I. He also wrote of his experience in the 29th Squadron's history:

Finding myself too low to jump, my only alternative was to pick out a field and fly it in. Hopefully the plane would not blow up before or during landing. When the fuselage made contact with the ground it created the most ungodly scraping, tearing and buckling sounds. The fuselage on my left started to cave in, wedging my foot between the rudder and fuselage. When the aircraft stopped I pulled my left leg back as far as I could and pulled my foot right out of my shoe. The cabin was full of smoke. I started for the jump door when I suddenly realized I would need that walking shoe and went back for it. The smoke was dense but I made it to the door with the shoe still in my hand. After jumping down to the ground I was greeted by the sight of submachineguns pointed at me. The Germans made me run with them to a farmhouse, one shoe still in hand. There were bullets flying around; we all ran in a crouch. I could hear fighter aircraft, machinegun, cannon and antiaircraft fire. The farmhouse was a German field hospital. The first one to greet me was the doctor, a captain, who was educated at Dayton University. He offered me a glass of milk. That night, with a Canadian POW, I was moved by truck to what was the beginning of a long, tough, trip east, to be a guest of the Germans for awhile!

✳   ✳   ✳   ✳

War correspondent Thomas Wolf was aboard 1st Lt. John L.
Ryan's plane (Chalk No. 25) in the lead of the three-ship element,
behind and left of Major Laird. All three C-46s came out undamaged. After returning to Achiet, he wrote his account, "Record Human Cargoes Drop East Of The Rhine." Its dateline was "Headquarters 313th Troop Carrier Group March 29." The following
excerpts are from the original copy before it was transmitted to his
London office. (Source: William W. Rose, pilot, 49th Squadron.)

Forgotten heroes of the Rhine crossing are the officers and
crews of the Troop Carrier Command. For some reason, it always works out that the last men to get credit in an airborne
operation are the airbearers who make the operation possible.
No mission is ever easy. Jack Ryan, pilot with whom I flew on a
recent Rhine crossing, summed it up: "As long as there's one
member of the Volkstürm left with one rifle, someone is going
to get hurt when you are flying at 600 feet."

Almost at the moment we cross the Rhine, which is too
fogged with battle to be clearly seen even at our low height. Formations start slowing down for a drop. Still in formation, they
will fly straight and level. They will fly incredibly slow to give
jumpers maximum safety. They will fly breathtakingly low.
Without arm or armor, they will face everything from flak guns
to squirrel rifles. One hit on the explosive laden parapacks hung
in bomb racks on the plane's belly means instant death. One
small hole in these gas tanks almost certainly means wings afire.
If one of these hundreds of pilots loses his nerve and breaks formation, the lives of thousands of men all over the drop zone are
endangered. This is war at its grimmest.

In an actual run, too much happens too quickly to record by
sequence. Planes wade miraculously through great black and
white fields of flak, bouncing on each explosion but keeping
their course, speed and height. Paratroops reach the drop zone
and are gone. Planes are hit and catch fire. With paratroops
safely out, it becomes a mad scramble, straining every bit of a
pilot's skill and courage to get out . . . a scramble of climbing and
diving aircraft, some coming full, others going out empty, others falling hysterically out of control. We creep agonizingly back
towards the Rhine at 200 miles per hour.

* * * *

The copilot, 2d Lt. Joe E. Haramy, in Chalk No. 36, had to take over the controls after 1st Lt. Donald W. Dunn was wounded and the plane was seriously damaged during the climb-out. With engine problems and flight controls crippled, Haramy set a southwest heading for the return route. Fifty miles after crossing the Rhine, an airfield was spotted, Y-32, just inside the Belgian border at Ophoven, where the 405th Fighter Group was based. Joe Haramy wrote about their odyssey:

> As the first of the formation approached the DZ, flak puffs began to appear among the planes. They seemed to have the range, for the flak burst very near the altitude of the formation. The paratroopers were beginning to drop in front and when they began pouring out of our flight leader's ship, I gave the green light and bell to our troopers. By this time, many planes were on fire, and I watched one go underneath us out of control and blazing. To the left, a Fortress [B-17] that had been cruising around was on fire, but still going straight and level. As soon as the troopers in our ship were out, I salvoed packs and we began a climbing turn to the right under full power.
>
> As soon as we were headed back toward the Rhine, the air got bumpy and I could feel that we were being hit. Just then there was an explosion in the cockpit which shattered the left windshield. I saw Dunn grasp his face, which was covered with blood, and run to the rear of the ship. Taking the stick, I noticed the ship was very nose heavy, so I rolled back the elevator trim until it would go no more. The ship was still nose heavy, and it took both hands to hold it. I asked the Radio Operator, Cpl. Norman Harris, to climb into the left seat to help hold back the pressure. Looking around the cockpit, I saw that the shell that had hit us in the front had come up through the instrument panel, knocking out the gyro horizon and runway localizer, and burst on the windshield. I also noticed a broken cable protruding from the throttle quadrant. Both rudder and elevator trim tab controls were inoperative. As soon as we had gotten back across the Rhine, the left engine started to function erratically. The RPM's would run high then low, and the prop pitch control had no effect. Then it started to cut out altogether, so I began a

single engine procedure, at which time the Crew Chief, T/Sgt. William Krebs, discovered the left-center gas tank had been shot out and was dry. After switching tanks, the left engine caught on again.

The crew chief and radio operator assisted Dunn back into the cockpit, although he was unable to see. We decided to go into the first field which turned out to be a fighter strip in Belgium. After one circle, we came in for a landing, both Dunn and I on the controls in order to hold enough back pressure on the stick. It was a good landing.

* * * *

The unpainted B-17 Joe Haramy saw burning was the same one that had arrived at Achiet on the 22d. The pilot, Lt. Col. Benton R. "Lucky" Baldwin, had been CO of the 29th Squadron until September 1943. In Sicily, he was moved to 52d Troop Carrier Wing headquarters, and assigned to planning.

Early on the 24th, the Flying Fortress left Achiet before the Commandos. It carried cameramen and newsmen to report on the largest airborne assault of World War II. Paris-based CBS newsman, Richard C. Hottelet, boarded the plane with his sound-recording equipment. His intent was to send his story to his boss, Edward R. Murrow, in London. Murrow, who headed the CBS European Bureau, was famous for his broadcasts to America from London. Hottelet wrote about his experience in *Jump Into Germany,* which appeared in an April 1945 issue of *Collier's* Magazine:

> The great airborne offensive across the northern Rhine on March 24th was probably one of the last big stories of the European war, and from a news as well as from a technical reporting angle, the Army wanted complete coverage. So the U.S. Troop Carrier Forces put aside a beautiful silver Flying Fortress, loaded it with their combat cameramen and observers, let me get on board with my sound-recording equipment and sent us out to cover the operation.
>
> The weather was on our side.
>
> To me the only worrying thing about the enterprise was the fact that I was not in the least worried.
>
> But this slight twinge disappeared after half an hour in the

Airfield B-54, Achiet, France, 24 March 1945. C-46 Commandos, 313th Troop Carrier Group, taking off with paratroopers of the 513th Parachute Infantry Regiment on Operation VARSITY. Note evidence of strong cross wind from right of runway with C-46 left of runway's centerline.
— Courtesy: 29th Squadron

Remains of 49th Squadron C-46 and farmhouse it destroyed. C-46 was so damaged on the VARSITY mission, it could not land. The crew bailed out over farmland adjacent to the airfield. — Courtesy: Blickensderfer

air. Because the sight of airfield after airfield in northern France loaded with planes and gliders taking off and ready to take off was too real a sign of strength to brook any doubt.

Colonel Joel O'Neal, Deputy Chief of Staff of U.S. Carrier Forces, put his flak suit on over his parachute harness and strapped the steel flaps of his flak helmet down over his ears. We all did the same. The three photographers, their cameras clicking away, jostled one another at the waist windows as we swooped around the drop ships.

P-Hour, the drop hour for the paratroops, was 10 A.M. Just after 9:45 we passed our last check point. It was called the IP, or Initial Point, the same as a bombing run. Its code name was Yalta. All of a sudden the ground below us, which had been golden in the morning sunlight, turned gray. For a moment I thought that we had run into clouds. It seemed impossible. Then we caught a whiff. It was chemical smoke. Below us and around us was a bank of misty smoke that ran for miles up and down the bank of the Rhine, across the river and over the east bank.

Here there was no sunlight; here in the center of green and fertile land was a clearly marked area of death. The smoke seemed a shroud. Outlines below us were indistinct. What had seemed warm now appeared ominously cold, and almost clammy. On our left was the first serial of paratroop pathfinders. We were flying at 700 feet.

And just at that moment we were over the first drop zone. It was 9:50, ten minutes early. On our left, paratroopers were tumbling out of the C-47s, their green camouflage chutes blending with the dark gray ground. The troop-carrier serial seemed like a snail, leaving a green trail as it moved along. And it was crawling indeed — about 115 miles an hour. Our big Fort seemed to me to be close to stalling speed.

It sounded like a riveting machine, a heavy one. For a split-second I didn't catch on. Then I smelled the explosive — a stench that always nauseates me. You get it in outward-bound bombers when the gunners clear their guns. But we had no gunners. Turret guns were taped up and our waist guns had been unmounted. We were here to photograph and record, not to fight. There was a sharp rap on the ship somewhere. We had been hit.

We turned and circled for a minute or two, and then joined

another serial going into its drop zone. On the ground we could see occasional gun flashes, but no sign of life apart from them. No flak was coming near so again a gradual relaxation made me see how tense I had become in every muscle. We watched the serial, with its fifteen tight little three-ship V formations, drop its load.

It suddenly seemed extremely silly to me that we should be there, because we were a huge bright silver B-17 flying along at almost stalling speed. We were probably the most conspicuous thing in the sky.

The Germans must have arrived at the same conclusion. We had been over the drop zone twenty or twenty-five minutes. We were turning again to pick up the first incoming serial of C-46s. These ships, the Curtiss Commandos, carried more paratroopers and jumped them out of two doors at once. They were used in this operation for the first time.

We were banking to head back to the Rhine and pick them up.

And then we really hit trouble. It may have been the same gun. I did not see it. Radio Operator Roy Snow watched the tracers come up from the ground and lifted his feet to let the shells pass under him. In the waist we heard the riveter again. A short burst, then a longer one. The heavy steel-scaled flak suit and heavy flak helmet, which had been weighing me down, now felt light and comforting. Then we got hit in a ripple. The ship shuddered, I grabbed my pipe. And then, as if it had been rehearsed, all five of us in the waist stepped into the flak suits, spread on the flooring.

Over the intercom, Snow was telling our pilot, Lt. Col. Benton Baldwin, that the left wing had been hit, and that fire was breaking out between the engines. The flak stopped. Baldwin was gaining altitude in a climbing turn. Smoke began to pour down through the plane, and in the left waist window. A tongue of flame licked back as far as the window, and the silver inner skin of the ship reflected its orange glow. The crew chief told Lieutenant Albert Richey that gasoline was sloshing around in the bomb bay.

This Fortress carried two thousand gallons of aviation fuel, which can almost ignite in a hot wind. One engine was burning;

the one next to it was catching fire. The ship was still under control. But there was no telling for how long.

As we staggered out, we watched the C-46s come in and apparently walk into a wall of flak. I could not see the flak, but one plane after another went down. All our attention was concentrated on our own ship. It could blow up in midair any moment. We moved close to the windows. From the pilot's compartment came streams of stinging smoke. The intercom went out.

Up in the cockpit, Colonel Baldwin was keeping the ship under control, watching the fire eat a larger and larger hole in the left wing like a smoldering cigarette in a tablecloth. Looking down on the wing from above, he could not see a large fire. The flame was mainly below the wing.

Suddenly we went into a sharp dip. Back aft we did not know what was happening. All we had was the smoke and the deafening noise, and the tiny fragments of molten metal which the wing was throwing back and which twinkled in the sun as they raced past the waist window.

We pulled off our flak suits and helmets. I reached down and buckled on my chest chute. It was obvious we would have to jump. But down below was still the cold, gray smoky country east of the Rhine. Impossible to tell what was happening down there. If it was not in enemy hands, it was a battlefield.

As we went into the dip, I thought the pilots had been hit, and I put my hands on the edge of the window to vault out. But the Colonel brought her back under control, and we hung on. There was no movement among the men in the waist. We stood and waited — for flak, or more flames or explosion or for the Rhine to slide by below. There was nothing else to do. After what seemed hours, the Rhine was below us at last. The left wing was blazing, but three motors were still running.

We were hardly across the river when Roy Snow came back and told us that the pilot wanted us to jump. That the Rhine River was all we had been waiting for.

Colonel O'Neal went back and began to struggle with the handle that jettisons the rear door. I jogged my chest pack up and down, made sure it was secure. The other men did the same. Colonel O'Neal was still wrestling with the door. I went back to help.

There was no panic. But if this telling sounds cool and collected, the actuality was not so. Uppermost in everyone's mind was just physically getting out of that ship. We were still flying at less than a thousand feet, which left not much time. I abandoned, with hardly a thought, my recording equipment and typewriter and notes and jacket in the radio compartment. Of the cameramen, only Quandt thought to take the film out of his camera. There was no point in trying to jump with anything in your hand because the opening of the chute will make you drop anything that is not tied to you.

The Colonel got the door open and crouched in it for a moment. I shouted, "Okay, Colonel, get going." He didn't hear, but tumbled out. I got to the doorway.

We were jumping at about six hundred feet, so I pulled the rip cord almost immediately.

I landed in a pasture. Trying to gauge my height to brace myself for the fall, I kept opening and closing my eyes, but was barely able to keep pace. I remembered to flex my knees. The next second I hit with a grunt. I snapped off the parachute and got to my feet. To my surprise I stayed there, getting my wind back.

All around us, as we stood on this approach route for the airborne forces, burning and disabled C-47s crashed into the fields.

After a while, I noticed that my eye was hurting, and found that the chest chute had given me the start of a beautiful shiner as it ripped up past my face. On hitching my way back to Paris next day, I found a telegram from my boss in London saying: "Better a purple eye than a Purple Heart."

The cameraman that remembered to take the film from his camera before jumping was Sergeant F. Quandt. He and other photographers for *Air Force*, the official service journal of the U.S. Army Air Forces (a monthly magazine), had been sent to Achiet with staff writer Capt. Eric Friedeim who was flown on the mission in a Commando.

* * * *

The 48th and 47th squadrons, the second serial of Commandos

from Achiet, were even less fortunate than those in the first serial. The leading three-ship element, headed by Maj. William G. Oliver (Chalk No. 37), received only damages with no harm to crew members. The only problem was in No. 38, when a bundle jammed in the door and twelve paratroopers could not jump. They returned with the plane to Achiet.

The first plane to be shot down was 1st Lt. Dudley B. Rose's (No. 44) in the third element. He managed to make the drop with both gasoline tanks ablaze. All crew members bailed out before the plane crashed and blew up on impact.

The crew of the plane flying in the left wing position (No. 45) was not as lucky. Pilot 2d Lt. Donald O. Shire, copilot John D. Stroud, and radio operator Sgt. Bernard Isenberg were in the burning ship during the crash-landing. The left wing struck the ground and the plane exploded. Only crew chief T/Sgt. Norman E. Rhoads, who was slightly wounded, had time to parachute.

Eric Friedheim was an observer in the lead plane of the 48th Squadron's second flight of nine C-46s. His account was published in the May 1945 issue of *Air Force*. The following excerpts are from his article, "Rhineland Rendezvous":

> I elected to fly with the 313th because this group was using the new Commandos. Each of our transports, with their greater payload, was carrying 30 paratroopers plus large quantities of supplies and ammunition. The C-46s of the 313th were transporting an entire paratroop regiment to the battle zone. The group was divided into two serials, and I had been assigned a place in the lead plane of the second serial. Our estimated time of arrival over the drop zone [was] 1020, and when I climbed aboard with 1st Lt. Bob Reeder shortly after 0700, the paratroopers already were in their places. They were quiet and tense as Reeder went forward with 2d Lt. Albert Strohm, the copilot, to warm up the engines.
>
> The run to the Rhine was smooth and uneventful. To our left we could see the column of C-47s, Horsas, CG-4As and giant Hamilcar gliders stretching back to the horizon. Occasionally our fighters knifed past the slow-moving stream, ranging ahead into the danger zones. Fifteen minutes before we reached the river, Reeder flashed the alert to the jumpmasters.

Tight-lipped, the troopers checked their weapons and made ready to hook up. The rest of us put on our flak suits. The three minute warning came as we flew over the Rhine, and Reeder brought the plane down to 600 feet and held her level. Haze and battle smoke shrouded the entire area. Along the east bank the ground was barely visible. Off to the right appeared a few black bursts of flak. Reeder kept straight on course, for the troop carriers are prohibited from taking evasive action before the troops have jumped.

Four miles in he rang the bell. The paratroopers streamed out of the Commando's two doors. They cleared the plane in seven seconds and Reeder immediately increased his speed. There was more flak now, dangerously close, but Reeder continued past the drop zone before trying to make his run. Ours being the lead plane, it was necessary for us to go in deeper to avoid jamming traffic behind.

Suddenly a string of bullets ripped through the plane's belly. All of us tried to lose ourselves inside our flak suits. Finally Reeder started his turn. He almost had the nose of the Commando pointed westward when we heard the ugly sound of metal slamming through the fuselage. Within seconds the starboard engine spouted flames. The ship shuddered from the impact of another burst, and fire danced across the left wing. Thick smoke billowed into the cabin from the sides. The navigator [1st Lt. John E. Hawkinson] rushed forward to the cockpit and Reeder gave the bailout order.

Ripping off the flak suit, I groped my way to the right door, pausing momentarily to look down. We had been climbing in the turn, and I judged our altitude was about 800 feet. While I was hesitating at the door, someone hurtled past shouting "Come on! What the hell are you waiting for?" I followed him out and found myself floating toward what appeared to be the vortex of a battle. I could see flashes of guns and hear bullets whipping past me. In the air the sky was filled with a tangle of gliders and transports, and I saw one spiral down and crash with a loud explosion in a field. Slowly I drifted over some buildings, and finally was jolted down beside some railway tracks.

Friedheim had parachuted somewhat south of the Hamminkeln railroad station in LZ U, minutes before the British Horsa gliders began landing. Ten minutes after crawling into a small lumber shed, he heard shouting in English. He crawled back out and yelled the pass word, "Thunder," as loud as he could. Two British airborne troopers covered him with tommy guns while he explained how he got there. After he gave his name, they became understandably doubtful. It was not until he was taken to their sergeant and questioned further that they became satisfied he was not a German. He was then told that the squad was preparing to capture the railroad station some 200 yards north of them.

"You can come along with us," the sergeant said. Friedheim was given a German pistol and ammunition that had been captured just minutes before. "Here you are, mate. You may need them." Luckily he did not.

The squad wormed its way up the tracks, close to a row of freight cars, and "reached the station without firing a shot . . . A quick search of the cellar flushed out a dozen German soldiers." In a farm yard across the road, there were a number of bodies — the result of a glider crashing into a farm house.

By 1100, after other British airborne troops moved in, the railroad station was converted into a British battalion command post. Among the first Americans to arrive was S/Sgt. Raymond A. Hill, radio operator of Reeder's C-46. He had parachuted close by the Issel Canal and was taken prisoner by a German who had watched him come down. When his captor was hit in the shoulder by machine-gun fire, he surrendered to Hill. Moments later, the wounded German was killed by another burst. The next morning, crew chief S/Sgt. Galen B. Boltjes turned up after a night of being pinned down in a field under fire from two sides.

Navigator John Hawkinson's right shin bone had been hit by small-arms fire, and after he received first aid, he arrived at a command post. Reeder and Strohm were reported by the 48th Squadron as Missing in Action.

*   *   *   *

Four other C-46s in the 48th Squadron's second flight behind Reeder were also shot down. The fate of the planes and crew members are summarized from 48th Squadron records by chalk number positions.

No. 49: Hit by antiaircraft fire. Belly of ship caught fire. Right wing blew off before hitting ground. All jumped except Navigator 2d Lt. Edward J. Musall who was listed KIA. Injured on jump were Pilot 1st Lt. Joe T. Henderson and Radio Operator John Badzo. Copilot Sheldon J. Witt and Crew Chief T/Sgt. Harry A. Mosbaugh were unharmed. A paratrooper who refused to drop with his platoon, jumped with the crew. He was shot in his right arm during the descent.

No. 50: Right wing on fire before crashing. Pilot 2d Lt. Gerald E. Hamilton and Copilot 2d Lt. Wayne Wilson were listed as MIA. Crew Chief T/Sgt. Wenzel T. Klimek and Radio Operator S/Sgt. Albert E. Lewis were unharmed.

No. 52: Crash landed and burned with all crew members, but one, aboard. Crew Chief T/Sgt. Charles L. Williams was thrown clear from the escape hatch and survived. KIAs were Pilot 1st Lt. James P. Claussen, Copilot 2d Lt. Ruben Levy, Navigator 1st Lt. Walter L. Ruzzo and Radio Operator S/Sgt. George J. Kuhn.

No. 54: Pilot's window and overhead electrical panel shot out. Pilot 1st Lt. Emanuel Cherkasky was wounded in his upper left arm, but he and Copilot 2d Lt. John F. Frazer landed the ship at Airfield A-87, near Charleroi.

The last two flights of the second serial from Achiet also suffered numerous loses as well as aircraft damage. The following summaries are from 47th Squadron reports and/or personal accounts:

No. 56: On return, southwest heading, right wing and gas tanks were afire with flames lapping into starboard jump door. Shortly after paratroop drop, Radio Operator S/Sgt. Reino J. Hyry bailed out. After right turn to return heading, Copilot 2d Lt. Quinton E. LeVan and Navigator P. Ketchum jumped. Pilot 1st Lt. Richard P. Sarrett was headed back out of the cockpit as Ketchum bailed out. Listed as MIAs were Sarrett and Hyry.

No. 59: Left engine shot out and right engine failed on the way out. Crash landed near Blerik, Holland, 28 miles SW of Wesel. All crew members unharmed. Crew picked up at Y-55 by Major Keller and returned to Achiet 25 March.

No. 62: Dived short of the DZ, crashed and exploded with all aboard, crew members and paratroops lost. The crew members were Pilot 1st Lt. Moorehead Phillips, Copilot 1st Lt. William C. Simmons, Crew Chief T/Sgt. Homer W. Lundine and Radio Operator S/Sgt. Harold M. Power.

No. 63: Front window shattered; flak hit hydraulic system under cockpit; hit in vertical stabilizer; shell through jump door exploding in roof; elevator trim tabs inoperative. Landing gear had to be cranked down by hand before landing without brakes at Airfield Y-32, Ophoven, Belgium. All crew members were unharmed. They were: Pilot 2d Lt. Robert J. Peterson, Jr., Copilot 2d Lt. John Stankik, Crew Chief T/Sgt. Vincent P. Gautreaux and Radio Operator Sgt. Angelo Petitti.

No. 71: Two flak holes in left wing, one was 5 ft. by 3 ft., another 1 ft. in diameter; hit in left prop blade. Small arms fire left gas tank; foot wide hole in left stabilizer; one in tail wheel nacelle. One crew member, Radio Operator Sgt. Augustine A. Raidy wounded in left thigh by shrapnel while over DZ. No.1 paratrooper hit in stomach prior to jump but pushed overboard. Because of gas leakage and general instability of aircraft, Pilot 1st Lt. Ernest Hammesfahr landed C-46 at Airfield A-92, St. Trond, Belgium. Others in the crew were Copilot 1st Lt. William C. Roley and Crew Chief T/Sgt. Charles H. Wendorf.

No. 72: Aircraft disabled by enemy ground fire, hit in nose, flames observed in pilots' compartment after paratroop jumped. Crew Chief T/Sgt. Edward J. Gardner, Jr. was the only survivor. He reported bailing out east of Rhine, southwest of DZ. When he jumped, Copilot 2d Lt. Robert M. Weiser and Radio Operator Sgt. Emmett L. Wolfe were leaving front section of plane, heading toward the jump door. Observer (Public Relations) 2d Lt. Charles A. Higgins was putting on his parachute. Pilot 1st Lt. Bert L. Blendinger was still in the cockpit setting the aircraft on automatic pilot. Gardner saw nothing of the plane after he had jumped. The other crew members were listed as MIA.

Eric Friedheim included his interview with the pilot, back at Achiet, in "Rhineland Rendezvous":

1st Lt. C. Koenig told how his right engine was blown out by a shell just after the last paratrooper had jumped. "Planes were burning and going down all around us," he continued. "We finally picked up enough airspeed to level off, but by then we were right on the deck and that's when we really got it. One shell burst through the plane and we were being peppered by small arms fire. Just as we were about to cross the river, a shell hit our left engine. Then we really became glider pilots. We picked out the nearest field and set her down. We all got out and started running, fearing the plane would explode. Some civilians were shouting at us but we didn't pay any attention. We didn't know we had landed in the middle of a mine field."

＊　＊　＊　＊

The last Commando, arriving far behind the rest of its squadron, was flown by Captain Scott. In his crew were copilot 2d Lt. Frederick C. Davis, navigator 2d Lt. Charles D. McCall, crew chief T/Sgt. Frank Joda, and radio operator S/Sgt. Vincent Russo.

After seeing the long glider formation crossing ahead of their route, Scott changed course, flew around it and crossed the Rhine at 1025. Because McCall could not pick up the Eureka signal, and because of poor visibility caused by haze and smoke, they were not sure they had passed the DZ until they saw the Issel River. During the turn back over the Issel Canal, they drew small-arms fire without apparent damage. As they approached the forest, they determined the location of the DZ, made a 180-degree turn, and headed back for the drop. Before they reached the objective, a glider formation blocked the way. Scott began a large 360-degree right turn and started again for the DZ. Over the Issel Canal, the plane received two flak bursts under and near the right door. While working with bundles at the door, Joda and paratrooper Kitson were wounded.

Just as they arrived at the DZ, more gliders appeared ahead and Scott veered right to miss them. By then, the C-46 was over the forest directly west of the DZ. After flying far enough to make a turn back toward the objective, his left rudder fell useless to the floor. He tried to bring the wing up with ailerons, but found them unworkable. He resorted to the rudder trim tab. The only logical thing to do was to hold the west-southwest heading.

Two times the paratroopers of 2d Platoon, F Company, had prepared to jump. Now it seemed they were on the way back. To Lieutenant Dean and the others, it was clear they would not be there "to get together" with the other platoons of Captain Reynolds' company. They asked to jump as soon as a drop area was seen. Scott found one just west of the Rhine and gave the green light. All but two paratroopers jumped, Sergeant Kitson, who had been wounded by flak, and one who had fainted.

After the flak hits, Russo was busy giving Joda first aid. Following the jump, the right engine began sputtering, and Russo ran forward and informed Scott that the right tank was spewing gasoline. Spotting a large, level field straight ahead, Scott started the approach at 110 MPH as Davis dropped half flaps. It was a smooth belly-landing in a field southwest of Eindhoven, Holland, close to Heeze. The paratrooper who had fainted took off on his own to find a way to rejoin his platoon, which had jumped forty miles back, south of Xanten. Kitson and Joda were taken to a hospital near Eindhoven. Kitson rejoined F Company two weeks later.

In 1990, Frank Joda recalled in a letter how Russo gave him first aid after he was hit by fragments of exploding flak.

> It busted my arm, breaking up the bones, the nerves and arteries as well. Shrapnel pierced 25 places on my body. After the troopers jumped, Vincent Russo put a tourniquet on my upper arm to stop the blood from spurting out. God bless him. He was probably more scared than I was.
>
> I remember being put on a litter and transported to a field hospital where I was put in plaster casts on my right arm and leg, put to sleep while shrapnel was removed from my stomach and other places. . . . After a few days there, I was taken to a hospital near Paris where I was readied for evacuation back to the States in a C-54 ambulance plane. Next it was the Army Hospital in Jackson, Mississippi; then the Mayo General Hospital near Galsburg, Illinois, about 200 miles from my home [River Grove, Illinois]. Here they tried their best to patch me up — with skin grafts to fill in the shrapnel holes. I was up and around in late summer of 1945 and discharged in August 1946.*

* * * *

Of the seventy-two Commandos from the 313th Troop Carrier Group, forty-nine returned to Airfield B-54 at Achiet. Over the

---

* Joda's account of his hospitalization is similar to what many of those seriously wounded in Operation VARSITY endured.

DZ, sixteen were shot down. Seven made emergency landings, or crash landed, on the way out — west of the Rhine. However, one of those that returned did not land. It was in No. 5 position in the 49th Squadron formation.

When pilot 1st Lt. Eugene Chiles, Jr. and copilot 2d Lt. Edward R. Hoffman began preparations for landing, they found the battle damage to the plane greater than had been estimated. The landing gear could not be lowered, even manually, and the flaps were out. After passing over the airfield at Achiet, it was decided that the crew should bail out over a rural area nearby. Radio operator S/Sgt. John E. Warren, Jr., and crew chief T/Sgt. Marvin H. Roth were first out. Abandoning a plane was not new to either of them — both were on their third combat mission. On their first, after dropping paratroopers of the 508th PIR, 82d Airborne Division, over the Cherbourg Peninsula at 0220, 6 June, their plane was so crippled that it was ditched in the English Channel. After three hours in life rafts, they were all rescued by a British torpedo boat. From South Hampton, it was hours later that they were flown to Airfield 484, Folkingham, England. This time, they were only a short jeep ride away from B-54, Achiet.

Although the first three Commandos of the formation did not return, the crews of the planes that followed them believed they had dropped the paratroops of the 513th PIR over DZ X, indicated by the 49th Squadron's records for the month of March 1945: "The mission was successful from the Squadron's standpoint as all troops except those from one aircraft [Scott's] were dropped on the DZ. . . ." *

* * * *

It did not take long for the first paratroops of Colonel Miller's 2d Battalion to learn they had landed in LZ R, the British sector. One of the first to jump, Allen Miller had the distinction of landing in a pigpen; a dubious honor he was never able to live down. The 1st

---

* Some days later, the 313th Troop Carrier Group accepted the fact that its Commandos had not dropped on the right DZ. At the same time, IX Troop Carrier Command prohibited combat use of the C-46 because of the vulnerability of its hydraulic control systems and its lack of self-sealing fuel tanks. The orders pulling the Commandos from service were posted on squadron bulletin boards throughout the 313th Group.

Battalion was also dropped in LZ R. The 3d Battalion landed farther east, at DZ U.

Most units of the 2d Battalion assembled and organized within thirty minutes while under intense fire. Captain Reynolds' F Company was missing its 2d Platoon and its executive officer, Lieutenant Dean. Bud Reynolds was dismayed: "Where are they? Here I am again without one of my platoons!" He did not know that they were at Xanten, west of the Rhine, until they showed up at DZ X.

Fighting and reconnoitering kept all units of the 513th PIR busy until afternoon. By 1230, Colonel Coutts had assembled most of his three battalions together a mile southwest of Hamminkeln. Moving south, they reached DZ X in midafternoon. There, defensive positions were set up for the night. On the days following the crossing of the Issel, the objective was to fight their way along the autobahn for fifty miles to Munster.

The Last Paradrops

At Mourmelon-le-Grand, forty-five C-47s of the 434th Troop Carrier Group began takeoffs at 0800. With paratroops of the 466th Parachute Field Artillery Battalion, theirs was the seventh serial scheduled to arrive at DZ X after the Commando serials. Beginning at 1023, 376 artillerymen and twelve howitzers were accurately dropped by forty-four C-47s. One C-47 had aborted on takeoff but the eleven paratroops and howitzers were flown in later by glider. All of the C-47s returned, although twenty-one suffered flak damage.

Without infantry to assist them, the artillerymen fought manfully until they were reached by glider troops landing at noon directly north of them at LZ N. While taking losses of their own, they killed some fifty Germans, took 320 prisoners and captured eighteen large weapons and eighteen machine guns.

Glider Troops to LZ S

First off the Coulommiers runway, at 0734, was Col. Donald J. French, commanding officer of the 437th Troop Carrier Group, with two gliders on tow behind his C-47. In one of the CG-4As was Col. James R. Pierce, commander of the 194th Glider Infantry Regiment, and twelve other glidermen. The first serial of thirty-six C-

47s and seventy-two CG-4As were assembled over the airfield and headed toward Wavre at 0823. Taking off at thirty-second intervals, the second serial was on its way close behind the first. Next to follow were the two thirty-six–plane-glider serials of three other groups: the 436th from Melun; the 435th from Brétigny; and the 439th from Chateaudun. The formation was over sixty miles long.

With few exceptions, all elements flew on course over the Rhine. Although the visibility was poor, flying at slower air speeds than the faster paratroop formations allowed them more time to observe landmarks. Another advantage was that their route toward LZ S was farther south, in the lee of the battle smoke.

On the final run in, after crossing the Rhine, the column was to split for two final approaches, one toward the northern part of the LZ and the other toward the southern part. The purpose was to avoid congestion in the glider landing patterns. Upon releasing, the gliders would land in pairs, in two separate flight patterns, into the wind after making 270-degree left turns.

Col. Adriel N. Williams, CO of the 436th, was piloting the lead plane of the third serial. From Shelbyville, Kentucky, he was one of the first pilots to drop paratroopers in training at Fort Benning, Georgia, on 16 August 1940. On the Rhine mission, he reported that the turbulence was the worst he had ever experienced. Flying at 110 MPH was a strenuous task for the pilots of fully loaded gliders, who alternated with their copilots for fifteen-minute stints at the controls from Wavre to the Rhine.

The problem was that Williams was ahead of schedule at Wavre. He corrected, climbing with his first two serials to 1,000 feet above the group ahead, which was flying at about the correct altitude of 600 feet. At the higher altitude, the glider pilots would have to fly much larger 270-degree turns, north of the LZ, before heading south to land.

Martin B. Wolfe, staff sergeant radio operator in one of the tow planes of the 81st Squadron behind Williams, wrote about the mission in his book *Green Light* and described the approach over the Rhine from Wavre:

> The picture worsened quickly after about 10:15. We had been pushed along by an unexpected tail wind, and our Group was too close to the serial in front of us. Colonel Williams tried to slow us down by "S-ing," that is, maneuvering in large curves

from left to right. But such curves were limited by the columns of planes to our left (the British) and our right (the paratroop planes). We crossed the Rhine when the serials in front of us were still launching their gliders over Wesel. To avoid a jam-up. Williams had to take us up over the prescribed height. This meant our gliders would be released higher than planned — and therefore subject to more flak on the way down.

*   *   *   *

Col. Frank MacNees, in the lead tow plane of his 435th Group, also avoided overrunning those of the 436th Group ahead by climbing to 2,000 feet. He also wanted to avoid the increasing flak at lower altitudes. Due to the battle smoke, the glider pilots could not see the ground clearly until they descended to about 1,200 feet to make their large, final approach patterns to LZ S. They carried troops with weapons and ammunition of the 681st Field Artillery Battalion.

"In the lead C-47 of the last two serials, flown by the 439th Group," wrote former Group CO Colonel Charles H. Young "was Maj. Woodrow T. Merrill, CO of the 91st Squadron. I was flying his right wing. Our serials, totaling 72 C-47s and 144 CG-4As, were loaded mostly with the 680th Glider Field Artillery Bn and some Hqs staff of the 681st. As we reached DZ W our serials split, and Woody led the northern stream toward the NW side of LZ S while I led the southern stream past the north edge of Wesel to the SW side of LZ S.

"As preceding serials overran each other, some gliders released high and I think Woody must have had to veer left to avoid them. Over half the gliders from the northern stream landed within a mile of the NW side of LZ S, while almost all others were within two miles — among friendly troops. I stayed on course in the smoke, however, and at least 57 gliders of the southern stream landed accurately in LZ S; nine more within a quarter mile. These descended through heavy AA fire and over half were hit on the way down. Our records show that a total of ten gliders were shot down, crashed, or missing, and more destroyed after landing. Three of our C-47s were shot down."

Reporters in Action

"All Was Clockwork" was the heading of the news article in the *Stars and Stripes*, 25 March 1945. Staff writer Russel Jones was in a tow plane of the 436th Group, flown by 1st Lt. D. F. Rhoades ("Dusty," naturally) of Maryland, Wisconsin, and his copilot, 2d Lt. C. W. Alderdyce of Toledo, Ohio. Jones wrote that during the approach to the LZ, "small-arms fire came up from the area northeast of Wesel." It was while Rhoades was "holding the plane steady in readiness for the release" that a plane several hundred yards in front suddenly burst into flames. "The fire swept down the hull of the big ship but the pilot held it steady until his gliders cut loose." The C-47 started a steep climb, "flipped over on its back and plunged down." Jones did not mention whether his pilot, Rhoades, had given his glider pilots a green light before they were to cut loose from his tow plane. He wrote:

> Just as we reached the landing zone, another C-47 plunged by us but no one said anything because Alderdyce, his face set, reached up and pulled the handle releasing our gliders; and our plane, suddenly free, surged and pushed us hard against our seats.

One of the daring staff writers from *Stars and Stripes* was Hamilton Whitman who rode with the glider troops of the 194th. He was in one of the CG-4As (Chalk No. 41) of the 77th Squadron, in the lead serial of Colonel MacNees' 435th Group. The following is from his account of the mission entitled *Airborne Attack!*, published in the "Warweek" section of *Stars and Stripes*, 1 April 1945.

> The air was thick with smoke from a British-laid screen along the river as the gliders came in over the Landing Zone. It was thick with flak, too, which reached a crescendo a few seconds after the glider pilots cut their tow lines and took it on their own. Maybe the Germans held their fire until the gliders cut loose. Maybe they were so surprised that they were only able to start firing then. Opinions in the 17th [Division] and among the glider and tow pilots vary on the point. All are agreed, however, that the stuff was thicker than the candles on Grandma's birthday cake.
>
> Talking to the pilots on the ground after the landings revealed one thing. The men who banked away from other ships, avoiding flak bursts whenever they saw another glider get hit, were the ones who got on the ground with only a hole or two in their craft. The pilots who just headed in for a field, ignoring the

flak, were the ones who, by and large, took the worst beating. Their hurried comments with the machine-gun fire hissing over head and the burp guns going from the woods, justified the evasive action some of them took.

The first job, when a glider gets on the ground, is to unload the cargo or get the men it carried into action.

That part of the job calls for coolness under fire and an ability to decide what is important and what must be done first. In the case of one glider in the Wesel mission, the cargo was a medical jeep, the complement — four medics, the pilot, the copilot and this correspondent.

The pilot, 2/Lt. John I. Love, of Youngstown, O., gave his first order while the glider was still in the air diving through the flak.

"Get those god-dammed doors open," he shouted over his shoulder.

Medics kicked out the escape panels and unlatched the swinging doors. Lt. Love, coming in at about 70 miles an hour, dragged his landing gear through the tops of a row of small trees to slow him down and then hit the field at about 60 mph. The wheels touched down, the glider rolled a few yards and then, as the weight settled, tipped up on its nose. For a breathless second it hung there.

Lt. Love, his copilot 2/Lt. Ray Niblo, of Dallas, Tex., the medics and the Warweek writer, tumbled head first through the doors and escape hatches.

There was some fire on the field from a German machine-gun in the woods, to the left rear of the glider. You could see the bullets cutting the grass ahead of the glider and a small plank which flipped into the air as the beaten zone [area swept by machine-gun fire] moved across.

"Get that jeep out," Lt. Love ordered.

The nose of the glider had been damaged in the landing and the cable device by which the nose lifts as the jeep moves forward, would not work. Men raised the tail of the glider by hand, put the tail props into position and then fisted open the damaged nose by sheer beef and back straining. The much-needed medical jeep rolled free.

Up to the moment that the jeep rolled out, with the blankets and litters, the morphine and bandages and blood plasma, the seven men of glider No. 41 had worked more like an engineer construction squad than seven field soldiers in the middle of a bullet-swept battlefield.

Then the training of the medics asserted itself and without another command they took off for the wrecked gliders in the next field where at least two badly wounded men could be seen in the splintered plywood, torn fabric and twisted duralumin tubing.

Spaced out, staggered — no man directly behind or directly beside any other, they moved across the field. The jeep made for the corner of the field, seeking an exit to the road.

The jeep bogged down in the ditch where it churned hopelessly for twenty endless minutes until one medic came back with an infantry man guarding a half dozen Krauts. They lifted the jeep on to firm ground from where it made the road without further trouble.

A stone farmhouse on the road was a temporary CP for the glider regiment and the men assembled there for orders. Then they moved into their assigned positions, digging in their machine-guns at the corner of a woods and building their foxholes for the night. With the first organization complete, the headquarters moved a couple of miles down the road. Wire crews went to work and before dark the whole area, roughly three by six miles in size, was linked up, coordinated and defended. The antitank guns and the airborne 75mm. howitzers were in place.

It was midnight before the Germans were able to counterattack — a try which was beaten back by the glider pilots, fighting as infantrymen. Four hours later the Krauts tried it again, from the other side of the area. Again they were beaten back.

* * * *

At first, DZ S was a scene of wild confusion, with at least 150 small battles raging at various locations. In any battle the concentration of combat units is important. Here it was no different. As was expected of them, many glider pilots fought through the afternoon and into the night with the 17th Airborne units they had carried in their gliders. The battles directly northeast of Wesel exemplified the contributions of glider pilots in Operation VARSITY once they had landed. Those actions described by Hamilton Whitman became known as "The Battle of 'Burp Gun Corner'."

The 435th Combat Team

Some glider copilots for the Operation VARSITY mission were rated power-plane pilots who were recent arrivals to the Troop Carrier groups. Their disgust at the assignment was evident. The glider pilots had been thoroughly trained for battle as infantrymen at Bowman Field, Louisville, Kentucky. While there, they had often been sent to Fort Knox to practice with infantry weapons — including mortars and bazookas — on the firing ranges. For the Rhine mission, glider pilots of the 435th Group received extra training.

A few weeks prior to the mission, General Miley was concerned about the strong German forces in and around Wesel. He decided that his 194th Glider Infantry and its accompanying 155th AA Battalion needed more support on the southern perimeter of LZ S. He asked 53d Troop Carrier Wing for glider pilots from one group to serve as a combat team. Thus group glider operations officers were sent to the 17th Airborne Division headquarters, at Châlons-Sur-Marne, where Miley explained the need for a volunteer. He got Maj. Charles O. Gordon, who placed himself and the glider pilots of his 435th Group (75th, 76th, 77th, and 78th squadrons) under the command of Colonel Pierce's 194th GIR, after landing.

The role of the 194th Glider Infantry and its attendant artillery was to occupy the southeast corner of the divisional sector bounded on the east and south by the Issel River and Canal. It was to make contact with the British commandos on the southwest, the 507th PIR to the west, and the 513th PIR on the north.

The 17th Division quickly sent personnel with the latest combat weapons and equipment to the 435th airfield (A-48) at Bretigny to specially train the 288 glider pilots under Major Gordon, now the commander of the 435th Combat Team.

Gordon wrote from Johnson City, Tennessee, about his team's exploits in the March 1990 issue of *Silent Wings:*

> We carried into combat the first 75mm recoilless rifle mounted on a jeep. This weapon, with its special airborne team, positioned itself along a route where it was believed the German

Top photo: At Airfield B-54, before VARSITY takeoffs, 24 March 1945. *From left* Lt. Col. William Filer, CO, 313th TC Group; Major Flynn, group communications officer; Ernest Anders, Filer's driver; and Robert Wilson, war correspondent. Filer was copilot and Wilson was a passenger in the lead plane of the 49th Squadron.　　— Courtesy: 29th Squadron

Bottom photo: CG-4A gliders after crash-landing north of Wesel, Germany, during Operation VARSITY, 24 March 1945.　　— Courtesy: Keys

troops in Wesel would retreat. The Germans changed their minds and after crossing the railroad near the LZ diverted to a small road which brought them to the intersection of Burp Gun Corner. Their strength was about the size of an infantry company. They were accompanied by two tanks and a towed flak gun. Our men rendered heavy fire when they reached the corner resulting in heavy casualties to the German troops. F/O Elbert Jella knocked out one tank with a bazooka and was recommended for the Bronze Star for his heroic action. The German tanks were successful in knocking out the airborne machine gun emplacement; however, the remaining tank and the German troops retreated.

A considerable number of Germans were killed and seriously wounded. They withdrew and surrendered the next morning at daylight. We were fortunate in that none of our men were lost in this particular battle.

I recall General Miley telling me later that during that first night the Germans attacked our perimeter in three locations and penetrated, causing casualties in two locations. We were the one location that did not give ground and, fortunately, had no casualties. I guess our concentration of fire really paid off.

We moved out at dusk early the second evening and marched through the woodland and up to the Rhine to a designated location where the Corps of Engineers, using assault boats, carried us across the Rhine, and there we spent the night. Early the next day we were conveyed to the nearest airfield where our C-47s picked us up and carried us back to A-48.

The Casualties

Of the 296 C-47 tow planes that reached LZ S, fourteen were reported as destroyed or missing, having been shot down after their gliders released. Eighteen glider pilots were killed, eighty wounded or injured, and three weeks later, thirty were still missing (they had been taken prisoners).

During and directly after the glider landings, the airborne troops of the 194th Glider Infantry Regiment, the 680th and the 681st field artillery battalions and the 155th Antiaircraft Battalion had over fifty killed and one hundred wounded or injured.

By the morning of the 25th, the 194th had taken about 1,150 German prisoners and had destroyed or captured ten tanks, two flak weapons, thirty-seven artillery pieces and ten 20mm antiaircraft guns.

Glider Troops to LZ N

Brig. Gen. Julian M. Chappell assigned Col. Frank X. Krebs' 440th Group to fly the first two of the last seven glider serials of Operation VARSITY. Three hundred fourteen C-47s with CG-4As on single tow were flown from four airfields of the 50th Wing, located west and southwest of Paris, and from one airfield of the 52d Wing, north of Paris. The objective, LZ N, was directly south of the British landing zones (LZ R and LZ U) directly below Hamminkeln.

On 21 March, inside the war room of the 440th headquarters at the Bricy-Orleans Airfield, Colonel Krebs and his staff finalized their flight plan. The two forty-five–plane-glider serials of the 440th were to carry a IX Troop Carrier Command Control Unit, as well as glider troops of the 17th Division: a reconnaissance platoon, the 139th Airborne Engineers Battalion, and the 517th Airborne Signal Company, together with their equipment. According to plans, they expected that the 513th PIR would have control of LZ N, after being dropped earlier, directly south of it on DZ X.

Colonel Krebs assigned himself as copilot to Lt. Col. Howard W. Cannon, operations officer of the 440th. It was not uncommon for group commanders to subordinate themselves, placing others in positions to earn higher awards (such as the Distinguished Flying Cross) on their second or third combat missions. (Krebs' choice was a reverse of their positions of the three prior missions: Normandy, southern France, and Holland.) Their glider pilot was Maj. Robert W. Wilson, of Los Angeles, 440th Group Glider Officer with IX TC Control personnel aboard.

On 22 March the briefing of the 95th, 96th, 97th, and 98th squadron staffs began with maps displayed and explained. "Those orange pins represent flak positions, but they expect to clean out most of them before Saturday [24 March]." Laughter followed. After many questions and answers, a final admonition was issued: "Don't forget to wear GI shoes."

At 1000 on the morning of the 23d, a mass briefing of power and glider pilots was held by the 440th Group staff at the Royal

Theatre in Orleans. Again the group's crews were reminded to wear their GI shoes.

That afternoon, ninety CG-4As were pulled along the outside edges of the runway, forty-five on each side. Down the center of the runway, C-47s, in pairs, taxied to their glider hookup positions. The giant concrete runway was 7,788 feet long and there were still over 4,000 feet available for the first takeoff.

At 0831, 24 March, Lieutenant Colonel Cannon pushed his throttles forward to start the takeoff. One after the other, the tow planes moved gently forward at twenty-second intervals, pulling taut the nylon tow ropes before applying full power. At 0848 Lt. Col. George M. Johnson, Jr., of Macon, Georgia, CO of the 96th Squadron, began his takeoff run to lead the second serial of forty-five planes and gliders.

The men on the ground heaved a concerted sigh of relief as they watched the skytrain fly back over the airfield in order: the first serial with twenty-three tow planes and gliders of the 95th Squadron and twenty-two of the 97th Squadron, and the second serial with twenty-two of the 96th Squadron and twenty-three of the 98th Squadron. They were formed in elements of four, echeloned to the right. The first disappointment came as one tow plane developed an engine problem and its glider was released over the airfield. A spare plane was ready to take the glider off again, in time to catch up with the formation.

Minutes later, with the formation out of sight, a tow plane with a propeller problem flew back over the airfield so its glider could release and land; then the C-47 landed. Aboard the CG-4A was the commander of the 139th Engineer Battalion, Lt. Col. Stanley T. B. Johnson, of Watsonville, California. The glider was quickly towed back to the head of the runway, but no tow plane was available. Johnson raged with impatience and worry. When the spare, with glider on tow, finally got into the air, it was about a half-hour behind the 440th Group's formation. As a solo flight, it would have to follow behind the next three serials from the 50th Wing as it joined up at the wing's departure point, "Slate," near Pontoise.

The timing of takeoffs and assembly of the serials following the 440th's departure from Pontoise went punctually. Lt. Col. William H. Parkhill, in the lead C-47 of forty-eight tug-glider combinations from his 441st Group at Dreux, having taken off at 0845, fell in close behind the 440th at 0940. From St. André de l'Eure, Col. Charles M.

Smith, CO of the 442d, led his forty-eight C-47s and CG-4As off at 0900 to swing over the airfield in full formation at 0935, and head for Pontoise, twenty minutes away. The fifth serial was flown from Chartres (50th Wing headquarters airfield) by the 441st and 442nd groups, each with twenty-four tugs and gliders.

The last two serials, each with forty gliders on tow from the 314th Group, 52d Wing, were in the air and assembled over the Poix airfield at 1045. They arrived at Wavre at 1150, to follow the leaders to the Rhine.

Over the Rhine and Back

In *Airborne Operations in World War II, European Theater*, September 1956, Dr. John C. Warren summarized the glider mission from Wavre to LZ N:

> Wind, turbulence, prop-wash, and the unduly slow air speed specified in the orders gradually distorted the glider formations, and caused the rear elements of the serials to stack up until they were some 400 feet or more above the leaders. On the other hand, all but one glider, which cut loose because of structural weakness, arrived at the Rhine squarely on course, within sighting distance of the white panels and yellow smoke which marked the point where they were to cross the river. Excellent fighter cover, both above and below their level, protected them as they approached the battle area. Between Warve and the Rhine eight flights of fighters were seen, and protection by one flight or more was continuous. No German fighters came forth to challenge them.
>
> Ground fire between the Rhine and the landing zone was remarkably meager and ineffective. There was only an occasional rattle of small-arms fire as the serials crossed the concave waist of the Diersfordter Wald. Most of the enemy in that part of the wood had already been dealt with by the 507th Parachute Infantry. Fire from the zone itself was hot enough to make Lt. Col. W. H. Parkhill of the 441st Group describe it as a flaming hellhole, but the shooting was directed at the gliders. The planes were mostly left alone.

At 1155, Major Wilson released his glider from Lieutenant

Colonel Cannon's tow plane over LZ N and began the perilous 270-degree descent to the left. Cannon then made a flat 180-degree right turn and some three minutes later, dropped the tow rope in the prescribed area west of the Rhine. Close behind, during the turn back, the C-47s of Maj. Walter P. Budd, Jr., and Lt. Frank T. Davey, of the 95th Squadron, were severely damaged. A 97th C-47, Lieutenant Sharkey's, had a hole in the cabin large enough for a person to crawl through.

The second serial was hit harder. The hazy sky was swarming with C-47s, and their pilots were maneuvering to avoid the anticipated and feared German flak around the Issel Canal area. Crew chiefs were busy in the cabins searching for signs of critical damage to their ships. During the turn back, a 20mm shell smashed into the nose of the lead ship of the 96th Squadron, Lieutenant Colonel Johnson's. While he was fully occupied stamping away at the fire on the left side of the cockpit, copilot Capt. James R. Robinson, of Shomac, Oklahoma, landed the plane at an emergency airfield near Eindhoven, Holland.

The 98th Squadron, last in the second serial, suffered the greatest losses. After three successive flak bursts, Lt. Edward J. Walters, of Junction City, Kansas, was unable to maintain altitude. He gave the order to his crew, "Bail out!" As they parachuted to safety, they watched their plane blow up and crash east of the Rhine.

Lt. David C. DeCou, of Larchmont, New York, flew his C-47 back over the Rhine with the right engine on fire. When the fuel tanks began burning, he ordered the bailout. Copilot Lt. Burns R. Eastman, of Pasadena, California, related his experience in his interrogation report:

> When I got to the door, the crew chief and radio operator were struggling with the door, which had jammed at the lower right hinge. After trying unsuccessfully to release it, the crew chief and I pushed against it as hard as we could to allow the radio operator to squeeze out the restricted opening. I then did the same for the crew chief, and finally squeezed through myself. It took me at least fifteen seconds to get through the opening. The pilot had stayed in the cockpit all this time, keeping the ship steady.

With one engine dead and not enough altitude to jump himself,

DeCou decided to fly the stricken plane into a plowed field. He reported his experience:

> Along the field's north edge was a highway which had heavy military traffic on it. Wishing to avoid piling up the ship across the highway and also to avoid a large herd of sheep on the north of the field, I dragged the right wing through some posts on the south edge of the field which caused a ground loop to the right, and the ship came to a halt about two-thirds of way across the field . . . I immediately removed the top escape hatch and went out over the nose, not knowing when the ship would blow up, having fully expected it to on first impact. Captain Thompson then buzzed the field and I waved an OK to him.

The Gliders' Release and Landings

Between each serial, seven-minute intervals had been carefully planned. However, Lieutenant Colonel Parkhill, with his forty-eight-plane-glider formation of the 441st Group, was six minutes early at Yalta before crossing the Rhine toward LZ N. Overrunning the lead serial of the 440th, he climbed from the approach altitude of 600 feet to 1,000 feet. Behind him some transports were near 2,000 feet when their gliders released. Others released too soon as well as too high at the west end of the zone. The formations were to split before the final approach in order to release in two columns of pairs, 1,800 feet apart. In the following serials, the lead elements approached at about the right altitude, but their rear elements were increasingly higher, some over 1,200 feet. In the last two serials, a few climbed to as high as 2,500 feet.

It was impossible for glider pilots releasing at the higher altitudes to fly the prescribed landing pattern. As a result, they made more turns before beginning the uniform 270-degree left turn before landing. On their descent, some even made two complete circles before starting the final landing pattern.

Another problem for the glider pilots was the visibility near the ground, about half a mile, due to battle smoke and haze. They could see the ground below them, but not until they were at about 200 feet could they see very far ahead or to the side.

Either by plan or because they could not see up through the

smoke and haze, the Germans in the LZ held their fire until the gliders were at about 500 feet. Some of the forty-five gliders of the first serial, those of the 95th and 97th squadrons, were damaged but landed safely. The gliders of the second serial of the 440th were less fortunate.

It was F/O Fred H. Daugherty's third combat mission. His 96th Squadron CG-4A was loaded with demolitions and men of the 139th Engineer Battalion. It was hit and exploded in midair, killing all aboard. At least one-fourth of the other gliders in the 96th and 98th squadrons, the second serial, were hit, suffering considerable damage and casualties during their landings. Four other glider pilots were killed and six were wounded on the ground, along with a higher number of glider troops.

The Germans seemed to have a detachment in every building or wooded area in and around LZ N. They directed heavy fire at the gliders which were vulnerable as they landed. Many glider troops were killed before they could exit the gliders, and many loads aboard the gliders were destroyed before they could be removed. LZ N was truly enemy-controlled territory.

One of the two gliders carrying medical personnel of the 139th landed close to a house where forty Germans were based. In spite of the enemy's small-arms fire, a medical officer and a medic leaped from the glider ahead of the glider pilots, all unharmed. Before the jeep driver could drive forward to lift the glider's nose section, he was killed by a direct mortar hit on the glider. With men and equipment from the other glider, the battalion surgeon set up an aid station some distance away to immediately tend the wounded in the area.

The forty-eight gliders of the third serial, those of the 441st Group, landed with very few casualties. It was the same for the forty-eight gliders of the fourth serial, the 442d Group. Directly after landing, glider troops and pilots were in pitched battle. Four glider pilots and more than twelve glider troops were killed during the afternoon and night.

Piloting the lead glider of the fifth and last serial of the 50th Wing from Chartres was Maj. Hugh J. Nevins, wing glider officer, and his copilot, 1st Lt. Robert M. Burke. Nevins wrote later of his experience on the mission in Milton Dank's *The Glider Gang*, 1977. He described it as a "very choppy" flight and many of his 17th Airborne troops became "deathly sick." He did not state his release altitude in his following account:

Unfortunately, we were above and parallel to the railroad track and embankment, which was infested with Germans and their efficient weapons. While keeping my left eye on my landing zone, I put the nose down and we were doing a whistling 120 miles per hour.... We were doing 100 miles per hour as I turned into the final approach, and had to do an immediate nose-high stall and left side-slip, which dropped us from one hundred miles an hour to fifty miles per hour instantly. Bob rode the controls with me, and we managed to get the left wing up just before contacting the ground some 100 hundred yards beyond a flaming C-46. The left landing gear sheared off in a ditch, and we ground looped left and stopped. We were "safe." Bob and I jumped out of the glider onto the ground, and were followed by the dull, airsick troops.

The landings were widely dispersed on and around LZ N. Of the 311 gliders that landed, about 200 were in the zone; less than fifteen were close, more than 3,000 feet away, with a few more than a mile and one-half from it. The eighty gliders of the last two serials, flown by the 314th Group from Poix, were to land in the southwest portion of LZ N. Some thirty-one mistakenly used the panel markings and smoke signals on DZ X for their objective. Seven of them landed at or on the north edges of LZ S. Nine glider pilots of the 314th were killed in action.

※　※　※　※

Rarely did more than four gliders in a formation land close together. Thus, the initial assembly of the airborne glider troops was by squads and pairs of squads, not by platoons and pairs of platoons as was possible after the earlier, more concentrated landings on LZ S. While the troops regrouped during the afternoon and into the night, continuous battles raged, quieting finally about 0530 on the 25th. The 139th Engineer Battalion was credited for doing the "lions share of the work in clearing the zone." The men of the 139th had killed eighty-three Germans and captured 315.

The victory exacted its costs. A number of glider troops and pilots were killed while still in their seats, and many loads of equipment were burned or destroyed by German mortar fire. In several battles, the airborne troops were pinned down for over two hours.

Of the glider pilots landing in and around LZ N, fourteen were dead, twenty-six wounded, and fifty-one missing, as of early April.

Glider Pilots Relieved

About 1,770 American glider pilots reached the battle area. Most of them were able to join up with units of the 17th Division. Each glider pilot had a map, about twenty by twenty-four inches in size, showing the DZs and LZs, roads, railroads, and wooded areas north of Wesel — the same map that was issued to soldiers of the 17th Airborne Division. For many of the glider pilots and glider troops, the maps proved invaluable for orientation and assembly after scattered landings.

The total glider pilot casualties numbered 106 wounded or injured, and as of 9 April, fifty-five were still missing in action.

Many glider pilots were in combat alongside units of the 17th Division until they were relieved by their airborne commanders. Early on the morning of the 25th, some 600 glider pilots were free to head for the assembly point near Wesel. There, in the late afternoon, they received another assignment. As guards, they marched about 2,500 German prisoners to the east bank of the Rhine, where MPs relieved them of their charges.

The glider pilots were ferried across the river in amphibious troop landing craft. From the west bank, it was a short trek to a British artillery base. They were greeted by a large sign which read:

THE RHINE
HOTEL

PARTIES CATERED FOR — GLIDER PILOTS — A SPECIALITY!
63 BEDROOMS. CONSTANT COLD WATER. NO BATHS.
DUKW HIRE SERVICE & TRIPS ACROSS THE RHINE.
PROPRIETORS — 52 (L) DIV.
RESIDENT MANAGERS — RASC 40 70

Hot food and drink were ready for them as they arrived. Then trucks carried them about fifty miles to a British fighter airfield, at Helmond, Netherlands, east of Eindhoven. There they were given cots, some in a maintenance hangar, until Troop Carrier C-47s began arriving the next day to fly them back to their airfields.

Other glider pilots were not relieved until late in the afternoon.

After hot meals that night, they were furnished cots in the tents of the Rhine Hotel. (The showers were cold!) It was the same for later arrivals during the next five days or so. Troop Carrier C-47s ran shuttle flights to Helmond to bring back not only glider pilots, but many wounded as well.

During the evening of the 25th, after one of the DUKWs unloaded glider pilots on the west bank of the Rhine, other troops were waiting to be loaded and ferried in the opposite direction. Among them were 1st Lt. Sam Dean and others with the 2d Platoon, F Company, 513th PIR. Around midday on the 26th, they reported to Captain Reynolds, in time for the reorganization of the 17th Division for battle. The first objective of the 513th PIR was Munster, Germany, fifty miles away.

* * * *

It was April in Paris, 1945, when the author met a classmate, Benjamin F. Sellers, for the first time since flying overseas together. He told how lucky he was during his glider flight with the 99th Squadron, 441st Troop Carrier Group. He added, "Guess what! I heard that Shinn is in Paris, too. He was not so lucky. He just got out of the hospital and is back with his 435th Group." It was by sheer coincidence that minutes later, John L. "Jack" Shinn came walking toward us carrying an inflated rubber "donut" in his hand. We found a bistro where we could talk, but before sitting down, Jack placed the "donut" on the bar stool. It was obvious that he didn't want to discuss what had happened, but he sadly told us about another classmate, Willard H. Van Eyck (Holland, Michigan), 77th Squadron, who had been killed on the mission. After a pause, Ben asked Jack how he had been wounded. About all he would say was, "After I got out of the glider, I hit the ground and kept my head low to the ground . . . but not enough of the rest of me!" Then he added, much more seriously, "That's enough battle stories for now." We drank to that.

Epilogue

MIAs and POWs

No one should ever forget the wives and families of those who were killed in action or reported missing in action. Although shocking, the first brief notification by telegram from the War Department was usually old news to families who had members in the service.

Mary, the wife of a glider pilot classmate of mine, Pete Houck, was living in Louisville, Kentucky, during the time of the Battle of the Bulge, as was my wife, Jane. Pete and I went overseas together but were assigned to different Troop Carrier groups in the ETO. Jane kept getting my letters during late December and early January, but Mary stopped getting any letters from Pete. It was hard, very hard, to keep going and hoping and praying, and praying and hoping some more, but that was what Mary did. Finally, on 24 January 1945, the "Missing in Action" telegram arrived. More waiting. On 11 March a letter came from the 94th Squadron's glider officer, Lieutenant Patterson, indicating that Pete was a POW. Another letter arrived 31 March from Maj. Ward Martindale, CO of the 94th, repeating the news. On 5 April came a welcome surprise. A battered postcard, the pre-printed kind, addressed by the POW and sent from the *stalags* arrived. It was from Pete and he said he was OK. It arrived without a date or a postmark. Lieutenant Patterson sent another letter that arrived on 9 April, telling Mary that from an investigation of two glider landings, Pete's glider had been found as well as a farmer who had witnessed his capture. The telegram from the War Department confirming that Pete was a POW arrived on 13 April!

* * * *

One of the more difficult cases that faced the War Department and the U.S. War Graves Administration involved S/Sgt. Joseph L. Smitrus, C-47 crew chief, 302d Squadron, 441st Troop Carrier Group. He was one of four crew members who, after parachuting from a burning C-47 on 23 December 1944, were captured near Bastogne. (See Chapter 16.)

For over three years, all that his mother, Mrs. Joseph F. Smitrus, New Brunswick, New Jersey, could learn from the War Department was that he had died during the march into Germany. Finding an ex-prisoner of war who knew where he was interred became her obsession. Her correspondence file grew thick with letters to and from veterans and the U.S. War Graves Administration in Washington. Smitty's fellow crew members were located, and from questionnaires, one noted that he was last seen at Gerolstein, Germany, headed toward Koblenz. After extensive investigations of the routes along which prisoners were marched into Germany, no record of his gravesite was found. In 1951 the Administration informed Mrs. Smitrus that the case had been closed.

She refused to give up her quest. In storybook fashion, she learned of a key person, a man named "Danny," who was living in New York City. In 1954, while visiting cousins there, she speculated on how far-fetched it would be to find Danny. The cousins were challenged, and for days they called the names in the New York City telephone directories that began with the letter D! They finally found Louis Denenberg, who was with Smitty when he died. Denenberg would have tried to find Mrs. Smitrus, had he known Smitty's full name.

The case was reopened, and this time the investigator was able to trace the march the prisoners had taken. He found an entry in the Koblenz Main Cemetery records, "One American Soldier P.O.W., name unknown" and initialed "B1." This stood for Bloemer's Funeral Home, where a certificate of death was filed for "American Prisoner of War Schmitt who died on the night of 10 January 1945."

The investigator followed the clue and found the grave of Smitrus in a plot for foreigners. The graves of another American soldier and eight Italians were also uncovered. Smitty's body was exhumed, and laboratory tests of teeth and an arm fracture agreed with his Army records.

Sergeant Smitrus was accorded full military honors on 25 July 1955 for his burial in New Brunswick, New Jersey. Louis Denenberg was there to see his comrade buried.

* * * *

Over the years, telegrams from the War Department sometimes left behind confusing records. Cecil King, who jumped in Sicily with the 82d Airborne Division, lives in Jacksonville, Florida (see Chapter 3). In 1990 he visited his hometown of Geneva, Pennsylvania, and stopped by the Veterans Office in the courthouse to check on his records. The director ran the check and said, "This can't be — you're dead!" He handed King a Veterans Graves Registration record that declared he had died in action on 5 May 1944. That was nearly a year after he had been captured by the Germans in Sicily.

Only the first telegram to his mother stating he was "Killed in Action" was on record. Later, she had received a second telegram saying he was "Missing in Action." Much later, a third telegram declared him a "Prisoner of War."

* * * *

Civilians Again

Most World War II veterans returned home with civilian endeavors foremost in mind. They had little interest in forming associations of their military units. Yet, they were always ready to relate and compare war stories with new friends and co-workers. If their military units had been together in battle, there was much more to talk about. My first such meeting was in 1948.

About a year after I started work with a consulting engineering firm (airport-airfield design), another civil engineer, Marshal M "Bud" Reynolds, joined the firm. It was but a few minutes after

Top photo: Glider pilots 2d Lts. Frank J. Hynes, 92d Squadron *left,* and Charles R. Brema, 93d Squadron *right,* 3 February 1945, 439th Troop Carrier airfield, Chateaudun, France. Both flew CG-4As with ammunition to Bastogne on 27 December 1944. Photo was taken for public relations news release by IX Troop Carrier Command to coincide with a bond tour in the U.S. that never materialized. Note new Griswold Nose on *Old Canvas Sides.* Few CG-4As were so equipped.

— Courtesy: Smithsonian Institution

Middle photo: Spring 1945. Children of Bastogne at play in remains of 2d Lt. Martin H. Sholnick's C-47, 92d Squadron.

— Courtesy: Hortense Martin

Bottom photo: Farm home of Pierson family at "Grand Vivier" where glider pilot F/O Henry H. Nowell found shelter, 28 December 1944.

— Courtesy: Meurisse

meeting him that I learned he had been a company commander in the 17th Airborne Division. My Troop Carrier group, the 313th, meant little to Bud until I mentioned that it flew C-46 Commandos on the last airborne operation in Europe. That rang a bell.

He and his men, F Company, 513th PIR, were flown in some of the planes of my squadron, the 49th. We would often rehash airborne operations after that. I learned many of his officers and men by name. He was proud of how they did in combat — one account was about a bayonet charge in the Ardennes during the Battle of the Bulge.

In 1949 our firm had a contract with the Civil Aviation Administration and sent a team to Korea to manage and operate the Kimpo Airport at Seoul. Reynolds was the engineer for facilities. I was in Alaska on an airport project when North Korea attacked South Korea on 25 June 1950. The first news, by radio and newspapers, mentioned attacks on Kimpo! Days later, I heard that all Americans had been flown out to Japan before 28 June.

Not until October 1950, when I arrived in Japan to head the firm's airfield planning-design services (under contract with the U.S. Air Force), did I learn the facts about the attack on Kimpo firsthand. Bud Reynolds gave me a copy of a six-page report which he had sent to our firm on 7 July 1950.

After two Yak fighter aircraft appeared over the airport before noon on Sunday, the 25th, a telephone call from the 5th U.S. Air Force at Itazuke, Japan, advised that a "State of War existed." That afternoon, Reynolds and two others mounted a .30-caliber machine gun (obtained from the U.S. Army) on the roof of the administration building. Another was borrowed from the Korean air force along with a crew to operate it.

The first two strafing attacks by four Yak fighters began after 4:00 P.M., hitting the Korean air force area and the administration building. They came before the machine-gun crews had completed sand-bagging their positions, but the crews did fire on the enemy planes during the second attack. Reynolds and his gun crew were the first Americans — civilians at that — to fire on the North Korean invaders.

Some American dependents were flown out by U.S. Air Force C-54s to Japan at 6:00 P.M. that evening. Others were driven to an evacuation ship in Inchon Harbor, and some awaited six C-54s which were due to arrive the next morning.

The night of 25 June was quiet for the machine-gun crews as they slept on the roof of the administration building. Early in the morning, they could hear artillery fire. In late afternoon, another Yak strafed the building. The machine gunners returned fire, but without results.

On Monday night, it was learned that the invaders were twelve miles northwest of Kimpo, in battle with South Korean infantry and tank forces. Early on the 27th, several truckloads of U.S. Diplomatic Mission personnel arrived for evacuation by five American C-54s. Minutes later, American F-80s and F-82s streaked overhead as the C-54s began their landings, a beautiful sight for the evacuees.

Reynolds remained behind to await another plane, the last from Itazuke, which would pick up "leftover personnel." Before departing Kimpo, he was intent on destroying the radio equipment aboard a MATS C-54 which had been damaged days before by the driver of a forklift. He didn't want the enemy to have use of the plane.

Bud's last and most difficult task was to say goodbye to the Koreans whom he had come to know so well — he felt like he and his group were a bunch of skunks running off and leaving the Koreans behind. He said he mimicked General MacArthur saying, "We shall return!"

The last time Bud and I rehashed experiences was in Honolulu, in September 1961, during a stopover on my way to Saigon, Viet Nam. We played golf together for the last time. In December I received a telegram in Saigon from our home office stating that Bud had suffered a fatal heart attack — ironic for one so young who had earned three Purple Hearts in World War II.

* * * *

Some veterans are still doing what they did during the war. One is Norman Vaughan, who headed the dog sled teams of the Air Transport Command Search and Rescue Service that were sent to the Ardennes in February 1945. Since then he has completed six Alaska Iditarod dog team races, the last one in 1990, at the age of eighty-four. During recent years, he participated in expeditions to Greenland for the recovery of P-38 and B-17 aircraft, missing since 1942. In December 1993, he went on another expedition with the last dog sled team in Anarctica. He hoped to be the first to scale Mount Vaughan, 10,302 feet high, a mountain that was named after him by Adm. Richard Byrd in 1930. He was unsuccessful in that attempt. However, on December 16, 1994, just a few days from his eighty-ninth birthday, Vaughan reached the summit of that mountain.

✻   ✻   ✻   ✻

Société Protectrice des Animaux

What a coincidence it was that the sled dogs of Operation WOOF-WOOF were sent to Spa, Belgium. S.P.A. is the abbreviation for the group in the French-speaking area of Belgium responsible for taking care of all lost or abandoned pets, such as dogs and cats. It can send anyone mistreating animals to court. But during February-March 1945, the citizens of Spa were more curious about than critical of the dog sled teams in town.

When I wrote my correspondent friend in Büllingen, André Meurisse, about Operation WOOF-WOOF, he lost little time in pursuing the subject with the local people. One was Mr. François Mathieu, who started his own investigations and found others who remembered the dogs. (Mr. Mathieu was a member of the Belgian Army battalion sent to Korea in 1951.) The following accounts are by five people whom he interviewed.

From Mr. Charles Close, eight years old in 1945: "Along with my game-pals I was often used to going to the Americans in the Château d'Alsa's property that was located less than one mile from my parent's property. Many sledge dogs were attached one to the other by groups on the snow covered lawn, some tied to trees. The dogs were very unruly and boisterous."

From Mr. Gilbert Grignard, then thirteen years old: "Some of the dogs were kept in the smaller building on the opposite side of the park. Those dogs looked to be wild and always getting themselves in affrays with others. When the U.S. Army men in charge of the dogs detected our presence they would give us 'sweeties' and then chase us away."

From Mr. Gilbert Bontemps, then thirty-three years old: "I think it was early February 1945 that I saw on the snow covered road running by the château, one herd of Husky dogs towing a jeep 'without' engine. Not long later we had heavy rainfalls and the snow quickly melted away. As to the dogs, I never saw them again."

André R. Meurisse, age forty-four, in Büllingen, Belgium, showing scar left by US Army surgeons when they saved his arm by removing shrapnel lodged deep in his arm (Sedan, France 1945). — Courtesy: Meurisse

Antoine Pierson (L), and Félix Debarcy (R), teenagers during WWII, remembered Nowell visiting the house. — Courtesy: Meurisse

From Mr. André Bouchoms, then thirteen years old: "I have no more recollections [than the others] about the dogs that were at Château d'Alsa but I did look into the book *Spa et Les Americains,* by Georges De Lame (deceased in 1983), local history writer and at that time, the Town of Spa's official representative to the American Forces Command there. From the book, he cited the dates of weather changes. From the first of the year, 'It kept snowing until 10 February 1945. Maximum snow cover went to 20 inches. It started to rain on 10 February and the snow began to melt away. The first spring's sun-rays appeared on 8 March.'"

Bouchoms added, "During the Nazi occupation of our country, the Château d'Alsa served as a school for the 'Hitler Youth' from the start of 1942 to early 1944. The Château was then owned by Count Van Den Burg, and before WWII, our King Léopold the Third stayed there a few times as did the famous French opera music composer, Charles Gounod."

From Mrs. Marie-José Bourguignon, then twenty-nine years old: "In early 1945 I was living in a house located some 200 yards away from the Château d'Alsa. I remember that some time in February, there were many dogs within the château's grounds enclosure. I cannot say how many of them were there, but I can attest that they were of five or six different breeds, some rather small and some real big. I also saw a herd of dogs towing a jeep occupied by at least 6 U.S. troopers. I can also attest that the château building was not only used by the dog teams' handlers but also by other U.S. Army men of a 'Secret' service related to the aerial photographs and that was part of First Army HQs. Members of that service used to come to my home when not on duty elsewhere. I do actually still exchange correspondence with one of them, Morris R. Rambo, Paris, Illinois."

I later learned from Morris Rambo that he was in the 654th Engineer Topographic Battalion, which kept the battle maps updated for the First Army. The unit was in Spa from 30 September until 18 December 1944, when it moved back with General Hodges to the First Army's rear headquarters, near Liege.

From Mr. and Mrs. Demaret: They are the current owners of the Château d'Alsa and they donated two rare photographs showing the Château as it appeared in 1945. Today, it is recognized for its outstanding restaurant and wooded park.

Appendix

Many veterans of IX Troop Carrier Command and the airborne divisions provided information to make this book possible. Those who were on missions of Operation REPULSE deserve special thanks. They are named here by their respective units.

439TH TROOP CARRIER GROUP

91st Squadron. Claude A. Berry, Tahlequah, OK; Robert R. Bisch, Safford, OK; Dick Fort, Stanwood, WA; John D. Hill, Dallas, TX; James F. Hurley, Far Hills, NJ; Duke F. Jarvis, Yakima, WA; Eric Rafter, Hermosa Beach, CA; George N. Weisfeld, Wyndoor, PA.

92d Squadron. Thomas F. Corrigan, Colorado Springs, CO; John J. Ginter, Jr., Stanford, CT; Harry G. Gutherless, North Platte, NB; Frank J. Hynes, Minneapolis, MN; Hollis W. Jones, Phoenix, AZ; E. B. Page, Lynnwood, WA; David Sill, Mobile, AL.

93d Squadron. Herbert W. Ballinger, Wichita, KS; Albert S. Barton, Dallas Center, IA; Richard W. Blake, Belvedere, IL; Fred O. Brauer, Missoula, MT; Robert Bullock, Murrysville, PA; Lloyd Clark, Belleville, IL; Paul O. Hower, El Dorado, KS; George Juneau, Everett, WA; Crawford D. Kinney, Hampden, ME; Robert L. Sakrison, Waunakee, WI; Robert Stout, River Vale, NJ; Edward L. Williams, Metairie, LA; Michael Zubritsky, Charleroi, PA.

94th Squadron. Emmett Avery, Richmond, VA; Pershing Y. Carlson, Bismark, ND; Francis L. Carroll, Las Vegas, NV; Jake W. Cratty, Los Altos Hills, CA; Phillip C. Hecker, Minnetonka, MN; Verbon E. "Pete" Houck, Wenatchee, WA; Ray Leonard, Casper, WY; Ernest Turner, Colonia, NJ; Meyer "Mike" Sheff, Flushing, NY.

440TH TROOP CARRIER GROUP

95th Squadron. Irvin G. Anderson, Ingram, TX; Warren de Beauclair, Pontiac, MI; William H. Lewis, Laguna Beach, CA; Luther J. Lizana,

Batesville, MS; George E. Morrow, San Gabriel, CA; Harvey D. Rideout, Sacramento, CA; George F. Wasson, Bethel Park, PA; Wilmer S. Weber, Philadelphia, PA; Michael E. Whitfill, Las Vegas, NV.

96th Squadron. William F. Byrd, Hiram, GA; Wendell Ebright, Lyons, KS; Roderick D. MacDougall, Lubbock, TX; Robert S. Mauck, Worthington, OH; Kent Maynard, Winnetka, IL; Robert H. Price, Albuquerque, NM; Al Sabon, Taylor, MI; Robert E. Thompson, Russell, KY; John H. Wesley, Chattanooga, TN.

97th Squadron. William W. Burnett, Tyler, TX; Joseph A. Purcell, Marion, OH; Vic Reinemer, Falls Church, VA.

98th Squadron. Charles F. Sutton, Wilmington, DE.

IX TROOP CARRIER PATHFINDER GROUP

James A. Bancroft, Chambersburg, PA; Joel L. Crouch, Honolulu, HI; Richard K. Jacobson, Arlington, VA; Lionel E. Wood, Estes Park, CO.

ARMY DIVISIONS

101st Airborne Division. John Agnew, Huntington Valley, PA.

17th Airborne Division. Samuel Calhoun, Fresno, CA; James W. Coutts, Kennett, MO; Royal Donovan, Naples, FL; Kenneth M. Kasse, Perrysville, OH; Joseph Kitson, New Windsor, NY; Sidney Laufer, Boca Raton, FL; William C. Mitchell, Eugene, OR; John O. Paul, Baton Rouge, LA.

Veterans closely associated with Operation REPULSE, as well as those who were on other airborne operations, contributed invaluable information and guidance during my research. They are listed here by their organizations and units:

50TH TROOP CARRIER WING

Headquarters. Julian M. Chappell, Americus, GA; Roy E. Weinzettel, San Antonio, TX.

439TH TROOP CARRIER GROUP

Headquarters, 439th Group. Noel F. Edmonds, Springfield, MO; Arthur Kaplan, Delray Beach, FL; Bernard G. Parks, Sunnymead, CA; Charles H. Young, Southlake, TX.

91st Squadron. Jack H. Beiser, Gardena, CA; Thomas J. Berry, Bridgeton, MO; Milton Dank, Wyncote, PA; John A. Neary, Phoenix, AZ; Harold J. Rhodehamel, Greenville, OH; Laverne C. Riley,

Chatsworth, CA; Frank Rossi, Northampton, MA; Norman C. Wilmeth, Guymon, OK.

92d Squadron. John A. Hinman, San Francisco, CA; Jack C. Holker, Minneapolis, MN; Melvin Kammen, Brunswick, NJ; Charles L. McBride, San Antonio, TX; Robert L. Pound, Severn, MD; John C. Vance, Wetumpk, AL.

93d Squadron. James H. Burnett, Luther, MT; Waverly M. Jarvis, Hollister, CA.

94th Squadron. James A. Bradley, Thomasville, GA; Melvin J. Brockman, Milwaukee, WI; Frank De Felitta, Los Angeles, CA; John L. Hoskins, Clearwater, FL; Robert L. Morehous, Louisville, KY; Clifford L. Mueller, Sedonia, AZ; John L. Patterson, Petosky, MI; Eugene F. Schwartz, Wilderville, OR.

440TH TROOP CARRIER GROUP

Headquarters. Frank K. Krebs, Accokeek, MD.

95th Squadron. Curlan McNeil, Germantown, TN; Donald M. Orcutt, Seattle, WA.

98th Squadron. William P. Asprey, Newton, NJ; Alfred H. Greiert, Canton, IL; Wilber Leonard, Olympia, WA; John L. Lowden, Wilmington, NC; Courtland G. Mabee, Houston, TX; Robert E. Mock, Federal Way, WA; Bascome L. Neal, Hampton, VA; James Shimek, Norco, CA; Walter F. Wilson, Davis, OK.

441ST TROOP CARRIER GROUP

99th Squadron. Benjamin F. Sellars, Austin, TX.

100th Squadron. Merrell R. Kirkpatrick, Wichita, KA.

61ST TROOP CARRIER GROUP

14th Squadron. John F. Skinner, Clarksburg, WV.

313TH TROOP CARRIER GROUP

29th Squadron. Joseph Harkiewicz, Orlando, FL.

47th Squadron. Robert D. Starkey, Austin, TX.

49th Squadron. Robert W. Blickensderfer, Coneaut, OH; Donald Collins, Ashville, OH; Frank Joda, River Grove, IL; Charles Konopa, Yuma, AZ; Elmer H. Munkvold, River Grove, IL; Donald Q. Paulsel, Pendelton, IN; William R. Pully, Richmond, VA; William W. Rose, Bothell, WA; Lucian M. Roy, Tallulah, LA; Robert F. Scott, New Braunfels, TX.

315TH TROOP CARRIER GROUP

Headquarters and 34th Squadron. William Brinson, Jacksonville, FL; Robert L. Cloer, Yuba City, CA

316TH TROOP CARRIER GROUP

37th Squadron. Samuel Fine, Glenwild, NY.

45th Squadron. H. B. McCullough, Raleigh, NC.

53D TROOP CARRIER WING

435TH TROOP CARRIER GROUP

75th Squadron. John L. Shinn, Fort Wayne, IN.

76th Squadron. Drew S. Anderson, Riverside, CA.

78th Squadron. William K. Horn, Dallas, TX.

ARMY DIVISIONS

101st Airborne Division. George Koskimaki, Northville, MI; Charles B. MacDonald, Arlington, VA; R. Bruce Middough, Manhattan Beach, CA; Joseph Kyle Perkins, Homosassa Springs, FL; George Rosie, Kalamazoo, MI.

82d Airborne Division. Milton V. Night, Lafayette, LA.

106th Infantry Division. Pete House, Jacksonville, FL.

Veterans who supplied additional information on airborne missions in the MTO and the ETO by organization and unit:

AIR SERVICE COMMAND HEADQUARTERS, WRIGHT FIELD, DAYTON, OH.

Glider Unit. Rolland F. Fetters, DeRidder, LA.

AIR TRANSPORT COMMAND

North Atlantic Division. Willis Patterson, Wooster, OH.

Search and Rescue Service. Hulen S. Dean, Conway, AR; Ed Moody, Rochester, NH; Richard S. Moulton, Holderness, NH; Norman D. Vaughan, Anchorage and Talkeetna, AK.

Many family members of deceased veterans were graciously willing to furnish information and records in their possession. They were:

Helen Billings (widow of Leroy Billings, ATC), Newport, NH; Mardell Parker (widow of Merlin E. Parker, ATC), Brainerd, MN;

Gary Purgett (son of Earl D. Purgett, 302d Sqdn, 441st TC Group), Ladysmith, WI; Vivian Schillinger (widow of Richard F. Schillinger, 91st Sqdn., 439th TC Group), Red Oak, IA; Polly Striplin (widow of Mack Striplin, 93d Sqdn., 439th TC Group), Freemont, CA.

EUROPE

Dave Benfield, Peterborough, England; John V. Nicholls, Brentwood, Essex, England.

Last, but far from least, is one who deserves very special recognition. André R. Meurisse, who lives in Büllingen, Belgium, furnished priceless information, both from his accumulated records and from his more recent investigations to find others who have firsthand recollections of the days during the Battle of the Bulge.

Top photo: Spring 1945. Children of Bastogne at play in remains of 2d Lt. Martin H. Skolnick's C-47, 92d Squadron. — Courtesy: Hortense Martin

Bottom photo: Remains of CG-4A glider directly north of Bastogne.
— Courtesy: Hortense Martin

Bibliography

Allen, Robert S. *The History of Patton's Third U.S. Army.* New York: The Vanguard Press, Inc., 1947.

Blair, Clay. *Ridgway's Paratroopers.* New York: Dial Press, 1985.

Blumenson, Martin. *The Battle of the Generals.* New York: William Morrow and Company, 1993.

Bradley, Omar N. *A Soldier's Story.* New York: Henry Holt and Company, 1951.

Brereton, Lewis H. *The Brereton Diaries.* New York: William Morrow and Company, 1946.

Breuer, William B. *Operation Torch.* New York: St. Martin's Press, 1985.

Churchill, Winston S. *The Second World War.* Vol. 5, *Closing the Ring;* Vol. 6, *Triumph and Tragedy.* Boston: Houghton Mifflin Company, 1951.

Colby, John. *War From The Ground Up.* Austin, TX: Eakin Press, 1991.

Cole, Hugh M. *The Ardennes, Battle of the Bulge. U.S. Army in World II,* Washington, DC: Government Printing Office, 1965.

Craven, W. F., and J. L. Cate, Editors. *Europe-Argument To V-E Day.* Vol. III, *The Army Air Forces in World War II.* Chicago: University of Chicago Press, 1956.

Dank, Milton. *The Glider Gang.* Philadelphia and New York: Lippincott Company, 1977.

Devlin, Gerard M. *Silent Wings.* New York: St. Martin's Press, 1985.

Eisenhower, Dwight D. *Report by the Supreme Commander to the Combined Chiefs of Staff on Operations in Europe of the Allied Expeditionary Force.* London: His Majesty's Stationary Office, 1946.

———. *Crusade in Europe.* Garden City, NY: Doubleday, 1948.

Fortune Magazine (Time, Inc.), *Troop Carrier Command.* October 1943.

Gabel, Kurt. *The Making of a Paratrooper.* University Press of Kansas, 1990.

Gavin, James M. *Airborne Warfare.* Washington, DC: Infantry Journal Press, 1947.

———. *On To Berlin: Battles of an Airborne Commander, 1943 to 1946.* New York: Viking Press, 1978.

Hagerman, Bart. *17th Airborne History.* Paducah, KY: Turner Publishing Co., 1987.

————. *War Stories*. Paducah, KY: Turner Publishing Company, 1993.

Harkiewicz, Joseph. *We Are The 29TH!* History of the 29th Troop Carrier Squadron, Special Edition for the 29th Squadron Association, 1990.

Huston, James A. *Out of the Blue*. Nashville, TN: The Battery Press, Inc., 1972.

Jablonski, Edward. *Flying Fortress*. Garden City, NY: Doubleday & Company, 1965.

Jones, James. *WW II*. New York: Grosset & Dunlap, 1975.

Keegan, John. *A History of Warfare*. New York: Alfred A. Knopf, 1993.

Kohn, Richard H., and Joseph P. Harahan, General Editors. *Condensed Analysis of the Ninth Air Force in the European Theater of Operations*. Washington, DC: Office of Air Force History, 1989.

Koskimaki, George E. *Hell's Highway*. Northville, MI: George E. Koskimaki, 1989.

Lewin, Ronald. *Montgomery As A Military Commander*. New York: Stein and Day, 1971.

Link, Mae Mills, and Hubert A. Coleman. *Medical Support of the Army Air Forces in World War II*. Washington, DC: Office of the Surgeon General, USAF, 1955.

Lowden, John L. *Silent Wings at War*. Washington, DC: Smithsonian Institution Press, 1992.

MacDonald, Charles B. *A Time For Trumpets*. New York: William Morrow and Company, Inc., 1985.

MacKenzie, Fred. *The Men Of Bastogne*. New York: David McKay Company, Inc., 1968.

Marshall, S. L. A. *Bastogne, The First Eight Days*. Washington DC: Infantry Journal Press, 1946.

Merriam, Robert E. *The Battle Of The Bulge*. New York: Ballantine Books, 1957.

Montgomery, Bernard L. *The Memoirs of Field-Marshal Montgomery*. Cleveland and New York: The World Publishing Co., 1958.

Mrazek, James E. *The Glider War*. New York: St. Martin's Press, 1975.

O'Brien, R. Edward. *With Geronimo Across Europe*. Sweetwater, TN: The 101st Airborne Division Association, 1990.

Parnell, Ben. *Carpetbaggers*. Austin, TX: Eakin Press, 1993.

Patton, George S., Jr. *War As I Knew It*. Boston: Houghton Mifffin Co., 1947.

Pogue, Forrest C. *The Supreme Command*. U.S. Army, World War II. Washington, DC: Government Printing Office, 1954.

Rust, Kenneth C. *The 9th Air Force In World War II*. Fallbrook, CA: Aero Publishers, Inc., 1967.

Ryan, Cornelius. *The Longest Day*. New York: Simon and Schuster, 1959.

————. *A Bridge Too Far*. New York: Simon and Schuster, 1974.

Thompson, Royce L. *Air Supply To Isolated Units, Ardennes Campaign*. OMH, Dept. of the Army. Feb. 1951 (Unpublished).

Toland, John. *Battle, The Story Of The Bulge*. New York: Random House, 1959.

Wallace, Brenton G. *Patton and His Third Army*. Harrisburg, PA: Military Service Publishing Co., 1946.

Warren, John C. *Airborne Missions in the Mediterranean, 1942-1945*. USAF Historical Studies: No. 74. Research Studies Institute, Air University, Maxwell AFB, Alabama. September 1955.

———. *Airborne Operations in World War II, European Theater.* USAF Historical Studies: No. 97. Research Studies Institute, Air University, Maxwell AFB, Alabama, 1956.

Wolfe, Martin. *Green Light.* Philadelphia, PA: University of Pennsylvania Press, 1984.

Yeager, Charles E. *Yeager, An Autobiography.* New York: Bantam Books, 1985.

Sources By Chapter

Introduction

Brereton, Lewis H. p 283
Letter: Young, Charles H. 15 Jan. 1943 with endorsements. National Archives, Suitland, MD.
Letter: Young, 25 Jan. 1945. From Lloyd G. Clark.

CHAPTER 1. Troop Carrier Command

Chappell, Julian M. Telephone interviews, 1987-1988.
Crouch, Joel L. Interview and correspondence, 1987-1992.
Fortune Magazine. Oct. 1943.
Huston, James A. pp 67-68, 122.
Warren, John C. USAF Historical Studies No. 74, pp 1-3.
Warren, John C. USAF Historical Studies No. 97, pp 32, 40-41, 70-71.
Young, Charles H. Interviews and correspondence, 1985-1992.

CHAPTER 2. Lesson One: North Africa

Breuer, William B. pp 97-101, 117-121, 148-156.
Huston, James A. pp 151-153.
Jablonski, Edward. pp 106-108.
Warren, John C. USAF Historical Studies No. 74, pp 3, 5-6, 9-13, 17-18, 56.

CHAPTER 3. Lesson Two: Sicily

Blair, Clay. pp 69-71, 102-103.
Bradley, Omar N. p 113.
Dank, Milton. p 82-84.
Devlin, Gerard M. pp 78, 105-106.
Fetters, Roland F. Unpublished Report: Overseas Assignment for the Investiga-

tion of Army Air Forces Glider Program in European Theater of Operations. Wright-Patterson AFB, Dayton, OH. 1943.
Mrazek, James E. pp 91-94.
Rust, Kenneth C. pp 36, 38.
Records of the 313th TC Group and 49th TC Squadron. HQ USAF Historical Research Center, Maxwell AFB, AL.
Warren, John C. USAF Historical Studies No. 74, pp 3-18, 23, 26, 29-30.

CHAPTER 4.   Lesson Three: Italy

Blair, Clay. pp 148, 150-151.
Churchill, Winston S. *The Second World War,* Volume 5, Closing The Ring. pp 26, 132, 141-147, 203-205, 210-217, 316-327, 421, 433-434, 460, 486.
Crouch, Joel L. Correspondence. 1991
Gavin, James M. *On To Berlin.* pp 58-62.
Green, Paul S. The Aborted Jump on Rome WWII, 82nd Airborne Division Assoc., Inc. Paraglide Fall Issue 1991. pp 39-44.
Knight, Milton V. Personal Interview. 1987.
Warren, John C. USAF Historical Studies No. 74. pp 37, 57-58, 60-62, 65-71.

CHAPTER 5.   From Allied Expeditionary Air Force to SHAEF-AIR

Brereton, Lewis H. p 228.
Churchill, Winston S. *The Second World War,* Volume 5, *Closing The Ring.* pp 316, 327-328, 333-334, 340, 410-419, 423-424.
Craven, W. F. and Cate, J. L. pp 5-6, 620-622.
Warren, John C. USAF Historical Studies No. 74. p 77.
Warren, John C. USAF Historical Studies No. 97. pp 4-5, 8-11.

CHAPTER 6.   IX Troop Carrier Command

Crouch, Joel L. Interview, Norfolk, VA. April 1987.
Knight, Milton V. Interview. Norfolk, VA. April 1987.
Records of the 313th Troop Carrier Group. National Archives, Suitland, MD.
Rust, Kenneth C. pp 54-55.
Warren, John C. USAF Historical Studies No. 97. pp 3-5, 16-19, 21-23.

CHAPTER 7.   Test One: Normandy

Bancroft, James A. The Pathfinder. Publication of the 9th Pathfinder Group Association, Vol. II, No. 3. July-August-September 1987.
Churchill, Winston S. *The Second World War,* Volume 5, *Closing The Ring.* pp 591-595.
Dank, Milton. pp 115-120.
Harkiewicz, Joseph. p 97.
Mrazek, James E. pp 105-106.

Records of 313th T.C. Group, National Archives, Suitland, MD.
Rust, Kenneth C. pp 54, 75.
Ryan, Cornelius. *The Longest Day.* pp 60, 62, 104, 107-110.
Smith, Ward. *Stars and Stripes,* June 12, 1944.
Warren, John C. USAF Historical Studies No. 97. pp 13, 21, 25-26, 28, 32-34, 36, 38, 40-41, 43, 48, 51, 55, 58-59, 61, 64-69, 71, 74-78, 224-225.

CHAPTER 8. Test Two: Southern France

Churchill, Winston S. *The Second World War,* Volume 5, *Closing The Ring.* pp 86, 345-346, 372-382, 408-413.
Churchill, Winston S. *The Second World War,* Volume 6, *Triumph and Tragedy.* pp 94-95.
Dank, Milton. pp 151, 156-157.
DZ Europe. The 440th Troop Carrier Group. (No Author.) Hollenbeck Press, Indianapolis, IN. 1946. pp 53-57, 75.
Krebs, Frank X. Speech at WWII Glider Pilot Association Reunion, Las Vegas, NV. September 1982. Copy furnished to author by Krebs, 1991.
Mrazek, James E. pp 189, 190-192.
Warren, John C. USAF Historical Studies No. 74. pp 77, 79-82, 86-87, 89, 91-92, 95-97, 99, 101-104, 110-112.
Wolfe, Martin. pp 261-262.

CHAPTER 9. First Allied Airborne Army

Brereton, Lewis H. p 228.
Craven, W. F. and Cate, J. L. pp 5-6, 561-562, 620-622.
Warren, John C. USAF Historical Studies No. 97. pp 5, 8-11, 82-83.

CHAPTER 10. Test Three: Holland

Blair, Clay. pp 136-137, 152-153, 169, 346, 350.
Devlin, Gerard M. pp 279-280.
DZ Europe. The 440th T.C. Group. (No Author.) Hollenbeck Press, Indianapolis, IN. 1946. pp 62-66.
Family Weekly. March 26, 1961. Escape To Freedom as told to Theodore Irwin by Howard W. Cannon.
Harkiewicz, Joseph. pp 118, 122, 126, 129-130.
Huston, James A. pp 183.
Krebs, Frank X. Copy of his speech given at WWII Glider Pilot Assoc. Reunion, Las Vegas, NV. 1982.
Letter from Brig. Gen. J. M. Gavin to Maj. Gen. P. L. Williams, 25 September 1944. Reproduced from IX T.C. Command Report on Operation MARKET, pp 75-76.
Records of the 313th T.C. Group and 49th T.C. Squadron. National Archives, Suitland, MD.
Ryan, Cornelius. *A Bridge Too Far.* pp 11-12, 135.

Warren, John C. USAF Historical Studies No. 97. pp 88-89, 101-102, 106, 112-114, 119-123, 125, 129-136, 138-139, 141-144, 153-155, 226-227.
Wolfe, Martin. pp 307-309.

CHAPTER 11.   The Autumn Fog

Blair, Clay. pp 356, 363, 376-378, 386-388, 392.
Cole, Hugh M. pp 137-140, 171-172, 315, 461.
Craven, W.F. and Cate, J. L. pp 673, 679, 681.
Eisenhower, Dwight D., Report by the Supreme Commander to the Combined Chiefs of Staff on Operations in Europe of the Allied Expeditionary Force. p 94.
Eisenhower, Dwight D., *Crusade in Europe.* pp 356-357.
House, Pete. Personal Experience Accounts, Jacksonville, FL. 1991.
MacDonald, Charles B. pp 125, 186-187, 345, 421-424, 443-444, 451, 480-481, 496, 505.
Montgomery, Bernard L. pp 275.
Pogue, Forrest C. pp 269, 271, 374, 378-379.
The G-3 Journal 106th Division. National Archives.
Thompson, Royce L. Air Supply to Isolated Units, Ardennes Campaign. OMH, Dept. of the Army. Feb. 1951 (Unpublished). pp 8, 11-18, 80-81.

CHAPTER 12.   On the Way to St. Vith

Records of the 435th T.C. Group and 75th and 76th T.C. Squadrons. HQ USAF Historical Research Center, Maxwell AFB, AL.
Rust, Kenneth C. pp 132.
Status of American Airfields in Western Europe. 1944. From Records in National Archives.
Thompson, Royce L. Air Supply to Isolated Units, Ardennes Campaigne. OMH, Dept. of the Army. Feb. 1951 (Unpublished). pp 19, 20-21.

CHAPTER 13.   DZ Marcouray

Cole, Hugh M. pp 353, 384.
MacDonald Charles B. pp 536-539, 554.
Report on Operation REPULSE. Headquarters, IX Troop Carrier Command to Commanding General, Army Air Forces, Washington, D.C., 3 Jan. 1945.
Report from IX Troop Carrier Statistical Control Office. 5 Jan. 1945.
Rust, Kenneth C. p 76.
Thompson, Royce L. Air Supply to Isolated Units, Ardennes Campaigne. OMH, Dept. of the Army. Feb. 1951 (Unpublished). pp 19-21.
Troop Carrier Unit Histories. For Dec. 1944. National Archives. 435 TC Group and 78th TC Squadron. 438th TC Group.

CHAPTER 14.   Bastogne Expectations

Thompson, Royce L. Air Supply to Isolated Units, Ardennes Campaigne. OMH, Dept. of the Army. Feb. 1951 (Unpublished). pp 83-94.

CHAPTER 15.   Pathfinders First

Agnew, John. Live from Bastogne. Article in *The Pathfinder,* 9th TC Command Pathfinder Association. Oct.-Nov. Dec. 1986.

Report of Airborne Pathfinder Operation 'Nuts.' XVIII Corps A/B Pathfinder Officer to Commanding General XVIII Corps (Airborne). 7 Jan. 1945. National Archives.

Report of Resupply Troops in Bastogne Area. Letter to CG, IX Troop Carrier Command from IX Troop Carrier Pathfinder Group (Prov), Joel L. Crouch. 29 Dec. 1944. National Archives.

Report on Operation REPULSE. Headquarters, IX Troop Carrier Command. To: Commanding General, Army Air Forces, Washington 25, D.C. 3 Jan. 1945. National Archives. pp 10-11.

Rust, Kenneth C. p 137.

Thompson, Royce L. Air Supply to Isolated Units, Ardennes Campaigne. OMH, Dept. of the Army. Feb. 1951 (Unpublished). pp 74, 88-90, 92-93, 96-98, 103-105.

CHAPTER 16.   The First Resupply Missions (23 December)

Anstey, Robert L. Narrative Report. Records of 441st Troop Carrier Group, 50th T.C. Wing, USAF HRC, Maxwell AFB, AL.

Brereton, Lewis H. pp 382-383.

Cole, Hugh M. p 470.

Frank L. Brown, Capt., XVIII Corps Pathfinder Office. Report of Airborne Pathfinder Operation 'Nuts,' to: Commanding General, XVIII Corps.

Jacobson, Richard K. Interview and correspondence with author. 1987.

MacDonald, Charles B. p 523.

Memorandum. A-2, Headquarters 50th Troop Carrier Wing, Analysis of Bastogne Resupply by Units of this Command. 18 Jan. 1945, USAF Historical Research Center, Maxwell AFB, AL.

Purgett, Gary. Reports by ex-POWs, with correspondence 1993.

Thompson, Royce L. Air Supply to Isolated Units, Ardennes Campaigne. OMH, Dept. of the Army. Feb. 1951 (Unpublished). pp 99-100, 103-106, 109.

CHAPTER 17.   Bastogne's Christmas Eve Presents

Historical Report, 435th T.C. Group. Dec. 1944.

Historical Report Form 34, Operation KANGAROO, IX Troop Carrier Command. 24 Dec. 1944.

Historical Reports, 435th T.C. Group and 77th T.C. Squadron, Dec. 1944

Historical Report, 72d T.C. Squadron. Dec. 1944.

IX T.C. Pathfinder Group. Report.

MacDonald, Charles B. pp 525-527.

MacKenzie, Fred. 213-215, 218.

Thompson, Royce L., Air Supply to Isolated Units, Ardennes Campaigne. OMH, Dept. of the Army. Feb. 1951 (Unpublished). pp 109, 112, 118-119.

CHAPTER 18.   Bleak Christmas

MacDonald, Charles B. pp 589-590.
MacKenzie, Fred. pp 234, 239.
Supplementary information, re: Mission of 101st A/B Officer (Addendum added 26 Mar. 1952). Four unnumbered pages following p 115.
Thompson, Royce L. Air Supply to Isolated Units, Ardennes Campaigne. OHM, Dept. of the Army. Feb. 1951 (Unpublished). pp 114-116, 120.

CHAPTER 19.   The Plans for Gliders

50th Troop Carrier Wing Hq. Historical Report. Dec. 1944. p 41.
Hq. IX T.C.C., Report on Operation REPULSE. p 8.
Historical Data, Hq. & Hq. Sq., 50th T.C. Wing, AAF, Book V.

CHAPTER 20.   Airborne Surgeons

Corwin, Charlton W. Jr. Interrogation, Hq 440th T.C.G. 30 Dec. 1944.
Corwin, Charlton W. Jr. Letter to Silent Wings Publication, Dallas, TX. Sept. 1978.
Dank, Milton. p 210.
Historical (Diary) Report, 95th T.C. Squadron. Dec. 1944.
Mauck, Robert S. Letters to author. 1989.
Thompson Royce L. Air Supply to Isolated Units, Ardennes Campaigne. OHM, Dept. of the Army. Feb. 1951 (Unpublished). pp 122-123.

CHAPTER 21.   Out of the Fog

435th T.C. Group, Unit History. Dec. 1944.
435th T.C. Group and 77th T.C. Squadron and Unit Histories. Dec. 1944
MacDonald, Charles B. p 530, 532.
90th T.C. Squadron, Unit History. Dec. 1944.
Rose, Zeno H., 1st Lt. Interrogation, 75th T.C. Sq., 435th T.C. Group
Thompson, Royce L. Air Supply to Isolated Units, Ardennes Campaigne. OHM, Dept. of the Army. Feb. 1951 (Unpublished). p 137.

CHAPTER 22.   Gasoline in Gliders

Dank, Milton. p 212
Devlin, Gerard M. p 293.
50th T.C. Wing Diary, Dec. 1944. pp 38-39.
Hq. IX T.C.C. Report on Operation REPULSE. p 8.
Historical Report, 97th T.C. Squadron. Dec. 1944.
Interrogation Reports, 95th T.C. Squadron.
MacDonald, Charles B. p 532.
III, The Phantom Corps. A History published by III Corps Hq., 15 Oct. 1945. p 9.
Thompson, Royce L. Air Supply to Isolated Units, Ardennes Campaigne. OMH, Dept. of the Army. Feb. 1951 (Unpublished). pp 125-126.

CHAPTER 23.   Ammunition Sky Train

Dank, Milton. pp 220-221.
Devlin, Gerard M. pp 296-297.
DZ Europe. History of 440th T.C. Group. Published by 440th T.C. Gp., pp 16-17.
439th T.C. Group, HQ. Diary, Dec. 1944. Written by 1st Lt. Arthur Kaplan, Group Historian.
Green, Billy J. Letter to 2nd Lt. Lester A. Nay, 96th Squadron, from field hospital near Sedan, France. 5 Jan. 1945.
Interrogation Statements, 1st Lt. Robert E. Stout. 93rd T.C. Squad.
Interrogation, S/Sgt. William M. Connarn, 91st T.C. Squadron. 31 Dec. 1944.
91st T.C. Squadron, Narrative History. Dec. 1944.
92d T.C. Squadron, Narrative History. Dec. 1944.
95th T.C. Squadron Report, Investigation of Lost Planes and Crews on Mission "REPULSE. 2 Feb. 1945.
Nowell, Henry H. Copy of Deposition filed with Veteran's Administration, Winston-Salem, NC. 20 May 1975. Also: Drew Anderson's records, Riverside, CA. Nov. 1986.
Rust, Kenneth C., p 76.
Schapiro, Sid, *Stars and Stripes.* 1 Feb. 1945.
Thompson, Royce L. Air Supply to Isolated Units, Ardennes Campaigne. OHM, Dept. of the Army. Feb. 1951 (Unpublished). pp 129, 132.

CHAPTER 24.   The Quick and the Dead

Dank, Milton. pp 221-222.
Devlin, Gerard M. pp 296-299.
Hower, Paul O. and Juneau, George W. Letters to author.
Interrogations — Reports of Glider Pilots.
Interrogations — Reports of Glider Pilots and C-47 Crews.
Nowell, Henry H. Deposition (Previous Chapter).
Rust, Kenneth C. p 137.
Squadrons' Records — Reports for Dec. 1944 and Jan. 1945.
Thompson, Royce L. Air Supply to Isolated Units, Ardennes Campaigne. OMH, Dept. of the Army. Feb. 1951 (Unpublished). p 132.
Warren, John C. USAF Historical Studies No. 97. pp 226-229.
Whitfill, Michael A. Personal account written later to author.

CHAPTER 25.   The Last Drop

IX T.C. Pathfinder Group. Report.
Memorandum. Summary of Operations of IX Troop Carrier Command, 27 Dec. 1944. To C.G. FAAA from HQ IX Troop Carrier Command. 28 Dec. 1944.
Operation Report Form 34, Operation KANGAROO, IX Troop Carrier Command. 27 Dec. 1944.
Squadron Diaries of 435th and 436th T.C. Groups. Dec. 1944.
Thompson, Royce L. Air Supply to Isolated Units, Ardennes Campaigne. OHM, Dept. of the Army. Feb. 1951 (Unpublished). p 133.

CHAPTER 26.   The 17th Airborne Division into Battle

Calhoun, Samuel. Correspondence with author. 1984-1993.
Headquarters 50th Troop Carrier Wing, Dec. 1944: Resume and Diary, USAF Historical Research Center, Maxwell AFB, AL.
Hq. IX T.C.C., Statistical Control Office, "Operation REPULSE." USAF Historical Research Center, Maxwell AFB, AL.
Huston, James A. pp 20, 173.
Link, Mae Mills and Coleman, Hubert A. p 96.
Report on Operation REPULSE. Headquarters IX Troop Carrier Command To: Commanding General, Army Air Forces, Wash. 25, DC., 3 Jan. 1945. National Archives. pp 9-10, 12, 14-16, 18.
Rust, Kenneth C. pp 54, 62.
SHAEF, Incoming Message from FAAA, Brereton. 25 Dec. 1944. USAF Historical Research Center, Maxwell AFB, AL.
Warren, John C. USAF Historical Studies No. 97. pp 98, 118, 158.

CHAPTER 27.   Operation WOOF-WOOF

Air Transport Command, European Division. Press Release, 1 Mar. 1945. Hq. USAF Historical Research Center, Maxwell AFB. AL.
Churchill, Winston S., *The Second World War,* Vol. 6 p 343.
Colby, John. pp 356-359.
Cole, Hugh M. pp 137-140.
The Daily Journal, International Falls, MN. March 10, 1976. Article: "George [Esslinger] and his jumping dogs."
Dean, Hulen S., Correspondence with author, 1990.
Historical Data, 98th Troop Carrier Squadron, Feb. 1945. HQ USAF Historical Research Center, Maxwell AFB, AL.
MacDonald, Charles B., pp 188, 419, 608-610.
Moody, Edward L. Correspondence with author. 1990.
Moulton, Richard S. Correspondence with author. 1993.
Patterson, Willis. Article in Tarpa Topics, TWA Retired Pilots Assoc. Magazine. Nov. 1987. Also correspondence with author, 1988.
Patton, George S. pp 225, 234-236.
Vaughan, Norman. Correspondence and telephone interviews with author. 1991-1993.
Wallace, Brenton, G. pp 165-171.

CHAPTER 28.   Invasion Plans, Over the Rhine

Blair, Clay. p 456.
Blickensderfer, Robert W. Operations Officer 49th Troop Carrier Squadron. Correspondence with author 1990-1992.
Calhoun, Samuel. Correspondence with author 1987-1992, and interview 1993.
Churchill, Winston S. *The Second World War,* Vol. 6, p 412
Devlin, Gerard M. p 316.
Harkiewicz, Joseph. pp 170, 172.

Huston, James A. pp 213, 217.

Mrazek, James E. pp 242-3.

Records of the 49th Squadron and 313th Troop Carrier Group. National Archives, Suitland, MD and USAF Historical Research Center, Maxwell AFB, AL.

Warren, John C. USAF Historical Studies No. 97, pp 156-9, 160-1, 163-4, 167-8, 170, 182-3.

CHAPTER 29.   Varsity Team in Action

Calhoun, Samuel. Correspondence with author. 1991-1992.

Churchill, Winston S. *The Second World War.* Vol. 6, p 413.

Dank, Milton. pp 227, 243-9, 251-3.

Devlin, Gerard M. p 321, 331.

DZ Europe. The T.C. Group (no author). Hollenbeck Press, Indianapolis, IN. 1946. pp 93, 97-103.

Eisenhower, Dwight D. *Crusade in Europe.* p 390.

Hagerman, Bart. p 58-59, 62-65.

Harkiewicz, Joseph. pp 175, 178, 183-6, 234, 274, 326.

Lowden, John L. pp 149, 153, 155.

Records of 29th, 48th, 49th Squadrons and 313th Troop Carrier Group. National Archives, Suitland, MD.

Rust, Kenneth C. p 166.

Warren, John C. USAF Historical Studies No. 97, pp 163, 174, 177-179, 180-188, 192, 203, 228.

Wolfe, Martin. pp 31, 389.

Index

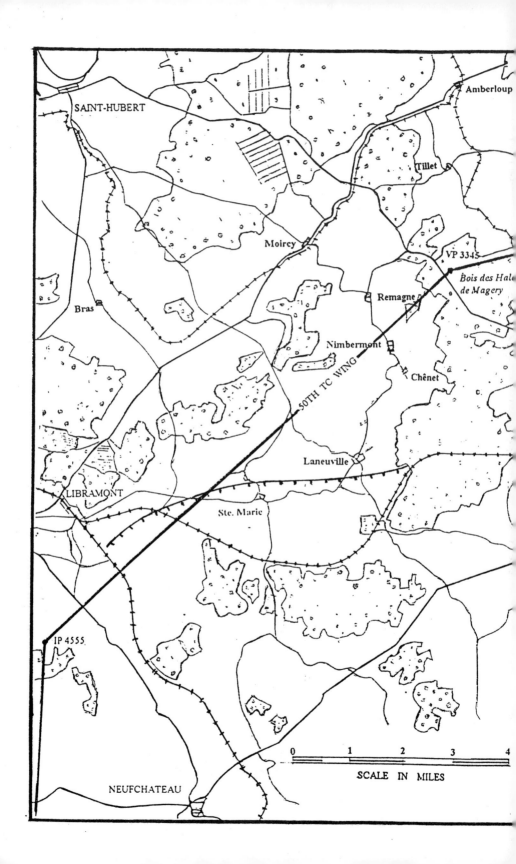

SAINT-HUBERT

Amberloup

Tillet

Moircy

VP 3345

Bois des Hal
de Magery

Bras

Remagne

Nimbermont

50TH TC WING

Chênet

Laneuville

LIBRAMONT

Ste. Marie

IP 4555

NEUFCHATEAU

| 0 | 1 | 2 | 3 | 4 |

SCALE IN MILES